Edwin F. Hatfield

The Chapel Hymn Book

with tunes - for the worship of God

Edwin F. Hatfield

The Chapel Hymn Book
with tunes - for the worship of God

ISBN/EAN: 9783337286798

Printed in Europe, USA, Canada, Australia, Japan

Cover: Foto ©Lupo / pixelio.de

More available books at **www.hansebooks.com**

THE
CHAPEL HYMN BOOK,

WITH TUNES;

FOR THE

WORSHIP OF GOD.

"In Psalms and Hymns and Spiritual Songs, singing, with grace in your hearts, to the Lord."—COL. III. 16.

IVISON, BLAKEMAN, TAYLOR & COMPANY,

NEW YORK AND CHICAGO.

1878.

Entered, according to Act of Congress, in the year 1873, by
EDWIN F. HATFIELD,
in the Office of the Librarian of Congress at Washington.

TAYLOR & BARWOOD, MUSIC ELECTROTYPERS,
27 Rose Street, New York.

PREFACE.

THE CHAPEL HYMN BOOK is an abridged edition of the CHURCH HYMN BOOK. It is designed for the Chapel, the Lecture-Room, the Social Meeting, and the Family. It aims, also, to meet the demands of missionary and feeble churches for a book less expensive than the more comprehensive and complete work.

To this end, the most familiar and best approved hymns and tunes of the CHURCH HYMN BOOK have been incorporated, without abridgment or alteration, and in the same order of topics, into this humbler selection. Both the hymns and the tunes of this MANUAL OF PRAISE are regarded as among the choicest in use among the churches of America. As the numbering of the larger work is attached to each of the hymns in this selection, both books may readily be used together.

The principles on which the original compilation was made are fully set forth in the preface to the CHURCH HYMN BOOK.

EDWIN F. HATFIELD.

New York, January 1, 1873.

CONTENTS.

	HYMNS.	PAGES.
I.—PREFACE		3
II.—HYMNS	1—752	5—268
I.—Hymns of Invocation	1—64	5—26
1. Morning and Evening	1—13	
2. Lord's Day	14—31	
3. Sanctuary	32—64	
II.—Hymns of Adoration	65—166	27—61
1. The Triune God	65—75	
2. The Eternal Father	76—130	
3. The Son of God	131—150	
4. The Holy Spirit	151—166	
III.—Hymns of Revelation	167—183	62—67
IV.—Hymns of Salvation	184—264	68—95
1. The Need of Salvation	184—189	
2. The Incarnation of Christ	190—205	
3. The Ministry of Christ	206—212	
4. The Atoning Sacrifice of Christ	213—229	
5. The Resurrection and Ascension of Christ	230—240	
6. The Royal Priesthood of Christ	241—264	
V.—Hymns of Reconciliation	265—362	96—130
1. Pardon offered	265—305	
2. Pardon sought	306—331	
3. Pardon found	332—362	
VI.—Hymns of Commemoration	363—396	131—141
VII.—Hymns of Aspiration	397—491	142—175
1. Of Love	397—419	
2. Of Faith	420—433	
3. Of Hope	434—452	
4. For Divine Fellowship	453—473	
5. For Divine Grace	474—491	
VIII.—Hymns of Tribulation	492—544	176—194
1. Spiritual Trouble	492—506	
2. Afflictions	507—544	
IX.—Hymns of Self-Examination	545—556	195—198
X.—Hymns of Church Relations	557—650	199—231
1. The Church	557—572	
2. The Ministry	573—584	
3. Baptism	585—587	
4. Covenant	588—593	
5. Church Fellowship	594—605	
6. Declensions	606—608	
7. Revival	609—616	
8. Missions	617—640	
9. Working and Giving	641—650	
XI.—Hymns for Special Occasions	651—676	232—240
1. Erection of Churches	651—656	
2. Festivals	657—665	
3. Fast-Days	666—668	
4. The Year and its Seasons	669—676	
XII.—Hymns on the Close of Probation	677—701	241—249
XIII.—Hymns of Glorification	702—752	250—268
1. The Resurrection	702—707	
2. The Judgment	708—717	
3. Heaven	718—752	
III.—DOXOLOGIES		269
IV.—INDEXES.—		270—292
1. Of Subjects		270—274
2. Of Scripture Texts		275—276
3. Of Tunes: (1.) Alphabetical		277—281
(2.) Metrical		281—283
4. Of Authors: (1.) Of Hymns		283—285
(2.) Of Tunes		285—286
5. Of Hymns		287—292

THE CHAPEL HYMN BOOK.

INVOCATION.

1.

The Blessed Trinity. (1.)

1 Holy, holy, holy! Lord God Almighty!
    Early in the morning our song shall rise to thee:
  Holy, holy, holy! merciful and mighty;
    God in Three Persons, blessèd Trinity!

2 Holy, holy, holy! all the saints adore thee,
    Casting down their golden crowns around the glassy sea;
  Cherubim and seraphim falling down before thee,
    Which wert, and art, and evermore shalt be.

3 Holy, holy, holy! though the darkness hide thee,
    Though the eye of sinful man thy glory may not see;
  Only thou art holy: there is none beside thee,
    Perfect in power, in love, and purity.

4 Holy, holy, holy! Lord God Almighty!
    All thy works shall praise thy name, in earth, and sky, and sea:
  Holy, holy, holy! merciful and mighty;
    God in Three Persons, blessèd Trinity. Amen.
                                    Reginald Heber, 1827.

INVOCATION.

DUKE STREET. L. M.
William Reeve, cir. 1790, or J. Hatton.

Awake, my soul! and, with the sun, Thy dai-ly stage of du-ty run;
Shake off dull sloth, and joy-ful rise, To pay thy morn-ing sac-ri-fice.

2. *A Morning Hymn.* (2.)

1 AWAKE, my soul! and, with the sun,
Thy daily stage of duty run;
Shake off dull sloth, and joyful rise,
To pay thy morning sacrifice.

2 Wake, and lift up thyself, my heart!
And with the angels bear thy part,
Who, all night long, unwearied sing,
High praise to the eternal King.

3 All praise to thee, who safe hast kept,
And hast refreshed me, whilst I slept;
Grant, Lord! when I from death shall wake,
I may of endless light partake.

4 Lord! I my vows to thee renew;
Disperse my sins as morning dew;
Guard my first springs of thought and will,
And with thyself my spirit fill.

5 Direct, control, suggest, this day,
All I design, or do, or say;
That all my powers, with all their might,
In thy sole glory may unite.

6 Praise God, from whom all blessings flow;
Praise him, all creatures here below!
Praise him above, ye heavenly host!
Praise Father, Son, and Holy Ghost.
Thomas Ken, 1697, a.

3. PSALM 17. (3.)

1 GLORY to thee, my God! this night,
For all the blessings of the light:
Keep me, Oh! keep me, King of kings!
Beneath thine own almighty wings.

2 Forgive me, Lord! for thy dear Son,
The ill that I this day have done;
That with the world, myself, and thee,
I, ere I sleep, at peace may be.

3 Teach me to live, that I may dread
The grave as little as my bed;
Teach me to die, that so I may
Rise glorious at the awful day.

4 Oh! may my soul on thee repose,
And may sweet sleep mine eyelids close:
Sleep, that shall me more vigorous make,
To serve my God when I awake.

5 When in the night I sleepless lie,
My soul with heavenly thoughts supply:
Let no ill dreams disturb my rest,
No powers of darkness me molest.
Thomas Ken, 1697, a.

4. *A Song for Morning or Evening.* (4.)

1 MY GOD! how endless is thy love!
Thy gifts are every evening new;
And morning mercies from above
Gently distill, like early dew.

2 Thou spread'st the curtains of the night,
Great Guardian of my sleeping hours!
Thy sovereign word restores the light,
And quickens all my drowsy powers.

3 I yield my powers to thy command;
To thee I consecrate my days;
Perpetual blessings, from thy hand,
Demand perpetual songs of praise.
Isaac Watts, 1709.

MORNING AND EVENING.

HURSLEY.   L. M.   *Adapted from Francis Jos. Haydn, 1732-1809.*

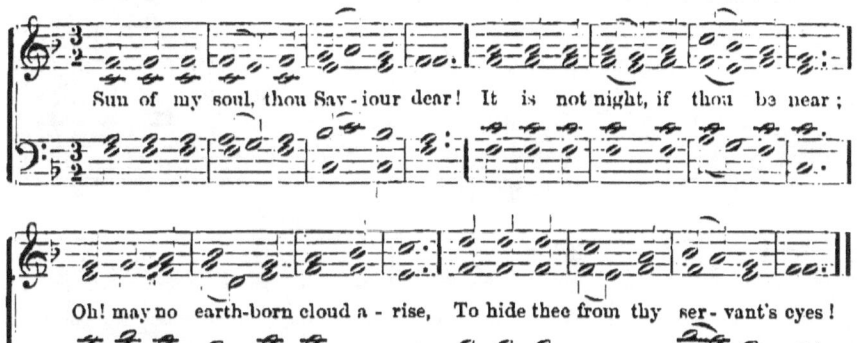

Sun of my soul, thou Saviour dear! It is not night, if thou be near;
Oh! may no earth-born cloud a-rise, To hide thee from thy servant's eyes!

5.   *Evening Hymn.*   (11.)

1 Sun of my soul, thou Saviour dear!
It is not night, if thou be near;
Oh! may no earth-born cloud arise,
To hide thee from thy servant's eyes!

2 When the soft dews of kindly sleep
My wearied eyelids gently steep,
Be my last thought, how sweet to rest
For ever on my Saviour's breast!

3 Abide with me from morn till eve,
For without thee I cannot live;
Abide with me when night is nigh,
For without thee I dare not die.

4 If some poor wandering child of thine
Have spurned to-day the voice divine,
Now, Lord! the gracious work begin;
Let him no more lie down in sin.

5 Watch by the sick; enrich the poor,
With blessings from thy boundless store;
Be every mourner's sleep to-night,
Like infant's slumbers, pure and light!

6 Come near and bless us when we wake,
Ere through the world our way we take;
Till, in the ocean of thy love,
We lose ourselves in heaven above.
John Keble, 1827

6.   PSALM 141.   (5.)

1 My God! accept my early vows,
Like morning incense in thy house;
And let my nightly worship rise
Sweet as the evening sacrifice.

2 Watch o'er my lips, and guard them, Lord!
From every rash and heedless word;
Nor let my feet incline to tread
The guilty path where sinners lead.

3 Oh! may the righteous, when I stray,
Smite and reprove my wandering way;
Their gentle words, like ointment shed,
Shall never bruise, but cheer my head.

4 When I behold them pressed with grief,
I'll cry to heaven for their relief;
And, by my warm petitions, prove
How much I prize their faithful love.
Isaac Watts, 1719.

7.   *An Evening Hymn.*   (10.)

1 Thus far the Lord has led me on,
Thus far his power prolongs my days;
And every evening shall make known
Some fresh memorial of his grace.

2 Much of my time has run to waste,
And I, perhaps, am near my home;
But he forgives my follies past,
He gives me strength for days to come.

3 I lay my body down to sleep,—
Peace is the pillow for my head;
While well-appointed angels keep
Their watchful stations round my bed.

4 Thus, when the night of death shall come,
My flesh shall rest beneath the ground,
And wait thy voice to rouse my tomb,
With sweet salvation in the sound.
Isaac Watts, 1709.

INVOCATION.

PETERBOROUGH.   C. M.   Ralph Harrison, 1786.

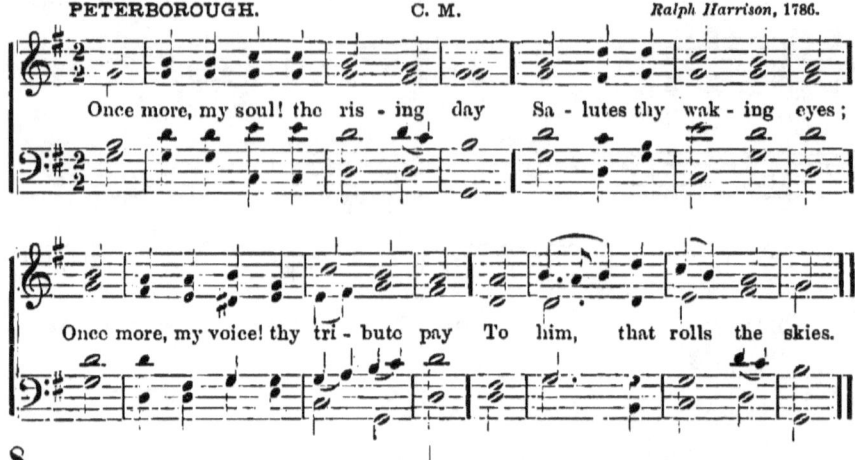

Once more, my soul! the ris-ing day Sa-lutes thy wak-ing eyes;
Once more, my voice! thy tri-bute pay To him, that rolls the skies.

8. *A Morning Song.* (14.)

1 Once more, my soul! the rising day
   Salutes thy waking eyes;
   Once more, my voice! thy tribute pay
   To him that rolls the skies.

2 Night unto night his name repeats,
   The day renews the sound;
   Wide as the heaven, on which he sits,
   To turn the seasons round.

3 'T is he supports my mortal frame,—
   My tongue shall speak his praise;
   My sins would rouse his wrath to flame,
   And yet his wrath delays.

4 Great God! let all my hours be thine,
   Whilst I enjoy the light;
   Then shall my sun in smiles decline,
   And bring a pleasing night.
   Philip Doddridge, 1740.

9. *The Twilight of Evening.* (17.)

1 I love to steal awhile away
   From every cumbering care,
   And spend the hours of setting day
   In humble, grateful prayer.

2 I love in solitude to shed
   The penitential tear,
   And all his promises to plead,
   Where none but God can hear.

3 I love to think on mercies past,
   And future good implore,
   And all my cares and sorrows cast
   On him whom I adore.

4 I love by faith to take a view
   Of brighter scenes in heaven;
   The prospect doth my strength renew,
   While here by tempests driven.

5 Thus, when life's toilsome day is o'er,
   May its departing ray
   Be calm as this impressive hour,
   And lead to endless day!
   Mrs. Phœbe H. Brown, 1825.

10. *An Evening Song.* (16.)

1 Now, from the altar of our hearts,
   Let incense flames arise;
   Assist us, Lord! to offer up
   Our evening sacrifice.

2 Awake, our love! awake, our joy!
   Awake, our hearts and tongue!
   Sleep not, when mercies loudly call;
   Break forth into a song.

3 Minutes and mercies multiplied
   Have made up all this day;
   Minutes came quick, but mercies were
   More fleet and free than they.

4 New time, new favors, and new joys,
   Do a new song require;
   Till we shall praise thee as we would,
   Accept our heart's desire.

5 Lord of our time! whose hand hath set
   New time upon our score;
   Thee may we praise for all our time,
   When time shall be no more!
   John Mason, 1683, c.

MORNING AND EVENING.

HOLLEY. 7s. 4 or 6 LINES. *George Hews, 1835.*

Soft-ly now the light of day Fades up-on my sight a-way;
Free from care, from la-bor free, Lord! I would commune with thee.

11. *Evening Contemplation.* (23.)

1 SOFTLY now the light of day
Fades upon my sight away;
Free from care, from labor free,
Lord! I would commune with thee.

2 Thou, whose all-pervading eye
Naught escapes, without, within!
Pardon each infirmity,
Open fault, and secret sin.

3 Soon, for me, the light of day
Shall for ever pass away;
Then, from sin and sorrow free,
Take me, Lord! to dwell with thee.

4 Thou who, sinless, yet hast known
All of man's infirmity!
Then, from thine eternal throne,
Jesus! look with pitying eye.
George W. Doane, 1826.

12. *The Round of daily Care.* (24.)

1 IN the morning hear my voice,
Let me in thy light rejoice;
God, my Sun! my strength renew,
Send thy blessing down like dew.

2 Through the duties of the day,
Grant me grace to watch and pray;
Live as always seeing thee,
Knowing,—Thou, God! seest me.

3 When the evening skies display
Richer pomp than noon's array,
Be the shades of death to me
Bright with immortality.

4 When the round of care is run,
And the stars succeed the sun,
Songs of praise with prayer unite,
Crown the day, and hail the night.

5 Thus with thee, my God! my Friend!
Time begin, continue, end,
While life's joys and sorrows pass,
Like the changes of the grass.
James Montgomery, 1825.

13. *Repose and Devotion.* (21.)

1 Now, from labor and from care,
Evening shades have set me free;
In the work of praise and prayer,
Lord! I would converse with thee;
Oh! behold me from above,
Fill me with a Saviour's love.

2 Sin and sorrow, guilt and woe,
Wither all my earthly joys;
Naught can charm me here below,
But my Saviour's melting voice;
Lord! forgive, thy grace restore,
Make me thine for evermore.

3 For the blessings of this day,
For the mercies of this hour,
For the gospel's cheering ray,
For the Spirit's quickening power,
Grateful notes to thee I raise;
Oh! accept my song of praise.
Thomas Hastings, 1831.

INVOCATION.

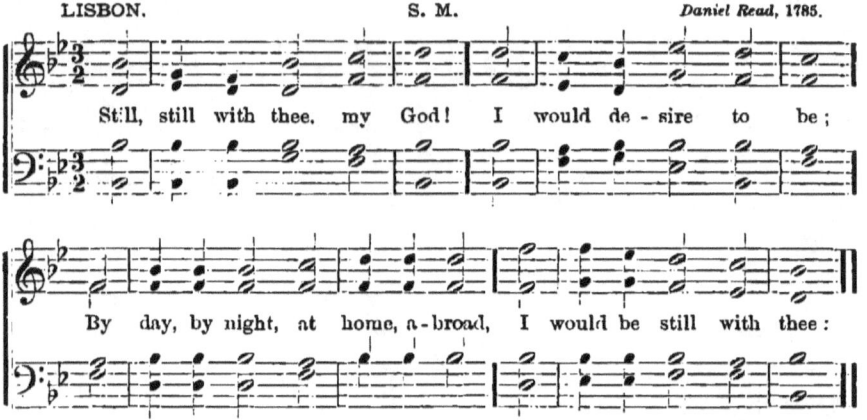

LISBON. S. M. Daniel Read, 1785.

Still, still with thee, my God! I would de-sire to be;
By day, by night, at home, a-broad, I would be still with thee:

14. *Ever with God.* (33.)

1 Still, still with thee, my God!
  I would desire to be;
  By day, by night, at home, abroad,
  I would be still with thee:

2 With thee, when dawn comes in,
  And calls me back to care;
  Each day returning to begin
  With thee, my God! in prayer:

3 With thee, amid the crowd
  That throngs the busy mart,
  To hear thy voice, 'mid clamor loud,
  Speak softly to my heart.

4 With thee, when day is done,
  And evening calms the mind:
  The setting, as the rising, sun
  With thee my heart would find.

5 With thee, when darkness brings
  The signal of repose,
  Calm in the shadow of thy wings,
  Mine eyelids I would close.

6 With thee, in thee, by faith
  Abiding I would be;
  By day, by night, in life, in death,
  I would be still with thee.
  James Drummond Burns, 1856.

15. *The Lord's Day and Public Worship.* (34.)

1 Welcome! sweet day of rest,
  That saw the Lord arise!
  Welcome to this reviving breast,
  And these rejoicing eyes!

2 The King himself comes near,
  And feasts his saints to-day;
  Here we may sit, and see him here,
  And love, and praise, and pray.

3 One day, amidst the place
  Where my dear God has been,
  Is sweeter than ten thousand days
  Of pleasurable sin.

4 My willing soul would stay,
  In such a frame as this,
  And sit and sing herself away
  To everlasting bliss.
  Isaac Watts, 1707.

16. *Sabbath Enjoyment.* (35.)

1 Sweet is the work, O Lord!
  Thy glorious acts to sing.
  To praise thy name, and hear thy word,
  And grateful offerings bring.

2 Sweet, at the dawning light,
  Thy boundless love to tell;
  And, when approach the shades of night,
  Still on the theme to dwell.

3 Sweet, on this day of rest,
  To join in heart and voice
  With those who love and serve thee best,
  And in thy name rejoice.

4 To songs of praise and joy
  Be every Sabbath given,
  That such may be our blest employ
  Eternally in heaven.
  Harriet Auber, 1829, a.

THE LORD'S DAY.

SABBATH. 7s. 6 or 8 LINES. *Lowell Mason, 1834.*

{ Safely thro' another week, God has brought us on our way ;
{ Let us now a blessing seek, [OMIT.....................] Waiting in his courts to-day ; Day of all the week the best, Emblem of e-ter-nal rest ; Day of all the week the best, Emblem of e-ter-nal rest.

17. *The Sabbath in the Sanctuary.* (37.)

1 SAFELY through another week,
   God has brought us on our way ;
  Let us now a blessing seek,
   Waiting in his courts to-day :
  Day of all the week the best,
  Emblem of eternal rest.

2 While we pray for pardoning grace,
   Through the dear Redeemer's name,
  Show thy reconciled face,
   Take away our sin and shame ;
  From our worldly cares set free,
  May we rest, this day, in thee.

3 Here we come thy name to praise ;
   May we feel thy presence near :
  May thy glory meet our eyes,
   While we in thy house appear ;
  Here afford us, Lord ! a taste
  Of our everlasting feast.

4 May thy gospel's joyful sound
   Conquer sinners, comfort saints ;
  Make the fruits of grace abound,
   Bring relief for all complaints :
  Thus may all our Sabbaths prove,
  Till we join the church above.
   John Newton, 1779, a.

18. *The God of the Sabbath.* (38.)

1 GREAT Creator ! who this day
   From thy perfect work didst rest,
  By the souls that own thy sway,
   Hallowed be its hours and blest ;
  Cares of earth aside be thrown,
  This day given to heaven alone.

2 Saviour ! who this day didst break
   The dark prison of the tomb,
  Bid my slumbering soul awake,
   Shine through all its sin and gloom :
  Let me, from my bonds set free,
  Rise from sin, and live to thee !

3 Blessed Spirit, Comforter !
   Sent this day from Christ on high,
  Lord ! on me thy gifts confer,
   Cleanse, illumine, sanctify ;
  All thine influence shed abroad,
  Lead me to the truth of God.
   Mrs. Julia Anne Elliott, 1835.

19. *The holy Day of Rest.* (39.)

1 WELCOME, sacred day of rest !
   Sweet repose from worldly care ;
  Day above all days the best,
   When our souls for heaven prepare :
  Day, when our Redeemer rose,
   Victor o'er the hosts of hell :
  Thus he vanquished all our foes ;
  Let our lips his glory tell.

2 Gracious Lord ! we love this day,
   When we hear thy holy word ;
  When we sing thy praise, and pray,
   Earth can no such joys afford :
  But a better rest remains,
   Heavenly Sabbaths, happier days,
  Rest from sin, and rest from pains,
  Endless joys, and endless praise.
   William Brown (?) 1822.

INVOCATION.

MARLOW. C. M.
English Melody.
Arr. by *Lowell Mason*, 1832.

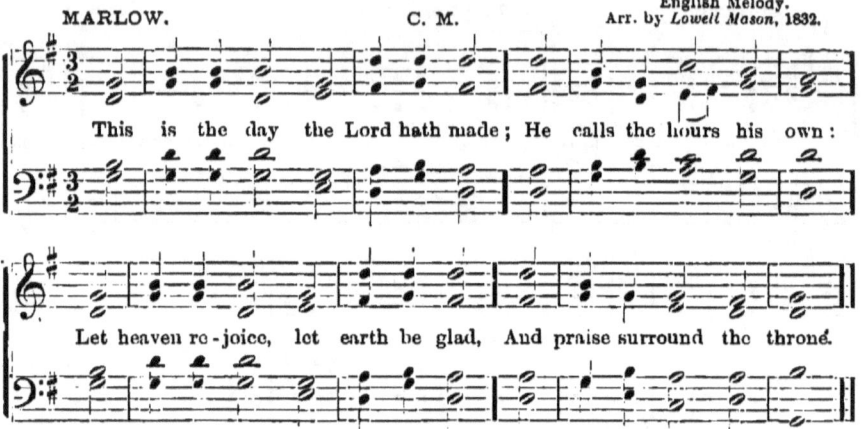

This is the day the Lord hath made; He calls the hours his own:
Let heaven re-joice, let earth be glad, And praise surround the throne.

20. PSALM 118. (49.)

1 This is the day the Lord hath made;
  He calls the hours his own:
Let heaven rejoice, let earth be glad,
  And praise surround the throne.

2 To-day he rose and left the dead,
  And Satan's empire fell;
To-day the saints his triumph spread,
  And all his wonders tell.

3 Hosanna to th' anointed King,
  To David's holy Son:
Help us, O Lord! descend, and bring
  Salvation from the throne.

4 Blest be the Lord, who comes to men,
  With messages of grace;
Who comes, in God his Father's name,
  To save our sinful race.

5 Hosanna, in the highest strains,
  The church on earth can raise!
The highest heavens, in which he reigns,
  Shall give him nobler praise.
    Isaac Watts, 1719.

21. PSALM 122. (50.)

1 With joy we hail the sacred day,
  Which God hath called his own;
With joy the summons we obey
  To worship at his throne.

2 Thy chosen temple, Lord! how fair!
  Where willing votaries throng,
To breathe the humble, fervent prayer,
  And pour the choral song.

3 Spirit of grace! Oh! deign to dwell
  Within thy church below;
Make her in holiness excel,
  With pure devotion glow.

4 Let peace within her walls be found;
  Let all her sons unite,
To spread with grateful zeal around
  Her clear and shining light.
    Harriet Auber, 1829.

22. Sabbath Morn. (51.)

1 How sweetly breaks the Sabbath dawn
  Along the eastern skies!
So, when the night of time hath gone,
  Eternity shall rise.

2 How softly spreads the Sabbath light!
  How soon the gloom hath fled!
So o'er the new-created sight
  Celestial bliss is spread.

3 What quiet reigns o'er earth and sea,
  Through all the stilly air!
So calm may we, this Sabbath, be,
  And free from worldly care.

4 Thus let thy peace, O Lord! pervade
  Our bosoms, all our days;
And let each passing hour be made
  A herald of thy praise.

5 This peace of God—how full! how sweet!
  It flows from Jesus' breast;
It makes our bliss on earth complete,
  It brings eternal rest.
    Edwin F. Hatfield, 1840.

THE LORD'S DAY.

Fre-quent the day of God re-turns, To shed its quickening beams; And yet how slow de-vo-tion burns, How lan-guid are its flames!

23. *Evening of the Lord's Day.* (55.)

1 FREQUENT the day of God returns
   To shed its quickening beams;
   And yet how slow devotion burns,
   How languid are its flames!

2 Accept our faint attempts to love,
   Our frailties, Lord! forgive;
   We would be like thy saints above,
   And praise thee while we live.

3 Increase, O Lord! our faith and hope,
   And fit us to ascend
   Where the assembly ne'er breaks up,
   The Sabbath ne'er will end:

4 Where we shall breathe in heavenly air,
   With heavenly lustre shine;
   For ever feed on heavenly fare,
   And feast on love divine;

5 Where we, in high seraphic strains,
   Shall all our powers employ,
   Delighted range th' ethereal plains,
   And take our fill of joy.
                    Simon Browne, 1720.

24. *The First Day of the Week.* (54.)

1 AND now another week begins,
   This day we call the Lord's;
   This day he rose, who bore our sins;—
   For so his word records.

2 Hark, how the angels sweetly sing!—
   Their voices fill the sky!
   They hail their great victorious King,
   And welcome him on high.

3 We'll catch the note of lofty praise;
   Their joys in part we feel;
   With them our thankful song we'll raise,
   And emulate their zeal.

4 Come, then, ye saints! and grateful sing
   Of Christ, our risen Lord,—
   Of Christ, the everlasting King,
   Of Christ, th' incarnate Word.

5 Hail! mighty Saviour! thee we hail!
   Who fill'st the throne above;
   Till heart and flesh together fail,
   We'll sing thy matchless love.
                    Thomas Kelly, 1809, a.

25. *Lord's Day Evening.* (57.)

1 WHEN, O dear Jesus! when shall I
   Behold thee all-serene,
   Blest in perpetual Sabbath-day,
   Without a veil between?

2 Assist me while I wander here,
   Amidst a world of cares;
   Incline my heart to pray with love,
   And then accept my prayers.

3 Spare me, my God! Oh! spare the soul
   That gives itself to thee;
   Take all that I possess below,
   And give thyself to me.

4 Thy Spirit, O my Father! give
   To be my guide and friend,
   To light my path to ceaseless joys,
   To Sabbaths without end.
                    John Cennick, 1743.

INVOCATION.

PORTUGAL.   L. M.   Thomas Thorley, 17—,

Sweet is the work, my God, my King! To praise thy name, give thanks, and sing;

To show thy love by morn-ing light, And talk of all thy truth at night.

26.   PSALM 92.   (43.)

1 SWEET is the work, my God, my King!
  To praise thy name, give thanks, and sing;
  To show thy love by morning light,
  And talk of all thy truth at night.

2 Sweet is the day of sacred rest;
  No mortal cares shall seize my breast;
  Oh! may my heart in tune be found,
  Like David's harp of solemn sound!

3 My heart shall triumph in my Lord,
  And bless his works, and bless his word;
  Thy works of grace, how bright they shine!
  How deep thy counsels! how divine!

4 Lord! I shall share a glorious part,
  When grace hath well refined my heart,
  And fresh supplies of joys are shed,
  Like holy oil to cheer my head.

5 Then shall I see, and hear, and know
  All I desired or wished below;
  And every power find sweet employ,
  In that eternal world of joy.
                Isaac Watts, 1719.

27.   *The Lord's Day.*   (17.)

1 THIS day the Lord hath called his own;
  Oh! let us then his praise declare,
  Fix our desires on him alone,
  And seek his face, with fervent prayer.

2 Lord! in thy love, would we rejoice,
  That bids the burdened soul be free;
  And, with united heart and voice,
  Devote these sacred hours to thee.

3 Now let the world's delusive things
  No more our groveling thoughts employ;
  But faith be taught to stretch her wings,
  In search of heaven's unfailing joy.

4 Oh! let these earthly Sabbaths, Lord!
  Be to our lasting welfare blessed;
  The purest comfort here afford,
  And fit us for eternal rest.
                William H. Bathurst, 1831.

28.   *The eternal Sabbath.*   (46.)

1 LORD of the Sabbath! hear our vows,
  On this thy day, in this thy house;
  And own, as grateful sacrifice,
  The songs, which from the desert rise.

2 Thine earthly Sabbaths, Lord! we love;
  But there 's a nobler rest above;
  To that our laboring souls aspire,
  With ardent pangs of strong desire.

3 No more fatigue, no more distress,
  Nor sin, nor hell shall reach the place;
  No groans to mingle with the songs,
  Which warble from immortal tongues.

4 No rude alarms of raging foes,
  No cares to break the long repose,
  No midnight shade, no clouded sun,
  But sacred, high, eternal noon.

5 O long expected day! begin;
  Dawn on these realms of woe and sin;
  Fain would we leave this weary road,
  And sleep in death to rise with God.
                Philip Doddridge, 1737.

THE LORD'S DAY.

29. *The Holy Day of Rest.* (60.)

1 O DAY of rest and gladness,
  O day of joy and light!
O balm of care and sadness,
  Most beautiful, most bright!
On thee, the high and lowly,
  Before th' eternal throne,
Sing Holy! Holy! Holy!
  To the great Three in One.

2 On thee, at the creation,
  The light first had its birth:
On thee, for our salvation,
  Christ rose from depths of earth;
On thee, our Lord, victorious,
  The Spirit sent from heaven,
And thus on thee, most glorious,
  A triple light was given.

3 Thou art a cooling fountain
  In life's dry dreary sand;
From thee, like Pisgah's mountain,
  We view our promised land:
A day of sweet reflection,
  A day of holy love,
A day of resurrection
  From earth to things above.

4 To-day on weary nations
  The heavenly manna falls;
To holy convocations
  The silver trumpet calls,
Where gospel light is glowing
  With pure and radiant beams,
And living water flowing
  With soul-refreshing streams.

5 New graces ever gaining
  From this our day of rest,
We reach the rest remaining
  To spirits of the blest:
To Holy Ghost be praises,
  To Father and to Son;
The church her voice upraises
  To thee, blest Three in One.
    Christopher Wordsworth, 1858.

30. *Welcome to the Sabbath.* (61.)

1 THY holy day's returning,
  Our hearts exult to see;
And, with devotion burning,
  Ascend, our God! to thee;
To-day, with purest pleasure,
  Our thoughts from earth withdraw
We search for sacred treasure,
  We learn thy holy law.

2 We join to sing thy praises,
  God of the Sabbath day!
Each voice in gladness raises
  Its loudest, sweetest lay;
Thy richest mercies sharing,
  Oh! fill us with thy love,
By grace our souls preparing
  For nobler praise above.
    Ray Palmer, 1865.

INVOCATION.

LISCHER. H. M. German. Arr. by Lowell Mason, 1841.

Welcome, delightful morn, Thou day of sacred rest!
I hail thy kind return; Lord! make these moments blest: From the low train of mortal toys,
I soar to reach immortal joys; I soar to reach immortal joys.

31. *The Sabbath welcomed.* (62.)

1 WELCOME, delightful morn,
  Thou day of sacred rest!
  I hail thy kind return;
  Lord! make these moments blest;
  From the low train of mortal toys,
  I soar to reach immortal joys.

2 Now may the King descend,
  And fill his throne of grace!
  Thy sceptre, Lord! extend,
  While saints address thy face:
  Let sinners feel thy quickening word,
  And learn to know and fear the Lord.

3 Descend, celestial Dove!
  With all thy quickening powers;
  Disclose a Saviour's love,
  And bless these sacred hours;
  Then shall my soul new life obtain,
  Nor Sabbaths e'er be spent in vain.
    Hayward, 1806.

32. PSALM 84. (65.)

1 LORD of the worlds above!
  How pleasant, and how fair,
  The dwellings of thy love,
  Thine earthly temples are!
  To thine abode my heart aspires,
  With warm desires to see my God.

2 Oh! happy souls who pray,
  Where God appoints to hear!
  Oh! happy men who pay
  Their constant service there!
  They praise thee still; and happy they
  Who love the way to Zion's hill.

3 They go from strength to strength,
  Through this dark vale of tears,
  Till each arrives at length,
  Till each in heaven appears;
  Oh! glorious seat, when God, our King,
  Shall thither bring our willing feet!
    Isaac Watts, 1719.

33. PSALM 43. (67.)

1 Now, to thy sacred house,
  With joy I turn my feet,
  Where saints, with morning-vows,
  In full assembly meet:
  Thy power divine shall there be shown,
  And from thy throne thy mercy shine.

2 Oh! send thy light abroad;
  Thy truth, with heavenly ray,
  Shall lead my soul to God,
  And guide my doubtful way;
  I'll hear thy word with faith sincere,
  And learn to fear and praise the Lord.

3 Here reach thy bounteous hand,
  And all my sorrows heal,
  Here health and strength divine,
  Oh! make my bosom feel;
  Like balmy dew, shall Jesus' voice
  My heart rejoice, my strength renew.

4 Now in thy holy hill,
  Before thine altar, Lord!
  My harp and song shall sound
  The glories of thy word;
  Henceforth to thee, O God of grace!
  A hymn of praise, my life shall be.
    Timothy Dwight, 1800.

THE SANCTUARY. 17

SICILY.   8s & 7s; or 8s, 7s & 4.   *Sicilian Melody.*

Come, thou soul-trans-form-ing Spir-it! Bless the sow-er and the seed;
Let each heart thy grace in-her-it: Raise the weak, the hun-gry feed:
From the gos-pel, from the gos-pel, Now sup-ply thy peo-ple's need.

34. *The Spirit and the Word.* (86.)

1 COME, thou soul-transforming Spirit!
Bless the sower and the seed;
Let each heart thy grace inherit;
Raise the weak, the hungry feed;
From the gospel,
Now supply thy people's need.

2 Oh! may all enjoy the blessing
Which thy word's designed to give;
Let us all, thy love possessing,
Joyfully the truth receive;
And for ever
To thy praise and glory live.
Jonathan Evans, 1784.

35. *Close of Worship.* (87.)

1 GOD of our salvation! hear us;
Bless, Oh! bless us, ere we go;
When we join the world, be near us,
Lest we cold and careless grow;
Saviour! keep us;
Keep us safe from every foe.

2 May we live in view of heaven,
Where we hope to see thy face;
Save us from unhallowed leaven,
All that might obscure thy grace;
Keep us walking
Each in his appointed place.

3 As our steps are drawing nearer
To our endless blissful home,
May our view of heaven grow clearer,
Hope more bright of joys to come;

And, when dying,
May thy presence cheer the gloom.
Thomas Kelly, 1809, a.

36. *A parting Blessing implored.* (84.)

1 LORD! dismiss us with thy blessing,
Fill our hearts with joy and peace;
Let us each, thy love possessing,
Triumph in redeeming grace;
Oh! refresh us,
Traveling through this wilderness.

2 Thanks we give and adoration,
For thy gospel's joyful sound;
May the fruits of thy salvation
In our hearts and lives abound;
May thy presence
With us, evermore, be found.

3 So, whene'er the signal's given,
Us from earth to call away,
Borne on angels' wings to heaven,
Glad the summons to obey,
We shall surely
Reign with Christ in endless day.
Walter Shirley, 1774.

37. *A parting Blessing.* (88.)

1 LORD! dismiss us with thy blessing;
Bid us all depart in peace;
Still on gospel manna feeding,
Pure seraphic joys increase.

2 Fill our hearts with consolation;
Unto thee our voices raise;
When we reach that blissful station,
We will give thee nobler praise.
Edward Smyth, 1774.

INVOCATION.

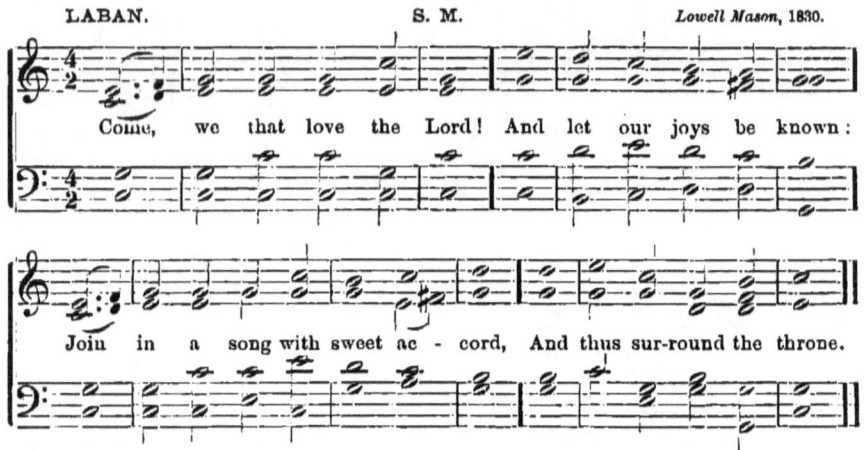

Come, we that love the Lord! And let our joys be known:
Join in a song with sweet ac-cord, And thus sur-round the throne.

38. *Heavenly Joy on Earth.* (73.)

1 Come, we that love the Lord!
  And let our joys be known:
Join in a song with sweet accord,
  And thus surround the throne.

2 Let those refuse to sing,
  That never knew our God;
But favorites of the heavenly King
  May speak their joys abroad.

3 The men of grace have found
  Glory begun below;
Celestial fruits on earthly ground
  From faith and hope may grow.

4 The hill of Zion yields
  A thousand sacred sweets,
Before we reach the heavenly fields,
  Or walk the golden streets.

5 Then let our songs abound,
  And every tear be dry; [ground,
We 're marching through Immanuel's
  To fairer worlds on high.
  Isaac Watts, 1707.

39. *The Pleasure of Social Worship.* (70.)

1 How charming is the place,
  Where my Redeemer God
Unveils the beauties of his face,
  And sheds his love abroad!

2 Not the fair palaces,
  To which the great resort,
Are once to be compared with this,
  Where Jesus holds his court.

3 Here on the mercy-seat,
  With radiant glory crowned,
Our radiant eyes behold him sit,
  And smile on all around.

4 To him, their prayers and cries
  Each humble soul presents;
He listens to their broken sighs,
  And grants them all their wants.

5 To them his sovereign will
  He graciously imparts;
And in return accepts, with smiles,
  The tribute of their hearts.

6 Give me, O Lord! a place
  Within thy blest abode,
Among the children of thy grace,
  The servants of my God.
  Samuel Stennett, 1772.

40. *Homage and Devotion.* (71.)

1 With joy, we lift our eyes
  To those bright realms above,
That glorious temple in the skies,
  Where dwells eternal love.

2 Before thy throne we bow,
  O thou almighty King!
Here we present the solemn vow,
  And hymns of praise we sing.

3 While in thy house we kneel,
  With trust and holy fear,
Thy mercy and thy truth reveal,
  And lend a gracious ear.
  Thomas Jervis, 1795, a.

THE SANCTUARY.

SILVER STREET. S. M. *Isaac Smith*, 1770.

Come, sound his praise abroad, And hymns of glory sing;
Jehovah is the sovereign God, The universal King.

41. PSALM 95. (76.)

1 Come, sound his praise abroad,
   And hymns of glory sing;
   Jehovah is the sovereign God,
   The universal King.

2 He formed the deeps unknown;
   He gave the seas their bound;
   The watery worlds are all his own,
   And all the solid ground.

3 Come, worship at his throne;
   Come, bow before the Lord;
   We are his works, and not our own;
   He formed us by his word.

4 To-day attend his voice,
   Nor dare provoke his rod;
   Come, like the people of his choice,
   And own your gracious God.

5 But, if your ears refuse
   The language of his grace,   [Jews,
   And hearts grow hard, like stubborn
   That unbelieving race; —

6 The Lord, in vengeance dressed,
   Will lift his hand and swear,—
   "You, that despised my promised rest,
   Shall have no portion there."
   Isaac Watts, 1719.

42. *Pleasures of spiritual Worship.* (77.)

1 How sweet to bless the Lord,
   And in his praises join,
   With saints his goodness to record,
   And sing his power divine!

2 These seasons of delight
   The dawn of glory seem.
   Like rays of pure, celestial light,
   Which on our spirits beam.

3 Thus may our joys increase,
   Our love more ardent grow,
   While rich supplies of Jesus' grace
   Refresh our souls below.

4 But, Oh! the bliss sublime,
   When joy shall be complete,
   In that unclouded, glorious clime,
   Where all thy servants meet!
   Anon., 1829.

43. *Close of Worship.* (78.)

1 Once more, before we part,
   Oh! bless the Saviour's name;
   Let every tongue and every heart
   Adore and praise the same.

2 Lord! in thy grace we came,
   That blessing still impart;
   We met in Jesus' sacred name,
   In Jesus' name we part.

3 Still on thy holy word
   Help us to feed, and grow,
   Still to go on to know the Lord,
   And practise what we know.

4 Now, Lord! before we part,
   Help us to bless thy name:
   Let every tongue and every heart
   Adore and praise the same.
   Joseph Hart, 1762, a.

INVOCATION.

HENDON. 7s. *Cæsar Malan,* 1830.

Lord! we come be-fore thee now: At thy feet we hum-bly bow; Oh! do not our suit dis-dain;—Shall we seek thee, Lord! in vain? Shall we seek thee, Lord! in vain?

44. *A Blessing humbly requested.* (89.)

1 Lord! we come before thee now:
At thy feet we humbly bow;
Oh! do not our suit disdain;—
Shall we seek thee, Lord! in vain?

2 Lord! on thee our souls depend,
In compassion, now descend;
Fill our hearts with thy rich grace,
Tune our lips to sing thy praise.

3 In thine own appointed way,
Now we seek thee, here we stay;
Lord! we know not how to go,
Till a blessing thou bestow.

4 Send some message, from thy word,
That may joy and peace afford;
Let thy Spirit now impart
Full salvation to each heart.

5 Comfort those who weep and mourn,
Let the time of joy return;
Those, that are cast down, lift up,
Strong in faith, and love, and hope.

6 Grant, that those who seek may find
Thee, a God sincere and kind:
Heal the sick, the captive free,
Let us all rejoice in thee.
William Hammond, 1745.

45. *A Day in the Lord's Courts.* (90.)

1 To thy temple I repair,
Lord! I love to worship there,
When, within the veil, I meet
Christ before the mercy-seat.

2 While thy glorious praise is sung,
Touch my lips, unloose my tongue,
That my joyful soul may bless
Thee, the Lord, my Righteousness.

3 While the prayers of saints ascend,
God of love! to mine attend;
Hear me, for thy Spirit pleads,
Hear, for Jesus intercedes.

4 While thy ministers proclaim
Peace and pardon in thy name,
Through their voice, by faith, may I
Hear thee speaking from the sky.

5 From thy house, when I return,
May my heart within me burn,
And at evening let me say,
"I have walked with God to-day."
James Montgomery, 1812.

46. *Peace through the Blood of Christ.* (95.)

1 Now may He, who, from the dead,
Brought the Shepherd of the sheep,
Jesus Christ, our King and Head,
All our souls in safety keep!

2 May he teach us to fulfill
What is pleasing in his sight;
Perfect us in all his will,
And preserve us day and night.

3 To that dear Redeemer's praise,
Who the covenant sealed with blood,
Let our hearts and voices raise
Loud thanksgivings to our God.
John Newton, 1779.

THE SANCTUARY.

COLCHESTER. C. M. From *Aaron Williams'* Coll., cir. 1760.

Oh! 't was a joy-ful sound, to hear Our tribes de-vout-ly say:—
"Up, Is-rael! to the tem-ple haste, And keep your fes-tal day!"

47.   PSALM 122.   (96.)

1 Oh! 't was a joyful sound, to hear
   Our tribes devoutly say :—
"Up, Israel! to the temple haste,
   And keep your festal day!"

2 At Salem's courts we must appear,
   With our assembled powers,
In strong and beauteous order ranged,
   Like her united towers.

3 Oh! ever pray for Salem's peace;
   For they shall prosperous be,
Thou holy city of our God!
   Who bear true love to thee.
Nahum Tate, 1696.

48.   PSALM 122.   (97.)

1 How did my heart rejoice, to hear
   My friends devoutly say,—
"In Zion let us all appear,
   And keep the solemn day!"

2 I love her gates, I love the road ;
   The church, adorned with grace,
Stands like a palace, built for God,
   To show his milder face.

3 Up to her courts, with joys unknown,
   The holy tribes repair ;
The Son of David holds his throne,
   And sits in judgment there.

4 He hears our praises and complaints ;
   And, while his awful voice
Divides the sinners from the saints,
   We tremble and rejoice.

5 Peace be within this sacred place,
   And joy a constant guest!
With holy gifts and heavenly grace,
   Be her attendants blest!

6 My soul shall pray for Zion still,
   While life or breath remains ;
There my best friends, my kindred, dwell,
   There God, my Saviour, reigns.
Isaac Watts, 1719.

49.   PSALM 5.   (99.)

1 LORD! in the morning thou shalt hear
   My voice ascending high ;
To thee will I direct my prayer,
   To thee lift up mine eye ;—

2 Up to the hills, where Christ is gone
   To plead for all his saints,
Presenting, at his Father's throne,
   Our songs and our complaints.

3 Thou art a God, before whose sight
   The wicked shall not stand ;
Sinners shall ne'er be thy delight,
   Nor dwell at thy right hand.

4 But to thy house will I resort,
   To taste thy mercies there
I will frequent thy holy court,
   And worship in thy fear.

5 Oh! may thy Spirit guide my feet,
   In ways of righteousness ;
Make every path of duty straight,
   And plain before my face.
Isaac Watts, 1719.

INVOCATION.

MEAR. C. M. Welsh Air. From Aaron Williams' Coll., cir. 1760.

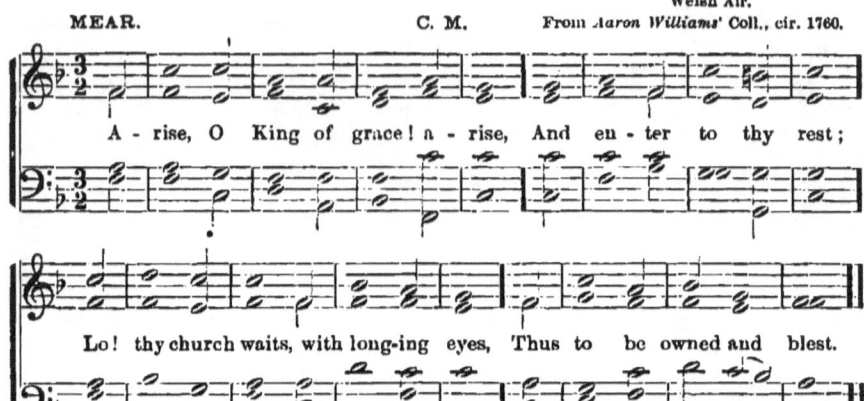

A-rise, O King of grace! a-rise, And en-ter to thy rest;
Lo! thy church waits, with long-ing eyes, Thus to be owned and blest.

50. PSALM 132. (102.)

1 ARISE! O King of grace! arise,
   And enter to thy rest;
Lo! thy church waits, with longing eyes,
   Thus to be owned and blest.

2 Enter, with all thy glorious train,
   Thy Spirit and thy word;
All that the ark did once contain
   Could no such grace afford.

3 Here, mighty God! accept our vows;
   Here let thy praise be spread:
Bless the provisions of thy house,
   And fill thy poor with bread.

4 Here let the Son of David reign,
   Let God's Anointed shine;
Justice and truth his court maintain,
   With love and power divine.

5 Here let him hold a lasting throne;
   And, as his kingdom grows,
Fresh honors shall adorn his crown,
   And shame confound his foes.
               Isaac Watts, 1719.

51. PSALM 27. (108.)

1 THE Lord of glory is my light,
   And my salvation too;
God is my strength; nor will I fear
   What all my foes can do.

2 One privilege my heart desires;
   Oh! grant me an abode
Among the churches of thy saints,
   The temples of my God.

3 There shall I offer my requests,
   And see thy beauty still;
Shall hear thy messages of love,
   And there inquire thy will.

4 When troubles rise, and storms appear,
   There may his children hide;
God has a strong pavillion, where
   He makes my soul abide.

5 Now shall my head be lifted high
   Above my foes around;
And songs of joy and victory
   Within thy temple sound.
               Isaac Watts, 1719.

52. *The Joys of Heaven.* (104.)

1 COME, Lord! and warm each languid heart,
   Inspire each lifeless tongue,
And let the joys of heaven impart
   Their influence to our song.

2 Then, to the shining seats of bliss,
   The wings of faith shall soar,
And all the charms of paradise
   Our raptured thoughts explore.

3 There shall the foll'wers of the Lamb
   Join in immortal songs;
And endless honors to his name
   Employ their tuneful tongues.

4 Lord! tune our hearts to praise and love,
   Our feeble notes inspire;
Till, in thy blissful courts above,
   We join the heavenly choir.
               Anne Steele, 1760.

THE SANCTUARY.

LANESBORO'.   C. M.   English Melody.

Early, my God! without delay, I haste to seek thy face; My thirsty spirit faints away, My thirsty spirit faints away, Without thy cheering grace.

53. PSALM 63. (105.)

1 EARLY, my God! without delay,
  I haste to seek thy face;
  My thirsty spirit faints away,
  Without thy cheering grace.

2 So pilgrims on the scorching sand,
  Beneath a burning sky,
  Long for a cooling stream at hand,
  And they must drink or die.

3 I've seen thy glory and thy power,
  Through all thy temple shine;
  My God! repeat that heavenly hour,
  That vision so divine.

4 Not all the blessings of a feast
  Can please my soul so well,
  As when thy richer grace I taste,
  And in thy presence dwell.

5 Not life itself, with all its joys,
  Can my best passions move;
  Or raise so high my cheerful voice,
  As thy forgiving love.

6 Thus, till my last expiring day,
  I'll bless my God and King;
  Thus will I lift my hands to pray,
  And tune my lips to sing.
                  Isaac Watts, 1719.

54. *Before Public Worship.* (110.)

1 LORD! when we bend before thy throne,
  And our confessions pour,
  Teach us to feel the sins we own,
  And hate what we deplore.

2 Our broken spirits, pitying, see;
  And penitence impart;
  Then let a kindling glance from thee
  Beam hope upon the heart.

3 When we disclose our wants in prayer,
  May we our wills resign;
  And not a thought our bosom share,
  Which is not wholly thine.

4 Let faith each meek petition fill,
  And waft it to the skies;
  And teach our hearts—'t is goodness still
  That grants it, or denies.
                  Joseph Dacre Carlyle, 1805.

55. *The Influences of the Spirit desired.* (107.)

1 GREAT Father of each perfect gift!
  Behold, thy servants wait;
  With longing eyes, and lifted hands,
  We flock around thy gate.

2 Oh! shed abroad that royal gift,—
  Thy Spirit from above,
  To bless our eyes with sacred light,
  And fire our hearts with love.

3 Blest Earnest of eternal joy!
  Declare our sins forgiven;
  And bear, with energy divine,
  Our raptured thoughts to heaven.

4 Diffuse, O God! the copious showers,
  That earth its fruit may yield,
  And change this barren wilderness,
  To Carmel's flowery field.
                  Philip Doddridge, 1736.

INVOCATION.

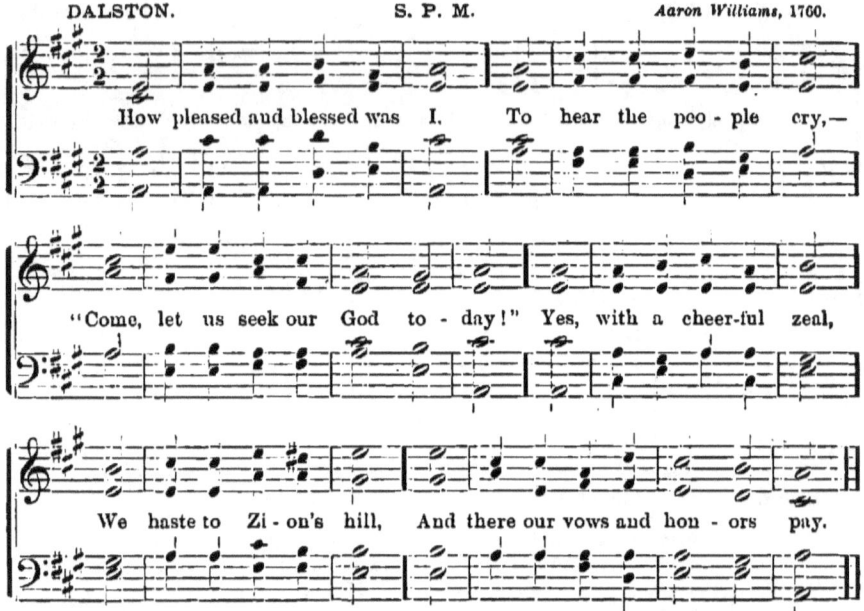

DALSTON. S. P. M. Aaron Williams, 1760.

How pleased and blessed was I, To hear the peo-ple cry,— "Come, let us seek our God to-day!" Yes, with a cheer-ful zeal, We haste to Zi-on's hill, And there our vows and hon-ors pay.

56. PSALM 122. (117.)

1 How pleased and blessed was I,
 To hear the people cry,—
  "Come, let us seek our God to-day!"
 Yes, with a cheerful zeal,
 We haste to Zion's hill,
  And there our vows and honors pay.

2 Zion! thrice happy place,
 Adorned with wondrous grace, [round;
  And walls of strength embrace thee
 In thee our tribes appear
 To pray, and praise, and hear
  The sacred gospel's joyful sound.

3 There David's greater Son
 Has fixed his royal throne;
  He sits for grace and judgment there:
 He bids the saint be glad,
 He makes the sinner sad,
  And humble souls rejoice with fear.

4 May peace attend thy gate,
 And joy within thee wait,
  To bless the soul of every guest!
 The man that seeks thy peace,
 And wishes thine increase,—
  A thousand blessings on him rest.

5 My tongue repeats her vows;
 "Peace to this sacred house!"
  For there my friends and kindred dwell:
 And, since my glorious God
 Makes thee his blest abode,
  My soul shall ever love thee well.
    Isaac Watts, 1719.

57. PSALM 93. (118.)

1 THE Lord Jehovah reigns,
 And royal state maintains,
  His head with awful glories crowned;
 Arrayed in robes of light,
 Begirt with sovereign might,
  And rays of majesty around.

2 Thy promises are true,
 Thy grace is ever new, [move;
  There fixed, thy church shall ne'er re-
 Thy saints, with holy fear,
 Shall in thy courts appear,
  And sing thine everlasting love.
    Isaac Watts, 1719.

THE SANCTUARY.

UXBRIDGE. L. M. *Lowell Mason,* 1830.

How pleasant, how di-vine-ly fair, O Lord of hosts! thy dwellings are!
With long de-sire my spir-it faints, To meet th' assemblies of thy saints.

58. PSALM 84. (119.)

1 How pleasant, how divinely fair,
  O Lord of hosts! thy dwellings are!
  With long desire my spirit faints,
  To meet th' assemblies of thy saints.

2 My flesh would rest in thine abode,
  My panting heart cries out for God:
  My God! my King! why should I be
  So far from all my joys, and thee?

3 Blest are the saints who sit on high,
  Around thy throne of majesty;
  Thy brightest glories shine above,
  And all their work is praise and love.

4 Blest are the souls, who find a place
  Within the temple of thy grace;
  There they behold thy gentler rays,
  And seek thy face, and learn thy praise.

5 Blest are the men, whose hearts are set
  To find the way to Zion's gate;   [road,
  God is their strength; and through the
  They lean upon their helper, God.

6 Cheerful they walk with growing strength,
  Till all shall meet in heaven at length;
  Till all before thy face appear,
  And join in nobler worship there.
  Isaac Watts, 1719.

59. PSALM 84. (120.)

1 GREAT God! attend while Zion sings
  The joy that from thy presence springs;
  To spend one day with thee on earth
  Exceeds a thousand days of mirth.

2 Might I enjoy the meanest place
  Within thy house, O God of grace!
  Not tents of ease, nor thrones of power,
  Should tempt my feet to leave thy door.

3 God is our sun, he makes our day;
  God is our shield, he guards our way
  From all th' assaults of hell and sin,
  From foes without, and foes within.

4 All needful grace will God bestow,
  And crown that grace with glory too;
  He gives us all things, and withholds
  No real good from upright souls.

5 O God, our King! whose sovereign sway
  The glorious hosts of heaven obey,
  And devils at thy presence flee;
  Blest is the man that trusts in thee!
  Isaac Watts, 1719.

60. *Love of Christ in the Heart.* (129.)

1 COME, dearest Lord! descend and dwell,
  By faith and love, in every breast;
  Then shall we know, and taste, and feel,
  The joys that cannot be expressed.

2 Come, fill our hearts with inward strength,
  Make our enlarged souls possess,
  And learn the height, and breadth, and
  Of thine immeasurable grace. [length,

3 Now to the God, whose power can do
  More than our thoughts or wishes know,
  Be everlasting honors done,
  By all the church, through Christ, his Son.
  Isaac Watts, 1709.

INVOCATION.

MENDON. L. M. Old German: arr. *Lowell Mason.* 1832.

Far from my thoughts, vain world! be gone; Let my re-li-gious hours a-lone;
Fain would mine eyes my Sav-iour see;— I wait a vis-it, Lord! from thee.

61. *The Enjoyment of Christ.* (125.)

1 FAR from my thoughts, vain world! be
Let my religious hours alone;   [gone;
Fain would mine eyes my Saviour see;—
I wait a visit, Lord! from thee.

2 My heart grows warm with holy fire,
And kindles with a pure desire;
Come, my dear Jesus! from above,
And feed my soul with heavenly love.

3 Blessed Jesus! what delicious fare—
How sweet thine entertainments are!
Never did angels taste above
Redeeming grace, and dying love.

4 Hail, great Immanuel, all-divine!
In thee thy Father's glories shine:
Thou brightest, sweetest, fairest one,
That eyes have seen, or angels known!
Isaac Watts, 1707.

62. *The Benefit of public Ordinances.* (122.)

1 AWAY from every mortal care,
  Away from earth, our souls retreat;
We leave this worthless world afar,
  And wait and worship near thy seat.

2 Lord! in the temple of thy grace
  We see thy feet, and we adore;
We gaze upon thy lovely face,
  And learn the wonders of thy power.

3 While here our various wants we mourn,
  United groans ascend on high;
And prayer brings down a quick return
  Of blessings in variety.

4 If Satan rage, and sin grow strong,
  Here we receive some cheering word;
We gird the gospel armor on,
  To fight the battles of the Lord.

5 Or, if our spirit faints and dies, [stings,
  Our conscience galled with inward
Here doth the righteous Sun arise,
  With healing beams beneath his wings.

6 Father! my soul would still abide
  Within thy temple, near thy side;
But, if my feet must hence depart,
  Still keep thy dwelling in my heart.
Isaac Watts, 1709.

63. PSALM 117. (124.)

1 FROM all that dwell below the skies,
  Let the Creator's praise arise;
Let the Redeemer's name be sung,
  Through every land, by every tongue.

2 Eternal are thy mercies, Lord!
  Eternal truth attends thy word;
Thy praise shall sound from shore to shore,
  Till suns shall rise and set no more.
Isaac Watts, 1719.

64. *Dismission.* (132.)

1 DISMISS us, with thy blessing, Lord!
  Help us to feed upon thy word;
All that has been amiss forgive,
  And let thy truth within us live.

2 Though we are guilty, thou art good;—
  Wash all our works in Jesus' blood;
Give every fettered soul release,
  And bid us all depart in peace.
Joseph Hart, 1762.

THE TRINITY.   27

STIRLING.　　　　　L. M.　　　　　Ralph Harrison, 1786.

Thee, thee we praise, O God! and own That thou, the Lord, art God a-lone;
Thy praise supreme all na-ture sings, E-ter-nal Fa-ther! King of kings!

65.　　*"Te Deum laudamus."*　　(133.)

1 THEE, thee we praise, O God! and own
That thou, the Lord, art God alone;
Thy praise supreme all nature sings,
Eternal Father! King of kings!

2 All angels and the cherubim,—
The heavenly host,—the seraphim,
Cease not to cry,—"Be thou adored,
O holy, holy, holy Lord!"

3 The heavens and earth are full of thee,—
Thy glory, power, and majesty;
Th' apostles, prophets, martyrs, raise
To thee their loudest songs of praise.

4 Thy holy church, o'er all the earth,
Exulting owns, with hallowed mirth,—
Infinite majesty is thine,
Father eternal! Power divine!

5 Thee, too, O Christ! they all confess,—
Thee, King of glory!—thee they bless;
The Father's Son thou art alone,—
Partaker of th' eternal throne.

6 Thee, Father, Son, and Holy Ghost!
Thy saints, with all the heavenly host,
Confess, proclaim, extol, adore,
From day to day, for evermore.
　　　　　　　Latin, *Ambrose* (?), 390.
　　　　　　　Tr., *Edwin F. Hatfield*, 1871.

66.　　*The Triune God.*　　(134.)

1 O HOLY, holy, holy Lord!
Bright in thy deeds and in thy name,
For ever be thy name adored,
Thy glories let the world proclaim!

2 O Jesus! Lamb once crucified
To take our load of sins away,—
Thine be the hymn, that rolls its tide
Along the realms of upper day!

3 O Holy Spirit! from above,
In streams of light and glory given,
Thou Source of ecstacy and love,
Thy praises ring through earth and heaven!

4 O God Triune! to thee we owe
Our every thought, our every song;
And ever may thy praises flow
From saint and seraph's burning tongue!
　　　　　　　James Wallis Eastburn, 1819.

67.　　*Prayer to the Trinity.*　　(137.)

1 FATHER of heaven! whose love profound
A ransom for our souls hath found,—
Before thy throne we sinners bend;
To us thy pard'ning love extend.

2 Alm'ghty Son—incarnate Word—
Our Prophet, Priest, Redeemer, Lord!
Before thy throne we sinners bend;
To us thy saving grace extend.

3 Eternal Spirit! by whose breath
The soul is raised from sin and death,—
Before thy throne we sinners bend;
To us thy quickening power extend.

4 Jehovah! Father, Spirit, Son!—
Mysterious Godhead—Three in One!
Before thy throne we sinners bend;
Grace, pardon, life, to us extend.
　　　　　　　J. Cooper (?), 1810.

ADORATION.

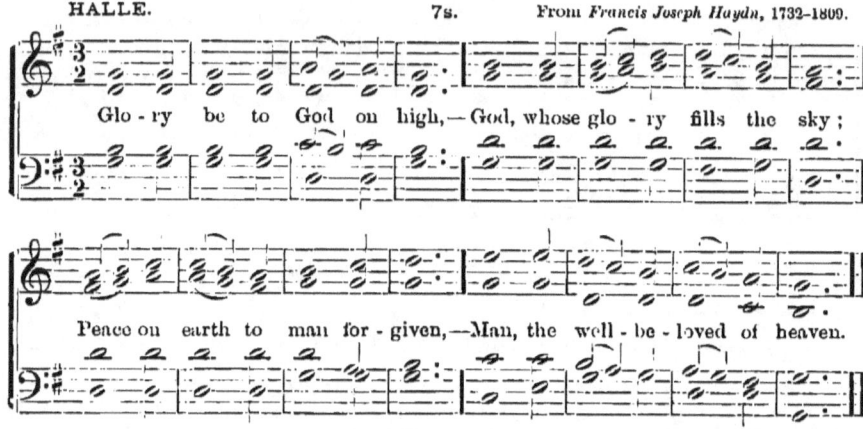

HALLE. 7s. From *Francis Joseph Haydn*, 1732-1809.

Glo-ry be to God on high,—God, whose glo-ry fills the sky;
Peace on earth to man for-given,—Man, the well-be-loved of heaven.

68. *Glory to the Triune God.* (143.)

1 Glory be to God on high.—
 God, whose glory fills the sky;
 Peace on earth to man forgiven,—
 Man, the well-beloved of heaven.

2 Sovereign Father, heavenly King!
 Thee we now presume to sing;
 Glad thine attributes confess,
 Glorious all, and numberless.

3 Hail, by all thy works adored!
 Hail, the everlasting Lord!
 Thee with thankful hearts we prove,—
 God of power, and God of love!

4 Christ our Lord and God we own,—
 Christ, the Father's only Son!
 Lamb of God, for sinners slain,
 Saviour of offending man.

5 Jesus! in thy name we pray,
 Take, Oh! take our sins away!
 Powerful Advocate with God!
 Justify us by thy blood.

6 Hear, for thou, O Christ! alone,
 Art with thy great Father one;
 One the Holy Ghost with thee;—
 One supreme eternal Three.
   Charles Wesley, 1739.

69. *Prayer to the Trinity.* (144.)

1 Holy Father! hear my cry;
 Holy Saviour! bend thine ear;
 Holy Spirit! come thou nigh:
 Father! Saviour! Spirit! hear.

2 Father! save me from my sin;
 Saviour! I thy mercy crave;
 Gracious Spirit! make me clean:
 Father! Son! and Spirit! save.

3 Father! let me taste thy love;
 Saviour! fill my soul with peace;
 Spirit! come my heart to move:
 Father! Son! and Spirit! bless.

4 Father! Son! and Spirit!—thou
 One Jehovah! shed abroad
 All thy grace within me now;
 Be my Father and my God.
   Horatius Bonar, 1857.

70. *Worship of the Trinity.* (145.)

1 Holy, holy, holy Lord!
 Self-existent Deity!
 By the hosts of heaven adored,
 Teach us how to worship thee:

2 Only uncreated Mind,
 Wonders in thy nature meet:
 Perfect unity combined
 With society complete.

3 All perfection dwells in thee,
 Now to us obscurely known,
 Three in one, and one in three,
 Great Jehovah, God alone!

4 Be our all, O Lord divine!
 Father! Saviour! Vital Breath!
 Body, spirit, soul be thine,
 Now, and at, and after death.
   John Ryland, 1780.

THE TRINITY.

HADDAM. H. M.
English.
Arr. *Lowell Mason,* 1822.

71. *Song of Praise to the Trinity.* (152.)

1 WE GIVE immortal praise
    To God, the Father's love,
For all our comforts here,
    And better hopes above :
He sent his own eternal Son
To die for sins that man had done.

2 To God, the Son, belongs
    Immortal glory too,
Who bought us with his blood
    From everlasting woe:
And now he lives, and now he reigns,
And sees the fruit of all his pains.

3 To God, the Spirit's name,
    Immortal worship give,
Whose new-creating power
    Makes the dead sinner live:
His work completes the great design,
And fills the soul with joy divine.

4 Almighty God! to thee
    Be endless honors done,—
The undivided Three,
    The great, mysterious One !
Where reason fails with all her powers,
There faith prevails and love adores.
Isaac Watts, 1709.

72. *Praise to the Trinity.* (153.)

1 To HIM that chose us first,
    Before the world began ;
To him that bore the curse,
    To save rebellious man ;
To him that formed our hearts anew,
Are endless praise and glory due.

2 The Father's love shall run
    Through our immortal songs;
We bring to God, the Son,
    Hosannas on our tongues ;
Our lips address the Spirit's name,
With equal praise, and zeal the same.

3 Let every saint above,
    And angel round the throne,
For ever bless and love
    The sacred Three in One:
Thus heaven shall raise his honors high,
When earth and time grow old and die.
Isaac Watts, 1709.

73. PSALM 134. (154.)

1 COME, bless Jehovah's name,
    Ye servants of the Lord !
Who, day and night, proclaim
    His grace, with glad accord ;
Within his house, lift up your song,
And swell his praises loud and long.

2 Lift up your hands, and bless
    The Lord who ever lives ;
And, in his courts, express
    The joy his presence gives;
The God of Zion, from above,
Will make your bosoms glow with love.

3 Your hallelujahs raise,
    To Father, Spirit, Son;
Extol, in loftiest praise,
    The great eternal One:
Within his house, lift up your song,
And swell his praises loud and long.
Edwin F. Hatfield, 1837.

ADORATION.

74. *The glorious Trinity.* (158.)

1 Come, thou almighty King!
 Help us thy name to sing,
  Help us to praise:
 Father! all-glorious,
 O'er all victorious,
 Come, and reign over us,
  Ancient of days!

2 Come, thou incarnate Word!
 Gird on thy mighty sword;
  Our prayer attend:
 Come, and thy people bless,
 And give thy word success;
 Spirit of holiness!
  On us descend.

3 Come, holy Comforter!
 Thy sacred witness bear,
  In this glad hour:
 Thou, who almighty art,
 Now rule in every heart,
 And ne'er from us depart,
  Spirit of power!

4 To the great One in Three
 The highest praises be,
  Hence, evermore!
 His sovereign majesty
 May we in glory see,
 And to eternity
  Love and adore.

Charles Wesley, 1757.

75. *Praise to the Three in One.* (159.)

1 Father of heaven above,
 Dwelling in light and love,
  Ancient of Days,
 Light unapproachable,
 Love inexpressible!
 Thee, the invisible,
  Laud we and praise.

2 Christ, the eternal Word,
 Christ, the incarnate Lord,
  Saviour of all,
 High throned above all light,
 God of God, Light of Light,
 Increate, infinite!
  On thee we call.

3 O God, the Holy Ghost!
 Whose fires of pentecost
  Burn evermore,
 In this far wilderness,
 Leave us not comfortless,
 Thee we love, thee we bless,
  Thee we adore.

4 Strike your harps, heavenly powers!
 With your glad chants shall ours
  Trembling ascend:
 All praise, O God! to thee,
 Three in one, one in three,
 Praise everlastingly,
  World without end.

Edward H. Bickersteth, 1871.

THE ETERNAL FATHER. 31

OLD HUNDREDTH. L. M. *Guillaume Franc*, 1543.

Before Jehovah's awful throne, Ye nations! bow with sacred joy;
Know that the Lord is God alone; He can create, and he destroy.

76. PSALM 100. (165.)

1 Before Jehovah's awful throne,
  Ye nations! bow with sacred joy;
  Know that the Lord is God alone;
  He can create, and he destroy.

2 His sovereign power, without our aid,
  Made us of clay, and formed us men;
  And when, like wandering sheep, we strayed,
  He brought us to his fold again.

3 We are his people, we his care,—
  Our souls, and all our mortal frame:
  What lasting honors shall we rear,
  Almighty Maker! to thy name?

4 We'll crowd thy gates with thankful songs,
  High as the heavens our voices raise;
  And earth, with her ten thousand tongues,
  Shall fill thy courts with sounding praise.

5 Wide as the world is thy command,
  Vast as eternity, thy love;
  Firm as a rock thy truth must stand,
  When rolling years shall cease to move.
  Isaac Watts, 1719, a.

77. PSALM 100. (166.)

1 All people, that on earth do dwell!
  Sing to the Lord with cheerful voice,
  Him serve with mirth, his praise forth tell,
  Come ye before him and rejoice.

2 Know that the Lord is God indeed:
  Without our aid he did us make;
  We are his flock, he doth us feed,
  And for his sheep, he doth us take.

3 Oh! enter, then, his gates with praise;
  Approach with joy his courts unto;
  Praise, laud, and bless his name always,
  For it is seemly so to do.

4 For why? the Lord, our God, is good,
  His mercy is for ever sure;
  His truth at all times firmly stood,
  And shall from age to age endure.
  William Kethe, 1562.

78. PSALM 148. (162.)

1 Loud hallelujahs to the Lord [dwell!
  From distant worlds where creatures
  Let heaven begin the solemn word,
  And sound it dreadful down to hell.

2 Mortals! can you refrain your tongue,
  When nature all around you sings?
  Oh! for a shout from old and young,
  From humble swains and lofty kings!

3 Wide as his vast dominion lies,
  Make the Creator's name be known:
  Loud as his thunder, shout his praise,
  And sound it lofty, as his throne.

4 Jehovah!—'t is a glorious word;
  Oh! may it dwell on every tongue;
  But saints, who best have known the Lord,
  Are bound to raise the noblest song.

5 Speak of the wonders of that love,
  Which Gabriel plays on every chord;
  From all below, and all above,
  Loud hallelujahs to the Lord.
  Isaac Watts, 1719.

ADORATION.

STONEFIELD.   L. M.   *Samuel Stanley, 1810.*

Ye nations round the earth! rejoice Before the Lord, your sovereign King;
Serve him with cheerful heart and voice; With all your tongues his glory sing.

79.
PSALM 100. (171.)

1 YE NATIONS round the earth! rejoice
   Before the Lord, your sovereign King;
Serve him with cheerful heart and voice;
   With all your tongues his glory sing.

2 The Lord is God; 't is he alone
   Doth life and breath and being give;
We are his work, and not our own;
   The sheep that on his pastures live.

3 Enter his gates with songs of joy;
   With praises to his courts repair;
And make it your divine employ,
   To pay your thanks and honors there.

4 The Lord is good, the Lord is kind;
   Great is his grace, his mercy sure;
And the whole race of man shall find
   His truth from age to age endure.
                  Isaac Watts, 1719.

80.
PSALM 145. (177.)

1 MY GOD! my King! thy various praise
   Shall fill the remnant of my days;
Thy grace employ my humble tongue,
   Till death and glory raise the song.

2 The wings of every hour shall bear
   Some thankful tribute to thine ear;
And every setting sun shall see
   New works of duty, done for thee.

3 Thy truth and justice I 'll proclaim:
   Thy bounty flows an endless stream,
Thy mercy swift, thine anger slow,
   But dreadful to the stubborn foe.

4 Thy works with sovereign glory shine,
   And speak thy majesty divine;
Let every realm, with joy, proclaim
   The sound and honor of thy name.

5 Let distant times and nations raise
   The long succession of thy praise;
And unborn ages make my song
   The joy and labor of their tongue.

6 But who can speak thy wondrous deeds?
   Thy greatness all our thoughts exceeds:
Vast and unsearchable thy ways,—
   Vast and immortal be thy praise.
                  Isaac Watts, 1719.

81.
The Majesty of God. (175.)

1 COME, O my soul! in sacred lays,
   Attempt thy great Creator's praise;
But Oh! what tongue can speak his fame?
   What mortal verse can reach the theme?

2 Enthroned amidst the radiant spheres,
   He glory, like a garment, wears;
To form a robe of light divine,
   Ten thousand suns around him shine.

3 In all our Maker's grand designs,
   Omnipotence with wisdom shines;
His works, thro' all this wondrous frame,
   Bear the great impress of his name.

4 Raised on devotion's lofty wing,
   Do thou, my soul! his glories sing;
And let his praise employ thy tongue,
   Till listening worlds applaud the song.
                 Thomas Blacklock, 1734.

THE ETERNAL FATHER.

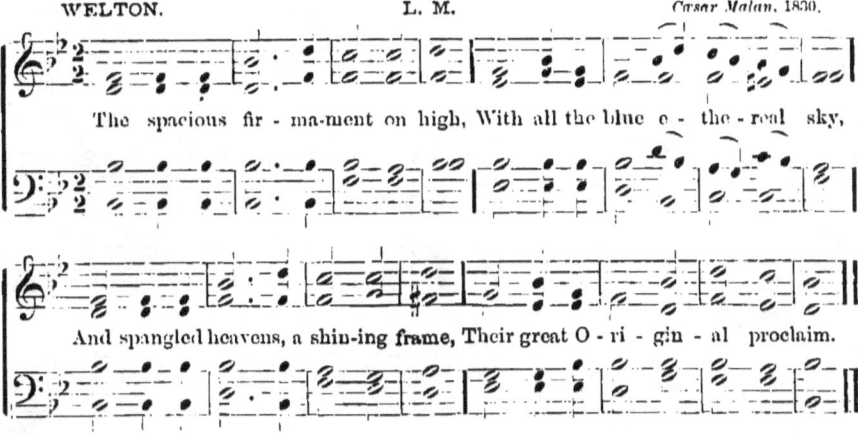

82.   PSALM 19.   (174.)

1 THE spacious firmament on high,
  With all the blue ethereal sky,
  And spangled heavens, a shining frame,
  Their great Original proclaim.

2 Th' unwearied sun, from day to day
  Does his Creator's power display,
  And publishes, to every land,
  The work of an almighty hand.

3 Soon as the evening shades prevail,
  The moon takes up the wondrous tale;
  And nightly, to the listening earth,
  Repeats the story of her birth:—

4 Whilst all the stars that round her burn,
  And all the planets in their turn,
  Confirm the tidings, as they roll,
  And spread the truth from pole to pole.

5 What though, in solemn silence, all
  Move round the dark terrestrial ball?
  What though no real voice, nor sound,
  Amidst their radiant orbs be found?—

6 In reason's ear they all rejoice,
  And utter forth a glorious voice,
  For ever singing as they shine,—
  "The hand that made us is divine."

  Joseph Addison, 1728.

83.   *The Wisdom and Knowledge of God.*   (176.)

1 AWAKE, my tongue! thy tribute bring
  To him, who gave thee power to sing;
  Praise him, who is all praise above,—
  The source of light, of truth, and love.

2 How vast his knowledge—how profound!
  A depth where all our thoughts are drowned;
  The stars he numbers:—and their names
  He gives to all these heavenly flames.

3 Through each bright world above, behold
  Ten thousand thousand charms unfold;
  Earth, air, and mighty seas combine,
  To speak his wisdom all-divine.

4 But, in redemption, Oh! what grace!—
  Its wonders, Oh! what thought can trace!
  Here wisdom shines for ever bright:—
  Praise him, my soul! with sweet delight.

  vs. 1–3, *John Needham,* 1768.

84.   *The Divine Perfections.*   (179.)

1 JEHOVAH reigns; his throne is high,
  His robes are light and majesty;
  His glory shines with beams so bright,
  No mortal can sustain the sight.

2 His terrors keep the world in awe;
  His justice guards his holy law;
  His love reveals a smiling face;
  His truth and promise seal the grace.

3 Through all his works his wisdom shines,
  And baffles Satan's deep designs;
  His power is sovereign to fulfill
  The noblest counsels of his will.

4 And will this glorious Lord descend
  To be my Father and my Friend?
  Then let my songs with angels join;
  Heaven is secure, if God be mine.

  Isaac Watts, 1709.

ADORATION.

ANGELS. L. M. Orlando Gibbons, 1623.

Bless, O my soul! the liv-ing God; Call home thy thoughts that rove a-broad;
Let all the powers, within me, join In work and wor-ship so di-vine.

85. PSALM 103. (180.)

1 BLESS, O my soul! the living God;
Call home thy thoughts that rove abroad;
Let all the powers, within me, join
In work and worship so divine.

2 Bless, O my soul! the God of grace;
His favors claim thy highest praise:
Why should the wonders he hath wrought
Be lost in silence, and forgot?

3 'T is he, my soul! that sent his Son,
To die for crimes which thou hast done:
He owns the ransom, and forgives
The hourly follies of our lives.

4 Let the whole earth his power confess,
Let the whole earth adore his grace:
The Gentile with the Jew shall join,
In work and worship so divine.
Isaac Watts, 1719.

86. *The Promises of God.* (181.)

1 PRAISE, everlasting praise, be paid
To him, that earth's foundations laid:
Praise to the God, whose strong decrees
Sway the creation, as he please.

2 Praise to the goodness of the Lord,
Who rules his people by his word;
And there, as strong as his decrees,
He sets his kindest promises.

3 Whence, then, should doubts and fears
arise?
Why trickling sorrows drown our eyes?
Slowly, alas! our mind receives
The comforts that our Maker gives.

4 Oh! for a strong, a lasting faith,
To credit what th' Almighty saith!
T' embrace the message of his Son,
And call the joys of heaven our own!

5 Then, should the earth's old pillars shake,
And all the wheels of nature break,
Our steady souls should fear no more,
Than solid rocks when billows roar.
Isaac Watts, 1707.

87. *The blessed Name.* (183.)

1 SING to the Lord a joyful song;
Lift up your hearts, your voices raise;
To us his gracious gifts belong,
To him our songs of love and praise.

2 For life and love, for rest and food,
For daily help and nightly care,
Sing to the Lord, for he is good,
And praise his name, for it is fair:

3 For strength to those who on him wait,
His truth to prove, his will to do,
Praise ye our God, for he is great,
Trust in his name, for it is true:

4 For joys untold that daily move
Round those who love his sweet employ,
Sing to our God, for he is love,
Exalt his name, for it is joy:

5 For life below, with all its bliss,
And for that life, more pure and high,
That inner life, which over this
Shall ever shine, and never die.
John S. B. Monsell, 1863.

THE ETERNAL FATHER. 35

LUTON. L. M. From *Aaron Williams'* Coll., 1760.

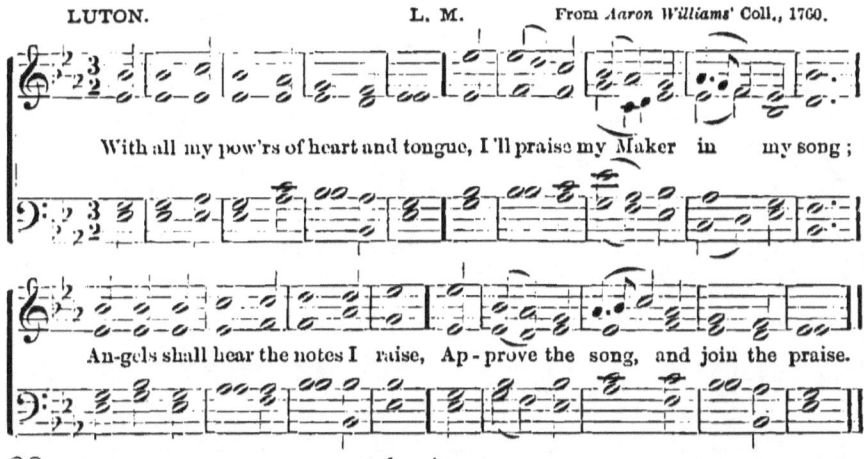

With all my pow'rs of heart and tongue, I'll praise my Maker in my song;
Angels shall hear the notes I raise, Approve the song, and join the praise.

88. Psalm 138. (186.)

1 With all my powers of heart and tongue,
I'll praise my Maker in my song;
Angels shall hear the notes I raise,
Approve the song, and join the praise.

2 To God I cried, when troubles rose;
He heard me, and subdued my foes;—
He did my rising fears control,
And strength diffused through all my soul.

3 Amid a thousand snares I stand,
Upheld and guarded by thy hand;
Thy words my fainting soul revive,
And keep my dying faith alive.

4 I'll sing thy truth and mercy, Lord!
I'll sing the wonders of thy word;
Not all thy works and names below
So much thy power and glory show.
Isaac Watts, 1719.

89. Psalm 103. (187.)

1 The Lord!—how wondrous are his ways!
How firm his truth! how large his grace!
He takes his mercy for his throne,
And thence he makes his glories known.

2 Not half so high, his power hath spread
The starry heavens above our head,
As his rich love exceeds our praise,—
Exceeds the highest hopes we raise.

3 Not half so far hath nature placed
The rising morning from the west,
As his forgiving grace removes
The daily guilt of those he loves.

4 How slowly doth his wrath arise!
On swifter wings salvation flies;
And, if he lets his anger burn,
How soon his frowns to pity turn!

5 But his eternal love is sure
To all the saints, and shall endure;
From age to age, his truth shall reign;
Nor children's children hope in vain.
Isaac Watts, 1719.

90. *Life-long Praise.* (182.)

1 God of my life! through all my days,
My grateful powers shall sound thy praise;
The song shall wake with opening light,
And warble to the silent night.

2 When anxious cares would break my rest,
And griefs would tear my throbbing breast,
Thy tuneful praises, raised on high,
Shall check the murmur and the sigh.

3 When death o'er nature shall prevail,
And all its powers of language fail;
Joy thro' my swimming eyes shall break,
And mean the thanks I cannot speak.

4 But, Oh! when that last conflict's o'er,
And I am chained to flesh no more,—
With what glad accents shall I rise
To join the music of the skies.

5 Soon shall I learn th' exalted strains,
Which echo o'er the heavenly plains,
And emulate, with joy unknown,
The glowing seraphs round thy throne.
Philip Doddridge, 1740.

ADORATION.

RAPTURE.   C. P. M.   Edward Harwood, 1707-1787.

Be-gin, my soul! th' exalt-ed lay, Let each en-raptured thought o-bey, And praise th' Almighty's name; Lo! heaven, and earth, and, seas, and skies, In one me-lo-dious con-cert rise, To swell th' inspir-ing theme.

91. PSALM 148. (189.)

1 BEGIN, my soul! th' exalted lay,
Let each enraptured thought obey,
  And praise th' Almighty's name;
Lo heaven, and earth, and seas, and skies,
In one melodious concert rise,
  To swell th' inspiring theme.

2 Ye angels! catch the thrilling sound,
While all th' adoring thrones around,
  His boundless mercy sing:
Let every listening saint above
Wake all the tuneful soul of love,
  And touch the sweetest string.

3 Let every element rejoice;
Ye thunders! burst, with awful voice,
  To him who bids you roll:
His praise in softer notes declare,
Each whispering breeze of yielding air!
  And breathe it to the soul.

4 Let man, by nobler passions swayed,
The feeling heart, the judging head,
  In heavenly praise employ;
Spread his tremendous name around,
Till heaven's broad arch rings back the
  The general burst of joy.   [sound,

John Ogilvie, 1749.

92. The Love of God. (190.)

1 My GOD! thy boundless love I praise;
How bright on high its glories blaze!
  How sweetly bloom below!
It streams from thine eternal throne,
Through heaven its joys for ever run,
  And o'er the earth they flow.

2 'T is love that paints the purple morn,
And bids the clouds, in air upborne,
  Their genial drops distill;
In every vernal beam it glows,
And breathes in every gale that blows,
  And glides in every rill.

3 But in thy word I see it shine
With grace and glories more divine,
  Proclaiming sins forgiven;   [way
There, faith, bright cherub, points the
To realms of everlasting day,
  And opens all her heaven.

4 Then let the love, that makes me blest,
With cheerful praise inspire my breast,
  And ardent gratitude;
And all my thoughts and passions tend
To thee, my Father and my Friend!
  My soul's eternal good.

Henry Moore, 1810.

THE ETERNAL FATHER.

93. PSALM 33. (193.)

1 YE HOLY souls! in God rejoice;
  Your Maker's praise becomes your voice;
  Great is your theme, your songs be new;
  Sing of his name, his word, his ways,
  His works of nature and of grace;—
  How wise and holy, just and true!

2 Justice and truth he ever loves;
  And the whole earth his goodness proves;
  His word the heavenly arches spread;
  How wide they shine from north to south!
  And, by the spirit of his mouth,
  Were all the starry armies made.

3 He gathers the wide-flowing seas,—
  Those watery treasures know their place,—
  In the vast storehouse of the deep;
  He spake—and gave all nature birth;
  And fires and seas, and heaven and earth,
  His everlasting orders keep.

4 Let mortals tremble, and adore
  A God of such resistless power,
  Nor dare indulge their feeble rage:
  Vain are your thoughts, and weak your hands;
  But his eternal counsel stands,
  And rules the world from age to age.
  Isaac Watts, 1719.

94. PSALM 146. (191.)

1 I'LL praise my Maker with my breath;
  And, when my voice is lost in death,
  Praise shall employ my nobler powers:
  My days of praise shall ne'er be past,
  While life, and thought, and being last,
  Or immortality endures.

2 Happy the man, whose hopes rely
  On Israel's God:—he made the sky,
  And earth, and seas, with all their train:
  His truth for ever stands secure;
  He saves th' oppressed, he feeds the poor,
  And none shall find his promise vain.

3 He loves his saints,—he knows them well,
  But turns the wicked down to hell;—
  Thy God, O Zion! ever reigns;
  Let every tongue, let every age,
  In this exalted work engage;
  Praise him in everlasting strains.

4 I'll praise him while he lends me breath,
  And, when my voice is lost in death,
  Praise shall employ my nobler powers:
  My days of praise shall ne'er be past,
  While life, and thought, and being last,
  Or immortality endures.
  Isaac Watts, 1719.

ADORATION.

HENRY. C. M. *Sylvanus B. Pond, 1835.*

The Lord descended from above, And bowed the heavens most high;
And underneath his feet he cast The darkness of the sky.

95. PSALM 18. (198.)

1 THE Lord descended from above.
  And bowed the heavens most high;
  And underneath his feet he cast
  The darkness of the sky.

2 On cherubim and seraphim,
  Full royally he rode,
  And, on the wings of mighty winds,
  Came flying all abroad.

3 He sat serene upon the floods,
  Their fury to restrain;
  And he, as sovereign Lord and King,
  For evermore shall reign.

Thomas Sternhold, 1549, a.

96. *Sovereignty and Grace.* (205.)

1 THE Lord! how fearful is his name!
  How wide is his command!
  Nature, with all her moving frame,
  Rests on his mighty hand.

2 Immortal glory forms his throne,
  And light, his awful robe;
  Whilst with a smile, or with a frown,
  He manages the globe.

3 A word of his almighty breath
  Can swell or sink the seas;
  Build the vast empires of the earth,
  Or break them as he please.

4 On angels, with unveiled face,
  His glory beams above;
  On men, he looks with softest grace,
  And takes his title, Love.

Isaac Watts, 1700, a.

97. *Our Heavenly Father.* (195.)

1 MY GOD! how wonderful thou art!
  Thy majesty how bright!
  How beautiful thy mercy-seat,
  In depths of burning light!

2 How dread are thine eternal years,
  O everlasting Lord!
  By prostrate spirits, day and night,
  Incessantly adored.

3 How beautiful, how beautiful,
  The sight of thee must be,
  Thine endless wisdom, boundless power,
  And awful purity!

4 Oh! how I fear thee, living God!
  With deepest, tenderest fears,
  And worship thee with trembling hope,
  And penitential tears.

5 Yet I may love thee too, O Lord!
  Almighty as thou art,
  For thou hast stooped to ask of me
  The love of this poor heart.

6 No earthly father loves like thee,
  No mother, half so mild,
  Bears and forbears as thou hast done
  With me, thy sinful child.

7 Father of Jesus, love's Reward!
  What rapture will it be,
  Prostrate before thy throne to lie,
  And gaze, and gaze on thee.

Frederick William Faber, 1849.

THE ETERNAL FATHER.

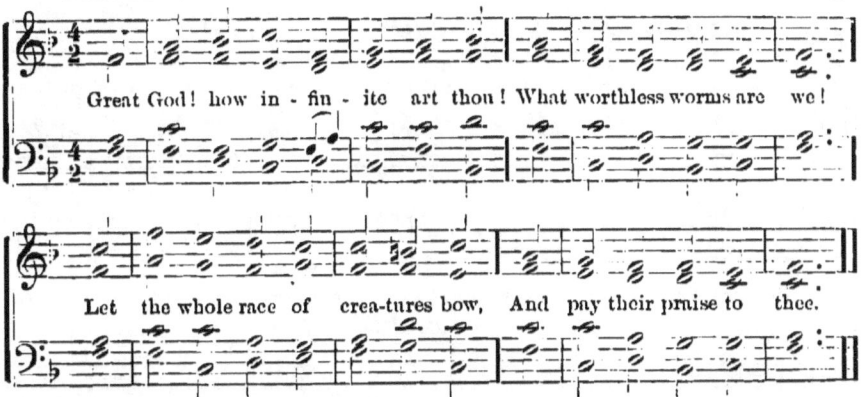

DUNDEE. (FRENCH.)   C. M.   Andre Hart's "Psalter," 1615.

Great God! how infinite art thou! What worthless worms are we!
Let the whole race of creatures bow, And pay their praise to thee.

98.   *God's eternal Dominion.*   (204.)

1 GREAT God! how infinite art thou!
   What worthless worms are we!
   Let the whole race of creatures bow,
   And pay their praise to thee.

2 Thy throne eternal ages stood,
   Ere seas or stars were made;
   Thou art the ever-living God,
   Were all the nations dead.

3 Eternity, with all its years,
   Stands present in thy view;
   To thee there's nothing old appears—
   Great God! there's nothing new.

4 Our lives through various scenes are drawn,
   And vexed with trifling cares;
   While thine eternal thought moves on
   Thine undisturbed affairs.

5 Great God! how infinite art thou!
   What worthless worms are we!
   Let the whole race of creatures bow,
   And pay their praise to thee.
              Isaac Watts, 1707.

99.   *God, the Thunderer.*   (203.)

1 SING to the Lord, ye heavenly hosts!
   And thou, O earth! adore;
   Let death and hell, through all their coasts,
   Stand trembling at his power.

2 His sounding chariot shakes the sky,
   He makes the clouds his throne;
   There all his stores of lightning lie,
   Till vengeance darts them down.

3 Think, O my soul! the dreadful day,
   When this incensed God
   Shall rend the sky, and burn the sea,
   And fling his wrath abroad.

4 What shall the wretch, the sinner, do?
   He once defied the Lord;
   But he shall dread the Thunderer now,
   And sink beneath his word.
              Isaac Watts, Aug. 20, 1697.

100.   *Creating Wisdom.*   (200.)

1 ETERNAL Wisdom! thee we praise,
   Thee the creation sings;
   With thy loved name, rocks, hills and seas,
   And heaven's high palace rings.

2 Thy hand, how wide it spread the sky!
   How glorious to behold!
   Tinged with a blue of heavenly dye,
   And starred with sparkling gold.

3 Thy glories blaze all nature round,
   And strike the gazing sight,
   Through skies, and seas, and solid ground,
   With terror and delight.

4 Infinite strength, and equal skill,
   Shine through the worlds abroad;
   Our souls with vast amazement fill,
   And speak the builder—God.

5 But the sweet beauties of thy grace
   Our softer passions move;
   Pity divine, in Jesus' face,
   We see, adore, and love.
              Isaac Watts, 1705.

ADORATION.

CAMBRIDGE. C. M. *John Randall, 1790.*

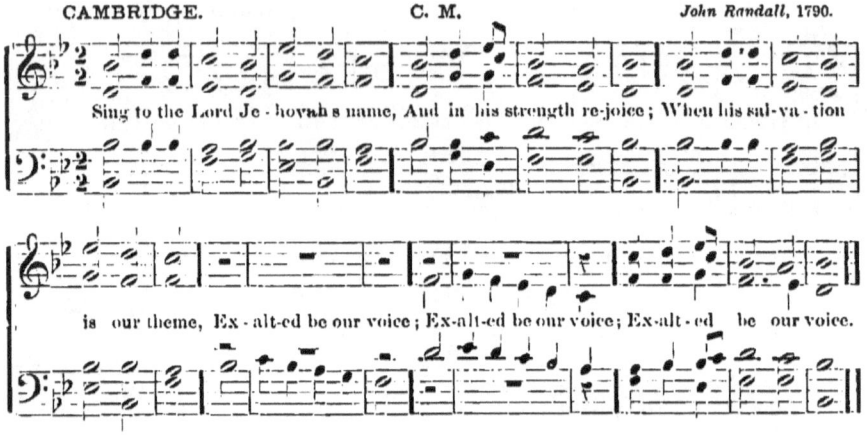

Sing to the Lord Jehovah's name, And in his strength rejoice; When his salvation is our theme, Exalted be our voice, Exalted be our voice, Exalted be our voice.

101. PSALM 95. (207.)

1 SING to the Lord Jehovah's name,
  And in his strength rejoice;
 When his salvation is our theme,
  Exalted be our voice.

2 With thanks, approach his awful sight,
  And psalms of honor sing:
 The Lord 's a God of boundless might,—
  The whole creation's King.

3 Come, and with humble souls adore;
  Come, kneel before his face;
 Oh! may the creatures of his power
  Be children of his grace!

4 Now is the time;—he bends his ear,
  And waits for your request;
 Come, lest he rouse his wrath, and swear,
  "Ye shall not see my rest."
            Isaac Watts, 1719.

102. PSALM 145. (218.)

1 LET every tongue thy goodness speak,
  Thou sovereign Lord of all!
 Thy strengthening hands uphold the weak,
  And raise the poor that fall.

2 When sorrow bows the spirit down,
  Or virtue lies distressed
 Beneath some proud oppressor's frown,
  Thou giv'st the mourners rest.

3 The Lord supports our tottering days,
  And guides our giddy youth:
 Holy and just are all his ways,
  And all his words are truth.

4 He knows the pain his servants feel;
  He hears his children cry;
 And, their best wishes to fulfill,
  His grace is ever nigh.

5 His mercy never shall remove
  From men of heart sincere;
 He saves the souls, whose humble love
  Is joined with holy fear.

6 My lips shall dwell upon his praise,
  And spread his fame abroad;
 Let all the sons of Adam raise
  The honors of their God.
            Isaac Watts, 1719.

103. PSALM 111. (216.)

1 SONGS of immortal praise belong
  To my almighty God;
 He has my heart, and he my tongue,
  To spread his name abroad.

2 How great the works his hand has wrought!
  How glorious in our sight!
 And men in every age have sought
  His wonders with delight.

3 How most exact is nature's frame!
  How wise th' eternal Mind!
 His counsels never change the scheme,
  That his first thoughts designed.

4 When he redeemed his chosen sons,
  He fixed his covenant sure;
 The orders, that his lips pronounce,
  To endless years endure.
            Isaac Watts, 1719.

THE ETERNAL FATHER.

Long as I live I'll bless thy name, My King! my God of love! My work and joy shall be the same, In the bright world a - bove.

104. PSALM 145. (213.)

1 Long as I live I 'll bless thy name,
   My King! my God of love!
   My work and joy shall be the same,
   In the bright world above.

2 Great is the Lord—his power unknown :
   And let his praise be great ;
   I 'll sing the honors of thy throne,
   Thy works of grace repeat.

3 Thy grace shall dwell upon my tongue ;
   And, while my lips rejoice,
   The men, that hear my sacred song,
   Shall join their cheerful voice.

4 Fathers to sons shall teach thy name,
   And children learn thy ways ;
   Ages to come thy truth proclaim,
   And nations sound thy praise.

5 The world is managed by thy hands ;
   Thy saints are ruled by love ;
   And thine eternal kingdom stands,
   Though rocks and hills remove.
   Isaac Watts, 1719.

105. *Endless Praise.* (214.)

1 Yes - I will bless thee, O my God !
   Through all my mortal days,
   And to eternity prolong
   Thy vast, thy boundless praise.

2 Nor shall my tongue alone proclaim
   The honors of my God :
   My life with all its active powers,
   Shall spread thy praise abroad.

3 Not death itself shall stop my song,
   Though death will close my eyes :
   My thoughts shall then to nobler heights
   And sweeter raptures rise.

4 There shall my lips, in endless praise,
   Their grateful tribute pay ;
   The theme demands an angel's tongue,
   And an eternal day.
   Ottiwell Heginbotham, 1768, a.

106. *"Te Deum laudamus."* (210.)

1 O God! we praise thee, and confess,
   That thou the only Lord
   And everlasting Father art,
   By all the earth adored.

2 To thee, all angels cry aloud ;
   To thee the powers on high,
   Both cherubim and seraphim,
   Continually do cry :—

3 O holy, holy, holy Lord !
   Whom heavenly hosts obey,
   The world is with the glory filled
   Of thy majestic sway !

4 The apostles' glorious company
   And prophets crowned with light,
   With all the martyrs' noble host,
   Thy constant praise recite.

5 The holy church throughout the world,
   O Lord! confesses thee,
   That thou th' eternal Father art,
   Of boundless majesty.
   Tate and Brady, 1703.

42 ADORATION.

AZMON. (DENFIELD.) C. M.
Carl Gotthelf Gläser, 1828.
arr., Lowell Mason, 1839.

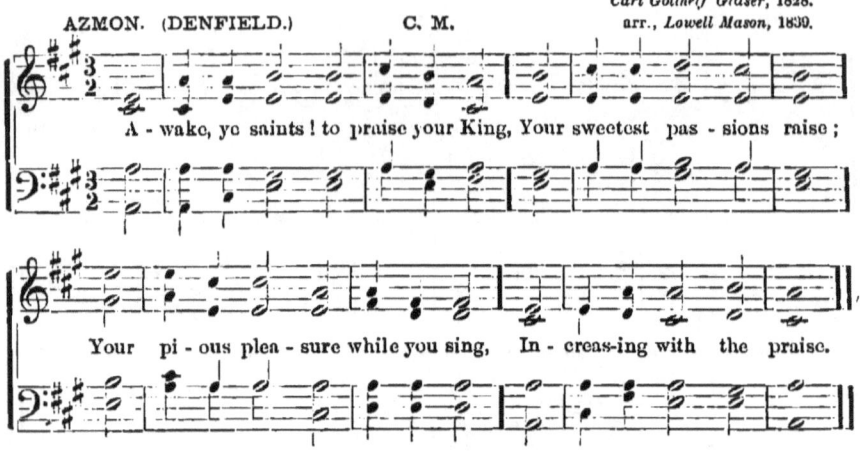

A-wake, ye saints! to praise your King, Your sweetest pas-sions raise;
Your pi-ous plea-sure while you sing, In-creas-ing with the praise.

107.   PSALM 145.   (219.)

1 Awake, ye saints! to praise your King,
    Your sweetest passions raise;
  Your pious pleasure, while you sing,
    Increasing with the praise.

2 Great is the Lord,—and works unknown
    Are his divine employ:
  But still his saints are near his throne,
    His treasure and his joy.

3 Heaven, earth and sea confess his hand;
    He bids the vapors rise;
  Lightning and storm, at his command,
    Sweep through the sounding skies.

4 Ye saints! adore the living God,
    Serve him with faith and fear;
  He makes the churches his abode,
    And claims your honors there.
        Isaac Watts, 1719; v. 4, a.

108.   PSALM 34.   (224.)

1 Through all the changing scenes of life,
    In trouble, and in joy,
  The praises of my God shall still
    My heart and tongue employ.

2 Of his deliverance I will boast,
    Till all, that are distressed,
  From my example comfort take,
    And charm their griefs to rest.

3 Oh! magnify the Lord with me,
    With me exalt his name;
  When in distress to him I called,
    He to my rescue came.

4 Oh! make but trial of his love;
    Experience will decide,
  How blest are they, and only they,
    Who in his truth confide.

5 Fear him, ye saints! and you will then
    Have nothing else to fear;
  Make you his service your delight,—
    Your wants shall be his care.
        Nahum Tate, 1696.

109.   PSALM 89.   (221.)

1 The mercies of my God and King
    My tongue shall still pursue;
  Oh! happy they who, while they sing
    Those mercies, share them too!

2 As bright and lasting as the sun,
    As lofty as the sky,
  From age to age, thy word shall run,
    And change and chance defy.

3 The covenant of the King of kings
    Shall stand for ever sure;
  Beneath the shadow of thy wings
    Thy saints repose secure.

4 Thine is the earth, and thine the skies,
    Created at thy will:
  The waves at thy command arise,
    At thy command are still.

5 In earth below, in heaven above,
    Who, who is Lord like thee?
  Oh! spread the gospel of thy love,
    Till all thy glories see!
        Henry Francis Lyte, 1834.

THE ETERNAL FATHER. 43

GENEVA. C. M. John Cole, 1805.

When all thy mercies, O my God! My rising soul surveys,
Transported with the view, I'm lost, In wonder, love, and praise.

110. *Thanks for providential favors.* (225.)

1 When all thy mercies, O my God!
My rising soul surveys,
Transported with the view, I'm lost
In wonder, love, and praise.

2 Unnumbered comforts, to my soul,
Thy tender care bestowed,
Before my infant heart conceived
From whom those comforts flowed.

3 When, in the slippery paths of youth,
With heedless steps, I ran,
Thine arm, unseen, conveyed me safe,
And led me up to man.

4 Ten thousand thousand precious gifts
My daily thanks employ;
Nor is the least a cheerful heart,
That tastes those gifts with joy.

5 Through every period of my life,
Thy goodness I 'll pursue ;
And after death, in distant worlds,
The glorious theme renew.

6 Through all eternity, to thee
A joyful song I 'll raise :
For, Oh! eternity's too short
To utter all thy praise!
Joseph Addison, 1712.

111. *The Goodness of God in his Works.* (226.)

1 Hail! great Creator, wise and good !
To thee our songs we raise ;
Nature, through all her various scenes,
Invites us to thy praise.

2 At morning, noon, and evening mild,
Fresh wonders strike our view ;
And, while we gaze, our hearts exult,
With transports ever-new.

3 Thy glory beams in every star,
Which gilds the gloom of night ;
And decks the smiling face of morn,
With rays of cheerful light.

4 And while, in all thy wondrous ways,
Thy varied love we see ;
Oh ! may our hearts, great God ! be led
Through all thy works to thee.
Anon., 1795.

112. Psalm 66. (227.)

1 Lift up to God the voice of praise,
Whose breath our souls inspired ;
Loud, and more loud, the anthem raise
With grateful ardor fired.

2 Lift up to God the voice of praise,
Whose goodness, passing thought,
Loads every minute, as it flies,
With benefits unsought.

3 Lift up to God the voice of praise,
From whom salvation flows,
Who sent his Son, our souls to save
From everlasting woes.

4 Lift up to God the voice of praise,
For hope's transporting rays, [death,
Which lights, through darkest shades of
To realms of endless day.
Ralph Wardlaw, 1803.

44 — ADORATION.

ST. JOHN'S.   C. M.   *Aaron Williams, cir. 1760.*

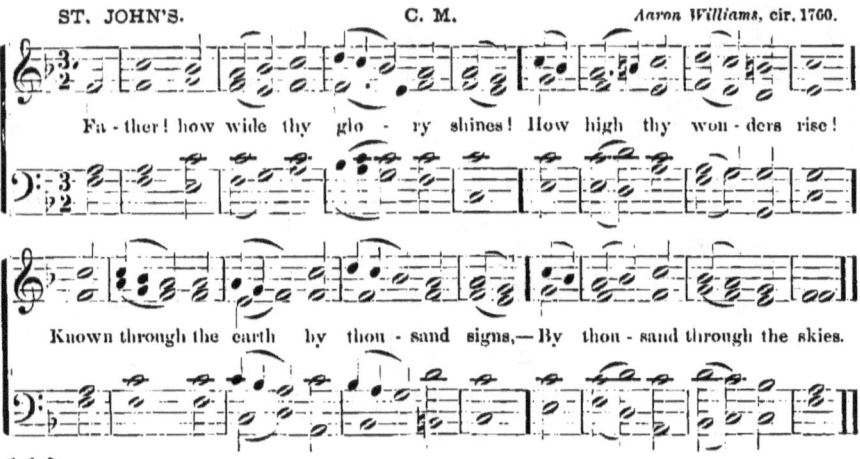

Father! how wide thy glo-ry shines! How high thy won-ders rise!
Known through the earth by thou-sand signs,— By thou-sand through the skies.

---

113.   *The Glories of Redemption.*   (231.)

1 Father! how wide thy glory shines!
    How high thy wonders rise! [signs,—
    Known through the earth by thousand
    By thousand through the skies.

2 Those mighty orbs proclaim thy power,
    Their motions speak thy skill;
    And, on the wings of every hour,
    We read thy patience still.

3 But, when we view thy strange design
    To save rebellious worms,
    Where vengeance and compassion join
    In their divinest forms,—

4 Here the whole Deity is known;
    Nor dares a creature guess,—
    Which of the glories brightest shone,
    The justice, or the grace.

5 Now the full glories of the Lamb
    Adorn the heavenly plains;
    Bright seraphs learn Immanuel's name,
    And try their choicest strains.

6 Oh! may I bear some humble part,
    In that immortal song;
    Wonder and joy shall tune my heart,
    And love command my tongue.
           Isaac Watts, 1706.

114.   *The Wonders of God's Love.*   (232.)

1 Ye humble souls! approach your God,
    With songs of sacred praise;
    For he is good, immensely good,
    And kind are all his ways.

2 All nature owns his guardian care,
    In him we live and move;
    But nobler benefits declare
    The wonders of his love.

3 He gave his Son, his only Son,
    To ransom rebel worms;
    'T is here he makes his goodness known
    In its divinest forms.

4 To this dear refuge, Lord! we come,
    'T is here our hope relies;—
    A safe defence, a peaceful home,
    When storms of trouble rise.
           Anne Steele, 1760.

115.   *God is Love.*   (230.)

1 Amid the splendors of thy state,
    My God! thy love appears,
    With the soft radiance of the moon
    Among a thousand stars.

2 Sinai, in clouds, and smoke, and fire,
    Thunders thy dreadful name!
    But Zion sings, in melting notes,
    The honors of the Lamb.

3 In all thy doctrines and commands,
    Thy counsels and designs,
    In every work thy hands have framed,
    Thy love supremely shines.

4 Angels and men! the news proclaim
    Through earth and heaven above,—
    The joyful and transporting news,—
    That God, the Lord, is love.
           Anon., 1800.

THE ETERNAL FATHER.

45

CLARENDON. C. M. *Isaac Tucker, 1800.*

Sweet is the mem'-ry of thy grace, My God, my heavenly King!
Let age to age thy right-eous-ness, In sounds of glo-ry sing.

116. PSALM 145. (234.)

1 SWEET is the mem'ry of thy grace,
   My God, my heavenly King!
  Let age to age thy righteousness,
   In sounds of glory, sing.

2 God reigns on high,—but ne'er confines
   His goodness to the skies; [shines.
  Through the whole earth his bounty
   And every want supplies.

3 With longing eyes, thy creatures wait
   On thee for daily food;
  Thy liberal hand provides their meat,
   And fills their mouths with good.

4 How kind are thy compassions, Lord!
   How slow thine anger moves!
  But soon he sends his pard'ning word
   To cheer the souls he loves.

5 Creatures, with all their endless race,
   Thy power and praise proclaim;
  But saints, who taste thy richer grace,
   Delight to bless thy name.
           Isaac Watts, 1719.

117. *Rejoicing in God, our Father.* (235.)

1 COME, shout aloud thy Father's grace,
   And sing the Saviour's love;
  Soon shall you join the glorious theme,
   In loftier strains above.

2 God, the eternal, mighty God,
   To dearer names descends;
  Calls you his treasure and his joy,
   His children and his friends.

3 My Father, God! and may these lips
   Pronounce a name so dear?
  Not thus could heaven's sweet harmony
   Delight my listening ear.

4 Thanks to my God for every gift,
   His bounteous hands bestow;
  And thanks eternal for that love,
   Whence all those comforts flow.
       Ottiwell Heginbotham, 1768.

118. *The Love of God.* (236.)

1 COME, ye that know and fear the Lord!
   And lift your souls above;
  Let every heart and voice accord,
   To sing that—God is love.

2 This precious truth his word declares,
   And all his mercies prove;
  Jesus, the Gift of gifts, appears,
   To show that—God is love.

3 Behold his patience lengthened out
   To those who from him rove,
  And calls effectual reach their hearts,
   To teach them—God is love.

4 The work begun is carried on,
   By power from heaven above;
  And every step, from first to last,
   Declares that—God is love.

5 Oh! may we all, while here below,
   This best of blessings prove;
  Till warmer hearts, in brighter worlds,
   Shall shout that—God is love.
           George Burder, 1784.

ADORATION.

ST. THOMAS. S. M. *William Tansur, 1768.*

Stand up, and bless the Lord, Ye people of his choice!
Stand up, and bless the Lord, your God, With heart, and soul, and voice,

119. *Exhortation to Praise.* (249.)

1 STAND up and bless the Lord,
  Ye people of his choice!
  Stand up, and bless the Lord, your God,
  With heart, and soul, and voice.

2 Though high above all praise,
  Above all blessing high,
  Who would not fear his holy name,
  And laud, and magnify?

3 Oh! for the living flame
  From his own altar brought,
  To touch our lips, our minds inspire,
  And wing to heaven our thought!

4 God is our strength and song,
  And his salvation ours:
  Then be his love in Christ proclaimed,
  With all our ransomed powers.

5 Stand up, and bless the Lord—
  The Lord, your God, adore,
  Stand up, and bless his glorious name,
  Henceforth, for evermore.
  James Montgomery, 1825.

120. *Sincere Praise.* (238.)

1 ALMIGHTY Maker, God!
  How wondrous is thy name!
  Thy glories, how diffused abroad,
  Through the creation's frame!

2 Nature, in every dress,
  Her humble homage pays;
  And finds a thousand ways t' express
  Thine undissembled praise.

3 My soul would rise and sing
  To her Creator, too;
  Fain would my tongue adore my King,
  And pay the worship due.

4 Let joy and worship spend
  The remnant of my days,
  And to my God my soul ascend,
  In sweet perfumes of praise.
  Isaac Watts, 1706.

121. PSALM 8. (242.)

1 O LORD, our heavenly King!
  Thy name is all-divine;
  Thy glories round the earth are spread,
  And o'er the heavens they shine.

2 When, to thy works on high,
  I raise my wondering eyes,
  And see the moon, complete in light,
  Adorn the darksome skies;—

3 When I survey the stars,
  And all their shining forms,—
  Lord! what is man, that worthless thing
  Akin to dust and worms?

4 Lord! what is worthless man,
  That thou shouldst love him so?
  Next to thine angels is he placed,
  And lord of all below.

5 How rich thy bounties are!
  And wondrous are thy ways;
  Of dust and worms, thy power can frame
  A monument of praise.
  Isaac Watts, 1719.

THE ETERNAL FATHER.

HARWICH. H. M. Johann Crüger, 1649. Adapted by *Lowell Mason*, 1822.

Ye tribes of Adam! join With heaven, and earth, and seas, And offer notes divine
To your Creator's praise: Ye holy throng of angels bright! In worlds of light, begin the song.

122. PSALM 148. (243.)

1 YE TRIBES of Adam! join
   With heaven, and earth, and seas,
And offer notes divine
   To your Creator's praise:
Ye holy throng of angels bright!
In worlds of light, begin the song.

2 Thou sun, with dazzling rays!
   And moon that rulest the night!
Shine to your Maker's praise,
   With stars of twinkling light:
His power declare, ye floods on high
And clouds that fly in empty air!

3 The shining worlds above
   In glorious order stand,
Or in swift courses move,
   By his supreme command:
He spake the word, and all their frame
From nothing came to praise the Lord.

4 Let all the nations fear
   The God that rules above;
He brings his people near,
   And makes them taste his love:
While earth and sky attempt his praise,
His saints shall raise his honors high.
                              Isaac Watts, 1719.

123. PSALM 148. (244.)

1 YE BOUNDLESS realms of joy!
   Exalt your Maker's name;
His praise your songs employ
   Above the starry frame:
Your voices raise, ye cherubim
And seraphim! to sing his praise.

2 Let all adore the Lord,
   And praise his holy name,
By whose almighty word
   They all from nothing came;
And all shall last, from changes free;
His firm decree stands ever fast.
                              Nahum Tate, 1696.

124. PSALM 136. (245.)

1 GIVE thanks to God most high,
   The universal Lord,—
The sovereign King of kings;
   And be his grace adored:
His power and grace are still the same;
And let his name have endless praise.

2 He saw the nations lie
   All perishing in sin;
And pitied the sad state
   The ruined world was in:
Thy mercy, Lord! shall still endure;
And ever sure abides thy word.

3 He sent his only Son
   To save us from our woe,
From Satan, sin, and death,
   And every hurtful foe:
His power and grace are still the same;
And let his name have endless praise.

4 Give thanks aloud to God,
   To God, the heavenly King;
And let the spacious earth
   His works and glories sing:
Thy mercy, Lord! shall still endure;
And ever sure abides thy word.
                              Isaac Watts, 1719.

ADORATION.

MANNHEIM. 8s & 7s. From *Ludwig von Beethoven*, 1800.

Praise the Lord; ye heavens! a-dore him; Praise him, an-gels in the height!
Sun and moon! re-joice be-fore him; Praise him, all ye stars of light!

125. PSALM 148. (249.)

1 Praise the Lord; ye heavens! adore him;
Praise him, angels in the height!
Sun and moon! rejoice before him;
Praise him, all ye stars of light!

2 Praise the Lord, for he hath spoken:
Worlds his mighty voice obeyed;
Laws, which never shall be broken,
For their guidance he hath made.

3 Praise the Lord, for he is glorious;
Never shall his promise fail;
God hath made his saints victorious,
Sin and death shall not prevail.

4 Praise the God of our salvation,
Hosts on high! his power proclaim;
Heaven and earth, and all creation!
Laud and magnify his name.
John Kempthorne, 1810.

126. *Praise for Grace.* (250.)

1 Lord! with glowing heart I'll praise thee
For the bliss thy love bestows:
For the pardoning grace that saves me,
And the peace that from it flows.

2 Help, O Lord! my weak endeavor;
This dull soul to rapture raise;
Thou must light the flame, or never
Can my love be warmed to praise.

3 Praise, my soul! the God that sought thee,
Wretched wanderer, far astray;
Found thee lost, and kindly brought thee
From the paths of death away.

4 Praise, with love's devoutest feeling,
Him who saw thy guilt-born fear,
And, the light of hope revealing,
Bade the blood-stained cross appear.

5 Lord! this bosom's ardent feeling
Vainly would my lips express;
Low before thy footstep kneeling,
Deign thy suppliant's prayer to bless.

6 Let thy grace, my soul's chief pleasure,
Love's pure flame within me raise;
And, since words can never measure,
Let my life show forth, thy praise.
Francis Scott Key, 1826.

127. *The Fountain of Grace.* (252.)

1 Blessed be thou, the God of Israel!
Thou, our Father, and our Lord:
Blessed thy majesty for ever!
Ever be thy name adored.

2 Thine, O Lord! are power and greatness,
Glory, victory, are thine own;
All is thine in earth and heaven,
Over all thy boundless throne.

3 Riches come of thee, and honor,
Power and might to thee belong;
Thine it is to make us prosper,
Only thine to make us strong.

4 Lord, our God! for these thy bounties,
Hymns of gratitude we raise;
To thy name, for ever glorious,
Ever we address our praise.
Henry U. Onderdonk, 1827.

THE ETERNAL FATHER.

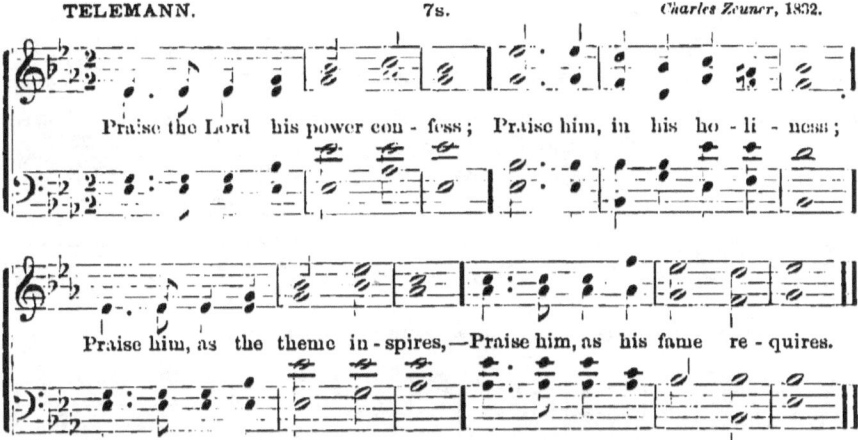

128. PSALM 150. (256.)

1 PRAISE the Lord—his power confess;
  Praise him, in his holiness;
  Praise him, as the theme inspires,—
  Praise him, as his fame requires.

2 Let the trumpet's lofty sound
  Spread its loudest notes around;
  Let the harp unite, in praise,
  With the sacred minstrel's lays.

3 Let the organ join to bless
  God, the Lord of righteousness;
  Tune your voice to spread the fame
  Of the great Jehovah's name.

4 All who dwell beneath his light!
  In his praise your hearts unite;
  While the stream of song is poured,
  Praise and magnify the Lord.
  William Wrangham, 1829.

129. PSALM 150. (257.)

1 PRAISE the Lord, his glories show,
  Saints, within his courts below!
  Angels, round his throne above!
  All that see and share his love!

2 Earth to heaven, and heaven to earth,
  Tell his wonders, sing his worth;
  Age to age, and shore to shore,
  Praise him, praise him, evermore!

3 Praise the Lord, his mercies trace;
  Praise his providence and grace—
  All that be for man hath done,
  All he sends us through his Son.

4 Strings and voices, hands and hearts!
  In the concert bear your parts:
  All that breathe! your Lord adore;
  Praise him, praise him, evermore!
  Henry Francis Lyte, 1834.

130. *Glory to God in the highest.* (258.)

1 SONGS of praise the angels sang,
  Heaven with hallelujahs rang,
  When Jehovah's work begun,—
  When he spake, and it was done.

2 Song of praise awoke the morn,
  When the Prince of peace was born;
  Songs of praise arose, when he
  Captive led captivity.

3 Heaven and earth must pass away,—
  Songs of praise shall crown that day;
  God will make new heavens, new earth,—
  Songs of praise shall hail their birth.

4 And can man alone be dumb,
  Till that glorious kingdom come?
  No!—the church delights to raise
  Psalms, and hymns, and songs of praise.

5 Saints below, with heart and voice,
  Still in songs of praise rejoice,
  Learning here, by faith and love,
  Songs of praise to sing above.

6 Borne upon their latest breath,
  Songs of praise shall conquer death;
  Then, amidst eternal joy,
  Songs of praise their powers employ.
  James Montgomery, 1819.

ADORATION.

ROTHWELL. L. M. *William Tansur*, cir. 1743.

Bright King of glo-ry, dreadful God! Our spir-its bow be-fore thy seat; To thee we lift an humble thought, And worship at thine awful feet; And worship at thine aw-ful feet.

131. *God, the Son, equal with the Father.* (275.)

1 BRIGHT King of glory, dreadful God!
  Our spirits bow before thy seat;
  To thee we lift an humble thought,
  And worship at thine awful feet.

2 A thousand seraphs, strong and bright,
  Stand round the glorious Deity;
  But who, amongst the sons of light,
  Pretends comparison with thee?

3 Yet there is one, of human frame,—
  Jesus, arrayed in flesh and blood,—
  Thinks it no robbery to claim
  A full equality with God.

4 Their glory shines with equal beams,
  Their essence is for ever one, [names,
  Though they are known by different
  The Father God, and God the Son.

5 Then let the name of Christ, our King,
  With equal honors be adored;
  His praise let every angel sing,
  And all the nations own their Lord.
  Isaac Watts, 1707.

132. *The Dominion of Christ.* (278.)

1 HAIL to the Prince of Life and peace,
  Who holds the keys of death and hell!
  The spacious world unseen is his,
  And sovereign power becomes him well.

2 In shame and torment once he died;—
  But now he lives for evermore:
  Bow down, ye saints! around his seat,
  And, all ye angel bands! adore!

3 So live for ever, glorious Lord!
  To crush thy foes, and guard thy friends;
  While all thy chosen tribes rejoice,
  That thy dominion never ends.

4 Worthy thy hand to hold the keys,
  Guided by wisdom and by love;
  Worthy to rule o'er mortal life,
  O'er worlds below, and worlds above.

5 For ever reign, victorious King! [known!
  Wide through the earth thy name be
  And call my longing soul to sing
  Sublimer anthems near thy throne.
  Philip Doddridge, 1740.

133. *Christ's Humiliation and Exaltation.* (277.)

1 WHAT equal honors shall we bring
  To thee, O Lord, our God, the Lamb!
  When all the notes, that angels sing,
  Are far inferior to thy name?

2 Worthy is he that once was slain,— [died,
  The Prince of peace, that groaned and
  Worthy to rise, and live, and reign,
  At his almighty Father's side.

3 Honor immortal must be paid,
  Instead of scandal and of scorn;
  While glory shines around his head,
  And a bright crown without a thorn.

4 Blessings for ever on the Lamb,
  Who bore the curse for wretched men!
  Let angels sound his sacred name,
  And every creature say,—Amen.
  Isaac Watts, 1707.

THE SON OF GOD.

TRURO. L. M. *Charles Burney*, cir. 1760.

Now to the Lord a no-ble song! A-wake, my soul! a-wake, my tongue!
Ho-san-na to th' e-ter-nal name, And all his boundless love pro-claim.

134. *Glory and Grace in Christ.* (285.)

1 Now to the Lord, a noble song!
 Awake, my soul! awake, my tongue!
 Hosanna to th' eternal name,
 And all his boundless love proclaim.

2 See where it shines in Jesus' face,—
 The brightest image of his grace!
 God, in the person of his Son,
 Has all his mightiest works outdone.

3 The spacious earth and spreading flood
 Proclaim the wise, the powerful God;
 And thy rich glories from afar
 Sparkle in every rolling star.

4 But in his looks a glory stands,
 The noblest labor of thy hands;
 The pleasing lustre of his eyes
 Outshines the wonders of the skies.

5 Grace!—'t is a sweet, a charming theme;
 My thoughts rejoice at Jesus' name:
 Ye angels! dwell upon the sound;
 Ye heavens! reflect it to the ground.

6 Oh! may I live to reach the place,
 Where he unveils his lovely face,
 Where all his beauties you behold,
 And sing his name to harps of gold.
 Isaac Watts, 1707.

135. *Christ, the supreme God and King.* (281.)

1 AROUND the Saviour's lofty throne,
 Ten thousand times ten thousand sing;
 They worship him as God alone,
 And crown him—everlasting King.

2 Approach, ye saints! this God is yours:
 'T is Jesus, fills the throne above:
 Ye cannot fail, while God endures;
 Ye cannot want, while God is love.

3 Jesus, thou everlasting King!
 To thee the praise of heaven belongs;
 Yet, smile on us who fain would bring
 The tribute of our humbler songs.

4 Though sin defile our worship here,
 We hope ere long thy face to view,
 In heaven with angels to appear,
 And praise thy name as angels do.
 Thomas Kelly, 1804, a.

136. *The Glories of Christ.* (279.)

1 Go, WORSHIP at Immanuel's feet;
 See in his face what wonders meet;
 Earth is too narrow to express
 His worth, his glory, or his grace.

2 The whole creation can afford
 But some faint shadows of my Lord;
 Nature, to make his beauties known,
 Must mingle colors not her own.

3 Nor earth, nor seas, nor sun, nor stars,
 Nor heaven, his full resemblance bears;
 His beauties we can never trace,
 Till we behold him face to face.

4 Oh! let me climb those higher skies,
 Where storms and darkness never rise;
 There he displays his powers abroad,
 And shines, and reigns, th' incarnate God.
 Isaac Watts, 1709.

ADORATION.

BEMERTON.   C. M.   *Henry W. Greatorex, 1849.*

Be-hold the glo-ries of the Lamb, A-midst his Fa-ther's throne!
Pre-pare new hon-ors for his name, And songs, be-fore un-known.

137.   *A new Song to the Lamb.*   (287.)

1 BEHOLD the glories of the Lamb,
   Amidst his Father's throne!
Prepare new honors for his name,
   And songs, before unknown.

2 Let elders worship at his feet,
   The church adore around,
With vials full of odors sweet,
   And harps of sweeter sound.

3 Those are the prayers of all the saints,
   And these the hymns they raise:
Jesus is kind to our complaints,
   He loves to hear our praise.

4 Now to the Lamb, that once was slain,
   Be endless blessings paid!
Salvation, glory, joy, remain
   For ever, on thy head!

5 Thou hast redeemed our souls with blood,
   Hast set the pris'ners free,
Hast made us kings and priests to God,
   And we shall reign with thee.
                     Isaac Watts, 1696.

138.   *The infinite Worth of Christ.*   (288.)

1 INFINITE excellence is thine,
   Thou lovely Prince of grace!
Thine uncreated beauties shine
   With never-fading rays.

2 Sinners, from earth's remotest end,
   Come bending at thy feet;
To thee their prayers and vows ascend,
   In thee their wishes meet.

3 Millions of happy spirits live
   On thine exhaustless store;
From thee they all their bliss receive,
   And still thou givest more.

4 Thou art their triumph and their joy;
   They find their all in thee:
Thy glories will their tongues employ
   Through all eternity.
                     John Fawcett, 1782.

139.   *The Glory of Christ in Heaven.*   (289.)

1 OH! THE delights, the heavenly joys,
   The glories of the place,
Where Jesus sheds the brightest beams
   Of his o'erflowing grace!

2 Sweet majesty and awful love
   Sit smiling on his brow;
And all the glorious ranks above,
   At humble distance bow.

3 Archangels sound his lofty praise
   Through every heavenly street;
And lay their highest honors down,
   Submissive, at his feet.

4 This is the man, th' exalted man,
   Whom we, unseen, adore;
But, when our eyes behold his face,
   Our hearts shall love him more.

5 Lord! how our souls are all on fire,
   To see thy blest abode;
Our tongues rejoice, in tunes of praise
   To our incarnate God.
                     Isaac Watts, 1707.

THE SON OF GOD.

Come, ye that love the Saviour's name, And joy to make it known! The sove-reign of your hearts pro-claim, And bow be-fore his throne.

140. *The King of Saints.* (290.)

1 COME, ye that love the Saviour's name,
 And joy to make it known!
 The sovereign of your hearts proclaim,
 And bow before his throne.

2 Behold your King your Saviour, crowned
 With glories all-divine!
 And tell the wondering nations round,
 How bright these glories shine.

3 Infinite power, and boundless grace,
 In him unite their rays;
 You, that have e'er beheld his face!
 Can you forbear his praise?

4 When, in his earthly courts, we view
 The glories of our King,
 We long to love as angels do,
 And wish like them to sing.

5 And shall we long and wish in vain?
 Lord! teach our songs to rise;
 Thy love can animate the strain,
 And bid it reach the skies.
 Anne Steele, 1760.

141. *Christ worshiped by all the Creation.* (291.)

1 COME, let us join our cheerful songs,
 With angels round the throne;
 Ten thousand thousand are their tongues,
 But all their joys are one.

2 "Worthy the Lamb that died," they cry,
 "To be exalted thus!"
 "Worthy the Lamb," our lips reply,
 "For he was slain for us!"

3 Jesus is worthy to receive
 Honor and power divine;
 And blessings, more than we can give,
 Be, Lord! for ever thine.

4 Let all that dwell above the sky,
 And air, and earth, and seas,
 Conspire to lift thy glories high,
 And speak thine endless praise.

5 The whole creation join in one,
 To bless the sacred name
 Of him, that sits upon the throne,
 And to adore the Lamb.
 Isaac Watts, 1707.

142. *The Love of Christ celebrated.* (296.)

1 To OUR Redeemer's glorious name,
 Awake the sacred song!
 Oh! may his love—immortal flame—
 Tune every heart and tongue.

2 His love what mortal thought can reach?
 What mortal tongue display?
 Imagination's utmost stretch,
 In wonder, dies away.

3 Dear Lord! while we adoring pay
 Our humble thanks to thee,
 May every heart with rapture say,—
 "The Saviour died for me!"

4 Oh! may the sweet, the blissful theme,
 Fill every heart and tongue,
 Till strangers love thy charming name,
 And join the sacred song.
 Anne Steele, 1760.

ADORATION.

WILMOT. 8s & 7s. *Carl Maria von Weber, 1786-1826.*

Mighty God! while angels bless thee, May an infant lisp thy name?
Lord of men, as well as angels! Thou art every creature's theme.

143. *Christ, the Creator and the Redeemer.* (304.)

1 MIGHTY God! while angels bless thee,
  May an infant lisp thy name?
  Lord of men, as well as angels!
  Thou art every creature's theme.

2 Lord of every land and nation!
  Ancient of eternal days!
  Sounded through the wide creation,
  Be thy just and lawful praise.

3 For the grandeur of thy nature,—
  Grand, beyond a seraph's thought;—
  For created works of power,
  Works with skill and kindness wrought;

4 For thy providence, that governs
  Through thine empire's wide domain,
  Wings an angel, guides a sparrow;—
  Blessed be thy gentle reign.

5 But thy rich, thy free redemption,
  Dark through brightness all along!—
  Thought is poor, and poor expression;
  Who dare sing that awful song?
  Robert Robinson, 1774.

144. *Christ adored.* (305.)

1 BRIGHTNESS of the Father's glory!
  Shall thy praise unuttered lie?
  Break, my tongue! such guilty silence,
  Sing the Lord who came to die:—

2 Did archangels sing thy coming?
  Did the shepherds learn their lays?—
  Shame would cover me ungrateful,
  Should my tongue refuse to praise!

3 From the highest throne of glory,
  To the cross of deepest woe,
  Came to ransom guilty captives!—
  Flow, my praise! for ever flow:

4 Re-ascend, immortal Saviour!
  Leave thy footstool, take thy throne;
  Thence return, and reign for ever;—
  Be the kingdom all thine own!
  Robert Robinson, 1774.

145. *Glory to the Lamb.* (306.)

1 HARK the notes of angels, singing,
  "Glory, glory to the Lamb!"
  All in heaven their tribute bringing,
  Raising high the Saviour's name.

2 Ye, for whom his life was given!
  Sacred themes to you belong;
  Come, assist the choir of heaven;
  Join the everlasting song.

3 See th' angelic hosts have crowned him,
  Jesus fills the throne on high:
  Countless myriads, hovering round him,
  With his praises rend the sky.

4 Filled with holy emulation,
  Let us vie with those above;
  Sweet the theme—a free salvation!
  Fruit of everlasting love.

5 Endless life in him possessing,
  Let us praise his precious name,
  Glory, honor, power, and blessing,
  Be for ever to the Lamb!
  Thomas Kelly, 1804.

THE SON OF GOD.

HARWELL. 8s, 7s & 7; or 8s & 7s. 8 LINES. Lowell Mason, 1840.

Hark! ten thousand harps and voices Sound the note of praise above, Jesus reigns, and heav'n rejoices;—Jesus reigns, the God of love: See! he sits on yonder throne; Jesus rules the world alone: See! he sits on yonder throne; Jesus rules the world alone.

146. *Christ enthroned and worshiped.* (307.)

1 HARK!—ten thousand harps and voices
　Sound the note of praise above,
Jesus reigns, and heaven rejoices;—
　Jesus reigns, the God of love:
See! he sits on yonder throne;
Jesus rules the world alone.

2 Jesus! hail! whose glory brightens
　All above, and gives it worth;
Lord of life! thy smile enlightens,
　Cheers, and charms thy saints on earth;
When we think of love like thine,
Lord! we own it love divine.

3 King of glory! reign for ever!
　Thine an everlasting crown;
Nothing, from thy love, shall sever
　Those whom thou hast made thine own;
Happy objects of thy grace,
Destined to behold thy face.

4 Saviour! hasten thine appearing;
　Bring—Oh! bring the glorious day,
When, the awful summons hearing,
　Heaven and earth shall pass away;—
Then, with golden harps, we'll sing,—
"Glory, glory to our King."
　　　　　　　Thomas Kelly, 1804.

147. PSALM 118. (308.)

1 CROWN his head with endless blessing,
　Who, in God the Father's name,
With compassions never ceasing,
　Comes salvation to proclaim.

Hail! ye saints! who know his favor,
　Who within his gates are found,—
There, on high exalt the Saviour,
　Let his courts with praise resound.

2 Jesus! thee our Saviour hailing,
　Thee our God in praise we own;
Highest honors, never failing,
　Rise eternal round thy throne;
Now, ye saints! his power confessing,
　In your grateful strains adore;
For his mercy, never ceasing,
　Flows, and flows for evermore.
　　　　　　William Goode, 1811.

148. *Jesus worshiped.* (309.)

1 JESUS! hail! enthroned in glory,
　There for ever to abide!
All the heavenly hosts adore thee,
　Seated at thy Father's side:
There for sinners thou art pleading,
　There thou dost our place prepare,
Ever for us interceding,
　Till in glory we appear.

2 Worship, honor, power, and blessing,
　Thou art worthy to receive;
Loudest praises without ceasing,
　Meet it is for us to give:
When we join th' angelic spirits,
　In their sweetest, noblest lays,
We will sing our Saviour's merits,
　Help to chant Immanuel's praise.
　　　　　　John Bakewell, 1760, a.

ADORATION.

NEW HAVEN.   6s & 4s.   *Thomas Hastings,* 1833.

Come, all ye saints of God! Publish thro' earth abroad, Je-sus's fame: Tell what his love has done; Trust in his name a-lone! Shout to his lofty throne,—"Worthy the Lamb!"

149.   *Praise to Jesus.*   (268.)

1 Come, all ye saints of God!
   Publish through earth abroad,
     Jesus's fame ;
   Tell what his love has done ;
   Trust in his name alone ;
   Shout to his lofty throne,—
     "Worthy the Lamb!"

2 Hence, gloomy doubts and fears !
   Dry up your mournful tears ;
     Join our glad theme ;
   Beauty for ashes bring,
   Strike each melodious string,
   Join heart and voice to sing,—
     "Worthy the Lamb!"

3 Hark ! how the choirs above,
   Filled with the Saviour's love,
     Dwell on his name !
   There, too, may we be found,
   With light and glory crowned,
   While all the heavens resound,—
     "Worthy the Lamb!"

              James Boden, 1801.

150.   *"Worthy the Lamb."*   (267.)

1 Glory to God on high !
   Let praises fill the sky ;
     Praise ye his name ;
   Angels ! his name adore,
   Who all our sorrows bore ;
   And, saints ! cry evermore,—
     "Worthy the Lamb!"

2 All they around the throne
   Cheerfully join in one,
     Praising his name ;
   We who have felt his blood
   Sealing our peace with God,
   Spread his dear fame abroad,—
     "Worthy the Lamb!"

3 To him our hearts we raise ;
   None else shall have our praise ;
     Praise ye his name ;
   Him, our exalted Lord,
   By us below adored,
   We praise with one accord,—
     "Worthy the Lamb!"

4 Join, all the human race !
   Our Lord and God to bless ;
     Praise ye his name ;
   In him we will rejoice ;
   Making a cheerful noise,
   And say, with heart and voice,—
     "Worthy the Lamb!"

5 Though we must change our place,
   Our souls sha'l never cease
     Praising his name ;
   To him we'll tribute bring,
   Laud him our gracious King,
   And, without ceasing, sing,—
     "Worthy the Lamb!"

              James Allen, 1761.

THE HOLY SPIRIT. 57

FEDERAL STREET. L. M. *Henry K. Oliver, 1832.*

E-ter-nal Spir-it! we con-fess, And sing the won-ders of thy grace; Thy pow'r conveys our bless-ings down, From God, the Fa-ther, and the Son.

151. *The Operations of the Holy Spirit.* (317.)

1 ETERNAL Spirit! we confess
And sing the wonders of thy grace;
Thy power conveys our blessings down,
From God, the Father, and the Son.

2 Enlightened by thy heavenly ray,
Our shades and darkness turn to day;
Thine inward teachings make us know
Our danger, and our refuge too.

3 Thy power and glory work within,
And break the chains of reigning sin;
Do our imperious lusts subdue,
And form our wretched hearts anew.

4 The troubled conscience knows thy voice,
Thy cheering words awake our joys;
Thy words allay the stormy wind,
And calm the surges of the mind.
Isaac Watts, 1709.

152. *The Work of the Holy Spirit.* (318.)

1 COME, sacred Spirit! from above,
And fill the coldest heart with love;
Soften to flesh the rugged stone,
And let thy godlike power be known.

2 Speak thou, and, from the haughtiest eyes,
Shall floods of pious sorrow rise;
While all their glowing souls are borne
To seek that grace, which now they scorn.

3 Oh! let a holy flock await,
Numerous around thy temple-gate!
Each pressing on with zeal to be
A living sacrifice to thee.
Philip Doddridge, 1740.

153. *The Teachings of the Spirit.* (319.)

1 COME, blessed Spirit! Source of Light!
Whose power and grace are unconfined,
Dispel the gloomy shades of night,
The thicker darkness of the mind.

2 To mine illumined eyes, display
The glorious truths thy word reveals,
Cause me to run the heavenly way,
Thy book unfold, and loose the seals.

3 Thine inward teachings make me know
The mysteries of redeeming love,
The emptiness of things below,
And excellence of things above.

4 While through this dubious maze I stray,
Spread, like the sun, thy beams abroad,
To show the dangers of the way,
And guide my feeble steps to God.
Benjamin Beddome, 1770.

154. *Prayer for spiritual Enjoyment.* (320.)

1 COME, Holy Spirit! calm my mind,
And fit me to approach my God;
Remove each vain, each worldly thought,
And lead me to thy blest abode.

2 Hast thou imparted to my soul
A living spark of heavenly fire?
Oh! kindle now the sacred flame;
Teach it to burn with pure desire.

3 A brighter faith and hope impart,
And let me now the Saviour see;
Oh! soothe and cheer my burdened heart,
And bid my spirit rest in thee.
Anon., 1826.

ADORATION.

BALERMA. C. M.
Spanish Melody.
Adapted by *R. Simpson*.

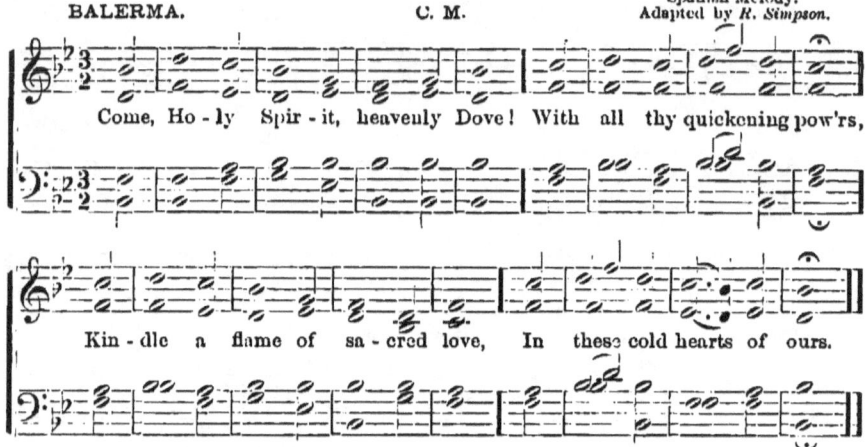

Come, Ho-ly Spir-it, heavenly Dove! With all thy quickening pow'rs,
Kin-dle a flame of sa-cred love, In these cold hearts of ours.

155. *Breathing after the Holy Spirit.* (321.)

1 Come, Holy Spirit, heavenly Dove!
  With all thy quickening powers,—
  Kindle a flame of sacred love,
  In these cold hearts of ours.

2 Look—how we grovel here below,
  Fond of these trifling toys!
  Our souls can neither fly nor go,
  To reach eternal joys.

3 In vain we tune our formal songs,
  In vain we strive to rise;
  Hosannas languish on our tongues,
  And our devotion dies.

4 Dear Lord! and shall we ever live,
  At this poor dying rate?
  Our love so faint, so cold to thee,
  And thine to us so great?

5 Come, Holy Spirit, heavenly Dove!
  With all thy quickening powers;
  Come, shed abroad a Saviour's love,
  And that shall kindle ours.
  Isaac Watts, 1707.

156. *The Descent of the Spirit.* (324.)

1 Spirit Divine! attend our prayers,
  And make this house thy home;
  Descend with all thy gracious powers,
  Oh! come, great Spirit! come.

2 Come as the light; to us reveal
  Our emptiness and woe:
  And lead us in those paths of life
  Where all the righteous go.

3 Come as the fire: and purge our hearts,
  Like sacrificial flame;
  Let our whole soul an offering be
  To our Redeemer's name.

4 Come as the dove; and spread thy wings,
  The wings of peaceful love;
  And let thy church on earth become
  Blessed as the church above.

5 Come as the wind; with rushing sound,
  And pentecostal grace,
  That all, of woman born, may see
  The glory of thy face.
  Andrew Reed, 1841.

157. *The Hope of Salvation.* (323.)

1 Eternal Spirit! God of truth!
  Our contrite hearts inspire;
  Kindle the flame of heavenly love,
  And feed the pure desire.

2 'T is thine to soothe the sorrowing soul,
  With guilt and fear oppressed;
  'T is thine to bid the dying live,
  And give the weary rest.

3 Subdue the power of every sin,
  Whate'er that sin may be;
  That we, in singleness of heart,
  May worship only thee.

4 Then with our spirits witness bear,
  That we're the sons of God;
  Redeemed from sin, and death, and hell,
  Through Christ's atoning blood.
  Thomas Cotterill, 1810.

THE HOLY SPIRIT.

DEDHAM. C. M. William Gardiner, 1830.

Spir-it of ho-li-ness! look down, Our faint-ing hearts to cheer;
And, when we trem-ble at thy frown, Oh! bring thy com-forts near.

158. *The Spirit of Adoption.* (327.)

1 SPIRIT of holiness! look down,
  Our fainting hearts to cheer;
And, when we tremble at thy frown,
  Oh! bring thy comforts near.

2 The fear, which thy convictions wrought,
  Oh! let thy grace remove;
And may the souls, which thou hast taught
  To weep, now learn to love.

3 Now let thy saving mercy heal
  The wounds it made before;
Now on our hearts impress thy seal,
  That we may doubt no more.

4 Complete the work thou hast begun,
  And make our darkness light,—
That we a glorious race may run,
  Till faith be lost in sight.

5 Then, as the wondering eyes discern
  The Lord's unclouded face,
In fitter language, we shall learn
  To sing triumphant grace.
               William Hiley Bathurst, 1830.

159. *The Outpouring of the Spirit.* (331.)

1 LET songs of praises fill the sky!
  Christ, our ascended Lord,
Sends down his Spirit from on high,
  According to his word.

2 The Spirit, by his heavenly breath,
  New life creates within;
He quickens sinners from the death
  Of trespasses and sin.

3 The things of Christ the Spirit takes,
  And to our heart reveals;
Our bodies he his temple makes,
  And our redemption seals.

4 Come, Holy Spirit! from above,
  With thy celestial fire;
Come, and with flames of zeal and love,
  Our hearts and tongues inspire.
               Thomas Cotterill, 1810, a.

160. *The new-creating Spirit.* (329.)

1 SPIRIT of power and might! behold
  A world by sin destroyed;
Creator Spirit! as of old,
  Move on the formless void.

2 Give thou the word; that healing sound
  Shall quell the deadly strife,
And earth again, like Eden crowned,
  Produce the tree of life.

3 If sang the morning stars for joy,
  When nature rose to view,
What strains will angel-harps employ,
  When thou shalt all renew?

4 And, if the sons of God rejoice
  To hear a Saviour's name,
How will the ransomed raise their voice,
  To whom the Saviour came?

5 So every kindred, tongue, and tribe,
  Assembling round the throne,
The new creation shall ascribe
  To sovereign love alone.
               James Montgomery, 1825.

ADORATION.

OLMUTZ. S. M.
From a Gregorian Chant; Adapted by *Lowell Mason*, 1832.

Come, Holy Spirit! come; Let thy bright beams arise;
Dispel the darkness from our minds, And open all our eyes.

161. *The sanctifying Spirit.* (334.)

1 Come, Holy Spirit! come;
  Let thy bright beams arise;
Dispel the darkness from our minds,
  And open all our eyes.

2 Revive our drooping faith,
  Our doubts and fears remove,
And kindle in our breasts the flame
  Of never-dying love.

3 Convince us of our sin;
  Then lead to Jesus' blood,
And to our wondering view reveal
  The secret love of God.

4 'T is thine to cleanse the heart,
  To sanctify the soul,
To pour fresh life on every part,
  And new-create the whole.

5 Dwell, therefore, in our hearts;
  Our minds from bondage free;
Then shall we know, and praise, and love,
  The Father, Son, and Thee.
    Joseph Hart, 1759.

162. *The Descent of the Spirit.* (335.)

1 Lord God, the Holy Ghost!
  In this accepted hour,
As on the day of pentecost,
  Descend in all thy power.

2 We meet with one accord
  In our appointed place,
And wait the promise of our Lord,
  The Spirit of all grace.

3 Like mighty rushing wind
  Upon the waves beneath,
Move with one impulse every mind,
  One soul, one feeling breathe.

4 The young, the old inspire
  With wisdom from above;
And give us hearts and tongues of fire,
  To pray, and praise, and love.

5 Spirit of light! explore,
  And chase our gloom away,
With lustre, shining more and more
  Unto the perfect day.
    James Montgomery, 1819.

163. *The Comforter.* (337.)

1 Blest Comforter Divine!
  Whose rays of heavenly love
Amid our gloom and darkness shine,
  And point our souls above;—

2 Thou! who with "still small voice,"
  Dost stop the sinner's way,
And bid the mourning saint rejoice,
  Though earthly joys decay;—

3 Thou! whose inspiring breath
  Can make the cloud of care,
And e'en the gloomy vale of death,
  A smile of glory wear;—

4 Thou! who dost fill the heart
  With love to all our race;—
Blest Comforter! to us impart
  The blessings of thy grace.
    Mrs. Lydia H. Sigourney, 1825.

THE HOLY SPIRIT.

PLEYEL. 7s. Adapted from *Ignace Pleyel*, cir. 1800.

Ho-ly Ghost! my soul in-spire; Spir-it of th' al-might-y Sire!
Spir-it of the Son di-vine! Com-fort-er! thy gifts be mine.

164. *Faith, Hope, and Love.* (340.)

1 HOLY Ghost! my soul inspire;
Spirit of th' almighty Sire!
Spirit of the Son divine!
Comforter! thy gifts be mine.

2 Holy Spirit! in my breast,
Grant that lively faith may rest;
And subdue each rebel thought
To believe what thou hast taught.

3 When around my sinking soul
Gathering waves of sorrow roll,
Spirit blest! the tempest still,
And with hope my bosom fill.

4 Holy Spirit! from my mind
Thought, and wish, and will unkind,
Deed and word unkind remove,
And my bosom fill with love.

5 Faith, and hope, and charity,
Comforter! descend from thee:
Thou th' anointing Spirit art;
These thy gifts to us impart!

6 Till our faith be lost in sight,
Hope be swallowed in delight,
Love return to dwell with thee,
In the threefold Deity.

Richard Mant, 1837.

165. *The indwelling Spirit.* (341.)

1 HOLY Ghost! with light divine,
Shine upon this heart of mine:
Chase the shades of night away,
Turn the darkness into day.

2 Holy Ghost! with power divine,
Cleanse this guilty heart of mine;
Long has sin, without control,
Held dominion o'er my soul.

3 Holy Ghost! with joy divine,
Cheer this saddened heart of mine;
Bid my many woes depart,
Heal my wounded, bleeding heart.

4 Holy Spirit! all-divine,
Dwell within this heart of mine;
Cast down every idol-throne,
Reign supreme,—and reign alone.

Andrew Reed, 1842.

166. *The sealing Spirit.* (342.)

1 GRACIOUS Spirit! Dove divine!
Let thy light within me shine;
All my guilty fears remove,
Fill me full of heaven and love.

2 Speak thy pardoning grace to me,
Set the burdened sinner free;
Lead me to the Lamb of God;
Wash me in his precious blood.

3 Life and peace to me impart,
Seal salvation on my heart;
Breathe thyself into my breast,—
Earnest of immortal rest.

4 Let me never from thee stray,
Keep me in the narrow way;
Fill my soul with joy divine,
Keep me, Lord! for ever thine.

John Stocker, 1776.

REVELATION.

MARRIOTT.   6s & 4s.   *Joseph Barnby,* 1867.

Thou! whose almighty word Chaos and darkness heard, And took their flight, Hear us, we humbly pray, And, where the gospel's day Sheds not its glorious ray, "Let there be light!"

---

167.   *The Light of Revelation.*   (347.)

1 Thou! whose almighty word
  Chaos and darkness heard,
    And took their flight,
  Hear us, we humbly pray,
  And, where the gospel's day
    Sheds not its glorious ray,
      "Let there be light!"

2 Thou! who didst come to bring,
  On thy redeeming wing,
    Healing and sight,
  Health to the sick in mind,
  Sight to the inly blind,—
  Oh! now to all mankind
    "Let there be light!"

3 Spirit of truth and love,
  Life-giving holy Dove!
    Speed forth thy flight:
  Move o'er the waters' face,
  Bearing the lamp of grace,
  And, in earth's darkest place,
    "Let there be light!"

4 Blessèd and holy Three,
  All-glorious Trinity,—
    Wisdom, Love, Might!
  Boundless as ocean's tide
  Rolling in fullest pride,
  Through the world, far and wide,—
    "Let there be light!"

         John Marriott, 1813.

168.   *The Diffusion of the Scriptures.*   (348.)

1 Lord of all power and might!
  Father of love and light!
    Speed on thy word:
  Oh! let the gospel sound
  All the wide world around,
  Wherever man is found:
    God speed his word!

2 Our thanks we give to thee;
  Thine let the glory be,—
    Glory to God!
  Thine was the mighty plan,
  From thee the work began,
  Away with praise of man,—
    Glory to God!

3 Lo! what embattled foes,
  Stern in their hate, oppose
    God's holy word!
  One for his truth we stand,
  Strong in his own right hand,
  Firm as a martyr-band:
    God shield his word!

4 Onward shall be our course,
  Despite of fraud or force:
    God bless his word!
  His word ere long shall run
  Free as the noonday sun;
  His purpose must be done:
    God bless his word!

         Hugh Stowell, 1852, a.

THE HOLY SCRIPTURES.

169.   PSALM 19.   (349.)

1 BEHOLD ! the lofty sky
   Declares its maker, God ;
   And all his starry worlds, on high,
   Proclaim his power abroad.

2 The darkness and the light
   Still keep their course the same ;
   While night to day, and day to night,
   Divinely teach his name.

3 In every different land.
   Their general voice is known ;
   They show the wonders of his hand,
   And orders of his throne.

4 Ye Christian lands ! rejoice ;
   Here he reveals his word ;
   We are not left to nature's voice,
   To bid us know the Lord.

5 His laws are just and pure,
   His truth without deceit ;
   His promises for ever sure,
   And his rewards are great.

6 While of thy works I sing,
   Thy glory to proclaim.
   Accept the praise, my God, my King !
   In my Redeemer's name.
                    Isaac Watts, 1719.

170.   PSALM 19.   (350.)

1 BEHOLD ! the morning sun
   Begins his glorious way ;
   His beams through all the nations run,
   And life and light convey.

2 But, where the gospel comes,
   It spreads diviner light ;
   It calls dead sinners from their tombs,
   And gives the blind their sight.

3 How perfect is thy word !
   And all thy judgments just ;
   For ever sure thy promise, Lord !
   And men securely trust.

4 My gracious God ! how plain
   Are thy directions given !
   Oh ! may I never read in vain,
   But find the path to heaven.

5 While, with my heart and tongue,
   I spread thy praise abroad ;
   Accept the worship and the song,
   My Saviour and my God !
                    Isaac Watts, 1719.

171.   *The Superiority of the Scriptures.*   (351.)

1 O LORD ! thy perfect word
   Directs our steps aright ;
   Nor can all other books afford
   Such profit or delight

2 Celestial beams it sheds,
   To cheer this vale below ;
   To distant lands its glory spreads,
   And streams of mercy flow.

3 True wisdom it imparts ;
   Commands our hope and fear ;
   Oh ! may we hide it in our hearts,
   And feel its influence there.
                    Benjamin Beddome, 1760.

REVELATION.

MEDFIELD. C. M. *William Mather, 1790.*

How precious is the book divine, By inspiration given!
Bright as a lamp its doctrines shine, To guide our souls to heaven.

172. *The Bible, our Light.* (355.)

1 How precious is the book divine,
   By inspiration given!
   Bright as a lamp its doctrines shine,
   To guide our souls to heaven.

2 Its light, descending from above,
   Our gloomy world to cheer,
   Displays a Saviour's boundless love,
   And brings his glories near.

3 It sweetly cheers our drooping hearts,
   In this dark vale of tears;
   Life, light, and joy, it still imparts,
   And quells our rising fears.

4 This lamp, through all the tedious night
   Of life, shall guide our way,
   Till we behold the clearer light
   Of an eternal day.
   John Fawcett, 1782.

173. *The Excellency of the Holy Scriptures.* (358.)

1 Father of mercies! in thy word,
   What endless glory shines!
   For ever be thy name adored,
   For these celestial lines.

2 Here, the fair tree of knowledge grows,
   And yields a free repast;
   Sublimer sweets than nature knows
   Invite the longing taste.

3 Here, the Redeemer's welcome voice
   Spreads heavenly peace around;
   And life, and everlasting joys
   Attend the blissful sound.

4 Oh! may these heavenly pages be
   My ever dear delight;
   And still new beauties may I see,
   And still increasing light.

5 Divine Instructor, gracious Lord!
   Be thou for ever near;
   Teach me to love thy sacred word,
   And view my Saviour there.
   Anne Steele, 1760.

174. *The Light and Glory of the Word.* (357.)

1 The Spirit breathes upon the word,
   And brings the truth to sight;
   Precepts and promises afford
   A sanctifying light.

2 A glory gilds the sacred page,
   Majestic, like the sun;
   It gives a light to every age;—
   It gives, but borrows none.

3 The hand, that gave it, still supplies
   The gracious light and heat;
   His truths upon the nations rise,—
   They rise, but never set.

4 Let everlasting thanks be thine,
   For such a bright display,
   As makes a world of darkness shine
   With beams of heavenly day.

5 My soul rejoices to pursue
   The steps of him I love,
   Till glory breaks upon my view,
   In brighter worlds above.
   William Cowper, 1772.

THE HOLY SCRIPTURES.

DEVIZES.   C. M.   *Isaac Tucker*, 1800.

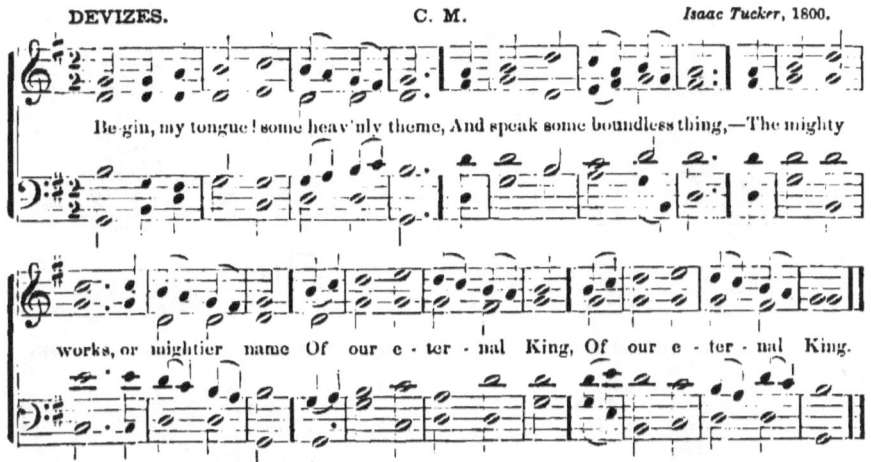

Be-gin, my tongue! some heav'nly theme, And speak some boundless thing,—The mighty works, or mightier name Of our e-ter-nal King, Of our e-ter-nal King.

175.   *The Faithfulness of God.*   (364.)

1 BEGIN, my tongue! some heavenly theme,
   And speak some boundless thing,—
   The mighty works, or mightier name
   Of our eternal King.

2 Tell of his wondrous faithfulness,
   And sound his power abroad;
   Sing the sweet promise of his grace,
   And the performing God.

3 Proclaim—"Salvation from the Lord,
   For wretched, dying men!"
   His hand has writ the sacred word,
   With an immortal pen.

4 Engraved as in eternal brass,
   The mighty promise shines,
   Nor can the powers of darkness raze
   Those everlasting lines.

5 His very word of grace is strong,
   As that which built the skies;
   The voice that rolls the stars along
   Speaks all the promises.

6 Oh! might I hear thy heavenly tongue
   But whisper,—"Thou art mine!"
   Those gentle words should raise my song,
   To notes almost divine.
                            Isaac Watts, 1707.

176.   PSALM 119.   (365.)

1 How shall the young secure their hearts,
   And guard their lives from sin?
   Thy word the choicest rules imparts
   To keep the conscience clean.

2 When once it enters to the mind,
   It spreads such light abroad;
   The meanest souls instruction find,
   And raise their thoughts to God.

3 'T is like the sun, a heavenly light,
   That guides us all the day;
   And, through the dangers of the night,
   A lamp to lead our way.

4 Thy precepts make me truly wise;
   I hate the sinner's road;
   I hate my own vain thoughts that rise,
   But love thy law, my God!

5 Thy word is everlasting truth;
   How pure is every page!
   That holy book shall guide our youth,
   And well support our age.
                            Isaac Watts, 1719.

177.   PSALM 89.   (366.)

1 BLESSED are the souls that hear and know
   The gospel's joyful sound;
   Peace shall attend the path they go,
   And light their steps surround.

2 Their joy shall bear their spirits up,
   Through their Redeemer's name;
   His righteousness exalts their hope,
   Nor Satan dares condemn.

3 The Lord, our glory and defence,
   Strength and salvation gives;
   Israel! thy King for ever reigns,
   Thy God for ever lives.
                            Isaac Watts, 1719.

REVELATION.

STONEFIELD. L. M.   *Samuel Stanley*, 1810.

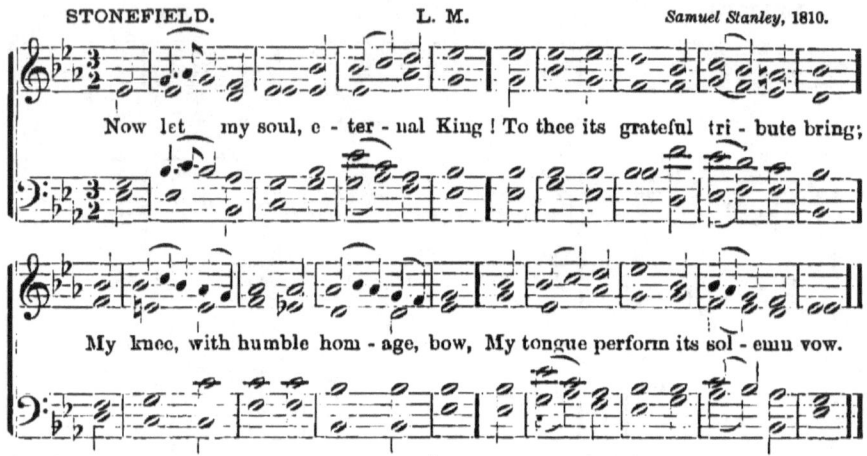

Now let my soul, e-ter-nal King! To thee its grateful tri-bute bring;
My knee, with humble hom-age, bow, My tongue perform its sol-emn vow.

178. *A Saviour seen in the Scriptures.* (367.)

1 Now let my soul, eternal King!
 To thee its grateful tribute bring;
 My knee, with humble homage, bow,
 My tongue perform its solemn vow.

2 All nature sings thy boundless love,
 In worlds below, and worlds above;
 But, in thy blessed word, I trace
 Diviner wonders of thy grace.

3 There, what delightful truths I read!
 There, I behold the Saviour bleed:
 His name salutes my listening ear,
 Revives my heart, and checks my fear.

4 There Jesus bids my sorrows cease,
 And gives my lab'ring conscience peace;
 Raises my grateful passions high,
 And points to mansions in the sky.

5 For love like this, Oh! let my song,
 Through endless years, thy praise prolong;
 Let distant climes thy name adore,
 Till time and nature are no more.
     Ottiwell Heginbotham, 1768.

179. Psalm 19. (368.)

1 The heavens declare thy glory, Lord!
 In every star thy wisdom shines;
 But, when our eyes behold thy word,
 We read thy name in fairer lines.

2 The rolling sun, the changing light,
 And nights and days thy power confess;
 But the blest volume thou hast writ
 Reveals thy justice and thy grace.

3 Sun, moon and stars convey thy praise,
 Round the whole earth, and never stand;
 So, when thy truth began its race,
 It touched and glanced on every land.

4 Nor shall thy spreading gospel rest,
 Till through the world thy truth has run;
 Till Christ has all the nations blessed,
 That see the light, or feel the sun.

5 Great Sun of righteousness! arise;
 Bless the dark world with heavenly light;
 Thy gospel makes the simple wise,
 Thy laws are pure, thy judgments right.

6 Thy noblest wonders here we view,
 In souls renewed, and sins forgiven;
 Lord! cleanse my sins, my soul renew,
 And make thy word my guide to heaven.
     Isaac Watts, 1719.

180. *The Law and Gospel contrasted.* (371.)

1 The law commands and makes us know
 What duties to our God we owe;
 But 't is the gospel must reveal
 Where lies our strength to do his will.

2 The law discovers guilt and sin,
 And shows how vile our hearts have been;
 Only the gospel can express
 Forgiving love and cleansing grace.

3 My soul! no more attempt to draw
 Thy life and comfort from the law;
 Fly to the hope the gospel gives;
 The man, that trusts the promise, lives.
     Isaac Watts, 1709.

THE HOLY SCRIPTURES. 67

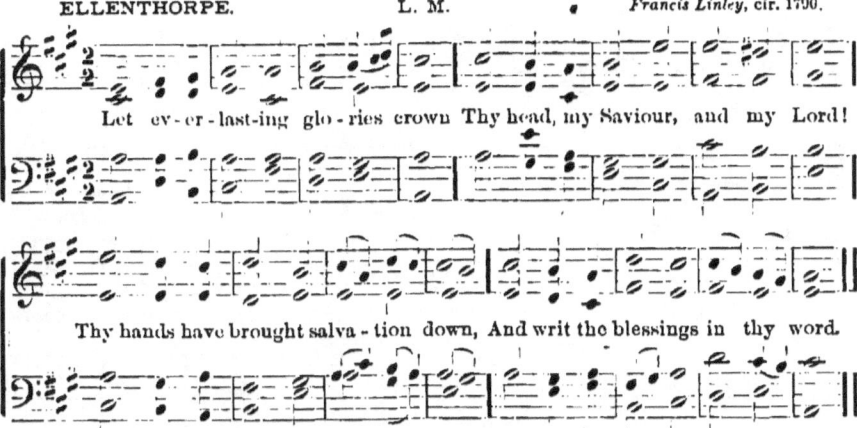

ELLENTHORPE. L. M. *Francis Linley*, cir. 1790.

Let ev-er-last-ing glo-ries crown Thy head, my Saviour, and my Lord!
Thy hands have brought salva-tion down, And writ the blessings in thy word.

181. *The Excellency of the Scriptures.* (373.)

1 Let everlasting glories crown
  Thy head, my Saviour, and my Lord!
  Thy hands have brought salvation down,
  And writ the blessings in thy word.

2 In vain the trembling conscience seeks
  Some solid ground to rest upon ;
  With long despair the spirit breaks,
  Till we apply to Christ alone.

3 How well thy blessed truths agree !
  How wise and holy thy commands !
  Thy promises —how firm they be !
  How firm our hope and comfort stands !

4 Should all the forms that men devise
  Assault my faith, with treacherous art,
  I'd call them vanity and lies,
  And bind the gospel to my heart.
  Isaac Watts, 1709.

182. *The Glory of the Scriptures.* (374.)

1 God, in the gospel of his Son,
  Makes his eternal counsels known ;
  'T is here his richest mercy shines,
  And truth is drawn in fairest lines.

2 Here, sinners of an humble frame
  May taste his grace and learn his name ;
  'T is writ in characters of blood,
  Severely just, immensely good.

3 Here, Jesus in ten thousand ways
  His soul-attracting charms displays,
  Recounts his poverty and pains,
  And tells his love in melting strains.

4 Wisdom its dictates here imparts,
  To form our minds, renew our hearts ;
  Its influence makes the sinner live,
  And bids the drooping saint revive.

5 Our raging passions it controls,
  And comfort yields to contrite souls ;
  It brings a better world in view,
  And guides us all our journey through.

6 May this blest volume ever lie
  Close to my heart, and near my eye,
  Till life's last hour my thoughts engage,
  And be my chosen heritage.
  Benjamin Beddome, 1787.

183. *The Power of divine Truth.* (375.)

1 This is the word of truth and love,
  Sent to the nations from above ;
  Jehovah here resolves to show
  What his almighty grace can do.

2 This remedy did wisdom find,
  To heal diseases of the mind ;—
  This sovereign balm, whose virtues can
  Restore the ruined creature, man.

3 The gospel bids the dead revive,—
  Sinners obey the voice, and live ;
  Dry bones are raised, and clothed afresh,
  And hearts of stone are turned to flesh.

4 May but this grace my soul renew,
  Let sinners gaze, and hate me too ;
  The word that saves me does engage
  A sure defence from all their rage.
  Isaac Watts, 1709.

SALVATION.

ROCKBRIDGE. (FOREST.) L. M.   Aaron Chapin, 1822.

Show pit-y, Lord! O Lord! for-give, Let a re-pent-ing reb-el live;
Are not thy mer-cies large and free? May not a sin-ner trust in thee?

184.   Psalm 51.   (382.)

1 Show pity, Lord! O Lord! forgive,
Let a repenting rebel live ;
Are not thy mercies large and free?
May not a sinner trust in thee?

2 My crimes are great, but not surpass
The power and glory of thy grace ;
Great God! thy nature hath no bound,
So let thy pardoning love be found.

3 Oh! wash my soul from every sin,
And make my guilty conscience clean ;
Here on my heart the burden lies,
And past offences pain my eyes.

4 My lips with shame my sins confess,
Against thy law, against thy grace ;
Lord! should thy judgments grow severe,
I am condemned, but thou art clear.

5 Should sudden vengeance seize my breath,
I must pronounce thee just in death ;
And, if my soul were sent to hell,
Thy righteous law approves it well.

6 Yet save a trembling sinner, Lord!
Whose hope, still hovering round thy word,
Would light on some sweet promise there,
Some sure support against despair.
                         Isaac Watts, 1719.

185.   *The first and second Adam.*   (380.)

1 Deep in the dust before thy throne,
Our guilt and our disgrace we own ;
Great God! we own th' unhappy name,
Whence sprung our nature and our shame.

2 But, whilst our spirits, filled with awe,
Behold the terrors of thy law,
We sing the honors of thy grace,
That sent to save our ruined race.

3 We sing thine everlasting Son,
Who joined our nature to his own ;
Adam, the second, from the dust,
Raises the ruins of the first.

4 Where sin did reign, and death abound
There have the sons of Adam found
Abounding life ; there glorious grace
Reigns thro' the Lord, our Righteousness.
                         Isaac Watts, 1709.

186.   *The Gospel, the Power of God.*   (381.)

1 What shall the dying sinner do,
That seeks relief for all his woe ?
Where shall the guilty conscience find
Ease for the torment of the mind?

2 How shall we get our crimes forgiven,
Or form our natures fit for heaven ?
Can souls, all o'er defiled with sin,
Make their own powers and passions clean ?

3 In vain we search, in vain we try,
Till Jesus brings his gospel nigh ;
'T is there such power and glory dwell,
As save rebellious souls from hell.

4 This is the pillar of our hope,
That bears our fainting spirits up ;
We read the grace, we trust the word,
And find salvation in the Lord.
                         Isaac Watts, 1707.

NEED OF SALVATION.

How sad our state by nature is! Our sin—how deep it stains!
And Satan binds our captive minds, Fast in his slavish chains.

187. *Pardon and Sanctification in Christ.* (385.)

1 How sad our state by nature is!
 Our sin—how deep it stains!
 And Satan binds our captive minds,
 Fast in his slavish chains.

2 But there's a voice of sovereign grace,
 Sounds from the sacred word;—
 "Ho! ye despairing sinners! come,
 And trust upon the Lord."

3 My soul obeys th' almighty call,
 And runs to this relief;
 I would believe thy promise, Lord!
 Oh! help my unbelief.

4 To the dear fountain of thy blood,
 Incarnate God! I fly;
 Here let me wash my spotted soul,
 From crimes of deepest dye.

5 A guilty, weak, and helpless worm,
 On thy kind arms I fall:
 Be thou my strength and righteousness,
 My Jesus, and my all.
 Isaac Watts, 1707.

188. *The Need of Regeneration.* (389.)

1 How helpless guilty nature lies,
 Unconscious of its load!
 The heart, unchanged, can never rise
 To happiness and God.

2 Can aught, beneath a power divine,
 The stubborn will subdue?
 'Tis thine, almighty Spirit! thine,
 To form the heart anew.

3 'Tis thine, the passions to recall,
 And upward bid them rise;
 To make the scales of error fall,
 From reason's darkened eyes.

4 To chase the shades of death away,
 And bid the sinner live;
 A beam of heaven, a vital ray,
 'Tis thine alone to give.

5 Oh! change these wretched hearts of ours,
 And give them life divine;
 Then shall our passions and our powers,
 Almighty Lord! be thine.
 Anne Steele, 1760.

189. *Regeneration.* (387.)

1 Nor all the outward forms on earth,
 Nor rites that God has given,
 Nor will of man, nor blood, nor birth,
 Can raise a soul to heaven.

2 The sovereign will of God alone
 Creates us heirs of grace;
 Born in the image of his Son,
 A new, peculiar race.

3 The Spirit, like some heavenly wind,
 Blows on the sons of flesh,
 New models all the carnal mind,
 And forms the man afresh.

4 Our quickened souls awake, and rise
 From the long sleep of death;
 On heavenly things we fix our eyes,
 And praise employs our breath.
 Isaac Watts, 1709.

SALVATION.

ANTIOCH.   C. M.

From *George Frederick Händel.*
Adapted *by Lowell Mason,* 1836.

Joy to the world, the Lord is come; Let earth receive her King; Let ev-ery heart prepare him room,

And heav'n and nature sing, And heav'n and nature sing, And heav'n, and heav'n and nature sing.

And heav'n and nature sing, And heav'n and nature sing, and heav'n, &c.

190.   PSALM 98.   (391.)

1 Joy to the world,—the Lord is come ;
   Let earth receive her King ;
   Let every heart prepare him room,
   And heaven and nature sing.

2 Joy to the earth,—the Saviour reigns :
   Let men their songs employ ; [plains
   While fields and floods, rocks, hills, and
   Repeat the sounding joy.

3 No more let sins and sorrows grow,
   Nor thorns infest the ground ;
   He comes to make his blessings flow,
   Far as the curse is found.

4 He rules the world with truth and grace,
   And makes the nations prove
   The glories of his righteousness,
   And wonders of his love.
                      Isaac Watts, 1709.

191.   *Christ's Mission.*   (392.)

1 HARK the glad sound ! the Saviour
     comes,—
   The Saviour promised long ;
   Let every heart prepare a throne,
   And every voice a song.

2 On him the Spirit, largely poured,
   Exerts his sacred fire ;
   Wisdom and might, and zeal and love
   His holy breast inspire.

3 He comes, the pris'ners to release,
   In Satan's bondage held,
   The gates of brass before him burst,
   The iron fetters yield.

4 He comes, from thickest films of vice,
   To clear the mental ray,
   And, on the eye-balls of the blind,
   To pour celestial day.

5 He comes, the broken heart to bind,
   The bleeding soul to cure ;
   And, with the treasures of his grace,
   T' enrich the humble poor.

6 Our glad hosannas, Prince of peace !
   Thy welcome shall proclaim,
   And heaven's eternal arches ring
   With thy beloved name.
                      Philip Doddridge, 1735.

192.   *The Angel's Song.*   (393.)

1 HIGH let us swell our tuneful notes,
   And join th' angelic throng ;
   For angels no such love have known,
   T' awake a cheerful song.

2 Good-will to sinful men is shown,
   And peace on earth is given ;
   For lo ! th' incarnate Saviour comes
   With messages from heaven.

3 Justice and grace, with sweet accord,
   His rising beams adorn ;
   Let heaven and earth in concert join,—
   To us a Saviour 's born.

4 Glory to God ! in highest strains,
   In highest worlds be paid ;
   His glory by our lips proclaimed,
   And by our lives displayed.
                      Philip Doddridge, 1740. *o.*

INCARNATION OF CHRIST.

CHRISTMAS. C. M. From *George Frederick Handel*, 1685–1759.

Mortals! awake, with angels join, And chant the solemn lay; Joy, love, and grati-tude, combine To hail th' auspicious day, To hail th' auspicious day.

193. *The Nativity of Christ.* (394.)

1 Mortals! awake, with angels join,
And chant the solemn lay;
Joy, love, and gratitude, combine
To hail th' auspicious day.

2 In heaven the rapturous song began,
And sweet seraphic fire
Through all the shining regions ran,
And strung and tuned the lyre.

3 Swift, through the vast expanse, it flew,
And loud the echo rolled;
The theme, the song, the joy was new,
'T was more than heaven could hold.

4 Down to the portals of the sky
Th' impetuous torrent ran ;
And angels rushed, with eager joy,
To bear the news to man.

5 Hark! the cherubic armies shout,
And glory leads the song;   [out
Good-will and peace are heard through-
Th' harmonious heavenly throng.

6 With joy the chorus we repeat—
"Glory to God on high!"
Good-will and peace are now complete :
Jesus was born to die.
        Samuel Medley, 1800.

194. *The Chorus of Angels.* (398.)

1 Calm on the listening ear of night,
Come heaven's melodious strains,
Where wild Judea stretches far
Her silver-mantled plains.

2 Celestial choirs, from courts above,
Shed sacred glories there,
And angels, with their sparkling lyres,
Make music on the air.

3 The answering hills of Palestine
Send back the glad reply ;
And greet, from all their holy heights,
The day-spring from on high.

4 O'er the blue depths of Galilee
There comes a holier calm,
And Sharon waves, in solemn praise,
Her silent groves of palm.

5 "Glory to God !" the sounding skies
Loud with their anthems ring,—
"Peace to the earth, good will to men,
From heaven's eternal King !"
        Edmund H. Sears, 1835.

195. *The Birth of Christ.* (396.)

1 To us a Child of hope is born,
To us a Son is given ;
Him shall the tribes of earth obey,
Him all the hosts of heaven.

2 His name shall be the Prince of Peace,
For evermore adored ;
The Wonderful, the Counselor,
The great and mighty Lord.

3 His power, increasing, still shall spread ;
His reign no end shall know ;
Justice shall guard his throne above,
And peace abound below.
        John Morrison, 1781.

SALVATION.

WARSAW. H. M. *Thomas Clark, 1804.*

Hark! hark! the notes of joy Roll o'er the heavenly plains, And se-raphs find em-ploy For their sublimest strains; Some new delight in heav'n is known; Loud ring the harps around the throne.

196. *Joy at Immanuel's Birth.* (400.)

1 Hark! hark!—the notes of joy
Roll o'er the heavenly plains,
And seraphs find employ
For their sublimest strains;
Some new delight in heaven is known;
Loud ring the harps around the throne.

2 Hark; hark!—the sounds draw nigh,
The joyful hosts descend;
Jesus forsakes the sky,
To earth his footsteps bend;
He comes to bless our fallen race;
He comes with messages of grace.

3 Bear—bear the tidings round;
Let every mortal know
What love in God is found,
What pity he can show;
Ye winds that blow! ye waves that roll!
Bear the glad news from pole to pole.

4 Strike—strike the harps again,
To great Immanuel's name;
Arise, ye sons of men!
And all his grace proclaim;
Angels and men! wake every string,
'T is God the Saviour's praise we sing.
Andrew Reed, 1842.

197. *The Birth of Christ.* (401.)

1 Hark! what celestial notes,
What melody we hear!
Soft on the morn it floats,
And fills the ravished ear:
The tuneful shell, the golden lyre,
And vocal choir, the concert swell.

2 Th' angelic hosts descend,
With harmony divine;
See how from heaven they bend,
And in full chorus join!
"Fear not," say they, "great joy we bring;
Jesus, your King, is born to-day.

3 Glory to God on high!
Ye mortals! spread the sound,
And let your raptures fly,
To earth's remotest bound:
For peace on earth, from God in heaven,
To man is given, at Jesus' birth."
Anon., 1778.

198. *Good-Will toward Men.* (402.)

1 Lo! God, our God, has come;
To us a Child is born,
To us a Son is given:
Bless, bless the blessed morn!
Oh! happy, lowly, lofty birth!
Now God, our God, has come to earth.

2 Rejoice! our God has come,
In love and lowliness;
The Son of God has come,
The sons of men to bless;
God with us now descends to dwell,—
God in our flesh — Immanuel.

3 Praise ye the Word made flesh;
True God, true man is he;
Praise ye the Christ of God;
To whom all glory be!
Praise ye the Lamb that once was slain,
Praise ye the King that comes to reign.
Horatius Bonar, 1868.

INCARNATION OF CHRIST.

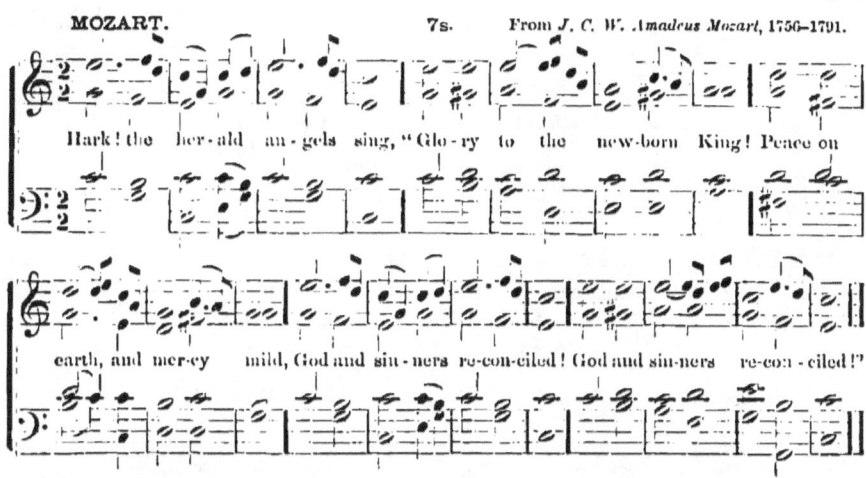

199. *The Nativity of Christ.* (403.)

1 HARK! the herald angels sing,—
"Glory to the new-born King!
Peace on earth, and mercy mild,
God and sinners reconciled!"

2 Joyful, all ye nations! rise,
Join the triumph of the skies;
Universal nature! say,—
"Christ, the Lord, is born to-day!"

3 Christ, by highest heaven adored,
Christ, the everlasting Lord:
Late in time behold him come,
Offspring of a virgin's womb!

4 Veiled in flesh, the Godhead see,
Hail th' incarnate Deity!
Pleased as man with men t' appear,
Jesus, our Immanuel here!

5 Hail the heavenly Prince of peace,
Hail the Sun of righteousness!
Light and life to all he brings,
Risen with healing in his wings.

6 Mild he lays his glory by,
Born that man no more may die;
Born to raise the sons of earth:
Born to give them second birth.
Charles Wesley, 1739.

200. *The Incarnate Deity.* (404.)

1 BRIGHT and joyful is the morn,
For to us a Child is born;
From the highest realms of heaven,
Unto us a Son is given.

2 On his shoulder he shall bear
Power and majesty, and wear,
On his vesture and his thigh,
Names most awful, names most high.

3 Wonderful in counsel, he,
Christ, th' incarnate Deity;
Sire of ages, ne'er to cease;
King of kings, and Prince of peace.

4 Come, and worship at his feet;
Yield to Christ the homage meet,
From his manger to his throne,
Homage due to God alone.
James Montgomery, 1825.

201. *The guiding Star.* (405.)

1 SONS of men! behold from far,
Hail the long-expected star!
Jacob's star, that gilds the night,
Guides bewildered nature right.

2 Fear not hence that ill should flow,
Wars or pestilence below;
Wars it bids and tumults cease,
Ushering in the Prince of peace.

3 Mild he shines on all beneath,
Piercing through the shades of death;
Scattering error's wide-spread night,
Kindling darkness into light.

4 Nations all, far off and near!
Haste to see your God appear;
Haste, for him your hearts prepare;
Meet him manifested there.
Charles Wesley, 1839.

SALVATION.

RUSSIA. (VESPER HYMN.) 8s & 7s. 8 LINES.

Dimitri S. Bartniansky, 1751-1825.
Adapted by *Lowell Mason.*

Hark! what mean those holy voices, Sweetly warbling in the skies?
Sure, th' angelic host rejoices— Loudest hallelujahs rise.
Listen to the wondrous story, Which they chant in hymns of joy;—
"Glory in the highest, glory; Glory be to God most high!"

---

202. *The Song of Angels.* (409.)

1 Hark! what mean those holy voices,
    Sweetly warbling in the skies?
  Sure, th' angelic host rejoices—
    Loudest hallelujahs rise.

2 Listen to the wondrous story,
    Which they chant in hymns of joy;—
  "Glory in the highest, glory;
    Glory be to God most high!

3 "Peace on earth, good-will from heaven,
    Reaching far as man is found;
  Souls redeemed, and sins forgiven;—
    Loud our golden harps shall sound.

4 "Christ is born, the great Anointed;
    Heaven and earth his glory sing:
  Glad, receive whom God appointed,
    For your Prophet, Priest, and King.

5 "Hasten, mortals! to adore him;
    Learn his name, and taste his joy;
  Till in heaven you sing before him,—
    Glory be to God most high!"

6 Let us learn the wondrous story
    Of our great Redeemer's birth,
  Spread the brightness of his glory,
    Till it cover all the earth.

John Cawood, 1825.

203. *The Worship of the Child Jesus.* (412.)

1 Come, ye lofty! come, ye lowly!
    Let your songs of gladness ring;
  In a stable lies the Holy,
    In a manger rests the King.

2 See, in Mary's arms reposing,
    Christ, by highest heaven adored;
  Come, your circle round him closing,
    Pious hearts that love the Lord!

3 Come, ye poor! no pomp of station
    Robes the Child your hearts adore;
  He, the Lord of all salvation,
    Shares your want, is weak and poor.

4 Come, ye gentle hearts and tender!
    Come, ye spirits keen and bold!
  All in all, your homage render,
    Weak and mighty, young and old!

5 High above a star is shining,
    And the wise men haste from far;
  Come, glad hearts, and spirits pining!
    For you all has risen the star.

6 Let us bring our poor oblations,
    Thanks and love and faith and praise;
  Come, ye people! come, ye nations!
    All in all, draw nigh to gaze.

Archer T. Gurney, 1860.

INCARNATION OF CHRIST.

GOULD.   11s & 10s.   S. P. W——, 1871.

Hail to the brightness of Zion's glad morning! Joy to the lands that in darkness have lain!

Hushed be the accents of sorrow and mourning! Zi-on in triumph begins her mild reign.

204. *Messiah's Advent.* (414.)

1 Hail to the brightness of Zion's glad morning!
Joy to the lands that in darkness have lain!
Hushed be the accents of sorrow and mourning!
Zion in triumph begins her mild reign.

2 Hail to the brightness of Zion's glad morning, [told!
Long by the prophets of Israel foretold!
Hail to the millions from bondage returning! [hold.
Gentiles and Jews the blest vision behold.

3 Lo! in the desert rich flowers are springing.
Streams ever copious are gliding along;
Loud from the mountain-top echoes are ringing, [song.
Wastes rise in verdure, and mingle in song.

4 See! from all lands, from the isles of the ocean,
Praise to Jehovah ascending on high;
Fallen are the engines of war and commotion,
Shouts of salvation are rending the sky.

5 Hail to the brightness of Zion's glad morning! [lain!
Joy to the lands that in darkness have lain!
Hushed be the accents of sorrow and mourning!
Zion in triumph begins her mild reign.

Thomas Hastings, 1830.

205. *Star of the East.* (415.)

1 Brightest and best of the sons of the morning! [thine aid;
Dawn on our darkness, and lend us thine aid;
Star of the East!—the horizon adorning,— [laid.
Guide where our infant Redeemer is laid.

2 Cold on his cradle, the dew-drops are shining; [the stall;
Low lies his head with the beasts of the stall;
Angels adore him, in slumber reclining,—
Maker, and Monarch, and Saviour of all.

3 Say, shall we yield him, in costly devotion,
Odors of Edom, and offerings divine,
Gems of the mountain, and pearls of the ocean, [mine?
Myrrh from the forest, or gold from the mine?

4 Vainly we offer each ample oblation,
Vainly with gifts would his favor secure;
Richer, by far, is the heart's adoration,—
Dearer to God are the prayers of the poor.

5 Brightest and best of the sons of the morning! [thine aid;
Dawn on our darkness, and lend us thine aid;
Star of the East!—the horizon adorning— [laid.
Guide where our infant Redeemer is laid.

Reginald Heber, 1827.

SALVATION.

ARNHEIM.   L. M.   *Samuel Holyoke, 1785.*

Now be my heart inspired to sing The glories of my Saviour King; Jesus, the Lord,—how heavenly fair His form! how bright his beauties are!

---

206.   PSALM 45.   (418.)

1 Now be my heart inspired to sing
   The glories of my Saviour King;
   Jesus, the Lord,—how heavenly fair
   His form! how bright his beauties are!

2 O'er all the sons of human race,
   He shines with a superior grace;
   Love from his lips divinely flows,
   And blessings all his state compose.

3 God, thine own God, has richly shed
   His oil of gladness on thy head;
   And, with his sacred Spirit, blessed
   His first-born Son above the rest.
                    Isaac Watts, 1719.

207.   *The Miracles of Christ.*   (419.)

1 BEHOLD! the blind their sight receive;
   Behold! the dead awake and live;
   The dumb speak wonders, and the lame
   Leap, like the hart, and bless his name.

2 Thus doth th' eternal Spirit own
   And seal the mission of the Son;
   The Father vindicates his cause,
   While he hangs bleeding on the cross.

3 He dies! the heavens in mourning stood;
   He rises, the triumphant God!
   Behold the Lord ascending high,
   No more to bleed, no more to die!

4 Hence, and for ever, from my heart,
   I bid my doubts and fears depart;
   And to those hands my soul resign,
   Which bear credentials so divine.
                    Isaac Watts, 1709.

208.   *The Teaching of Jesus.*   (420.)

1 How sweetly flowed the gospel's sound
   From lips of gentleness and grace,
   When list'ning thousands gathered round,
   And joy and reverence filled the place!

2 From heav'n he came, of heav'n he spoke,
   To heaven he led his followers' way;
   Dark clouds of gloomy night he broke,
   Unveiling an immortal day.

3 "Come, wanderers! to my Father's home,
   Come, all ye weary ones! and rest:"
   Yes, sacred Teacher! we will come,
   Obey thee, love thee, and be blest.
                    John Bowring, 1823.

209.   *The Example of Christ.*   (422.)

1 MY DEAR Redeemer, and my Lord!
   I read my duty in thy word;
   But in thy life the law appears,
   Drawn out in living characters.

2 Such was thy truth, and such thy zeal,
   Such deference to thy Father's will,
   Such love and meekness, so divine,
   I would transcribe, and make them mine.

3 Cold mountains and the midnight air
   Witnessed the fervor of thy prayer;
   The desert thy temptations knew,
   Thy conflict and thy victory too.

4 Be thou my pattern; make me bear
   More of thy gracious image here;
   Then God, the Judge, shall own my name,
   Amongst the followers of the Lamb.
                    Isaac Watts, 1709.

THE MINISTRY OF CHRIST.

Be-hold where, in the Friend of man, Ap-pears each grace di-vine!
The vir-tues all in Je-sus met, With mildest ra-diance shine.

210. *The Example of Christ.* (425.)

1 BEHOLD where, in the Friend of man,
  Appears each grace divine!
  The virtues, all in Jesus met,
  With mildest radiance shine.

2 To spread the rays of heavenly light,
  To give the mourner joy,
  To preach glad tidings to the poor,
  Was his divine employ.

3 Midst keen reproach, and cruel scorn,
  Patient and meek he stood;
  His foes, ungrateful, sought his life;
  He labored for their good.

4 In the last hour of deep distress,
  Before his Father's throne,
  With soul resigned, he bowed, and said,
  "Thy will, not mine, be done!"

5 Be Christ our pattern and our guide;
  His image may we bear;
  Oh! may we tread his sacred steps,
  And his bright glories share.
  William Enfield, 1802.

211. *Christ's Compassion to the Weak.* (428.)

1 WITH joy we meditate the grace
  Of our High-Priest above;
  His heart is made of tenderness,
  His bowels melt with love.

2 Touched with a sympathy within,
  He knows our feeble frame;
  He knows what sore temptations mean,
  For he has felt the same.

3 But spotless, innocent, and pure,
  The great Redeemer stood;
  While Satan's fiery darts he bore,
  And did resist to blood.

4 He, in the days of feeble flesh,
  Poured out his cries and tears;
  And, in his measure, feels afresh
  What every member bears.

5 Then let our humble faith address
  His mercy and his power;
  We shall obtain delivering grace,
  In the distressing hour.
  Isaac Watts, 1709.

212. *The Way, the Truth, and the Life.* (430.)

1 THOU art the Way;—to thee alone
  From sin and death we flee;
  And he, who would the Father seek,
  Must seek him, Lord! by thee.

2 Thou art the Truth;—thy word alone
  True wisdom can impart;
  Thou only canst inform the mind,
  And purify the heart.

3 Thou art the Life;—the rending tomb
  Proclaims thy conquering arm;
  And those, who put their trust in thee,
  Nor death nor hell shall harm.

4 Thou art the Way, the Truth, the Life;
  Grant us that Way to know,
  That Truth to keep, that Life to win,
  Whose joys eternal flow.
  George W. Doane, 1824.

SALVATION.

BAVARIA. 8s & 7s. 6 or 8 lines. *German.*

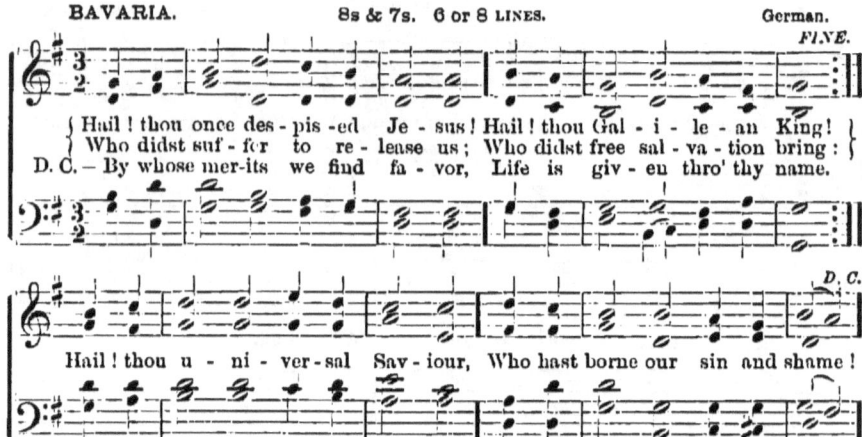

Hail! thou once despised Jesus! Hail! thou Galilean King!
Who didst suffer to release us; Who didst free salvation bring:
By whose merits we find favor, Life is given thro' thy name.
Hail! thou universal Saviour, Who hast borne our sin and shame!

213. *The Paschal Lamb.* (434.)

1 HAIL! thou once despiséd Jesus!
Hail! thou Galilean King!
Who didst suffer to release us;
Who didst free salvation bring;
Hail! thou universal Saviour,
Who hast borne our sin and shame!
By whose merits we find favor,
Life is given, through thy name.

2 Paschal Lamb, by God appointed!
All our sins on thee were laid;
By almighty love anointed,
Thou hast full atonement made;
Every sin may be forgiven,
Through the virtue of thy blood;
Opened is the gate of heaven;
Peace is made 'twixt man and God.
      John Bakewell, 1760.

214. *The great Atonement.* (435.)

1 GREAT High Priest! we view thee stooping,
With our names upon thy breast,
In the garden, groaning, drooping,
To the ground with horrors pressed:
Weeping angels stood confounded
To behold their Maker thus,
And can we remain unwounded
When we know 't was all for us?

2 On the cross thy body broken
Cancels every penal tie;
Tempted souls! produce this token,
All demands to satisfy:

All is finished; do not doubt it;
But believe your dying Lord;
Never reason more about it,
Only take him at his word.

3 Lord! we fain would trust thee solely;
'T was for us thy blood was spilled;
Bruiséd Bridegroom! take us wholly;
Take and make us what thou wilt;
Thou hast borne the bitter sentence
Passed on man's devoted race;
True belief and true repentance
Are thy gifts, thou God of grace!
      Joseph Hart, 1759.

215. *The Finished Redemption.* (436.)

1 HARK! the voice of love and mercy
Sounds aloud from Calvary;
See!—it rends the rocks asunder,
Shakes the earth, and veils the sky:
"It is finished!"
Hear the dying Saviour cry.

2 "It is finished!"—Oh! what pleasure
Do these charming words afford!
Heavenly blessings, without measure,
Flow to us from Christ the Lord:
"It is finished!"
Saints! the dying words record.

3 Tune your harps anew, ye seraphs!
Join to sing the pleasing theme;
All on earth, and all in heaven!
Join to praise Immanuel's name:
Hallelujah!
Glory to the bleeding Lamb!
      Jonathan Evans, 1787.

THE ATONING SACRIFICE.

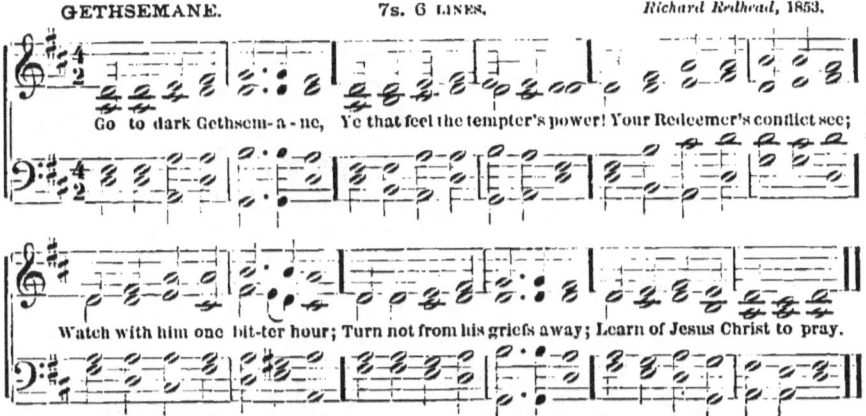

GETHSEMANE. 7s. 6 LINES. *Richard Redhead*, 1853.

Go to dark Gethsem-a-ne, Ye that feel the tempter's power! Your Redeemer's conflict see;
Watch with him one bit-ter hour; Turn not from his griefs away; Learn of Jesus Christ to pray.

216. *Christ, our Example in Suffering.* (442.)

1 Go to dark Gethsemane,
  Ye that feel the tempter's power!
Your Redeemer's conflict see;
  Watch with him one bitter hour;
Turn not from his griefs away;
Learn of Jesus Christ to pray.

2 Follow to the judgment-hall,
  View the Lord of life arraigned;
Oh! the wormwood and the gall!
  Oh! the pangs his soul sustained!
Shun not suffering, shame, or loss;
Learn of him to bear the cross.

3 Calvary's mournful mountain climb;
  There, adoring at his feet,
Mark that miracle of time,—
  God's own sacrifice complete:
"It is finished," hear him cry;
Learn of Jesus Christ to die.

4 Early hasten to the tomb,
  Where they laid his breathless clay;
All is solitude and gloom;—
  Who hath taken him away?
Christ is risen!—he meets our eyes;
Saviour! teach us so to rise.
James Montgomery, 1819.

217. *The Garden Scene.* (443.)

1 SURELY Christ thy griefs hath borne;
  Weeping soul! no longer mourn;
View him bleeding on the tree,
  Pouring out his life for thee:
There thine every sin he bore:
Weeping soul! lament no more.

2 All thy crimes on him were laid;
  See! upon his blameless head
Wrath its utmost vengeance pours,
  Due to my offence and yours:
Wounded in our stead he is,
Bruised for our iniquities.

3 Weary sinner! keep thine eyes
  On th' atoning sacrifice;
There th' incarnate Deity
  Numbered with transgressors see!
There his Father's absence mourns,
Nailed, and bruised, and crowned with thorns.

4 See thy God his head bow down;
  Hear the Man of sorrows groan,
For thy ransom there condemned,
  Stripped, derided, and blasphemed:
Bleeds the Guiltless for th' unclean,
Made an offering for thy sin.

5 Cast thy guilty soul on him,
  Find him mighty to redeem:
At his feet thy burden lay,
  Look thy doubts and cares away:
Now, by faith, the Son embrace,
Plead his promise, trust his grace.

6 Lord! thine arm must be revealed,
  Ere I can by faith be healed:
Since I scarce can look to thee,
  Cast a gracious eye on me:
At thy feet myself I lay;
Shine, Oh! shine my fears away!
Augustus M. Toplady, 1759.

SALVATION.

218. *At the Cross.* (447.)

1 O Jesus! sweet the tears I shed,
  While at thy cross I kneel,
  Gaze at thy wounded, fainting head,
  And all thy sorrows feel.

2 My heart dissolves to see thee bleed,
  This heart so hard before ;
  I hear thee for the guilty plead,
  And grief o'erflows the more.

3 'T was for the sinful thou didst die,
  And I a sinner stand :
  What love speaks from thy dying eye,
  And from each piercéd hand.

4 I know this cleansing blood of thine
  Was shed, dear Lord! for me,—
  For me, for all,—Oh! grace divine!—
  Who look by faith on thee.

5 O Christ of God! O spotless Lamb!
  By love my soul is drawn ;
  Henceforth, for ever, thine I am ;
  Here life and peace are born.

6 In patient hope, the cross I'll bear,
  Thine arm shall be my stay ;
  And thou, enthroned, my soul shalt spare,
  On thy great judgment-day.
  Ray Palmer, 1867.

219. *"Vexilla Regis prodeunt."* (448.)

1 The royal banner is unfurled,
  The cross is reared on high,
  On which the Saviour of the world
  Is stretched in agony.

2 See! through his holy hands and feet
  The cruel nails they drive :
  Our ransom thus is made complete,
  Our souls are saved alive.

3 And see! the spear that pierced his side,
  And shed that sacred flood,
  That holy reconciling tide,
  The water and the blood.

4 Hail, holy cross! from thee we learn
  The only way to heaven :
  And, Oh! to thee may sinners turn,
  And look, and be forgiven.

5 So let us praise the Saviour's name,
  And, with exulting cry,
  The triumph of the cross proclaim
  To all eternity.
  Lat., *Venantius Fortunatus*, 580.
  Tr., *John Chandler*, 1837.

220. *"Lugete, Pacis Angeli!"* (449.)

1 Angels! lament ; behold! your God
  Man's sinful likeness wears ;
  Behold! upon th' accursed tree
  Man's sins the Saviour bears.

2 O Christ! with wondering minds we see
  What mighty love was thine ;
  Did God consent to suffer thus ?
  And, Oh! shall man repine ?

3 No, Saviour! no ; the power of death
  Thy cross hath overcome,
  To save us, not from earthly woe,
  But from th' eternal doom.
  Lat., *Charles Coffin*, 1720.
  Tr., *John Chandler*, 1837.

THE ATONING SACRIFICE.

221. *Christ, the living Fountain.* (450.)

1 THERE is a fountain filled with blood,
   Drawn from Immanuel's veins;
And sinners, plunged beneath that flood,
   Lose all their guilty stains.

2 The dying thief rejoiced to see
   That fountain in his day;
And there have I, as vile as he,
   Washed all my sins away.

3 Dear dying Lamb! thy precious blood
   Shall never lose its power,
Till all the ransomed church of God
   Be saved, to sin no more.

4 E'er since, by faith, I saw the stream
   Thy flowing wounds supply,
Redeeming love has been my theme,
   And shall be, till I die.

5 Then, in a nobler, sweeter song,
   I'll sing thy power to save, [tongue
When this poor lisping, stammering
   Lies silent in the grave.
         William Cowper, 1779.

222. *Godly Sorrow at the Cross.* (451.)

1 ALAS! and did my Saviour bleed?
   And did my Sovereign die?
Would he devote that sacred head,
   For such a worm as I?

2 Was it for crimes that I had done,
   He groaned upon the tree?
Amazing pity!—grace unknown!
   And love beyond degree!

3 Well might the sun in darkness hide,
   And shut his glories in,
When God, the mighty Maker, died,
   For man the creature's sin.

4 Thus might I hide my blushing face,
   While his dear cross appears;
Dissolve my heart in thankfulness,
   And melt mine eyes to tears.

5 But drops of grief can ne'er repay
   The debt of love I owe;
Here, Lord! I give myself away;—
   'T is all that I can do.
         Isaac Watts, 1707.

223. *Christ crucified.* (452.)

1 BEHOLD the Saviour of mankind
   Nailed to the shameful tree!
How vast the love that him inclined
   To bleed and die for thee!

2 Hark! how he groans, while nature shakes,
   And earth's strong pillars bend!
The temple's veil in sunder breaks,
   The solid marbles rend.

3 'T is done; the precious ransom 's paid;
   "Receive my soul!" he cries:
See where he bows his sacred head!
   He bows his head and dies.

4 But soon he'll break death's envious chain,
   And in full glory shine;
O Lamb of God! was ever pain,
   Was ever love, like thine?
         Samuel Wesley, Sr., 1709.

SALVATION.

BOYLSTON. S. M. *Lowell Mason, 1832.*

Not all the blood of beasts, On Jew-ish al-tars slain, Could give the guilt-y conscience peace, Or wash a-way the stain.

224. *Christ, our Sacrifice.* (444.)

1 Not all the blood of beasts,
 On Jewish altars slain,
Could give the guilty conscience peace,
 Or wash away the stain.

2 But Christ, the heavenly Lamb,
 Takes all our sins away;—
A sacrifice of nobler name,
 And richer blood than they.

3 My faith would lay her hand
 On that dear head of thine,
While, like a penitent, I stand,
 And there confess my sin.

4 My soul looks back to see
 The burdens thou didst bear,
When hanging on the cursèd tree,—
 And hopes her guilt was there.

5 Believing, we rejoice
 To see the curse remove;
We bless the Lamb with cheerful voice,
 And sing his bleeding love.
  Isaac Watts, 1709.

225. *"Sacvo Dolorum Turbine."* (445.)

1 O'erwhelmed in depths of woe,
 Upon the tree of scorn,
Hangs the Redeemer of mankind,
 With racking anguish torn.

2 The sun withdraws his light;
 The mid-day heavens grow pale,
The moon, the stars, the universe,
 Their Maker's death bewail.

3 Shall man alone be mute?
 Come, youth and hoary hairs!
Come, rich and poor! come, all mankind!
 And bathe those feet in tears.

4 Come, fall before his cross,
 Who shed for us his blood;
Who died, the victim of pure love,
 To make us sons of God.

3 Jesus! all praise to thee,
 Our Joy and endless Rest!
Be thou our Guide while pilgrims here,
 Our Crown amid the blest!
  Lat., *Roman Breviary.*
  Tr., *Edward Caswall, 1849.*

226. *Christ, suffering for our Sins.* (446.)

1 Like sheep we went astray,
 And broke the fold of God,—
Each wandering in a different way,
 But all the downward road.

2 How dreadful was the hour,
 When God our wanderings laid,
And did at once his vengeance pour,
 Upon the Shepherd's head!

3 How glorious was the grace,
 When Christ sustained the stroke!
His life and blood the Shepherd pays,
 A ransom for the flock.

4 But God shall raise his head,
 O'er all the sons of men,
And make him see a numerous seed,
 To recompense his pain.
  Isaac Watts, 1709.

THE ATONING SACRIFICE. 83

HAMBURG. L. M. Gregorian. Adapted by *Lowell Mason*, 1825.

When I sur-vey the won-drous cross, On which the Prince of glo-ry died,
My richest gain I count but loss, And pour contempt on all my pride.

227. *Crucifixion to the World.* (462.)

1 When I survey the wondrous cross,
On which the Prince of glory died,
My richest gain I count but loss,
And pour contempt on all my pride.

2 Forbid it, Lord! that I should boast,
Save in the death of Christ, my God :
All the vain things that charm me most,
I sacrifice them to his blood.

3 See! from his head, his hands, his feet,
Sorrow and love flow mingled down ;
Did e'er such love and sorrow meet?
Or thorns compose so rich a crown ?

4 His dying crimson, like a robe,
Spreads o'er his body on the tree ;
Then am I dead to all the globe,
And all the globe is dead to me.

5 Were the whole realm of nature mine,
That were a present far too small ;
Love so amazing, so divine,
Demands my soul, my life, my all.
Isaac Watts, 1707.

228. *The Wonders of the Cross.* (466.)

1 Nature, with open volume, stands
To spread her Maker's praise abroad ;
And every labor of his hands
Shows something worthy of a God.

2 But, in the grace that rescued man,
His brightest form of glory shines ;
Here, on the cross, 't is fairest drawn
In precious blood, and crimson lines.

3 Here I behold his inmost heart, [join,
Where grace and vengeance strangely
Piercing his Son with sharpest smart,
To make the purchased pleasures mine.

4 Oh! the sweet wonders of that cross,
Where God, the Saviour, loved and died !
Her noblest life my spirit draws [side.
From his dear wounds and bleeding

5 I would for ever speak his name,
In sounds to mortal ears unknown ;
With angels join to praise the Lamb,
And worship at his Father's throne.
Isaac Watts, 1707.

229. *" It is finished!"* (467.)

1 "'T is finished!"- so the Saviour cried,
And meekly bowed his head, and died ;
"'T is finished!'—yes, the race is run,
The battle fought, the vict'ry won.

2 "'T is finished!"—this my dying groan,
Shall sins of every kind atone ;
Millions shall be redeemed from death,
By this my last expiring breath."

3 "'T is finished!"—Heaven is reconciled,
And all the powers of darkness spoiled :
Peace, love, and happiness, again
Return, and dwell with sinful men.

4 "'T is finished!"—let the joyful sound
Be heard through all the nations round :
"'T is finished!"—let the echo fly,
Thro' heaven and hell, thro' earth and sky.
Samuel Stennett, 1787.

SALVATION.

MESSIAH. 7s. 8 LINES.
From *L. J. F. Herold*, 1791–1833.
Adapted by *George Kingsley*, 1838.

Sing, O heav'ns! O earth! rejoice; Angel harp, and human voice! Round him, as he rises, raise
D. C.—And to Christ, gone up on high,
Your ascending Saviour's praise. Bruis'd is the serpent's head; Hell is vanquished, death is dead;
Cap-tive is cap-tiv-i-ty.

230. *Resurrection and Ascension of Christ.* (476.)

1 Sing, O heavens! O earth! rejoice;
Angel harp, and human voice!
Round him, as he rises, raise
Your ascending Saviour's praise.

2 Bruisèd is the serpent's head;
Hell is vanquished, death is dead;
And to Christ, gone up on high,
Captivity.

3 All his work and warfare done,
He into his heaven is gone;
And, beside his Father's throne,
Now is pleading for his own.

4 Sing, O heavens! O earth! rejoice;
Angel harp, and human voice!
Round him, in his glory, raise
Your ascended Saviour's praise.
John S. B. Monsell, 1862.

231. *The Ascension of Christ.* (477.)

1 Hail the day that sees him rise,
Ravished from our wishful eyes!
Christ, awhile to mortals given,
Reascends his native heaven.

2 There the pompous triumph waits;
Lift your heads, eternal gates!
Wide unfold the radiant scene;
Take the King of glory in!

3 Him though highest heaven receives,
Still he loves the earth he leaves;
Though returning to his throne,
Still he calls mankind his own.

4 See! he lifts his hands above!
See! he shows the prints of love!
Hark! his gracious lips bestow
Blessings on his church below!

5 Still for us his death he pleads;
Prevalent, he intercedes;
Near himself prepares our place,
Harbinger of human race.

6 There we shall with thee remain,
Partners of thine endless reign;
There thy face unclouded see,
Find our heaven of heavens in thee.
Charles Wesley, 1739.

232. *The Resurrection of Christ.* (474.)

1 "Christ, the Lord, is risen to-day!"
Sons of men, and angels! say;
Raise your joys and triumphs high;
Sing, ye heavens! and, earth! reply.

2 Love's redeeming work is done;
Fought the fight, the battle won;
Lo! our Sun's eclipse is o'er;
Lo! he sets in blood no more.

3 Vain the stone, the watch, the seal;
Christ hath burst the gates of hell;
Death in vain forbids his rise:
Christ has opened paradise.

4 Lives again our glorious King!
"Where, O death! is now thy sting?"—
Dying once, he all doth save;
"Where thy victory, O Grave!"
Charles Wesley, 1739.

CHRIST'S RESURRECTION.

STOW. H. M.
English Melody.
Adapted by *Lowell Mason*, 1832.

Yes, the Redeemer rose; The Saviour left the dead; And, o'er our hellish foes, High raised his conqu'ring head: In wild dismay, the guards around Fell to the ground, and sunk away.

233. *The Resurrection of Christ.* (481.)

1 Yes, the Redeemer rose;
  The Saviour left the dead;
  And, o'er our hellish foes,
    High raised his conquering head:
  In wild dismay, the guards around
  Fell to the ground, and sunk away.

2 Lo! the angelic bands
    In full assembly meet,
  To wait his high commands,
    And worship at his feet:
  Joyful they come, and wing their way,
  From realms of day, to such a tomb.

3 Then back to heaven they fly,
    And the glad tidings bear;
  Hark! as they soar on high,
    What music fills the air!
  Their anthems say,—"Jesus, who bled,
  Hath left the dead;—he rose to-day."

4 Ye mortals! catch the sound,—
    Redeemed by him from hell;
  And send the echo round
    The globe, on which you dwell;
  Transported, cry.—"Jesus, who bled,
  Hath left the dead, no more to die."

5 All hail! triumphant Lord!
    Who sav'st us with thy blood:
  Wide be thy name adored,
    Thou rising, reigning God!
  With thee we rise, with thee we reign,
  And empires gain, beyond the skies.
                Philip Doddridge, 1740.

234. *The Condescension and Love of Christ.* (480.)

1 Come, every pious heart,
    That loves the Saviour's name!
  Your noblest powers exert,
    To celebrate his fame;
  Tell all above, and all below,
  The debt of love to him you owe.

2 Such was his zeal for God,
    And such his love for you,
  He freely undertook
    What Gabriel could not do;
  His every deed of love and grace,
  All words exceed, and thoughts surpass.

3 He left his starry crown,
    And laid his robes aside;
  On wings of love came down,
    And wept, and bled, and died;
  What he endured, Oh! who can tell,
  To save our souls from death and hell?

4 From the dark grave he rose,
    The mansion of the dead;
  And thence his mighty foes,
    In glorious triumph led;
  Up through the sky the Conqueror rode,
  And reigns on high, the Saviour God.

5 Jesus! we ne'er can pay
    The debt we owe thy love,
  Yet tell us how we may
    Our gratitude approve:
  Our hearts, our all, to thee we give;
  The gift, though small, thou wilt receive.
                Samuel Stennett, 1787.

SALVATION.

PARK STREET. L. M. From *Frederick M. A. Venua*, cir. 1810.

Now for a tune of loft-y praise To great Je-ho-vah's e-qual Son! A-wake, my voice! in heavenly lays, Tell the loud wonders he hath done; Tell the loud wonders he hath done.

235. *Christ's sufferings and Glory.* (483.)

1 Now for a tune of lofty praise
 To great Jehovah's equal Son!
Awake, my voice! in heavenly lays,
 Tell the loud wonders he hath done.

2 Sing—how he left the worlds of light,
 And the bright robes he wore above,—
How swift and joyful was his flight,
 On wings of everlasting love.

3 Deep in the shades of gloomy death,
 Th' almighty Captive pris'ner lay;
Th' almighty Captive left the earth,
 And rose to everlasting day.

4 Amongst a thousand harps and songs,
 Jesus, the God, exalted reigns;
His sacred name fills all their tongues,
 And echoes through the heavenly plains.
  Isaac Watts, 1707.

236. PSALM 24. (486.)

1 Our Lord is risen from the dead;
 Our Jesus is gone up on high;
The powers of hell are captive led,
 Dragged to the portals of the sky.

2 There his triumphal chariot waits,
 And angels chant the solemn lay;—
"Lift up your heads, ye heavenly gates!
 Ye everlasting doors! give way."

3 "Loose all your bars of massy light,
 And wide unfold th' ethereal scene;
He claims these mansions as his right;
 Receive the King of glory in."

4 "Who is the King of glory?—who?"
 "The Lord, that all our foes o'ercame,
The world, sin, death, and hell o'erthrew;
 And Jesus is the Conqueror's name."

5 Lo! his triumphal chariot waits,
 And angels chant the solemn lay:—
"Lift up your heads, ye heavenly gates!
 Ye everlasting doors! give way."

6 "Who is the King of glory?—who?"—
 "The Lord, of glorious power possessed;
The King of saints and angels too;
 God over all, for ever blessed."
  Charles Wesley, 1741.

237. PSALM 68. (485.)

1 Lord! when thou didst ascend on high,
 Ten thousand angels filled the sky;
Those heavenly guards around thee wait,
 Like chariots that attend thy state.

2 Not Sinai's mountain could appear
 More glorious, when the Lord was there;
While he pronounced his dreadful law,
 And struck the chosen tribes with awe.

3 How bright the triumph none can tell,
 When the rebellious powers of hell,
That thousand souls had captive made,
 Were all in chains, like captives, led.

4 Raised by his Father to the throne,
 He sent the promised Spirit down,
With gifts and grace for rebel men,
 That God might dwell on earth again.
  Isaac Watts, 1719.

CHRIST'S RESURRECTION.

ST. MARTIN'S.   C. M.   *William Tansur*, 1735.

Oh! for a shout of sacred joy, To God, the sovereign King! Let every land their tongues employ, And hymns of triumph sing.

238.   PSALM 47.   (489.)

1 Oh! for a shout of sacred joy
   To God, the sovereign King!
   Let every land their tongues employ,
   And hymns of triumph sing.

2 Jesus, our God, ascends on high;
   His heavenly guards around,
   Attend him rising through the sky,
   With trumpets' joyful sound.

3 While angels shout and praise their King,
   Let mortals learn their strains;
   Let all the earth his honor sing;—
   O'er all the earth he reigns.

4 Rehearse his praise with awe profound;
   Let knowledge lead the song;
   Nor mock him with a solemn sound
   Upon a thoughtless tongue.

5 In Israel stood his ancient throne:—
   He loved that chosen race;
   But now he calls the world his own,
   And heathens taste his grace.
             Isaac Watts, 1719.

239.   PSALM 47.   (492.)

1 Arise! ye people! and adore;
   Exulting strike the chord;
   Let all the earth, from shore to shore,
   Confess th' almighty Lord.

2 Hark! the glad shouts, wide echoing round,
   Th' ascending God proclaim;
   Th' angelic choir respond the sound,
   And shake creation's frame.

3 They sing of death and hell o'erthrown
   In that triumphant hour;
   And God exalts his conquering Son
   To the right hand of power.

4 Arise, ye people! and adore;
   Exulting strike the chord:
   Let all the earth, from shore to shore,
   Confess th' almighty Lord.
             Harriet Auber, 1819.

240.   *Resurrection and Ascension of Christ.*   (493.)

1 Hosanna to the Prince of light,
   That clothed himself in clay,
   Entered the iron gates of death,
   And tore the bars away.

2 Death is no more the king of dread,
   Since our Immanuel rose;
   He took the tyrant's sting away,
   And spoiled our hellish foes.

3 See how the Conqueror mounts aloft,
   And to his Father flies,
   With scars of honor in his flesh,
   And triumph in his eyes.

4 Raise your devotion, mortal tongues!
   To reach his blessed abode;
   Sweet be the accents of your songs
   To our incarnate God.

5 Bright angels! strike your loudest strings,
   Your sweetest voices raise;
   Let heaven, and all created things,
   Sound our Immanuel's praise.
             Isaac Watts, 1707.

SALVATION.

DARWELL. H. M. — John Darwell, cir. 1750.

Rejoice! the Lord is King!—Your God and King adore; Mortals! give thanks and sing, And triumph evermore; Lift up your hearts, lift up your voice, Rejoice! again, I say,—rejoice!

241. *The Reign of Christ.* (501.)

1 Rejoice! the Lord is King!—
  Your God and King adore;
  Mortals! give thanks, and sing,
    And triumph evermore:
  Lift up your hearts,—lift up your voice,
  Rejoice! again, I say,—rejoice!

2 His kingdom cannot fail;
  He rules o'er earth and heaven;
  The keys of death and hell
    Are to our Jesus given;
  Lift up your hearts,—lift up your voice,
  Rejoice! again, I say,—rejoice!

3 He all his foes shall quell,
  Shall all our sins destroy;
  And every bosom swell
    With pure seraphic joy:
  Lift up your hearts,—lift up your voice,
  Rejoice! again, I say,—rejoice!

4 Rejoice in glorious hope;
  Jesus, the Judge, shall come,
  And take his servants up
    To their eternal home:
  We soon shall hear th' archangel's voice,
  The trump of God shall sound,—Rejoice!
                    Charles Wesley, 1746.

242. *The Offices of Christ.* (502.)

1 Great Prophet of our God!
  Our tongues would bless thy name;
  By thee the joyful news
    Of our salvation came:
  The joyful news of sins forgiven,
  Of hell subdued, and peace with heaven.

2 Jesus, our great High-Priest,
  Hath shed his blood and died;
  My guilty conscience needs
    No sacrifice beside;
  His precious blood did once atone;
  And now it pleads before the throne.

3 O thou almighty Lord,
  Our Conqueror and our King!
  Thy sceptre and thy sword,
    Thy reigning grace we sing;
  Thine is the power; Oh! make us sit,
  In willing bonds, beneath thy feet.
                    Isaac Watts, 1709, a.

243. *The Cross celebrated.* (503.)

1 Ye saints! your music bring,
    Attuned to sweetest sound;
  Strike every trembling string,
    Till earth and heaven resound:
  The triumphs of the cross we sing:
  Awake, ye saints! each joyful string.

2 The cross—the cross alone—
    Subdued the powers of hell;
  Like lightning from his throne,
    The prince of darkness fell:
  The triumphs of the cross we sing;
  Awake, ye saints! each joyful string.

3 The cross has power to save,
    From all the foes that rise;
  The cross has made the grave
    A passage to the skies:
  The triumphs of the cross we sing;
  Awake, ye saints! each joyful string.
                    Andrew Reed, 1817.

CHRIST'S ROYAL PRIESTHOOD.

ROSEFIELD. 7s. 4 or 6 LINES. Cæsar Malan, 1830.

Glo-ry, glo-ry to our King! Crowns un-fad-ing wreathe his head;
Je-sus, is the name we sing,—Je-sus ris-en from the dead;
Je-sus, Conqueror o'er the grave, Je-sus, might-y now to save.

244. *Christ enthroned.* (504.)

1 GLORY, glory to our King!
 Crowns unfading wreathe his head;
Jesus is the name we sing,—
 Jesus, risen from the dead;
Jesus, Conqueror o'er the grave;
 Jesus, mighty now to save.

2 Jesus is gone up on high:
 Angels come to meet their King;
Shouts triumphant rend the sky,
 While the Victor's praise they sing:
"Open now, ye heavenly gates!
 'T is the King of glory waits."

3 Now behold him high enthroned,
 Glory beaming from his face,
By adoring angels owned,
 God of holiness and grace!
Oh! for hearts and tongues to sing—
 "Glory, glory to our King!"

4 Jesus! on thy people shine;
 Warm our hearts and tune our tongues,
That with angels we may join,
 Share their bliss, and swell their songs:
Glory, honor, praise, and power,
 Lord! be thine for evermore!
  Thomas Kelly, 1804.

245. *The Coronation of Christ.* (505.)

1 CROWNS of glory, ever bright,
 Rest upon the Victor's head;
Crowns of glory are his right,—
 His, "who liveth and was dead."

2 He subdued the powers of hell;
 In the fight he stood alone;
All his foes before him fell,
 By his single arm o'erthrown.

3 His, the fight, the arduous toil,
 His, the honors of the day,
His, the glory and the spoil,
 Jesus bears them all away.

4 Now proclaim his deeds afar;
 Fill the world with his renown:
His alone, the Victor's car,
 His, the everlasting crown!
  Thomas Kelly, 1804.

246. *The Victor's Triumph.* (506.)

1 SONS of Zion! raise your songs;
 Praise to Zion's King belongs;
His, the victor's crown and fame:
 Glory to the Saviour's name!

2 Sore the strife, but rich the prize;
 Precious in the Victor's eyes:
Glorious is the work achieved,—
 Satan vanquished, man relieved!

3 Sing we then the Victor's praise;
 Go ye forth and strew the ways;
Bid him welcome to his throne:
 He is worthy, he alone!

4 Place the crown upon his brow;
 Every knee to him shall bow:
Him the brightest seraph sings;
 Heaven proclaims him "King of kings!"
  Thomas Kelly, 1820.

SALVATION.

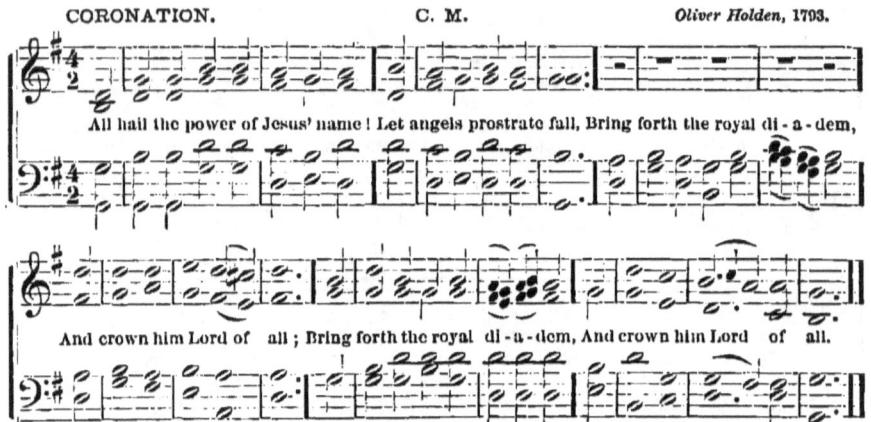

CORONATION.   C. M.   Oliver Holden, 1793.

All hail the power of Jesus' name! Let angels prostrate fall, Bring forth the royal di-a-dem, And crown him Lord of all; Bring forth the royal di-a-dem, And crown him Lord of all.

247.   *Crowning Jesus Lord of all.*   (516.)

1 ALL hail the power of Jesus' name!
   Let angels prostrate fall ;
  Bring forth the royal diadem,
   And crown him Lord of all.

2 Crown him, ye martyrs of our God !
   Who from his altar call ;
  Extol the stem of Jesse's rod,
   And crown him Lord of all.

3 Ye chosen seed of Israel's race !
   Ye ransomed from the fall !
  Hail him, who saves you by his grace,
   And crown him Lord of all.

4 Sinners ! whose love can ne'er forget
   The wormwood and the gall,
  Go, spread your trophies at his feet,
   And crown him Lord of all.

5 Let every kindred, every tribe,
   On this terrestrial ball,
  To him all majesty ascribe,
   And crown him Lord of all.

6 Oh ! that with yonder sacred throng,
   We at his feet may fall ;
  We 'll join the everlasting song,
   And crown him Lord of all.
             Edward Perronet, 1780, a.

248.   *The mighty Conqueror.*   (533.)

1 JESUS, immortal King ! arise !
   Assume, assert thy sway ;
  Till earth, subdued, its tribute bring,
   And distant lands obey.

2 Ride forth, victorious Conqueror ! ride,
   Till all thy foes submit ;
  And all the powers of hell resign
   Their trophies at thy feet.

3 Send forth thy word, and let it fly,
   This spacious earth around ;
  Till every soul, beneath the sun,
   Shall hear the joyful sound.

4 From sea to sea, from shore to shore,
   May Jesus be adored ;
  And earth, with all her millions, shout
   Hosannas to the Lord.
           A. C. Hobart Seymour, 1810.

249.   *The wondrous Name.*   (518.)

1 JESUS ! the name high over all,
   In hell, or earth, or sky ;
  Angels and men before it fall,
   And devils fear and fly.

2 Jesus ! the name to sinners dear,
   The name to sinners given ;
  It scatters all their guilty fear ;
   It turns their hell to heaven.

3 Oh ! that the world might taste and see
   The riches of his grace ;
  The arms of love that compass me,
   Would all mankind embrace.

4 His only righteousness I show,
   His saving truth proclaim :
  'T is all my business here below,
   To cry, "Behold the Lamb !"
           Charles Wesley, 1749.

CHRIST'S ROYAL PRIESTHOOD.

250. *Access to the Throne of Grace.* (525.)

1 Come, let us lift our joyful eyes,
 Up to the courts above,
 And smile to see our Father there,
 Upon a throne of love.

2 Now we may bow before his feet,
 And venture near the Lord:
 No fiery cherub guards his seat,
 Nor double flaming sword.

3 The peaceful gates of heavenly bliss
 Are opened by the Son;
 High let us raise the notes of praise,
 And reach th' almighty throne.

4 To thee ten thousand thanks we bring,
 Great Advocate on high;
 And glory to th' eternal King,
 That lays his fury by.
   Isaac Watts, 1719.

251. Psalm 46. (526.)

1 Hail, mighty Jesus! how divine
 Is thy victorious sword!
 The stoutest rebel must resign,
 At thy commanding word.

2 Deep are the wounds thine arrows give,
 They pierce the hardest heart;
 Thy smiles of grace the slain revive,
 And joy succeeds to smart.

3 Still gird thy sword upon thy thigh,
 Ride with majestic sway;
 Go forth, sweet Prince! triumphantly,
 And make thy foes obey.

4 And, when thy victories are complete,
 When all the chosen race
 Shall round the throne of glory meet,
 To sing thy conquering grace,

5 Oh! may my humble soul be found,
 Among that favored band;
 And I, with them, thy praise will sound,
 Throughout Immanuel's land.
   Benjamin Wallin, 1776.

252. *Praise to the Redeemer.* (527.)

1 Plunged in a gulf of dark despair,
 We wretched sinners lay,
 Without one cheerful beam of hope,
 Or spark of glimmering day.

2 With pitying eyes the Prince of grace
 Beheld our helpless grief;
 He saw, and—Oh! amazing love!—
 He ran to our relief.

3 Down from the shining seats above,
 With joyful haste he fled,
 Entered the grave in mortal flesh,
 And dwelt among the dead.

4 Oh! for this love let rocks and hills
 Their lasting silence break;
 And all harmonious human tongues
 The Saviour's praises speak.

5 Angels! assist our mighty joys;
 Strike all your harps of gold;
 But, when you raise your highest notes,
 His love can ne'er be told.
   Isaac Watts, 1707.

92 SALVATION.

WARWICK. C. M. *Samuel Stanley, cir. 1810.*

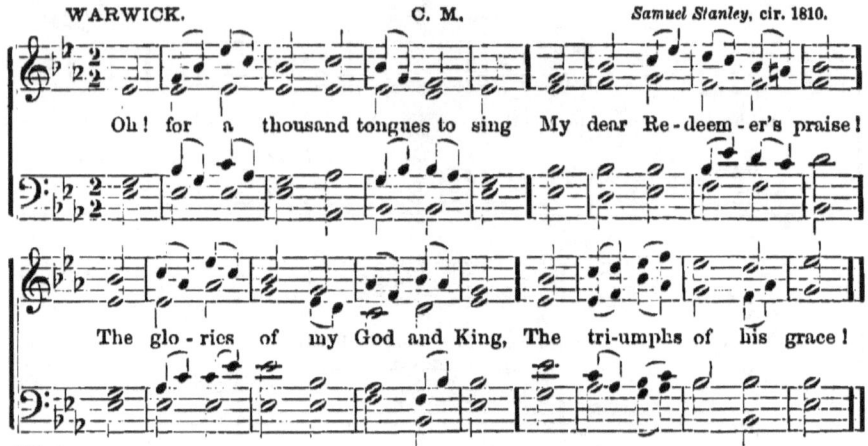

Oh! for a thousand tongues to sing My dear Redeemer's praise!
The glories of my God and King, The triumphs of his grace!

253. *The saving Name.* (519.)

1 Oh! for a thousand tongues to sing
  My dear Redeemer's praise!
  The glories of my God and King,
  The triumphs of his grace!

2 My gracious Master and my God!
  Assist me to proclaim,
  To spread, through all the earth abroad,
  The honors of thy name.

3 Jesus—the name that charms our fears,
  That bids our sorrows cease;
  'T is music in the sinner's ears;
  'T is life, and health, and peace.

4 He breaks the power of canceled sin,
  He sets the pris'ner free;
  His blood can make the foulest clean;
  His blood availed for me.

5 He speaks,—and, listening to his voice,
  New life the dead receive;
  The mournful, broken hearts rejoice;
  The humble poor believe.
  Charles Wesley, 1740.

254. *God reconciled in Christ.* (520.)

1 Dearest of all the names above,
  My Jesus and my God!
  Who can resist thy heavenly love,
  Or trifle with thy blood?

2 'T is by the merits of thy death,
  The Father smiles again;
  'T is by thine interceding breath,
  The Spirit dwells with men.

3 Till God in human flesh I see,
  My thoughts no comfort find;

  The holy, just, and sacred Three
  Are terrors to my mind.

4 But, if Immanuel's face appear,
  My hope, my joy begins;
  His name forbids my slavish fear,
  His grace removes my sins.

5 While Jews on their own law rely,
  And Greeks of wisdom boast;—
  I love th' incarnate mystery,
  And there I fix my trust.
  Isaac Watts, 1709.

255. *The Sympathy of Jesus.* (522.)

1 Come, let us join in songs of praise
  To our ascended Priest;
  He entered heaven, with all our names
  Engraven on his breast.

2 Below he washed our guilt away,
  By his atoning blood;
  Now he appears before the throne,
  And pleads our cause with God.

3 Clothed with our nature still. he knows
  The weakness of our frame,
  And how to shield us from the foes
  Which he himself o'ercame.

4 Nor time, nor distance, e'er shall quench
  The fervors of his love;
  For us he died in kindness here,
  Nor is less kind above.

5 Oh! may we ne'er forget his grace,
  Nor blush to wear his name:
  Still may our hearts hold fast his faith,
  Our mouths his praise proclaim.
  Anon., 1818.

CHRIST'S ROYAL PRIESTHOOD.

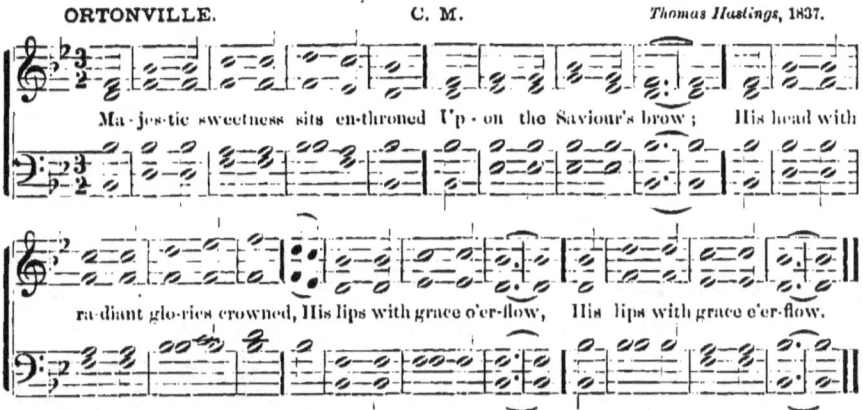

ORTONVILLE. C. M. *Thomas Hastings*, 1837.

Ma-jes-tic sweetness sits en-throned Up-on the Saviour's brow; His head with ra-diant glo-ries crowned, His lips with grace o'er-flow, His lips with grace o'er-flow.

256. *The Excellencies of Jesus.* (528.)

1 MAJESTIC sweetness sits enthroned
  Upon the Saviour's brow;
  His head with radiant glories crowned,
  His lips with grace o'erflow.

2 No mortal can with him compare
  Among the sons of men;
  Fairer is he, than all the fair
  That fill the heavenly train.

3 He saw me plunged in deep distress;
  He flew to my relief;
  For me he bore the shameful cross,
  And carried all my grief.

4 To him I owe my life and breath,
  And all the joys I have;
  He makes me triumph over death,
  And saves me from the grave.

5 To heaven, the place of his abode,
  He brings my weary feet;
  Shows me the glories of my God,
  And makes my joys complete.

6 Since from his bounty I receive
  Such proofs of love divine,
  Had I a thousand hearts to give,
  Lord! they should all be thine.
  Samuel Stennett, 1787.

257. *Redeeming Love.* (531.)

1 COME, heavenly Love! inspire my song
  With thine immortal flame;
  And teach my heart, and teach my tongue,
  The Saviour's lovely name.

2 The Saviour! Oh! what endless charms
  Dwell in the blissful sound!
  Its influence every fear disarms,
  And spreads sweet comfort round.

3 Th' almighty Former of the skies
  Stooped to our vile abode;
  While angels viewed with wondering eyes,
  And hailed th' incarnate God.

4 Oh! the rich depths of love divine!
  Of bliss, a boundless store!
  Dear Saviour! let me call thee mine;
  I cannot wish for more.

5 On thee alone my hope relies,
  Beneath thy cross I fall;
  My Lord, my Life, my Sacrifice,
  My Saviour, and my All!
  Anne Steele, 1760.

258. *"Jesu! nostra Redemptio."* (521.)

1 O CHRIST! our Hope, our heart's Desire,
  Redemption's only Spring!
  Creator of the world art thou,
  Its Saviour and its King.

2 How vast the mercy and the love,
  Which laid our sins on thee,
  And led thee to a cruel death,
  To set thy people free!

3 But now the bonds of death are burst,
  The ransom has been paid:
  And thou art on thy Father's throne,
  In glorious robes arrayed.

4 O Christ! be thou our present joy,
  Our future great reward!
  Our only glory may it be
  To glory in the Lord!
  Lat., *Ambrose* (?), 390.
  Tr., *John Chandler*, 1837.

SALVATION.

DOVER. S. M. English Melody.

A-wake, and sing the song Of Mo-ses and the Lamb;
Wake, ev-ery heart, and ev-ery tongue! To praise the Sav-iour's name.

259. *The Song of Moses and the Lamb.* (510.)

1 AWAKE, and sing the song
Of Moses and the Lamb;
Wake, every heart, and every tongue!
To praise the Saviour's name.

2 Sing of his dying love;
Sing of his rising power;
Sing—how he intercedes above
For those whose sins he bore.

3 Sing, till we feel our hearts
Ascending with our tongues;
Sing, till the love of sin departs,
And grace inspires our songs.

4 Sing on your heavenly way,
Ye ransomed sinners! sing;
Sing on, rejoicing, every day,
In Christ, th' eternal King.

5 Soon shall ye hear him say,
"Ye blessèd children! come;"
Soon will he call you hence away,
And take his wanderers home.

William Hammond, 1745.
Altered, by *Martin Madan,* 1760.

260. *The atoning Blood.* (511.)

1 How heavy is the night
That hangs upon our eyes,
Till Christ, with his reviving light,
Over our souls arise!

2 Our guilty spirits dread
To meet the wrath of heaven;
But, in his righteousness arrayed,
We see our sins forgiven.

3 Unholy and impure
Are all our thoughts and ways;
His hands infected nature cure,
With sanctifying grace.

4 The powers of hell agree
To hold our souls in vain:
He sets the sons of bondage free,
And breaks the cursèd chain.

5 Lord! we adore thy ways
To bring us near to God;
Thy sovereign power, thy healing grace
And thine atoning blood.

Isaac Watts, 1709.

261. *The Song of the Seraphs.* (513.)

1 CROWN him with many crowns,
The Lamb upon his throne;
Hark! how the heavenly anthem drowns
All music but its own!

2 Awake, my soul! and sing
Of him who died for thee;
And hail him as thy matchless King,
Through all eternity.

3 Crown him, the Lord of love!
Behold his hands and side,—
Rich wounds, yet visible above
In beauty glorified:

4 Crown him, the Lord of peace!
Whose power a sceptre sways,
From pole to pole, that wars may cease,
Absorbed in prayer and praise:

5 Crown him, the Lord of years!
The Potentate of time,
Creator of the rolling spheres,
Ineffably sublime!

Matthew Bridges, 1852.

CHRIST'S ROYAL PRIESTHOOD.

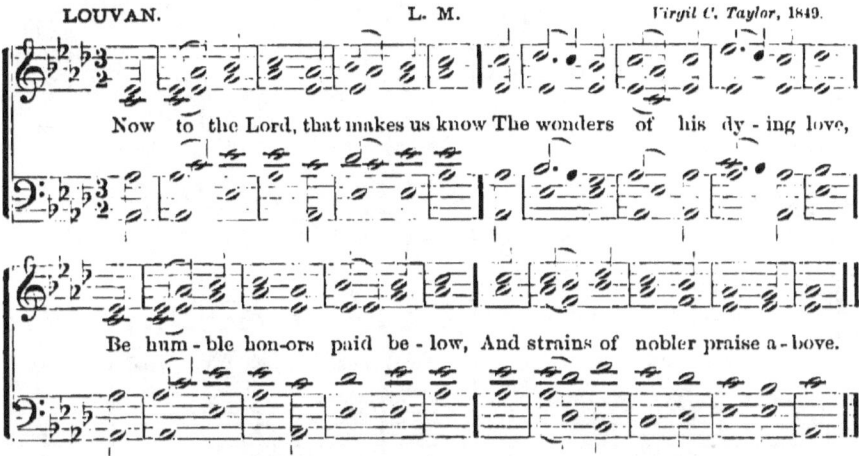

LOUVAN. L. M. Virgil C. Taylor, 1849.

Now to the Lord, that makes us know The wonders of his dy-ing love,
Be hum-ble hon-ors paid be-low, And strains of nobler praise a-bove.

262. *Christ, our Priest, King, and Judge.* (537.)

1 Now to the Lord, that makes us know
The wonders of his dying love,
Be humble honors paid below,
And strains of nobler praise above.

2 'T was he that cleansed our foulest sins,
And washed us in his richest blood;
'T is he that makes us priests and kings,
And brings us rebels near to God.

3 To Jesus, our atoning Priest,
To Jesus, our superior King,
Be everlasting power confessed,
And every tongue his glory sing.

4 Behold on flying clouds he comes,
And every eye shall see him move;
Tho' with our sins we pierced him once,
Still he displays his pardoning love.

5 The unbelieving world shall wail,
While we rejoice to see the day;
Come, Lord! nor let thy promise fail,
Nor let thy chariots long delay.
Isaac Watts, 1707.

263. *The Intercession of Christ.* (541.)

1 He lives, the great Redeemer lives:—
What joy the blest assurance gives!—
And now, before his Father, God,
Pleads the full merits of his blood.

2 Repeated crimes awake our fears,
And justice, armed with frowns, appears;
But, in the Saviour's lovely face,
Sweet mercy smiles, and all is peace.

3 Hence, then, ye black, despairing thoughts!
Above our fears, above our faults,
His powerful intercessions rise,
And guilt recedes, and terror dies.

4 In every dark, distressful hour,
When sin and Satan join their power,
Let this dear hope repel the dart,
That Jesus bears us on his heart.

5 Great Advocate, almighty Friend,—
On him our humble hopes depend:
Our cause can never, never fail,
For Jesus pleads, and must prevail.
Anne Steele, 1760.

264. *Christ in Glory.* (536.)

1 Descend from heaven, immortal Dove!
Stoop down and take us on thy wings,
And mount, and bear us far above
The reach of these inferior things.

2 Oh! for a sight, a pleasing sight
Of our almighty Father's throne!
There sits our Saviour, crowned with light,
Clothed in a body like our own.

3 Adoring saints around him stand,
And thrones and powers before him fall;
The God shines gracious thro' the man,
And sheds sweet glories on them all.

4 Oh! what amazing joys they feel,
While to their golden harps they sing,
And sit on every heavenly hill,
And spread the triumphs of their King!
Isaac Watts, 1707.

RECONCILIATION.

BELMONT. (VISITATION.) 8s, 7s & 4. Anon., 1830.

Come, ye sin-ners! poor and wretch-ed, Weak and wound-ed, sick and sore;
D. C.—He is a - ble, he is a - ble, He is will - ing; doubt no more.

Je - sus read - y stands to save you, Full of pit - y, joined with power;

265. *Welcome to Jesus Christ.* (552.)

1 Come, ye sinners! poor and wretched,
  Weak and wounded, sick and sore;
Jesus ready stands to save you,
  Full of pity, joined with power;
    He is able,
  He is willing; doubt no more.

2 Ho! ye needy! come and welcome,
  God's free bounty glorify;
True belief, and true repentance,
  Every grace that brings us nigh,
    Without money,
  Come to Jesus Christ and buy.

3 Let not conscience make you linger,
  Nor of fitness fondly dream;
All the fitness he requireth,
  Is to feel your need of him;
    This he gives you;
  'T is the Spirit's rising beam.
                                    Joseph Hart, 1759.

266. *Come and Welcome.* (553.)

1 Come, ye weary, heavy laden!
  Bruised and mangled by the fall;
If you tarry till you're better,
  You will never come at all;
    Not the righteous,—
  Sinners Jesus came to call.

2 View him prostrate in the garden;
  Lo! your Maker prostrate lies;
On the bloody tree behold him!
  Hear him cry, before he dies,—
    "It is finish'd!"
  Sinner! will not this suffice?

3 Lo! th' incarnate God, ascended,
  Pleads the merit of his blood;
Venture on him, venture wholly;
  Let no other trust intrude:
    None but Jesus
  Can do helpless sinners good.

4 Saints and angels, joined in concert,
  Sing the praises of the Lamb;
While the blissful seats of heaven
  Sweetly echo with his name;
    Hallelujah!
  Sinners here may sing the same.
                                    Joseph Hart, 1759.

267. *The healing Fountain.* (554.)

1 Come to Calv'ry's holy mountain,
  Sinners, ruined by the fall!
Here a pure and healing fountain
  Flows to you,—to me,—to all,—
    In a full perpetual tide,
  Opened when our Saviour died.

2 Come, in sorrow and contrition,
  Wounded, impotent, and blind;
Here the guilty, free remission,—
  Here the troubled, peace may find;
    Health this fountain will restore;
  He that drinks shall thirst no more:—

3 He that drinks shall live for ever,—
  'T is a soul-renewing flood;
God is faithful: God will never
  Break his covenant in blood,—
    Signed, when our Redeemer died,
  Sealed, when he was glorified.
                                    James Montgomery, 1825.

PARDON OFFERED.

ZION.   8s, 7s & 4.   *Thomas Hastings, 1830.*

{ Come, ye souls, by sin af-flict-ed! Bowed with fruitless sor-row down, }
{ By the per-fect law con-vict-ed! Through the cross, be-hold the crown; }

Look to Je-sus; Mercy flows thro' him a-lone; Look to Je-sus; Mercy flows thro' him a-lone.

268.   *Welcome to the Saviour.*   (555.)

1 Come, ye souls, by sin afflicted!
   Bowed with fruitless sorrow down,
By the perfect law convicted,
   Through the cross, behold the crown;
      Look to Jesus;
Mercy flows through him alone.

2 Take his easy yoke, and wear it;
   Love will make obedience sweet;
Christ will give you strength to bear it,
   While his wisdom guides your feet
      Safe to glory,
Where his ransomed captives meet.

3 Sweet, as home to pilgrims weary,
   Light to newly-opened eyes,
Or full springs in deserts dreary,
   Is the rest the cross supplies;
      All, who taste it,
Shall to rest immortal rise.
                Joseph Swain, 1792.

269.   *The Gospel Message.*   (556.)

1 Sinners! will you scorn the message
   Sent in mercy from above?
Every sentence, Oh! how tender!
   Every line is full of love;
      Listen to it;
Every line is full of love.

2 Hear the heralds of the gospel,
   News from Sion's King proclaim, -
"Pardon to each rebel sinner;
   Free forgiveness in his name!"
      How important!
"Free forgiveness in his name!"

3 Who hath our report believed?
   Who received the joyful word?
Who embraced the news of pardon,
   Offered to you by the Lord?
      Can you slight it?
Offered to you by the Lord.

4 O ye angels! hovering round us,—
   Waiting spirits! speed your way,
Haste ye to the court of heaven,
   Tidings bear without delay, -
      Rebel sinners
Glad the message will obey.
                Jonathan Allen, 1801, a.

270.   *The Voice of Mercy.*   (557.)

1 Listen, sinner! mercy hails you;
   With her sweetest voice she calls;
Bids you hasten to the Saviour,
   Ere the hand of justice falls:
      Listen, sinner!
'Tis the voice of mercy calls.

2 See! the storm of vengeance gathering
   O'er the path you dare to tread!
Hark! the awful thunders rolling
   Loud and louder o'er your head!
      Flee, O sinner!
Lest the lightnings strike you dead.

3 Haste, ah! hasten to the Saviour,
   Sue his mercy while you may;
Soon the day of grace is over;—
   Soon your life will pass away;
      Hasten, sinner!
You must perish, if you stay.
                Andrew Reed, 1817.

RECONCILIATION.

CAMBRIDGE. C. M. John Randall, 1790.

Sal-vation! Oh! the joy-ful sound; 'T is pleasure to our ears; A sovereign balm for ev-ery wound, A cordial for our fears; A cordial for our fears; A cor-dial for our fears.

271. *Salvation.* (558.)

1 SALVATION!—Oh! the joyful sound;
 'T is pleasure to our ears;
 A sovereign balm for every wound,
 A cordial for our fears.

2 Buried in sorrow and in sin,
 At hell's dark door we lay;
 But we arise, by grace divine,
 To see a heavenly day.

3 Salvation!—let the echo fly
 The spacious earth around;
 While all the armies of the sky
 Conspire to raise the sound.
 Isaac Watts, 1707.

272. *Christ's Commission.* (559.)

1 COME, happy souls! approach your God,
 With new melodious songs,
 Come, render to almighty grace,
 The tribute of your tongues.

2 So strange, so boundless was the love
 That pitied dying men,
 The Father sent his equal Son
 To give them life again.

3 Thy hands, dear Jesus! were not armed
 With a revenging rod,
 No hard commission to perform
 The vengeance of a God.

4 But all was mercy, all was mild,
 And wrath forsook the throne,
 When Christ on the kind errand came,
 And brought salvation down.

5 Here, sinners! you may heal your wounds,
 And wipe your sorrows dry;
 Trust in the mighty Saviour's name,
 And you shall never die.

6 See, dearest Lord! our willing souls
 Accept thine offered grace;
 We bless the great Redeemer's love,
 And give the Father praise.
 Isaac Watts, 1707.

273. *Welcome to the Young.* (562.)

1 YE HEARTS, with youthful vigor warm!
 In smiling crowds draw near;
 And turn from every mortal charm,
 A Saviour's voice to hear.

2 He, Lord of all the worlds on high,
 Stoops to converse with you;
 And lays his radiant glories by,
 Your friendship to pursue.

3 The soul, that longs to see his face,
 Is sure his love to gain;
 And those, that early seek his grace,
 Shall never seek in vain.

4 What object, Lord! my soul should move,
 If once compared with thee?
 What beauty should command my love,
 Like what in Christ I see?

5 Away, ye false, delusive toys!
 Vain tempters of the mind;
 'T is here I fix my lasting choice,
 And here, true bliss I find.
 Philip Doddridge, 1740.

PARDON OFFERED.

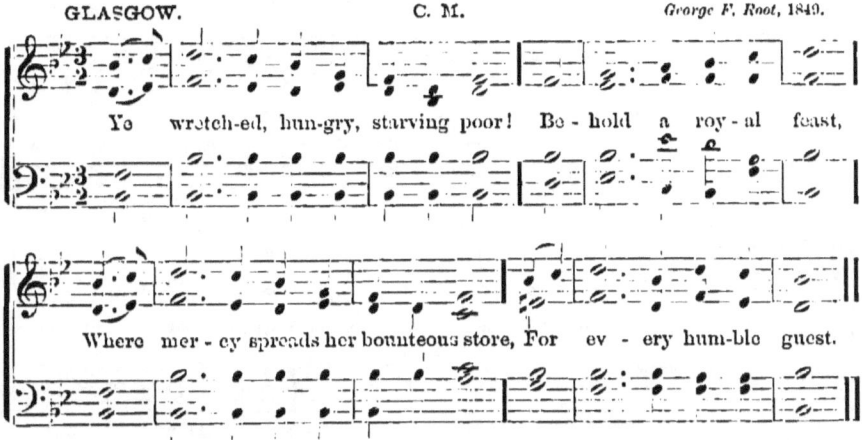

274. *The Gospel Feast.* (561.)

1 YE WRETCHED, hungry, starving poor!
    Behold a royal feast,
  Where mercy spreads her bounteous store,
    For every humble guest.

2 See, Jesus stands with open arms;
    He calls,—he bids you come;
  Guilt holds you back, and fear alarms;
    But, see! there yet is room.

3 Room, in the Saviour's bleeding heart;
    There love and pity meet;
  Nor will he bid the soul depart,
    That trembles at his feet.

4 Oh! come, and, with his children, taste
    The blessings of his love:
  While hope attends the sweet repast
    Of nobler joys above.

5 There, with united heart and voice,
    Before th' eternal throne,
  Ten thousand thousand souls rejoice,
    In ecstasies unknown.

6 And yet ten thousand thousand more
    Are welcome still to come;
  Ye longing souls! the grace adore,
    Approach, there yet is room.
            Anne Steele, 1760.

275. *The Call of Divine Mercy.* (574.)

1 SINNERS! the voice of God regard;
    'T is Mercy speaks to-day;
  He calls you by his sovereign word,
    From sin's destructive way.

2 Like the rough sea, that cannot rest,
    You live, devoid of peace;
  A thousand stings, within your breast,
    Deprive your souls of ease.

3 But he, that turns to God, shall live,
    Through his abounding grace;
  His mercy will the guilt forgive
    Of those that seek his face.

4 Bow to the sceptre of his word,
    Renouncing every sin;
  Submit to him, your sovereign Lord,
    And learn his will divine.

5 His love exceeds your highest thoughts;
    He pardons like a God;
  He will forgive your numerous faults,
    Through a Redeemer's blood.
            John Fawcett, 1782.

276. *The Way to Zion.* (563.)

1 INQUIRE, ye pilgrims! for the way
    That leads to Zion's hill,
  And thither set your steady face,
    With a determined will.

2 Come, let us to his temple haste,
    And seek his favor there;
  Before his footstool, humbly bow,
    And pour out fervent prayer.

3 Come, let us join our souls to God
    In everlasting bands;
  And seize the blessings he bestows,
    With eager hearts and hands.
            Philip Doddridge, 1740.

RECONCILIATION.

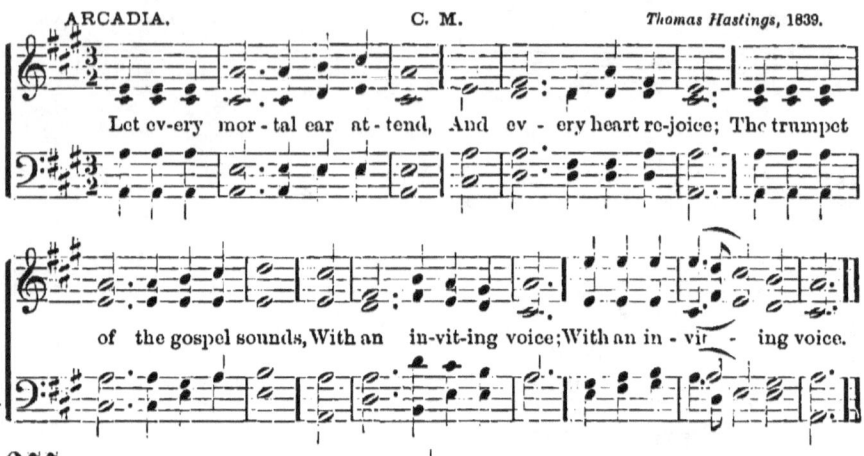

ARCADIA. C. M. Thomas Hastings, 1839.

Let ev-ery mor-tal ear at-tend, And ev-ery heart re-joice; The trumpet of the gospel sounds, With an in-vit-ing voice; With an in-vit-ing voice.

277. *The spiritual Banquet.* (564.)

1 Let every mortal ear attend,
  And every heart rejoice :
  The trumpet of the gospel sounds,
  With an inviting voice.

2 Ho! all ye hungry, starving souls!
  That feed upon the wind,
  And vainly strive, with earthly toys,
  To fill an empty mind ;—

3 Eternal wisdom has prepared
  A soul-reviving feast,
  And bids your longing appetites,
  The rich provision taste.

4 Ho! ye that pant for living streams,
  And pine away and die!
  Here you may quench your raging thirst,
  With springs that never dry.

5 Rivers of love and mercy here
  In a rich ocean join ;
  Salvation in abundance flows,
  Like floods of milk and wine.

6 The happy gates of gospel grace
  Stand open night and day ;
  Lord! we are come to seek supplies,
  And drive our wants away.
  Isaac Watts, 1707.

278. *The Saviour's Invitation.* (568.)

1 The Saviour calls ; let every ear
  Attend the heavenly sound ;
  Ye doubting souls! dismiss your fear,
  Hope smiles reviving round.

2 For every thirsty, longing heart,
  Here streams of bounty flow,
  And life, and health, and bliss impart,
  To banish mortal woe.

3 Ye sinners! come ; 't is mercy's voice :
  The gracious call obey :
  Mercy invites to heavenly joys,—
  And can you yet delay ?

4 Dear Saviour! draw reluctant hearts ;
  To thee let sinners fly,
  And take the bliss thy love imparts,
  And drink and never die.
  Anne Steele, 1760.

279. *The Saviour at the Door.* (569.)

1 Amazing sight! the Saviour stands,
  And knocks at every door ;
  Ten thousand blessings in his hands,
  To satisfy the poor.

2 "Behold!" he saith, " I bleed and die
  To bring you to my rest ;
  Hear, sinners! while I 'm passing by,
  And be for ever blessed.

3 " Will you despise my bleeding love,
  And choose the way to hell?
  Or, in the glorious realms above,
  With me, for ever dwell ?

4 " Say, will you hear my gracious voice,
  And have your sins forgiven ?
  Or will you make that wretched choice,
  And bar yourselves from heaven ?"
  Anon., 1825.

PARDON OFFERED. 101

WOODLAND.   C. M.   *Nathaniel D. Gould*, 1832.

Would'st thou eternal life obtain? Now to the cross repair; There stand, and gaze, and weep, and pray, Where Jesus breathes his life away; Eternal life is there.

280. *Life at the Cross.* (570.)

1 WOULD'ST thou eternal life obtain?
  Now to the cross repair:
  There stand, and gaze, and weep, and pray,
  Where Jesus breathes his life away;
  Eternal life is there.

2 Go;—'t is the Son of God expires!
  Approach the shameful tree;
  See, quivering there, the mortal dart,
  In the Redeemer's loving heart,
  O sinful soul! for thee.

3 Go;—there, from every streaming wound,
  Flows rich atoning blood;
  That blood can cleanse the deepest stain,
  Bid frowning justice smile again,
  And seal thy peace with God.

4 Go;—at that cross thy heart, subdued,
  With thankful love shall glow;
  By wondrous grace thy soul set free,
  Eternal life, from Christ, to thee,
  A vital stream shall flow.
  Ray Palmer, 1862.

281. *The repenting Sinner returning.* (567.)

1 COME, humble sinner! in whose breast,
  A thousand thoughts revolve;
  Come, with your guilt and fear oppressed,
  And make this last resolve:—

2 "I'll go to Jesus, though my sin
  Hath like a mountain rose;
  I know his courts, I'll enter in,
  Whatever may oppose.

3 "Prostrate I'll lie before his throne,
  And there my guilt confess;
  I'll tell him I'm a wretch undone,
  Without his sovereign grace.

4 "I'll to the gracious King approach,
  Whose sceptre pardon gives;
  Perhaps he may command my touch,
  And then the suppliant lives.

5 "Perhaps he will admit my plea,
  Perhaps will hear my prayer;
  But, if I perish, I will pray,
  And perish only there.

6 "I can but perish if I go,
  I am resolved to try;
  For, if I stay away, I know
  I must for ever die."
  Edmund Jones, 1777.

282. *The Fountain of living Waters.* (565.)

1 OH! what amazing words of grace
  Are in the gospel found,
  Suited to every sinner's case
  Who knows the joyful sound!

2 Come then, with all your wants and wounds,
  Your every burden bring;
  Here love, eternal love, abounds,—
  A deep, celestial spring.

3 This spring with living waters flows,
  And living joy imparts;
  Come, thirsty souls! your wants disclose,
  And drink with thankful hearts.
  Samuel Medley, 1789.

RECONCILIATION.

GOLDEN HILL.   S. M.   *Aaron Chapin, cir. 1823.*

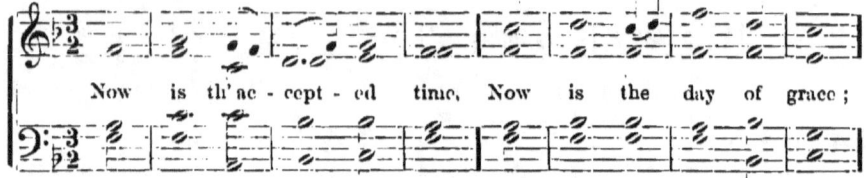
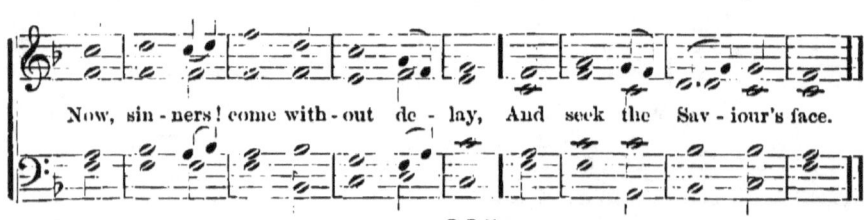

Now is th' ac-cept-ed time, Now is the day of grace;
Now, sin-ners! come with-out de-lay, And seek the Sav-iour's face.

283.   *The accepted Time.*   (548.)

1 Now is th' accepted time,
  Now is the day of grace;
Now, sinners! come, without delay,
  And seek the Saviour's face.

2 Now is th' accepted time,
  The Saviour calls to-day;
Pardon and peace he freely gives:—
  Then why should you delay?

3 Now is th' accepted time,
  The gospel bids you come;
And every promise, in his word,
  Declares there yet is room.
                John Dobell, 1806.

284.   *To-Day.*   (549.)

1 To-day the Saviour calls;
  Ye wretched wanderers! come;
O ye benighted, dying souls!
  Why will you longer roam?

2 To-day the Saviour calls;
  Oh! hearken to him now!
Within these consecrated walls,
  To Jesus come and bow.

3 To-day the Saviour calls;
  To him for refuge fly;
For soon the storm of justice falls,
  And death is ever nigh.

4 The Spirit calls to-day;
  Yield to his saving power;
Oh! do not grieve him now away,—
  'T is mercy's tender hour.
                Anon., 1831, a.

285.   *To-Day.*   (550.)

1 YE SINNERS! fear the Lord,
  While yet 't is called to-day;
Soon will the awful voice of death
  Command your souls away.

2 Soon will the harvest close,
  The summer soon be o'er;
And soon your injured angry God
  Will hear your prayers no more.

3 Then, while 't is called to-day,
  Oh! hear the gospel's sound;
Come, sinners! haste. Oh! haste away,
  While pardon may be found.
               Timothy Dwight, 1800, a.

286. *The Voice of the Spirit and the Bride.* (547.)

1 THE Spirit, in our hearts,
  Is whispering,—"Sinner! come!"
The bride, the church of Christ, proclaims,
  To all his children,—"Come!"

2 Let him that heareth say,
  To all about him,—"Come!"
Let him that thirsts for righteousness
  To Christ, the Fountain, come.

3 Yes, whosoever will,
  Oh! let him freely come,
And freely drink the stream of life;
  'T is Jesus bids him come.

4 Lo! Jesus, who invites,
  Declares,—"I quickly come:"
Lord! even so; I wait thine hour;
  Jesus, my Saviour! come!
              Henry U. Onderdonk, 1826.

PARDON OFFERED.

ZEPHYR. L. M. William B. Bradbury, 1844.

"Come hither, all ye weary souls! Ye heavy laden sinners! come;
I'll give you rest from all your toils, And raise you to my heavenly home.

287. *Christ's Invitation to Sinners.* (576.)

1 " Come hither, all ye weary souls!
  Ye heavy-laden sinners! come;
  I'll give you rest from all your toils,
  And raise you to my heavenly home.

2 "They shall find rest, that learn of me;
  I'm of a meek and lowly mind;
  But passion rages like the sea,
  And pride is restless as the wind.

3 "Blessed is the man, whose shoulders take
  My yoke, and bear it with delight;
  My yoke is easy to his neck, [light."
  My grace shall make the burden

4 Jesus! we come at thy command,
  With faith, and hope, and humble zeal;
  Resign our spirits, to thy hand,
  To mould and guide us, at thy will.
  Isaac Watts, 1709.

288. *Rest for the weary Penitent.* (577.)

1 Come, weary souls! with sin distressed,
  The Saviour offers heavenly rest;
  The kind, the gracious call obey,
  And cast your gloomy fears away.

2 Here mercy's boundless ocean flows,
  To cleanse your guilt, and heal your woes;
  Pardon, and life, and endless peace; —
  How rich the gift, how free the grace!

3 Lord! we accept, with thankful heart,
  The hope thy gracious words impart;
  We come, with trembling; yet rejoice,
  And bless the kind inviting voice.

4 Dear Saviour! let thy powerful love
  Confirm our faith, our fears remove;
  And sweetly influence every breast,
  And guide us to eternal rest.
  Anne Steele, 1760.

289. *Christ at the door.* (578.)

1 Behold! a stranger's at the door!
  He gently knocks, — has knocked before;
  Has waited long — is waiting still;
  You treat no other friend so ill.

2 But will he prove a friend indeed?
  He will — the very friend you need;
  The Man of Nazareth. — 't is he,
  With garments dyed at Calvary.

3 Oh! lovely attitude! — he stands
  With melting heart, and laden hands:
  Oh! matchless kindness! — and he shows
  This matchless kindness to his foes.

4 Rise, touched with gratitude divine,
  Turn out his enemy and thine, —
  That hateful hell-born monster, sin, —
  And let the heavenly stranger in.

5 Admit him, ere his anger burn;
  His feet departed ne'er return;
  Admit him, — or the hour 's at hand,
  When, at his door, denied you 'll stand.
  Joseph Grigg, 1765.

RECONCILIATION.

BERA. L. M. *John E. Gould*, 1849.

Come, let our voic-es join to raise A sacred song of sol-emn praise;
God is a sovereign King;—re-hearse His honors in ex-alt-ed verse.

290. PSALM 95. (579.)

1 Come, let our voices join to raise
A sacred song of solemn praise;
God is a sovereign King; rehearse
His honors in exalted verse.

2 Come, let our souls address the Lord,
Who framed our natures with his word;
He is our Shepherd;—we the sheep,
His mercy chose, his pastures keep.

3 Come, let us hear his voice to-day,
The counsels of his love obey;
Nor let our hardened hearts renew
The sins and plagues that Israel knew.

4 Look back, my soul! with holy dread,
And view those ancient rebels dead:
Attend the offered grace to-day
Nor lose the blessing by delay.

5 Seize the kind promise, while it waits,
And march to Zion's heavenly gates;
Believe,—and take the promised rest;
Obey,—and be for ever blessed.
Isaac Watts, 1719.

291. *The Strivings of the Spirit.* (582.)

1 Say, sinner! hath a voice within
Oft whispered to thy secret soul,
Urged thee to leave the ways of sin,
And yield thy heart to God's control?

2 Sinner! it was a heavenly voice,—
It was the Spirit's gracious call;
It bade thee make the better choice,
And haste to seek in Christ thine all.

3 Spurn not the call to life and light:
Regard, in time, the warning kind;
That call thou may'st not always slight,
And yet the gate of mercy find.

4 God's Spirit will not always strive
With hardened, self-destroying man;
Ye, who persist his love to grieve,
May never hear his voice again.

5 Sinner! perhaps, this very day,
Thy last accepted time may be;
Oh! should'st thou grieve him now away,
Then hope may never beam on thee.
Mrs. Ann B. Hyde, 1825.

292. *Life, the only accepted Time.* (581.)

1 While life prolongs its precious light,
Mercy is found and peace is given;
But soon, ah! soon,—approaching night
Shall blot out every hope of heaven.

2 While God invites, how blessed the day!
How sweet the gospel's charming sound!
Come, sinners! haste, Oh! haste away,
While yet a pard'ning God he's found.

3 Soon, borne on time's most rapid wing,
Shall death command you to the grave,
Before his bar your spirits bring,
And none be found to hear, or save.

4 In that lone land of deep despair,
No Sabbath's heavenly light shall rise;
No God regard your bitter prayer,
Nor Saviour call you to the skies.
Timothy Dwight, 1800.

PARDON OFFERED.

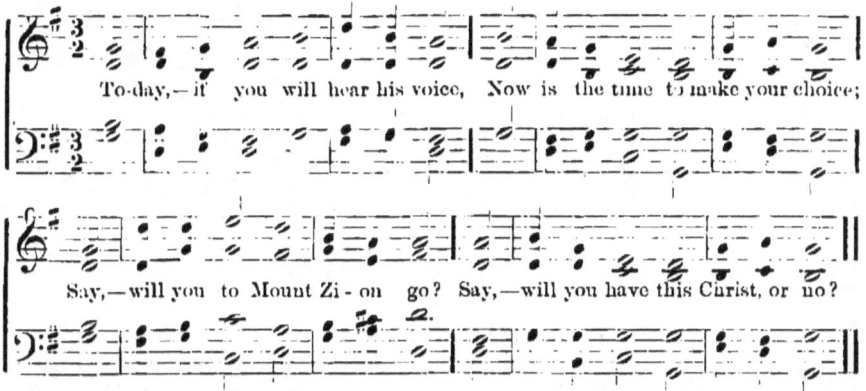

293. *The happy Choice.* (585.)

1 To-day,—if you will hear his voice,—
Now is the time to make your choice;
Say,—will you to Mount Zion go?
Say,—will you have this Christ, or no?

2 Ye wandering souls, who find no rest!
Say,—will you be for ever blessed?
Will you be saved from sin and hell?
Will you with Christ in glory dwell?

3 Come now, dear youth! for ruin bound,
Obey the gospel's joyful sound ;
Come, go with us, and you shall prove
The joys of Christ's redeeming love.

4 Once more we ask you in his name,—
For yet his love remains the same,—
Say,—will you to Mount Zion go?
Say,—will you have this Christ, or no?
Anon., 1808, a.

294. *The Waters of Life.* (586.)

1 "Ho! EVERY one that thirsts! draw nigh!"—
'T is God invites the fallen race ;
"Mercy and free salvation buy,
Buy wine, and milk, and gospel grace.

2 "Nothing ye in exchange shall give,—
Leave all you have and are behind ;
Frankly the gift of God receive,—
Pardon and peace in Jesus find.

3 "Come to the living waters, come,
Sinners! obey your Maker's call ;
Return, ye weary wanderers! home,
And find my grace is free for all."
Charles Wesley, 1740.

295. *The Sinner entreated.* (587.)

1 RETURN! O wanderer! return,
And seek an injured Father's face ;
Those warm desires that in thee burn,
Were kindled by reclaiming grace.

2 Return, O wanderer! return,
He hears thy deep repentant sigh ;
He saw thy softened spirit mourn,
When no intruding ear was nigh.

3 Return! O wanderer! return,
Thy Saviour bids thy spirit live ;
Go to his bleeding feet, and learn
How freely Jesus can forgive.

4 Return, O wanderer! return,
And wipe away the falling tear ;
'T is God, who says—"No longer mourn!"
'T is mercy's voice invites thee near.
William B. Collyer, 1812.

296. *The Mercy of God in Christ.* (583.)

1 NOT to condemn the sons of men,
Did Christ, the Son of God appear ;
No weapons in his hands are seen,
No flaming sword, nor thunder there.

2 Such was the pity of our God,
He loved the race of man so well,
He sent his Son, to bear our load
Of sins, and save our souls from hell.

3 Sinners! believe the Saviour's word,
Trust in his mighty name and live ;
A thousand joys his lips afford,
His hands a thousand blessings give.
Isaac Watts, 1709.

RECONCILIATION.

MARTYN. 7s. 6 or 8 lines. S. B. Marsh, 1836.

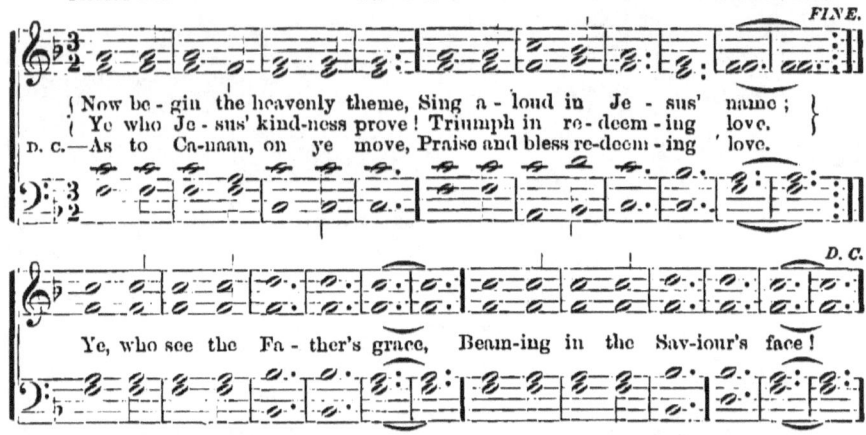

Now be-gin the heavenly theme, Sing a-loud in Je-sus' name;
Ye who Je-sus' kind-ness prove! Triumph in re-deem-ing love.
D. C.—As to Ca-naan, on ye move, Praise and bless re-deem-ing love.

Ye, who see the Fa-ther's grace, Beam-ing in the Sav-iour's face!

297. *Redeeming Love.* (596.)

1 Now begin the heavenly theme,
  Sing aloud in Jesus' name;
  Ye, who Jesus' kindness prove!
  Triumph in redeeming love.

2 Ye, who see the Father's grace
  Beaming in the Saviour's face!
  As to Canaan on ye move,
  Praise, and bless redeeming love.

3 Mourning souls! dry up your tears;
  Banish all your guilty fears;
  See your guilt and curse remove,—
  Canceled by redeeming love.

4 Ye, alas! who long have been
  Willing slaves of death and sin!
  Now from bliss no longer rove,
  Stop, and taste redeeming love.

5 Welcome all, by sin oppressed,—
  Welcome to his sacred rest!
  Nothing brought him from above,—
  Nothing but redeeming love.

6 Hither, then, your music bring;
  Strike aloud each joyful string;
  Mortals! join the hosts above,—
  Join to praise redeeming love.
  Martin Madan, (?) 1763.

298. *Expostulation.* (594.)

1 Sinners! turn, why will you die?
  God, your Maker, asks you—Why?
  God, who did your being give,
  Made you with himself to live,—
  He the fatal cause demands,
  Asks the work of his own hands,—
  Why, ye thankless creatures! why
  Will ye cross his love, and die?

2 Sinners! turn, why will you die?
  God, your Saviour, asks you—Why?
  God, who did your souls retrieve,
  Died himself, that you might live;
  Will you let him die in vain?
  Crucify your Lord again?
  Why, ye ransomed sinners! why
  Will you slight his grace, and die?

3 Sinners! turn, why will you die?
  God, the Spirit, asks you—why?
  God, who all your lives hath strove,
  Wooed you to embrace his love:
  Will you not the grace receive?
  Will you still refuse to live?
  Why, ye long-sought sinners! why
  Will you grieve your God, and die?
  Charles Wesley, 1756.

299. *The Saviour's Call.* (595.)

1 Come! ye weary sinners! come:
  All, who groan beneath your load;
  Jesus calls his wanderers home;
  Hasten to your pardoning God:
  Come, ye guilty souls oppressed!
  Answer to the Saviour's call;
  "Come, and I will give you rest;
  Come, and I will save you all."
  Charles Wesley, 1742.

PARDON OFFERED.

MOUNT CALVARY. 7s, 6 lines. From *Johann Rosenmüller*, 1655.

Hearts of stone! relent; relent; Break, by Jesus' cross subdued;
See his body mangled, rent, Stained and covered with his blood!
Sinful soul! what hast thou done? Crucified th' eternal Son!

300. *Repentance at the Cross.* (599.)

1 Hearts of stone! relent, relent;
  Break, by Jesus' cross subdued;
  See his body, mangled, rent,
  Stained and covered with his blood!
  Sinful soul! what hast thou done?
  Crucified th' eternal Son!

2 Yes, thy sins have done the deed;
  Driven the nails that fixed him there;
  Crowned with thorns his sacred head;
  Plunged into his side the spear;
  Made his soul a sacrifice,—
  While for sinful man he dies.

3 Wilt thou let him bleed in vain.—
  Still to death thy Lord pursue?
  Open all his wounds again,
  And the shameful cross renew?
  No; - with all my sins I'll part,
  Saviour! take my broken heart.
  Ger., John Kruger, 1640.
  Tr., by *Charles Wesley*, 1745.

301. *Come and welcome.* (600.)

1 From the cross uplifted high,
  Where the Saviour deigns to die,
  What melodious sounds I hear,
  Bursting on my ravished ear!—
  "Love's redeeming work is done,—
  Come and welcome, sinner! come.

2 Spread for thee, the festal board
  See with richest dainties stored;
  To thy Father's bosom pressed,
  Yet again a child confessed,
  Never from his house to roam;
  Come and welcome, sinner! come.

3 Soon the days of life shall end;
  Lo! I come, your Saviour, Friend,
  Safe your spirits to convey
  To the realms of endless day,
  Up to my eternal home;
  Come and welcome, sinner! come!"
  Thomas Haweis, 1792.

302. *Looking to Jesus.* (601.)

1 Ye that in his courts are found,
  Listening to the joyful sound,
  Lost and helpless as ye are,
  Sons of sorrow, sin and care!
  Glorify the King of kings,
  Take the peace the gospel brings.

2 Turn to Christ your longing eyes,
  View his bloody sacrifice,
  See in him your sins forgiven,
  Pardon, holiness and heaven;
  Glorify the King of kings,
  Take the peace the gospel brings.
  Rowland Hill, 1774.

RECONCILIATION.

LENOX. H. M. *J. Edson,* 1782.

Blow ye the trumpet, blow!—The gladly solemn sound,—Let all the nations know, To earth's remotest bound,

The year of jubilee is come, The year of jubilee is come; Return, ye ransomed sinners! home.

---

303. *The Jubilee proclaimed.* (591.)

1 Blow ye the trumpet,—blow!—
  The gladly solemn sound ;—
Let all the nations know,
  To earth's remotest bound,—
The year of jubilee is come ;
Return, ye ransomed sinners ! home.

2 Jesus, our great High Priest,
  Hath full atonement made ;
Ye weary spirits ! rest,
  Ye mournful souls ! be glad ;
The year of jubilee is come ;
Return, ye ransomed sinners ! home.

3 Ex'ol the Lamb of God,—
  The all-atoning Lamb ;
Redemption in his blood,
  Throughout the world, proclaim ;
The year of jubilee is come ;
Return, ye ransomed sinners ! home.

4 Ye slaves of sin and hell !
  Your liberty receive ;
And safe in Jesus dwell,
  And blest in Jesus live ;
The year of jubilee is come ;
Return, ye ransomed sinners ! home.

5 Ye, who have sold for naught
  Your heritage above !
Shall have it back unbought,
  The gift of Jesus' love ;
The year of jubilee is come ;
Return, ye ransomed sinners ! home.

6 The gospel trumpet hear,
  The news of heavenly grace ;
And, saved from earth, appear
  Before your Saviour's face ;
The year of jubilee is come ;
Return, ye ransomed sinners! home.
                    Charles Wesley, 1755.

304. *Yet there is Room.* (592.)

1 Ye dying sons of men,
  Immerged in sin and woe !
The gospel's voice attend,
  While Jesus sends to you ;
Ye perishing and guilty ! come ;
In Jesus' arms there yet is room.

2 No longer now delay,
  Nor vain excuses frame ;
He bids you come to-day,
  Though poor, and blind, and lame ;
All things are ready, sinners ! come,
For every trembling soul there's room.

3 Believe the heavenly word,
  His messengers proclaim ;
He is a gracious Lord,
  And faithful is his name ;
Backsliding souls ! return and come,
Cast off despair, there yet is room.

4 Compelled by bleeding love,
  Ye wandering sheep ! draw near;
Christ calls you from above,
  His charming accents hear ;
Let whosoever will now come,
In mercy's arms there still is room.
                    James Boden, 1777.

PARDON OFFERED.

SCOTLAND. 12s. *John Clarke*, cir. 1800.

The voice of free grace cries, "Escape to the mountain; For Adam's lost race, Christ hath opened a foun-tain; For sin and un-cleanness, and ev-ery trans-gres-sion, His blood flows most freely in streams of sal-va-tion; His blood flows most freely, in streams of sal-va-tion.
Hal-le-lu-jah to the Lamb, who hath purchased our pardon! We'll praise him a-gain, when we pass o-ver Jordan! We'll praise him a-gain, when we pass o-ver Jordan!

305.   *The Voice of Free Grace.*   (606.)

1 THE voice of free grace cries,—"Escape to the mountain ;
For Adam's lost race, Christ hath opened a fountain ;
For sin, and uncleanness, and every transgression,
His blood flows most freely, in streams of salvation."
Hallelujah to the Lamb, who hath purchased our pardon!
We'll praise him again, when we pass over Jordan.

2 Ye souls that are wounded! repair to the Saviour ;
He calls you in mercy, 't is infinite favor ;
Your sins are increased as high as a mountain,—
His blood can remove them, it flows from the fountain.
Hallelujah, &c.

3 Now Jesus, our King, reigns triumphantly glorious ;
O'er sin, death, and hell, he is more than victorious ;
With shouting proclaim it, Oh! trust in his passion,
He saves us most freely, Oh! glorious salvation!
Hallelujah, &c.

4 Our Jesus his name now proclaims all victorious,
He reigns over all, and his kingdom is glorious :
To Jesus, we'll join with the great congregation,
In triumph, ascribing to him our salvation.
Hallelujah, &c.

5 With joy shall we stand, when escaped to the shore ;
With harps in our hands, we will praise him the more ;
We'll range the sweet plains on the banks of the river,
And sing of salvation for ever and ever!
Hallelujah to the Lamb, who hath purchased our pardon!
We'll praise him again, when we pass over Jordan!

Richard Burdsall, 1806, a.

RECONCILIATION.

YOAKLEY.   L. M.   *William Yoakley.*

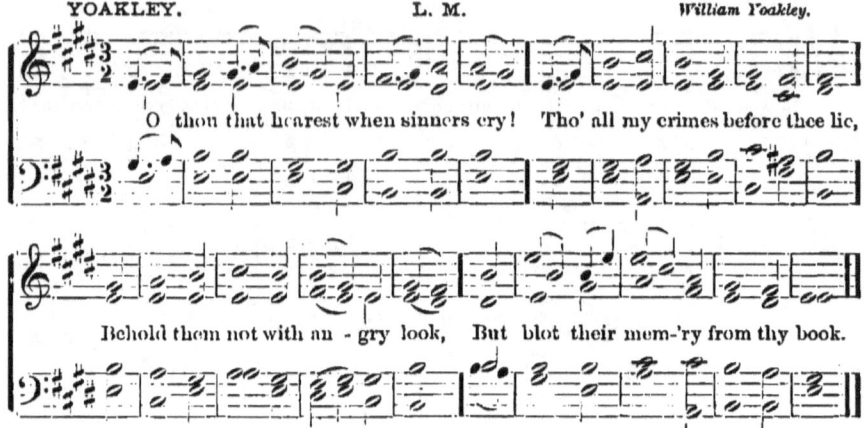

O thou that hearest when sinners cry! Tho' all my crimes before thee lie,
Behold them not with an-gry look, But blot their mem'ry from thy book.

306.   PSALM 51.   (610.)

1 O THOU, that hearest when sinners cry!
  Though all my crimes before thee lie,
  Behold them not with angry look,
  But blot their mem'ry from thy book.

2 Create my nature pure within,
  And form my soul averse to sin;
  Let thy good Spirit ne'er depart,
  Nor hide thy presence from my heart.

3 I cannot live without thy light,
  Cast out and banished from thy sight:
  Thy holy joys, my God! restore,
  And guard me, that I fall no more.

4 Though I have grieved thy Spirit, Lord!
  His help and comfort still afford;
  And let a wretch come near thy throne,
  To plead the merits of thy Son.
  Isaac Watts, 1719.

307.   PSALM 51.   (611.)

1 A BROKEN heart, my God, my King!
  Is all the sacrifice I bring;
  The God of grace will ne'er despise
  A broken heart for sacrifice.

2 My soul lies humbled in the dust,
  And owns thy dreadful sentence just;
  Look down, O Lord! with pitying eye,
  And save the soul condemned to die.

3 Then will I teach the world thy ways;
  Sinners shall learn thy sovereign grace;
  I'll lead them to my Saviour's blood,
  And they shall praise a pard'ning God.

4 Oh! may thy love inspire my tongue!
  Salvation shall be all my song;
  And all my powers shall join to bless
  The Lord, my strength, and right. ousness.
  Isaac Watts, 1719.

308.   *Seeking Rest in Christ.*   (613.)

1 OH! that my load of sin were gone!
  Oh, that I could at last submit!
  At Jesus' feet to lay it down,—
  To lay my soul at Jesus' feet!

2 Rest for my soul I long to find;
  Saviour of all! if mine thou art,
  Give me thy meek and lowly mind,
  And stamp thine image on my heart.

3 Break off the yoke of inbred sin,
  And fully set my spirit free;
  I cannot rest, till pure within,
  Till I am wholly lost in thee.

4 Fain would I learn of thee, my God!
  Thy light and easy burden prove,—
  The cross, all stained with hallowed blood,
  The labor of thy dying love.

5 I would, but thou must give the power;
  My heart from every sin release;
  Bring near, bring near the joyful hour,
  And fill me with thy perfect peace!

6 Come, Lord! the drooping sinner cheer,
  Nor let thy chariot wheels delay;
  Appear, in my poor heart appear!
  My God, my Saviour! come away!
  Charles Wesley, 1742.

PARDON SOUGHT.

SUPPLICATION. L. M. From *Wolfgang A. Mozart*, 1756-1791.

Oh! for a glance of heavenly day, To take this stubborn stone a-way,
And thaw, with beams of love divine, This heart, this frozen heart of mine.

309. *The stony Heart.* (616.)

1 Oh! for a glance of heavenly day,
To take this stubborn stone away,
And thaw, with beams of love divine,
This heart, this frozen heart, of mine!

2 The rocks can rend; the earth can quake;
The seas can roar; the mountains shake;
Of feeling, all things show some sign,
But this unfeeling heart of mine.

3 To hear the sorrows thou hast felt,
Dear Lord! an adamant would melt;
But I can read each moving line,
And nothing move this heart of mine.

4 Thy judgments, too, unmoved I hear,—
Amazing thought!—which devils fear;
Goodness and wrath in vain combine
To stir this stupid heart of mine.

5 But something yet can do the deed;
And, Lord! that something much I need;
Thy Spirit can from dross refine,
And move, and melt this heart of mine.
Joseph Hart, 1762.

310. *The Prayer of the Prodigal.* (617.)

1 With broken heart and contrite sigh,
A trembling sinner, Lord! I cry;
Thy pardoning grace is rich and free;
O God! be merciful to me!

2 I smite upon my troubled breast,
With deep and conscious guilt oppressed;
Christ and his cross my only plea;
O God! be merciful to me!

3 Far off I stand with tearful eyes,
Nor dare uplift them to the skies;
But thou dost all my anguish see;
O God! be merciful to me!

4 Nor alms, nor deeds, that I have done,
Can for a single sin atone;
To Calvary alone I flee;
O God! be merciful to me!

5 And when, redeemed from sin and hell,
With all the ransomed throng I dwell,
My raptured song shall ever be,
God has been merciful to me!
Cornelius Elven, 1852.

311. *The departing Spirit stayed.* (615.)

1 Stay, thou insulted Spirit! stay,
Though I have done thee such despite;
Nor cast the sinner quite away,
Nor take thine everlasting flight.

2 Though I have most unfaithful been
Of all who e'er thy grace received;
Ten thousand times thy goodness seen,
Ten thousand times thy goodness grieved;

3 Yet, Oh! the chief of sinners spare,
In honor of my great High Priest;
Nor, in thy righteous anger, swear
T' exclude me from thy people's rest.

4 Now, Lord! my weary soul release,
Upraise me with thy gracious hand;
And guide into thy perfect peace,
And bring me to the promised land.
Charles Wesley, 1749.

RECONCILIATION.

ARMENIA.   C. M.   *Sylvanus B. Pond, 1835.*

Oh! that thou would'st, the heavens rent, In majesty come down! Stretch out thine arm omnipotent, And seize me for thine own.

312. *All-subduing Grace.* (619.)

1 Oh! that thou wouldst, the heavens rent,
  In majesty come down;
Stretch out thine arm omnipotent,
  And seize me for thine own!

2 Descend, and let thy lightning burn
  The stubble of thy foe:
My sins o'erturn, o'erturn, o'erturn,
  And make the mountains flow.

3 Thou my impetuous spirit guide,
  And curb my headstrong will;
Thou only canst drive back the tide,
  And bid the sun stand still.

4 What, though I cannot break my chain,
  Or e'er throw off my load?
The things impossible to men
  Are possible to God.
    Charles Wesley, 1740.

313. *Pardoning Love.* (620.)

1 How oft, alas! this wretched heart
  Has wandered from the Lord!
How oft my roving thoughts depart,
  Forgetful of his word!

2 Yet sovereign mercy calls—"Return!"
  Dear Lord! and may I come?
My vile ingratitude I mourn;
  Oh! take the wanderer home.

3 And canst thou, wilt thou, yet forgive,
  And bid my crimes remove?
And shall a pardoned rebel live
  To speak thy wondrous love?

4 Almighty grace! thy healing power,
  How glorious, how divine!
That can, to life and bliss, restore
  So vile a heart as mine!

5 Thy pard'ning love, so free, so sweet,
  Dear Saviour! I adore;
Oh! keep me at thy sacred feet,
  And let me rove no more.
    Anne Steele, 1760.

314. *Contrition.* (621.)

1 O Thou, whose tender mercy hears
  Contrition's humble sigh;
Whose hand, indulgent, wipes the tears
  From sorrow's weeping eye!

2 See low before thy throne of grace,
  A wretched wanderer mourn:
Hast thou not bid me seek thy face?
  Hast thou not said—"Return?"

3 And shall my guilty fears prevail
  To drive me from thy feet?
Oh! let not this dear refuge fail,
  This only safe retreat!

4 Absent from thee, my Guide! my Light!
  Without one cheering ray, [night,
Through dangers, fears, and gloomy
  How desolate my way!

5 Oh! shine on this benighted heart,
  With beams of mercy shine!
And let thy healing voice impart
  A taste of joy divine.
    Anne Steele, 1760.

PARDON SOUGHT.

MANOAH.   C. M.   From *Rossini*, 1792-1868.

Ap-proach, my soul! the mer-cy seat, Where Je-sus an-swers prayer;
There hum-bly fall be-fore his feet, For none can per-ish there.

315.   *Coming to Christ.*   (622.)

1 APPROACH, my soul! the mercy-seat,
   Where Jesus answers prayer;
   There humbly fall before his feet,
   For none can p'rish there.

2 Thy promise is my only plea,
   With this I venture nigh:
   Thou callest burdened souls to thee,
   And such, O Lord! am I.

3 Bowed down beneath a load of sin,
   By Satan sorely pressed,
   By war without and fears within,
   I come to thee for rest.

4 Be thou my shield and hiding-place,
   That, sheltered near thy side,
   I may my fierce accuser face,
   And tell him—"Thou hast died."

5 Oh! wondrous love,—to bleed and die,
   To bear the cross and shame,
   That guilty sinners, such as I,
   Might plead thy gracious name!
          John Newton, 1779.

316.   *The Friend of Sinners.*   (623.)

1 JESUS! thou art the sinner's friend;
   As such I look to thee;
   Now, in the fullness of thy love,
   O Lord! remember me.

2 Remember thy pure word of grace,—
   Remember Calvary;
   Remember all thy dying groans,
   And, then, remember me.

3 Thou wondrous Advocate with God!
   I yield myself to thee;
   While thou art sitting on thy throne,
   Dear Lord! remember me.

4 Lord! I am guilty—I am vile,
   But thy salvation's free;
   Then, in thine all abounding grace,
   Dear Lord! remember me.

5 And, when I close my eyes in death,
   When creature-helps all flee,
   Then, O my dear Redeemer God!
   I pray, remember me.
          Richard Burnham, 1783, a.

317.   PSALM 51.   (624.)

1 O GOD of mercy! hear my call,
   My loads of guilt remove;
   Break down this separating wall,
   That bars me from thy love.

2 Give me the presence of thy grace;
   Then my rejoicing tongue
   Shall speak aloud thy righteousness,
   And make thy praise my song.

3 No blood of goats, nor heifer slain,
   For sin could e'er atone:
   The death of Christ shall still remain
   Sufficient and alone.

4 A soul, oppressed with sin's desert,
   My God will ne'er despise;
   An humble groan, a broken heart,
   Is our best sacrifice.
          Isaac Watts, 1719.

RECONCILIATION.

WINDSOR (DUNDEE.) C. M. *George Kirby, Este's Psalter, 1592.*

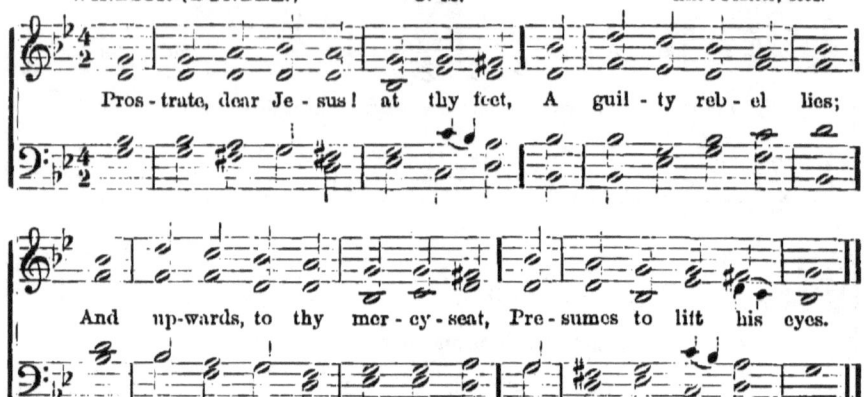

Pros-trate, dear Jesus! at thy feet, A guilty rebel lies;
And upwards, to thy mercy-seat, Presumes to lift his eyes.

---

318. *The Penitent.* (628.)

1 PROSTRATE, dear Jesus! at thy feet,
   A guilty rebel lies;
   And upwards, to thy mercy-seat,
   Presumes to lift his eyes.

2 Oh! let not justice frown me hence;
   Stay, stay the vengeful storm;
   Forbid it, that Omnipotence
   Should crush a feeble worm.

3 If tears of sorrow would suffice
   To pay the debt I owe,
   Tears should, from both my weeping eyes,
   In ceaseless torrents flow.

4 But no such sacrifice I plead
   To expiate my guilt;
   No tears, but those which thou hast shed,
   No blood, but thou hast spilt.

5 Think of thy sorrows, dearest Lord!
   And all my sins forgive;
   Justice will well approve the word,
   That bids the sinner live.
                    Samuel Stennett, 1787.

319. *The heavenly Guest.* (625.)

1 AND will the Lord thus condescend
   To visit sinful worms?
   Thus at the door shall mercy stand,
   In all her winning forms?

2 Shall Jesus for admission sue,—
   His charming voice unheard?
   And this vile heart, his rightful due,
   Remain for ever barred?

3 'T is sin, alas! with tyrant power,
   The lodging has possessed;
   And crowds of traitors bar the door,
   Against the heavenly guest.

4 Lord! rise in thine all-conquering grace,
   Thy mighty power display;
   One beam of glory from thy face
   Can drive my foes away.

5 Ye dangerous inmates! hence depart;
   Dear Saviour! enter in,
   And guard the passage to my heart,
   And keep out every sin.
                    Anne Steele, 1760.

320. *Inconstancy deplored.* (627.)

1 WITH tears of anguish I lament,
   Here at thy feet, my God!
   My passion, pride, and discontent,
   And vile ingratitude.

2 Sure there was ne'er a heart so base,
   So false, as mine has been—
   So faithless to its promises,
   So prone to every sin?

3 How long, dear Saviour! shall I feel
   These struggles in my breast?
   When wilt thou bow my stubborn will,
   And give my conscience rest?

4 Break, sovereign grace! Oh! break the charm,
   And set the captive free;
   Reveal, almighty God! thine arm,
   And haste to rescue me.
                    Samuel Stennett, 1787.

PARDON SOUGHT. 115

EVEN ME. 8 7, 8 7, 6 7, or 8s & 7s. 8 LINES. *William B. Bradbury, 1862.*

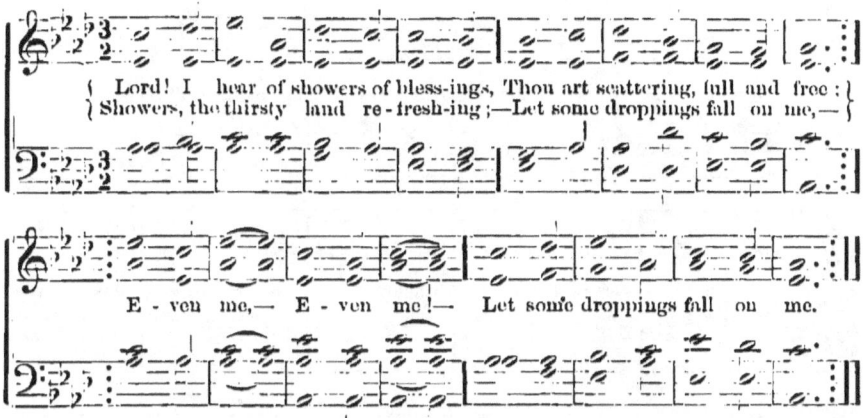

{ Lord! I hear of showers of bless-ings, Thou art scattering, full and free : }
{ Showers, the thirsty land re-fresh-ing ;— Let some droppings fall on me,— }
E - ven me,— E - ven me!— Let some droppings fall on me.

321. *Pass me not.* (636.)

1 Lord! I hear of showers of blessing,
  Thou art scattering full and free ;
Showers, the thirsty land refreshing ;
  Let some droppings fall on me,—
Even me,—even me !
Let some droppings fall on me.

2 Pass me not, O gracious Father !
  Sinful though my heart may be ;
Thou might'st curse me, but the rather
  Let thy mercy light on me,—
Even me, &c.

3 Pass me not, O tender Saviour !
  Let me love and cling to thee ;
I am longing for thy favor ;
  When thou comest, call for me,—
Even me, &c.

4 Pass me not, O mighty Spirit !
  Thou canst make the blind to see ;
Witness of Jesus' merit,
  Speak the word of power to me,—
Even me, &c.

5 Have I long in sin been sleeping,
  Long been slighting, grieving thee?
Has the world my heart been keeping?
  Oh! forgive and rescue me,—
Even me, &c.

6 Love of God, so pure and changeless,—
  Blood of God, so rich and free,—
Grace of God, so strong and boundless,—
  Magnify them all in me,—
Even me, &c.

7 Pass me not, this lost one bringing,
  Satan's slave thy child shall be,
All my heart to thee is springing ;
  Blessing others, Oh! bless me,—
Even me, &c.
Elizabeth Codner, 1860.

322. *Self-Consecration.* (637.)

1 Take me, O my Father! take me,
  Take me, save me, through thy Son ;
That, which thou wouldst have me, make me,
  Let thy will in me be done.

2 Long from thee my footsteps straying,
  Thorny proved the way I trod :
Weary come I now, and praying—
  Take me to thy love, my God!

3 Fruitless years with grief recalling,
  Humbly I confess my sin ;
At thy feet, O Father! falling,
  To thy household take me in.

4 Freely now to thee I proffer
  This relenting heart of mine ;
Freely, life and soul I offer—
  Gift unworthy love like thine.

5 Once the world's Redeemer dying
  Bore our sins upon the tree ;
On that sacrifice relying,
  Now I look in hope to thee.

6 Father! take me ; all forgiving,
  Fold me to thy loving breast ;
In thy love for ever living,
  I must be for ever blest !
Ray Palmer, 1865.

RECONCILIATION.

HOLLINGSIDE. 7s. 8 LINES. John B. Dykes, 1861.

Saviour! when, in dust, to thee Low we bow th' adoring knee; When, repentant, to the skies Scarce we lift our weeping eyes; Oh! by all thy pains and woe Suffered once for man below, Bending from thy throne on high, Hear our solemn Litany.

323. *The penitential Plea.* (631.)

1 SAVIOUR! when, in dust, to thee
Low we bow th' adoring knee;
When, repentant, to the skies
Scarce we lift our weeping eyes;
Oh! by all thy pains and woe
Suffered once for man below,
Bending from thy throne on high,
Hear our solemn Litany!

2 By thy helpless infant years,
By thy life of want and tears,
By thy days of sore distress
In the savage wilderness;
By the dread mysterious hour
Of th' insulting tempter's power,
Turn, Oh! turn a favoring eye;
Hear our solemn Litany!

3 By thine hour of dire despair;
By thine agony of prayer;
By the cross, the nail, the thorn,
Piercing spear, and torturing scorn;
By the gloom that veiled the skies
O'er the dreadful sacrifice;
Listen to our humble cry,
Hear our solemn Litany!

4 By thy deep expiring groan;
By the sad sepulchral stone;
By the vault, whose dark abode
Held in vain the rising God:
Oh! from earth to heaven restored,
Mighty re-ascended Lord!
Listen, listen to the cry
Of our solemn Litany!
                    Robert Grant, 1815.

324. *Deep Contrition.* (632.)

1 SOVEREIGN Ruler, Lord of all!
Prostrate at thy feet I fall;
Hear, Oh! hear my ardent cry,
Frown not, lest I faint and die:
Vilest of the sons of men,—
Worst of rebels I have been;
Oft abused thee to thy face,
Trampled on thy richest grace.

2 Justly might thy vengeful dart
Pierce this broken, bleeding heart;
Justly might thy kindled ire
Blast me in eternal fire:
But with thee there 's mercy found,
Balm to heal my every wound ·
Thou canst soothe the troubled breast,
Give the weary wanderer rest.
                    Thomas Raffles, 1812.

PARDON SOUGHT. 117

ALETTA. 7s. 4 or 6 LINES. William B. Bradbury, 1856.

Depth of mer-cy! can there be Mer-cy still re-served for me?
Can my God his wrath for-bear? Me, the chief of sin-ners, spare?

325. *The Chief of Sinners.* (633.)

1 DEPTH of mercy, can there be
Mercy still reserved for me?
Can my God his wrath forbear?
Me, the chief of sinners, spare?

2 I have long withstood his grace,
Long provoked him to his face;
Would not hearken to his calls;
Grieved him by a thousand falls.

3 Kindled his relentings are;
Me he now delights to spare;
Cries,—"How shall I give thee up?"—
Lets the lifted thunder drop.

4 There for me the Saviour stands;
Shows his wounds, and spreads his hands;
God is love; I know, I feel;
Jesus weeps, and loves me still.

5 Jesus! answer from above;
Is not all thy nature love?
Bow thine ear, in mercy bow,
Pardon and accept me now.

6 Now incline me to repent;
Let me now my fall lament;
Now my foul revolt deplore;
Weep, believe, and sin no more.
Charles Wesley, 1740.

326. *Pleading with Jesus.* (634.)

1 THOU, who didst on Calvary bleed!
Thou, who dost for sinners plead!
Help me in my time of need,
Jesus, Saviour! hear my cry.

2 In my darkness and my grief,
With my heart of unbelief,
I, who am of sinners chief,
Jesus! lift to thee mine eye.

3 Foes without and fears within,
With no plea thy grace to win,
But that thou canst save from sin,
Jesus! to thy cross I fly.

4 There on thee I cast my care,
There to thee I raise my prayer,
Jesus! save me from despair,
Save me, save me, or I die.

5 When the storms of trial lower,
When I feel temptation's power,
In the last and darkest hour,
Jesus, Saviour! be thou nigh.
James Drummond Burns, 1856.

327. *God's Help entreated.* (635.)

1 O THOU God, who hearest prayer,
Every hour, and every where!
Listen to my feeble breath,
Now I touch the gates of death;
For his sake whose blood I plead,
Hear me in the hour of need.

2 Hear and save me, gracious Lord!
For my trust is in thy word;
Wash me from the stain of sin,
That thy peace may rule within;
May I know myself thy child,
Ransomed, pardoned, reconciled.
Josiah Conder, 1836.

RECONCILIATION.

328. *Preparation for the Judgment.* (640.)

1 When thou, my righteous Judge! shalt come
To take thy ransomed people home,
Shall I among them stand?
Shall such a worthless worm as I,
Who sometimes am afraid to die,
Be found at thy right hand?

2 I love to meet among them now,
Before thy gracious feet to bow,
Though vilest of them all ;
But, can I bear the piercing thought,
What, if my name should be left out,
When thou for them shalt call ?

3 Prevent, prevent it by thy grace ;
Be thou, dear Lord ! my hiding-place,
In this th' accepted day ;
Thy pardoning voice, Oh ! let me hear,
To still my unbelieving fear,
Nor let me fall, I pray.

4 Among thy saints let me be found,
Whene'er th' archangel's trump shall
To see thy smiling face ; [sound,
Then loudest of the throng I 'll sing,
While heaven's resounding mansions ring
With shouts of sovereign grace.
Selina Shirley, 1772, a.

329. *The Surrender of the Heart.* (641.)

1 Lord ! thou ha t won : at length I yield ;
My heart, by mighty grace compelled,
Surrenders all to thee :
Against thy terrors long I strove ;
But who can stand against thy love ?
Love conquers even me.

2 Now, Lord ! I would be thine alone ;
Come, take possession of thine own,
For thou hast set me free ;
Released from Satan's hard command,
See all my powers waiting stand,
To be employed by thee.
John Newton, 1779.

330. *Christ, the only Refuge.* (642.)

1 O thou, that hear'st the prayer of faith !
Wilt thou not save a soul from death,
That casts itself on thee?
I have no refuge of my own,
But fly to what my Lord hath done,
And suffered once for me.

2 Slain in the guilty sinner's stead,
His spotless righteousness I plead,
And his availing blood ;
Thy merit, Lord ! my robe shall be ;
Thy merit shall atone for me,
And bring me near to God.

3 Then snatch me from eternal death,
The Spirit of adoption breathe,
His consolation send ;
By him some word of life impart,
And sweetly whisper to my heart,
"Thy Maker is thy Friend."

4 The king of terrors then would be
A welcome messenger to me,
That bids me come away ;
Unclogged by earth, or earthly things,
I 'd mount upon his sable wings,
To everlasting day.
Augustus M. Toplady, 1776.

PARDON SOUGHT. 119

GANGES. C. P. M. Old Melody.

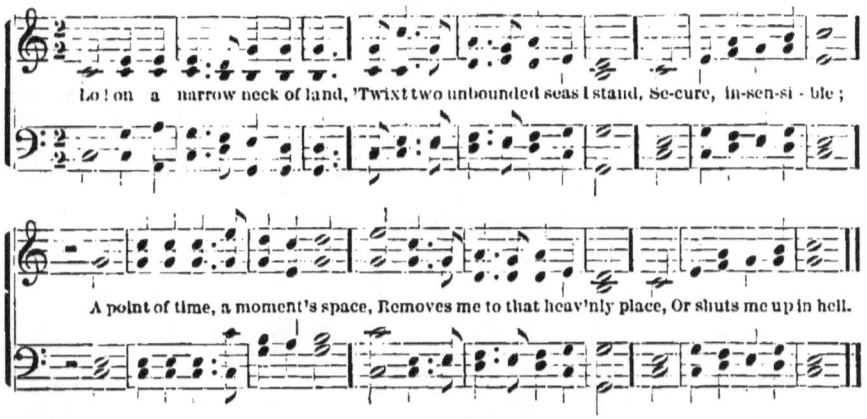

Lo! on a narrow neck of land, 'Twixt two unbounded seas I stand, Secure, in-sen-si-ble; A point of time, a moment's space, Removes me to that heav'nly place, Or shuts me up in hell.

331. *The Brink of Eternity.* (643.)

1 Lo! on a narrow neck of land,
 'Twixt two unbounded seas, I stand,
  Secure, insensible;
 A point of time, a moment's space,
 Removes me to that heavenly place,
  Or shuts me up in hell.

2 O God! mine inmost soul convert,
 And deeply, on my thoughtful heart,
  Eternal things impress:
 Give me to feel their solemn weight,
 And tremble on the brink of fate,
  And wake to righteousness.

3 Before me place, in dread array,
 The pomp of that tremendous day,
  When thou, with clouds, shalt come
 To judge the nations at thy bar;
 And tell me, Lord! shall I be there
  To meet a joyful doom!

4 Be this my one great business here,—
 With serious industry and fear,
  Eternal bliss t' ensure;
 Thine utmost counsel to fulfill,
 And suffer all thy righteous will,
  And to the end endure.

5 Then, Saviour! then my soul receive,
 Transported from this vale to live,
  And reign with thee above;
 Where faith is sweetly lost in sight,
 And hope, in full, supreme delight,
  And everlasting love.
        Charles Wesley, 1749.

332. *The New-Birth.* (644.)

1 Awaked by Sinai's awful sound,
 My soul in bonds of guilt I found,
  And knew not where to go;
 Eternal truth did loud proclaim,
 "The sinner must be born again,"
  Or sink to endless woe.

2 When to the law I trembling fled,
 It poured its curses on my head,
  I no relief could find;
 This fearful truth increased my pain,
 "The sinner must be born again,"
  And whelmed my tortured mind.

3 Again did Sinai's thunders roll,
 And guilt lay heavy on my soul,
  A vast oppressive load:
 Alas. I read and saw it plain,
 "The sinner must be born again,"
  Or drink the wrath of God.

4 The saints I heard with rapture tell,
 How Jesus conquered death and hell,
  And broke the fowler's snare;
 Yet, when I found this truth remain,
 "The sinner must be born again,"
  I sunk in deep dispair.

5 But while I thus in anguish lay,
 The gracious Saviour passed this way,
  And felt his pity move;
 The sinner, by his justice slain,
 Now by his grace is born again,
  And sings redeeming love.
        Samson Ockum, 1760.
     Altered by *Asahel Nettleton*, 1825.

RECONCILIATION.

BARTIMEUS.   8s & 7s. 4 or 6 LINES.   Daniel Read, 1804.

"Mer-cy, O thou Son of Da-vid!" Thus the blind Bar-tim-eus prayed;
"Oth-ers by thy word are sav-ed, Now to me af-ford thine aid."

333. *The blind Man healed.* (645.)

1 "Mercy, O thou Son of David!"
 Thus the blind Bartimeus prayed;
 "Others by thy word are saved,
 "Now to me afford thine aid."

2 Many for his crying chid him,
 But he called the louder still;
 Till the gracious Saviour bid him,—
 "Come, and ask me what you will."

3 Money was not what he wanted,
 Though by begging used to live;
 But he asked, and Jesus granted,
 Alms which none but he could give:

4 "Lord! remove this grievous blindness,
 "Let mine eyes behold the day!"
 Straight he saw, and, won by kindness,
 Followed Jesus in the way.

5 Oh! methinks, I hear him praising,
 Publishing to all around,
 "Friends! is not my case amazing?
 "What a Saviour I have found!

6 "Oh! that all the blind but knew him,
 "And would be advised by me!
 "Surely would they hasten to him,
 "He would cause them all to see."
 John Newton, 1779.

334. *Looking to the Cross.* (646.)

1 Sweet the moments, rich in blessing,
 Which before the cross I spend,
 Life, and health, and peace possessing,
 From the sinner's dying Friend!

2 Here I'll sit, for ever viewing
 Mercy's streams in streams of blood:
 Precious drops! my soul bedewing,
 Plead, and claim my peace, with God.

3 Truly blessed is this station,
 Low before his cross to lie,
 While I see divine compassion
 Floating in his languid eye.

4 Here it is I find my heaven,
 While upon the Lamb I gaze;
 Love I much?—I've much forgiven,—
 I'm a miracle of grace.

5 Love and grief my heart dividing,
 With my tears his feet I'll bathe;
 Constant still in faith abiding,—
 Life deriving from his death.
 James Allen, 1757.
 Altered, by *Walter Shirley,* 1776.

335. *The Surrender.* (647.)

1 Welcome, welcome, dear Redeemer!
 Welcome to this heart of mine;
 Lord! I make a full surrender,
 Every power and thought be thine;
 Thine entirely,—
 Through eternal ages thine.

2 Known to all to be thy mansion,
 Earth and hell will disappear;
 Or in vain attempt possession,
 When they find the Lord is near:—
 Shout, O Zion!
 Shout, ye saints! the Lord is here.
 W—— M——, 1794.

PARDON FOUND. 121

336. *Forsaking All for Christ.* (648.)

1 Jesus! I my cross have taken,
    All to leave, and follow thee;
Destitute, despised, forsaken,
    Thou, from hence, my all shalt be;
Perish every fond ambition,
    All I've sought, and hoped, and known!
Yet how rich is my condition!
    God and heaven are still my own.

2 Let the world despise and leave me;
    They have left my Saviour, too;
Human hearts and looks deceive me;
    Thou art not, like man, untrue;
And, while thou shalt smile upon me,
    God of wisdom, love, and might!
Foes may hate, and friends may shun me;
    Show thy face, and all is bright.

3 Go, then, earthly fame and treasure!
    Come, disaster, scorn, and pain!
In thy service, pain is pleasure,
    With thy favor, loss is gain:
I have called thee, — "Abba Father!"
    I have stayed my heart on thee:
Storms may howl, and clouds may gather,
    All must work for good to me.

4 Man may trouble and distress me;
    'T will but drive me to thy breast;
Life with trials hard may press me,
    Heaven will bring me sweeter rest:

Oh! 't is not in grief to harm me;
    While thy love is left to me;
Oh! 't were not in joy to charm me,
    Were that joy unmixed with thee.
                        Henry Francis Lyte, 1829.

337. *Much forgiven.* (649.)

1 Hail! my ever blessed Jesus!
    Only thee I wish to sing;
To my soul, thy name is precious,
    Thou, my Prophet, Priest, and King:
Oh! what mercy flows from heaven!
    Oh! what joy and happiness!
Love I much? I've much forgiven;
    I'm a miracle of grace.

2 Once with Adam's race in ruin,
    Unconcerned in sin I lay;
Swift destruction still pursuing,
    Till my Saviour passed by:
Witness, all ye host of heaven!
    My Redeemer's tenderness;
Love I much? I've much forgiven;
    I'm a miracle of grace.

3 Shout, ye bright angelic choir!
    Praise the Lamb enthroned above;
Whilst, astonished, I admire
    God's free grace, and boundless love:
That blest moment, I received him,
    Filled my soul with joy and peace:
Love I much? I've much forgiven;
    I'm a miracle of grace.
                        John Wingrove, 1806.

RECONCILIATION.

INVERNESS. S. M. Lowell Mason, 1835.

And can I yet de-lay, My lit-tle all to give?
To tear my soul from earth a-way, For Jesus to receive?

338. *Resignation to Christ.* (655.)

1 And can I yet delay
  My little all to give?
  To tear my soul from earth away,
  For Jesus to receive?

2 Nay, but I yield, I yield,
  I can hold out no more;
  I sink, by dying love compelled,
  And own thee, Conqueror!

3 Though late, I all forsake;
  My friends, my all resign:
  Gracious Redeemer! take, Oh! take,
  And seal me ever thine!

4 Come, and possess me whole,
  Nor hence again remove;
  Settle and fix my wavering soul
  With all thy weight of love.

5 My one desire be this,
  Thine only love to know:
  To seek and taste no other bliss,
  No other good below.

6 My Life, my Portion thou!
  Thou all-sufficient art;
  My Hope, my heavenly Treasure! now
  Enter and keep my heart.
  Charles Wesley, 1740.

339. *Submission to Christ.* (356.)

1 Jesus! I come to thee,
  A sinner doomed to die;
  My only refuge is thy cross,—
  Here at thy feet I lie.

2 Can mercy reach my case,
  And all my sins remove?
  Break, O my God! this heart of stone,
  And melt it by thy love.

3 Too long my soul has gone,
  Far from my God, astray;
  I've sported on the brink of hell,
  In sin's delusive way.

4 But, Lord! my heart is fixed,—
  I hope in thee alone;
  Break off the chains of sin and death,
  And bind me to thy throne.

5 Thy blood can cleanse my heart,
  Thy hand can wipe my tears;—
  Oh! send thy blessed Spirit down,
  To banish all my fears.
  Nathan S. S. Beman, 1832.

340. Psalm 32. (657.)

1 Oh! blessed souls are they,
  Whose sins are covered o'er;—
  Divinely blessed, to whom the Lord
  Imputes their guilt no more.

2 They mourn their follies past,
  And keep their hearts with care;
  Their lips and lives, without deceit,
  Shall prove their faith sincere.

3 While I concealed my guilt,
  I felt the festering wound;
  Till I confessed my sins to thee,
  And ready pardon found.
  Isaac Watts, 1719.

PARDON FOUND.

341. *Jesus is mine.* (660.)

1 Now I have found a Friend;
   Jesus is mine;—
His love shall never end;
   Jesus is mine:
Though earthly joys decrease,
Though earthly friendships cease,
Now I have lasting peace;
   Jesus is mine.

2 Though I grow poor and old,
   Jesus is mine;
Though I grow faint and cold,
   Jesus is mine:
He shall my wants supply;
His precious blood is nigh,
Naught can my hope destroy;
   Jesus is mine.

3 When earth shall pass away,—
   Jesus is mine,—
In the great judgment day,—
   Jesus is mine,—
Oh! what a glorious thing,
Then to behold my King,
On tuneful harp to sing,
   Jesus is mine.

4 Father! thy name I bless;
   Jesus is mine;
Thine was the sovereign grace;
   Praise shall be thine;
Spirit of holiness!
Sealing the Father's grace,
Thou mad'st my soul embrace
   Jesus, as mine.

Henry Hope, 1852.

342. *Parting with the World.* (661.)

1 Pass away, earthly joy!—
   Jesus is mine!
Break every mortal tie;
   Jesus is mine:
Dark is the wilderness;
Distant the resting-place;
Jesus alone can bless;
   Jesus is mine.

2 Tempt not my soul away;
   Jesus is mine:
Here would I ever stay;
   Jesus is mine:
Perishing things of clay,
Born but for one brief day!
Pass from my heart away,
   Jesus is mine.

3 Farewell, ye dreams of night!
   Jesus is mine:
Mine is a dawning bright,
   Jesus is mine:
All, that my soul has tried,
Left but a dismal void;
Jesus has satisfied;
   Jesus is mine.

4 Farewell, mortality!
   Jesus is mine:
Welcome, eternity!
   Jesus is mine:
Welcome, ye scenes of rest!
Welcome, ye mansions blest!
Welcome, a Saviour's breast;
   Jesus is mine.

Mrs. Horatio Bonar, 1845.

RECONCILIATION.

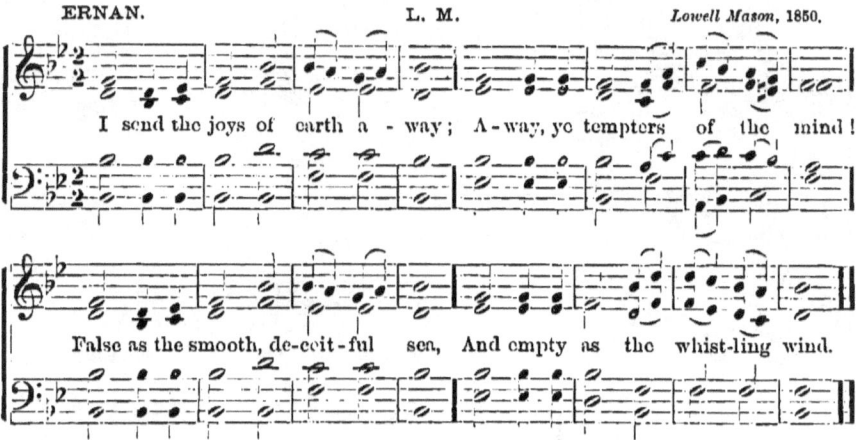

ERNAN. L. M. Lowell Mason, 1850.

I send the joys of earth a-way; A-way, ye tempters of the mind!
False as the smooth, de-ceit-ful sea, And empty as the whist-ling wind.

343. *Parting with carnal Joys.* (667.)

1 I SEND the joys of earth away;
   Away, ye tempters of the mind!
   False as the smooth, deceitful sea,
   And empty as the whistling wind.

2 Your streams were floating me along,
   Down to the gulf of black despair:
   And, whilst I listened to your song,
   Your streams had e'en conveyed me there.

3 Lord! I adore thy matchless grace,
   That warned me of that dark abyss,
   That drew me from those treacherous seas,
   And bade me seek superior bliss.

4 Now, to the shining realms above, [eyes;
   I stretch my hands, and glance mine
   Oh! for the pinions of a dove,
   To bear me to the upper skies.

5 There, from the bosom of my God,
   Oceans of endless pleasure roll;
   There would I fix my last abode,
   And drown the sorrows of my soul.
   Isaac Watts, 1707.

344. *Renouncing All for Christ.* (668.)

1 COME, Saviour, Jesus! from above;
   Assist me with thy heavenly grace;
   Empty my heart of earthly love,
   And for thyself prepare the place.

2 Oh! let thy sacred presence fill,
   And set my longing spirit free,
   Which pants to have no other will,
   But day and night to feast on thee.

3 That path, with humble speed, I'll seek,
   In which my Saviour's footsteps shine;
   Nor will I hear, nor will I speak,
   Of any other love but thine.

4 Henceforth may no profane delight
   Divide this consecrated soul;
   Possess it thou, who hast the right,
   As Lord and Master of the whole.

5 Nothing on earth do I desire,
   But thy pure love within my breast;
   This, only this, will I require,
   And freely give up all the rest.
   From the French, John Wesley, 1739.

345. *Entire Consecration.* (669.)

1 Now I resolve, with all my heart,
   With all my powers, to serve the Lord;
   Nor from his precepts e'er depart,
   Whose service is a rich reward.

2 Oh! be his service all my joy!—
   Around let my example shine,
   Till others love the blest employ,
   And join in labors so divine.

3 Be this the purpose of my soul,
   My solemn, my determined choice,
   To yield to his supreme control,
   And, in his kind commands, rejoice.

4 Oh! may I never faint nor tire,
   Nor wandering leave his sacred ways;
   Great God! accept my soul's desire,
   And give me strength to live thy praise.
   Anne Steele, 1760.

PARDON FOUND.

WOODWORTH. L. M. *William B. Bradbury*, 1849.

Just as I am, with-out one plea, But that thy blood was shed for me, And that thou bid'st me come to thee, O Lamb of God! I come—I come!

346. *Just as I am.* (670.)

1 Just as I am, without one plea,
  But that thy blood was shed for me,
  And that thou bid'st me come to thee,
    O Lamb of God! I come—I come!

2 Just as I am, and waiting not
  To rid my soul of one dark blot,
  To thee, whose blood can cleanse each spot,
    O Lamb of God! I come—I come!

3 Just as I am, though tossed about
  With many a conflict, many a doubt,
  Fightings and fears within, without.
    O Lamb of God! I come—I come!

4 Just as I am, poor, wretched, blind;
  Sight, riches, healing of the mind,
  Yea, all I need, in thee to find,
    O Lamb of God! I come—I come!

5 Just as I am; thou wilt receive,
  Wilt welcome, pardon, cleanse, relieve;
  Because thy promise I believe,
    O Lamb of God! I come—I come!

6 Just as I am; thy love unknown
  Has broken every barrier down;
  Now, to be thine, yea, thine alone,
    O Lamb of God! I come, I come!
                    Charlotte Elliott, 1836.

347. *Christ and his Righteousness.* (671.)

1 No more, my God! I boast no more,
  Of all the duties I have done;
  I quit the hopes I held before,
    To trust the merits of thy Son.

2 Now, for the love I bear his name,
  What was my gain, I count but loss;
  My former pride I call my shame,
    And nail my glory to his cross.

3 Yes, and I must, and will, esteem
  All things but loss for Jesus' sake;
  Oh! may my soul be found in him,
    And of his righteousness partake.

4 The best obedience of my hands
  Dares not appear before thy throne;
  But faith can answer thy demands,
    By pleading what my Lord has done.
                    Isaac Watts, 1709.

348. *The Convert.* (672.)

1 Far from thy fold, O God! my feet
  Once moved in error's devious maze;
  Nor found religious duties sweet,
  Nor sought thy face, nor loved thy ways.

2 With tenderest voice thou bad'st me flee
  The paths which thou couldst ne'er approve;
  And gently drew my soul to thee.
  With cords of sweet eternal love.

3 Now to thy footstool, Lord! I fly,
  And low in self-abasement fall;
  A vile, a helpless worm, I lie.
  And thou, my God! art all in all.

4 Dearer—far dearer—to my heart,
  Than all the joys that earth can give;
  From fame, from wealth, from friends I'd part,
  Beneath thy countenance to live.
                    Eleanor Tatlock, 1798.

RECONCILIATION.

ILLINOIS.   L. M.   *Jonathan Spilman,* 1835.

Je-sus, my All, to heaven is gone, He whom I fix my hopes up-on;
His track I see, and I'll pur-sue The nar-row way, till him I view.

349.   *Way to Canaan.*   (673.)

1 JESUS, my All, to heaven is gone,
 He whom I fix my hopes upon;
 His track I see, and I'll pursue
 The narrow way, till him I view.

2 The way the holy prophets went,
 The road that leads from banishment,
 The King's highway of holiness,
 I'll go; for all his paths are peace.

3 This is the way I long have sought,
 And mourned because I found it not;
 My grief, my burden long has been,
 Because I could not cease from sin.

4 The more I strove against its power,
 I sinned and stumbled but the more;
 Till late I heard my Saviour say,
 "Come hither, soul! I am the way."

5 Lo! glad I come! and thou, blest Lamb!
 Shalt take me to thee as I am;
 Nothing but sin I thee can give;
 Nothing but love shall I receive.

6 Then will I tell, to sinners round,
 What a dear Saviour I have found;
 I'll point to thy redeeming blood,
 And say -Behold the way to God!
            John Cennick, 1743, a.

350.   *The Voice of Mercy.*   (674.)

1 I HEAR a voice that comes from far;
 From Calvary it sounds abroad;
 It soothes my soul, and calms my fear;
 It speaks of pardon bought with blood.

2 And is it true, that many fly
 The sound that bids my soul rejoice;
 And rather choose with fools to die,
 Than turn an ear to mercy's voice?

3 Alas for those!—the day is near,
 When mercy will be heard no more;
 Then will they ask in vain to hear
 The voice, they would not hear before.

4 With such, I own, I once appeared,
 But now I know how great their loss;
 For sweeter sounds were never heard,
 Than mercy utters from the cross.

5 But let me not forget to own,
 That, if I differ aught from those,
 'T is due to sovereign grace alone,
 That oft selects its proudest foes.
            Thomas Kelly, 1809.

351. *Joy in Heaven for a repenting Sinner.* (675.)

1 WHO can describe the joys that rise,
 Through all the courts of paradise,
 To see a prodigal return,
 To see an heir of glory born?

2 With joy the Father doth approve
 The fruit of his eternal love;
 The Son with joy looks down, and sees
 The purchase of his agonies.

3 The Spirit takes delight to view
 The holy soul he formed anew;
 And saints and angels join to sing
 The growing empire of their King.
            Isaac Watts, 1709.

PARDON FOUND.

VALENTIA. (FLORENCE.) C. M.
Maximilian Eberwein, 1775–1831.
Adapted by George Kingsley, 1853.

Oh! gift of gifts! Oh! grace of faith! My God! how can it be
That thou, who hast dis-cern-ing love, Shouldst give that gift to me?

352. *The Grace of Faith.* (676.)

1 Oh! gift of gifts! Oh! grace of faith!
  My God! how can it be
That thou, who hast discerning love,
  Shouldst give that gift to me?

2 How many hearts thou mightst have had
  More innocent than mine!
How many souls more worthy far
  Of that sweet touch of thine!

3 Ah! grace! into unlikeliest hearts
  It is thy boast to come,
The glory of thy light to find
  In darkest spots a home.

4 The crowd of cares, the weightiest cross,
  Seem trifles less than light;
Earth looks so little, and so low,
  When faith shines full and bright.

5 Oh! happy, happy that I am!
  If thou canst be, O faith!
The treasure, that thou art in life,
  What wilt thou be in death?

6 Thy choice, O God of goodness! then
  I lovingly adore:
Oh! give me grace to keep thy grace,
  And grace t' inherit more.
  Frederick Wm. Faber, 1848.

353. *Lost and found.* (677.)

1 Amazing grace! how sweet the sound!
  That saved a wretch like me;
I once was lost, but now am found,
  Was blind, but now I see.

2 'T was grace that taught my heart to fear,
  And grace my fears relieved;
How precious did that grace appear,
  The hour I first believed!

3 Through many dangers, toils and snares,
  I have already come;
'T is grace has brought me safe thus far,
  And grace will lead me home.

4 Yes, when this flesh and heart shall fail,
  And mortal life shall cease,
I shall possess, within the veil,
  A life of joy and peace.

5 The earth shall soon dissolve like snow,
  The sun forbear to shine;
But God, who called me here below,
  Will be for ever mine.
  John Newton, 1779.

354. *Self-Denial for Christ.* (678.)

1 And must I part with all I have,
  My dearest Lord! for thee?
It is but right, since thou hast done
  Much more than this for me.

2 Yes, let it go; one look from thee
  Will more than make amends
For all the losses, I sustain,
  Of credit, riches, friends.

3 Ten thousand worlds, ten thousand lives,
  How worthless they appear,
Compared with thee, supremely good,
  Divinely bright and fair!
  Benjamin Beddome, 1787.

RECONCILIATION.

MORAVIAN. C. M. 8 LINES. German.

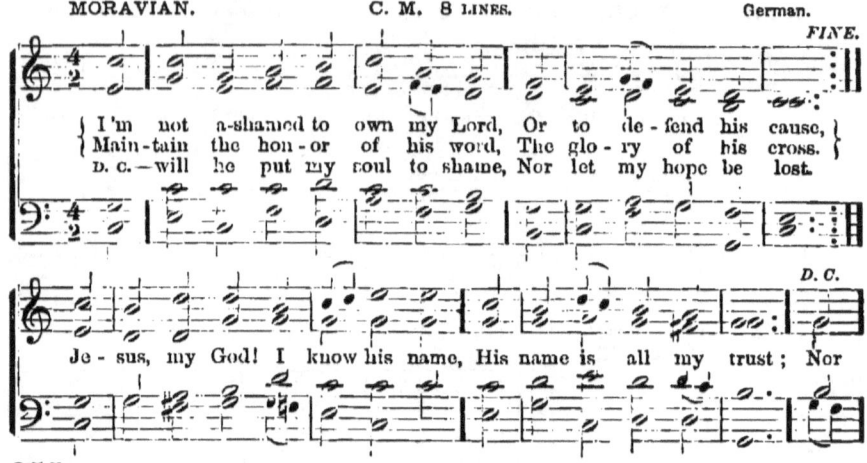

I'm not a-shamed to own my Lord, Or to de-fend his cause;
Main-tain the hon-or of his word, The glo-ry of his cross.
D. C.—will he put my soul to shame, Nor let my hope be lost.

Je-sus, my God! I know his name, His name is all my trust; Nor

355. *Not ashamed of Christ.* (382.)

1 I'M not ashamed to own my Lord,
Or to defend his cause.
Maintain the honor of his word,
The glory of his cross.

2 Jesus, my God!—I know his name,
His name is all my trust;
Nor will he put my soul to shame,
Nor let my hope be lost.

3 Firm as his throne his promise stands,
And he can well secure
What I've committed to his hands,
Till the decisive hour.

4 Then will he own my worthless name,
Before his Father's face,
And, in the new Jerusalem,
Appoint my soul a place.
Isaac Watts, 1709.

356. PSALM 126. (383.)

1 WHEN God revealed his gracious name,
And changed my mournful state,
My rapture seemed a pleasing dream,
The grace appeared so great.

2 The world beheld the glorious change,
And did thy hand confess;
My tongue broke out in unknown strains,
And sung surprising grace.

3 "Great is the work!"— my neighbors
And owned the power divine; [cried,
"Great is the work!"— my heart re-
"And be the glory thine." [plied,—

4 The Lord can clear the darkest skies,
Can give us day for night;
Make drops of sacred sorrow rise
To rivers of delight.

5 Let those, that sow in sadness, wait
Till the fair harvest come;
They shall confess their sheaves are great,
And shout the blessings home.

6 Though seed lie buried long in dust,
It sha'n't deceive their hope;
The precious grain can ne'er be lost,
For grace insures the crop.
Isaac Watts, 1719.

357. *Joy over the Penitent.* (684.)

1 OH! how divine, how sweet the joy,
When but one sinner turns,
And, with an humble, broken heart,
His sins and errors mourns!

2 Pleased with the news, the saints below,
In songs, their tongues employ;
Beyond the skies the tidings go,
And heaven is filled with joy.

3 Well-pleased, the Father sees, and hears
The conscious sinner's moan;
Jesus receives him in his arms,
And claims him for his own.

4 Nor angels can their joys contain,
But kindle with new fire:
"The sinner lost is found!" they sing,
And strike the sounding lyre.
John Needham, 1768. a.

PARDON FOUND.

BETHLEHEM. C. M. *Spencer Madan, d. 1813.*

A-wake, my heart! a-rise, my tongue! Prepare a tune-ful voice; Pre-pare a tune-ful voice; In God, the life of all my joys. A-loud will I re-joice.

358. *The Robe of Righteousness.* (688.)

1 Awake, my heart! arise, my tongue!
  Prepare a tuneful voice;
  In God, the life of all my joys,
  Aloud will I rejoice.

2 'T is he adorned my naked soul,
  And made salvation mine;
  Upon a poor polluted worm,
  He makes his graces shine.

3 And, lest the shadow of a spot
  Should on my soul be found,
  He took the robe the Saviour wrought,
  And cast it all around.

4 How far the heavenly robe exceeds
  What earthly princes wear!
  These ornaments, how bright they shine!
  How white the garments are!

5 Strangely, my soul! art thou arrayed
  By the great sacred Three!
  In sweetest harmony of praise,
  Let all thy powers agree.
  Isaac Watts, 1707.

359. *Redemption and Protection.* (689.)

1 Arise, my soul! my joyful powers!
  And triumph in my God;
  Awake my voice! and loud proclaim
  His glorious grace abroad.

2 He raised me from the deeps of sin,
  The gates of gaping hell;
  And fixed my standing more secure,
  Than 't was before I fell.

3 The arms of everlasting love,
  Beneath my soul he placed;
  And on the rock of ages set
  My slippery footsteps fast.

4 The city of my blessed abode
  Is walled around with grace;
  Salvation for a bulwark stands,
  To shield the sacred place.

5 Arise, my soul! awake, my voice!
  And tunes of pleasure sing;
  Loud hallelujahs shall address
  My Saviour and my King.
  Isaac Watts, 1707.

360. *The Pearl of great Price.* (690.)

1 Ye glittering toys of earth! adieu;
  A nobler choice be mine;
  A real prize attracts my view,
  A treasure all divine.

2 Begone, unworthy of my cares,
  Ye flattering baits of sense!
  Inestimable worth appears,—
  The pearl of price immense.

3 Jesus, to multitudes unknown,—
  Oh! name, divinely sweet!—
  Jesus! in thee, in thee alone,
  Wealth, honor, pleasure meet.

4 Should earth's vain treasures all depart,
  Of this dear gift possessed,
  I'd clasp it to my joyful heart,
  And be for ever blessed.
  Anne Steele, 1760.

RECONCILIATION.

BETHESDA. H. M. *Maurice Greene*, d. 1755.

Come, my fond fluttering heart! Come, struggle to be free;
Thou and the world must part, However hard it be:
My trembling spi-rit owns it just, But cleaves yet clo-ser to the dust.

361.   *Renouncing the World.*   (691.)

1 COME, my fond fluttering heart!
  Come, struggle to be free;
Thou and the world must part,
  However hard it be:
My trembling spirit owns it just,
But cleaves yet closer to the dust.

2 Ye tempting sweets! forbear;
  Ye dearest idols! fall;
My love ye must not share,
  Jesus shall have it all:
'T is bitter pain,—'t is cruel smart,—
But, Oh! thou must consent, my heart!

3 Ye fair enchanting throng!
  Ye golden dreams! farewell!
Earth has prevailed too long,
  And now I break the spell:
Farewell, ye joys of early years!—
Jesus! forgive these parting tears.

4 In Gilead there is balm,
  A kind Physician there,
My fevered mind to calm,
  To bid me not despair:
Dear Saviour! help me, set me free,,
And I will all resign to thee.

5 Oh! may I feel thy worth,
  And let no idol dare,—
No vanity of earth,
  With thee, my Lord! compare:
Now bid all worldly joys depart,
And reign supremely in my heart.

  Jane Taylor, 1812, a.

362.   *Intercession and Pardon.*   (692.)

1 ARISE, my soul! arise;
  Shake off thy guilty fears;
The bleeding Sacrifice
  In my behalf appears:
Before the throne my Surety stands,
My name is written on his hands.

2 He ever lives above,
  For me to intercede;
His all-redeeming love,
  His precious blood, to plead;
His blood atoned for all our race,
And sprinkles now the throne of grace.

3 Five bleeding wounds he bears,
  Received on Calváry;
They pour effectual prayers,
  They strongly plead for me:
"Forgive him, Oh! forgive," they cry,
"Nor let that ransom'd sinner die."

4 The Father hears him pray,
  His dear anointed One:
He cannot turn away
  The presence of his Son:
His Spirit answers to the blood,
And tells me, I am born of God.

5 My God is reconciled;
  His pardoning voice I hear;
He owns me for his child;
  I can no longer fear:
With confidence I now draw nigh,
And "Father, Abba, Father!" cry.

  Charles Wesley, 1742.

THE LORD'S SUPPER. 131

ROCK OF AGES. (TOPLADY.) 7s. 6 LINES.   Thomas Hastings, 1830.

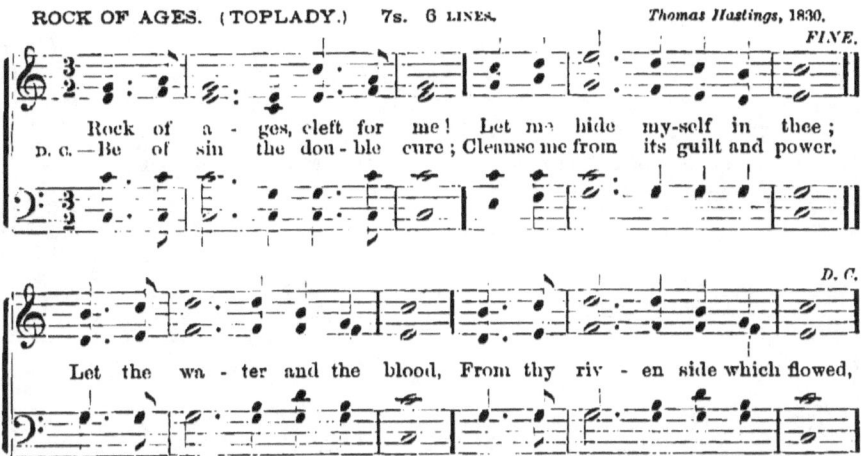

Rock of a-ges, cleft for me! Let me hide my-self in thee;
D. C.—Be of sin the dou-ble cure; Cleanse me from its guilt and power.

Let the wa-ter and the blood, From thy riv-en side which flowed,

363.   *The Rock of Ages.*   (697.)

1 Rock of ages, cleft for me!
Let me hide myself in thee;
Let the water and the blood,
From thy riven side which flowed,
Be of sin the double cure;
Cleanse me from its guilt and power.

2 Not the labors of my hands
Can fulfill the law's demands;
Could my zeal no respite know,
Could my tears for ever flow,
All for sin could not atone;
Thou must save, and thou alone.

3 Nothing in my hand I bring;
Simply to thy cross I cling;
Naked, come to thee for dress,
Helpless, look to thee for grace;
Foul, I to the fountain fly,
Wash me, Saviour! or I die.

4 Whilst I draw this fleeting breath,
When my eye-lids close in death,
When I soar to worlds unknown,
See thee on thy judgment throne,
Rock of ages, cleft for me!
Let me hide myself in thee.
     Augustus M. Toplady, 1776.

364.   *The living Food.*   (698.)

1 Bread of heaven! on thee I feed,
For thy flesh is meat, indeed;
Ever may my soul be fed
With this true and living Bread;
Day by day, with strength supplied,
Through the life of him who died.

2 Vine of heaven! thy blood supplies
This blest cup of sacrifice;
'T is thy wounds my healing give;
To thy cross I look, and live;
Thou, my Life! Oh! let me be
Rooted, grafted, built on thee.
     Josiah Conder, 1824.

365.   *Jesus only.*   (699.)

1 Blessed Saviour! thee I love,
All my other joys above:
All my hopes in thee abide,
Thou my Hope, and naught beside:
Ever let my glory be,
Only, only, only thee.

2 Once again beside the cross,
All my gain I count but loss;
Earthly pleasures fade away,—
Clouds they are that hide my day;
Hence, vain shadows! let me see
Jesus crucified for me.

3 Blessed Saviour! thine am I,
Thine to live, and thine to die;
Height, or depth, or creature power,
Ne'er shall hide my Saviour more;
Ever shall my glory be,
Only, only, only thee.
     George Duffield, 1850.

COMMEMORATION.

NETTLETON. 8s & 7s. 6 or 8 LINES. *Asahel Nettleton, 1825.*

Come, thou Fount of ev-ery bless-ing! Tune my heart to sing thy grace;
Streams of mer-cy nev-er ceas-ing, Call for songs of loud-est praise;
D. C.—Praise the mount; I'm fixed up-on it, Mount of God's un-chang-ing love.

Teach me some me-lo-dious son-net. Sung by flam-ing tongues a-bove;

---

366. *A Memorial of Praise.* (710.)

1 Come, thou Fount of every blessing!
Tune my heart to sing thy grace;
Streams of mercy, never ceasing,
Call for songs of loudest praise;
Teach me some melodious sonnet,
Sung by flaming tongues above;
Praise the mount; I'm fixed upon it,
Mount of God's unchanging love.

2 Here I raise my Eben-Ezer;
Hither by thy help I'm come;
And I hope, by thy good pleasure,
Safely to arrive at home;
Jesus sought me when a stranger,
Wandering from the fold of God;
He, to rescue me from danger,
Interposed with precious blood.

3 Oh! to grace how great a debtor,
Daily I'm constrained to be!
Let that grace now, like a fetter,
Bind my wandering heart to thee;
Prone to wander, —Lord! I feel it;
Prone to leave the God I love;
Here's my heart; Oh! take and seal it;
Seal it from thy courts above.
Robert Robinson, 1758.

367. *Remembrance of Christ.* (714.)

1 Jesus spreads his banner o'er us,
Cheers our famished souls with food;
He the banquet spreads before us,
Of his mystic flesh and blood;
Precious banquet; bread of heaven;
Wine of gladness, flowing free;—
May we taste it, kindly given,
In remembrance, Lord! of thee.

2 In thy holy incarnation,
When the angels sang thy birth;
In thy fasting and temptation;
In thy labors on the earth;
In thy trial, and rejection;
In thy sufferings on the tree;
In thy glorious resurrection;
May we, Lord! remember thee.
Roswell Park, 1836.

368. *Christ seen at his Table.* (715.)

1 While, in sweet communion, feeding
On this earthly bread and wine,
Saviour! may we see thee bleeding
On the cross, to make us thine:
Now, our eyes for ever closing
To this fleeting world below;
On thy gentle breast reposing,
Teach us, Lord! thy grace to know.

2 Though unseen, be ever near us,
With the still small voice of love;
Whispering words of peace to cheer us,
Every doubt and fear remove;
Bring before us all the glory
Of thy life, and death of woe;
And, with hopes of endless glory,
Wean our hearts from all below.
Edward Denny, 1839.

THE LORD'S SUPPER.

RATHBUN. 8s & 7s. Ithamar Conkey, 1851.

In the cross of Christ I glory, Towering o'er the wrecks of time;
All the light of sacred story Gathers round its head sublime.

369. *Glorying in the Cross.* (710.)

1 IN THE cross of Christ I glory,
  Towering o'er the wrecks of time ;
  All the light of sacred story
  Gathers round its head sublime.

2 When the woes of life o'ertake me,
  Hopes deceive, and fears annoy,
  Never shall the cross forsake me :
  Lo ! it glows with peace and joy.

3 When the sun of bliss is beaming
  Light and love upon my way,
  From the cross the radiance, streaming,
  Adds more lustre to the day.

4 Bane and blessing, pain and pleasure,
  By the cross are sanctified ;
  Peace is there, that knows no measure,
  Joys that through all time abide.

5 In the cross of Christ I glory,
  Towering o'er the wrecks of time ;
  All the light of sacred story
  Gathers round its head sublime.
                          John Bowring, 1825.

370. *The Threefold Love.* (712.)

1 SEE, Oh ! see, what love the Father
  Hath bestowed upon our race!
  How he bends, with sweet compassion,
  Over us his beaming face !
  See how he his best and dearest,
  For the very worst, hath given,—
  His own Son for us poor sinners ;
  See, Oh! see the love of heaven !

2 See, Oh ! see, what love the Saviour,
  Also, hath on us bestowed !
  How he bled for us and suffered,
  How he bore the heavy load !
  On the cross and in the garden,
  Oh ! how sore was his distress !
  Is not this a love, that passeth
  Aught that tongue can e'er express ?

3 See, Oh ! see, what love is shown us,
  Also, by the Holy Ghost !
  How he strives with us, poor sinners,
  Even when we sin the most,
  Teaching, comforting, correcting,
  Where he sees it needful is !
  Oh ! what heart would not be thankful
  For a threefold love like this !
                  Ger., *Carl J. P. Spitta*, 1833.
                  Tr., *Richard Massie*, 1859.

371. *The Close of the Feast.* (718.)

1 FROM the table now retiring,
  Which for us the Lord hath spread,
  May our souls, refreshment finding,
  Grow, in all things, like our Head !

2 His example by beholding,
  May our lives his image bear ;
  Him our Lord and Master calling,
  His commands may we revere.

3 Love to God and man displaying,
  Walking steadfast in his way.
  Joy attend us in believing,
  Peace from God, through endless day.
                              Anon., 1812.

COMMEMORATION.

DETROIT. S. M. Eurotas P. Hastings, 1846.

Did Christ o'er sinners weep? And shall our cheeks be dry?
Let floods of penitential grief Burst forth from every eye.

372. *Repentance at the Cross.* (706.)

1 Did Christ o'er sinners weep?
   And shall our cheeks be dry?
Let floods of penitential grief
   Burst forth from every eye.

2 The Son of God in tears
   The wondering angels see!
Be thou astonished, O my soul!
   He shed those tears for thee.

3 He wept, that we might weep;—
   Each sin demands a tear;—
In heaven alone no sin is found,
   There is no weeping there.
                Benjamin Beddome, 1787.

373. *Salvation by Grace.* (703.)

1 Grace!—'t is a charming sound,
   Harmonious to mine ear;
Heaven with the echo shall resound,
   And all the earth shall hear.

2 Grace first contrived a way
   To save rebellious man;
And all the steps that grace display,
   Which drew the wondrous plan.

3 Grace led my wandering feet
   To tread the heavenly road;
And new supplies each hour I meet,
   While pressing on to God.

4 Grace all the work shall crown,
   Through everlasting days;
It lays in heaven the topmost stone,
   And well deserves the praise.
                Philip Doddridge, 1740.

374. *The Feast of Love.* (708.)

1 Sweet feast of love divine!
   'T is grace, that makes us free
To feed upon this bread and wine,
   In memory, Lord! of thee.

2 That blood, that flowed for sin,
   In symbol here we see,
And feel the blessed pledge within,
   That we are loved of thee.

3 Oh! if this glimpse of love
   Is so divinely sweet,
What will it be, O Lord! above,
   Thy gladdening smile to meet?—

4 To see thee face to face,
   Thy perfect likeness wear,
And all thy ways of wondrous grace
   Through endless years declare!
                Edward Denny, 1839.

375. *The Living Bread.* (709.)

1 Thee, King of saints! we praise
   For this, our living bread;
Nourished by thy preserving grace,
   And at thy table fed.

2 Yet still a higher seat
   We in thy kingdom claim,
Who here begin, by faith, to eat
   The supper of the Lamb.

3 That glorious, heavenly prize
   We surely shall attain,
And, in the palace of the skies,
   With thee for ever reign.
                Charles Wesley, 1745.

THE LORD'S SUPPER. 135

HEBRON.   **L. M.**   *Lowell Mason, 1830.*

My gra-cious Lord! I own thy right, To ev-ery ser-vice I can pay,
And call it my su-preme de-light, To hear thy dic-tates and o - bey.

376.   *Living to Christ alone.*   (725.)

1 MY GRACIOUS Lord! I own thy right
To every service I can pay,
And call it my supreme delight,
To hear thy dictates and obey.

2 What is my being, but for thee,
Its sure support, its noblest end?
Thine ever-smiling face to see,
And serve the cause of such a Friend.

3 I would not breathe for worldly joy,
Or to increase my worldly good;
Nor future days or powers employ,
To spread a sounding name abroad.

4 'T is to my Saviour I would live,
To him, who for my ransom died;
Nor could untainted Eden give
Such bliss as blossoms at his side.

5 His work my hoary age shall bless,
When youthful vigor is no more;
And my last hour of life confess
His love hath animating power.
                       Philip Doddridge, 1740.

377.   *Showing forth Christ's Death.*   (726.)

1 O JESUS! bruised and wounded more
Than bursted grape, or bread of wheat,
The Life of life within our souls,
The Cup of our salvation sweet;

2 We come to show thy dying hour,
Thy streaming vein, thy broken flesh;
And still the blood is warm to save,
And still the fragrant wounds are fresh.

3 O Heart! that, with a double tide
Of blood and water maketh pure;
O Flesh! once offered on the cross,
The gift that makes our pardon sure;

4 Let never more our sinful souls
The anguish of thy cross renew;
Nor forge again the cruel nails,
That pierced thy victim body through.
                       Mrs. Cecil F. Alexander, 1859.

378.   *Communion with Christ at his Table.*   (727.)

1 To JESUS, our exalted Lord,—
Dear name, by heaven and earth adored!
Fain would our hearts and voices raise
A cheerful song of sacred praise.

2 But all the notes which mortals know
Are weak, and languishing, and low;
Far, far above our humble songs,
The theme demands immortal tongues.

3 Yet, while around his board we meet,
And worship at his glorious feet,
Oh! let our warm affections move,
In glad returns of grateful love.

4 Let faith our feeble senses aid,
To see thy wondrous love displayed,—
Thy broken flesh, thy bleeding veins,
Thy dreadful agonizing pains.

5 Let humble, penitential woe,
With painful, pleasing anguish, flow;
And thy forgiving smiles impart
Life, hope, and joy to every heart.
                       Anne Steele, 1760.

COMMEMORATION.

WINDHAM.   L. M.   *Daniel Read, 1785.*

'T was on that dark, that dole-ful night, When powers of earth and hell a-rose A-gainst the Son of God's de-light, And friends betrayed him to his foes.

379.   *The Lord's Supper instituted.*   (722.)

1 'T was on that dark, that doleful night,
When powers of earth and hell arose
Against the Son of God's delight,
And friends betrayed him to his foes:

2 Before the mournful scene began, [brake:
He took the bread, and blessed, and
What love through all his actions ran!
What wondrous words of grace he spake!

3 "This is my body, broke for sin;
Receive and eat the living food:"—
Then took the cup, and blessed the wine,
"'T is the new covenant in my blood."

4 "Do this," he cried, "till time shall end,
In mem'ry of your dying Friend;
Meet, at my table, and record
The love of your departed Lord."

5 Jesus! thy feast we celebrate;
We show thy death, we sing thy name,
Till thou return, and we shall eat
The marriage supper of the Lamb.
                 Isaac Watts, 1707.

380.   *The good Shepherd.*   (723.)

1 THOU! whom my soul admires, above
All earthly joy, and earthly love,—
Tell me, dear Shepherd! let me know,
Where doth thy sweetest pasture grow?

2 Where is the shadow of that rock,
That from the sun defends thy flock?
Fain would I feed among thy sheep,—
Among them rest, among them sleep.

3 Why should thy bride appear, like one
That turns aside to paths unknown?
My constant feet would never rove,—
Would never seek another love.

4 The footsteps of thy flock I see;
Thy sweetest pastures here they be;
A wondrous feast thy love prepares,
Bought with thy wounds, and groans, and tears.

5 His dearest flesh he makes my food,
And bids me drink his richest blood:
Here to these hills my soul will come,
Till my belovéd leads me home.
                 Isaac Watts, 1707.

381.   *Not ashamed of Christ.*   (719.)

1 AT THY command, our dearest Lord!
Here we attend thy dying feast;
Thy blood, like wine, adorns thy board,
And thine own flesh feeds every guest.

2 Our faith adores thy bleeding love,
And trusts for life in one that died;
We hope for heavenly crowns above,
From a Redeemer crucified.

3 Let the vain world pronounce it shame,
And fling their scandals on thy cause;
We come to boast our Saviour's name,
And make our triumphs in his cross.

4 With joy we tell the scoffing age,
He that was dead has left his tomb;
He lives above their utmost rage,
And we are waiting till he come.
                 Isaac Watts, 1707.

THE LORD'S SUPPER.

382. *The Day of Espousals.* (728.)

1 Jesus, thou everlasting King!
 Accept the tribute which we bring;
 Accept the well-deserved renown,
 And wear our praises as thy crown.

2 Let every act of worship be,
 Like our espousals, Lord! to thee;—
 Like the dear hour, when, from above,
 We first received thy pledge of love.

3 The gladness of that happy day,—
 Our hearts would wish it long to stay;
 Nor let our faith forsake its hold,
 Nor comfort sink, nor love grow cold.

4 Each foll'wing minute as it flies,
 Increase thy praise, improve our joys;
 Till we are raised to sing thy name,
 At the great supper of the Lamb.
 Isaac Watts, 1707.

383. *"Jesu, Dulcedo Cordium!"* (729.)

1 Jesus, thou Joy of loving hearts!
 Thou Fount of life! thou Light of men!
 From the best bliss that earth imparts,
 We turn unfilled to thee again.

2 Thy truth unchanged hath ever stood;
 Thou savest those that on thee call;
 To them that seek thee, thou art good,
 To them that find thee,—All in all!

3 We taste thee, O thou living Bread!
 And long to feast upon thee still;
 We drink of thee, the Fountain Head,
 And thirst, our souls from thee to fill.

4 Our restless spirits yearn for thee,
 Where'er our changeful lot is cast;
 Glad, when thy gracious smile we see,
 Blest, when our faith can hold thee fast.

5 O Jesus! ever with us stay;
 Make all our moments calm and bright;
 Chase the dark night of sin away;
 Shed o'er the world thy holy light.
 Lat., Bernard, of Clairvaux, 1140.
 Tr., Ray Palmer, 1833.

384. *"Jesu! dulcis Memoria."* (730.)

1 Jesus! how sweet thy mem'ry is!
 Thinking of thee is truest bliss;
 Beyond all honeyed sweets below
 Thy presence is it here to know.

2 Tongue cannot speak a lovelier word,
 Naught more melodious can be heard,
 Naught sweeter can be thought upon,
 Than Jesus Christ, God's only Son.

3 Jesus! thou Hope of those who turn,
 Gentle to those who pray and mourn,
 Ever to those who seek thee, kind,—
 What must thou be to those who find?

4 Jesus! thou dost true pleasures bring,
 Light of the heart, and living Spring!
 Higher than highest pleasures roll,
 Or warmest wishes of the soul.

5 Lord! in our bosoms ever dwell,
 And of our souls the night dispel;
 Pour on our inmost mind the ray;
 And fill our earth with blissful day.
 Lat., Bernard, of Clairvaux, 1140.
 Tr., James W. Alexander, 1859.

COMMEMORATION.

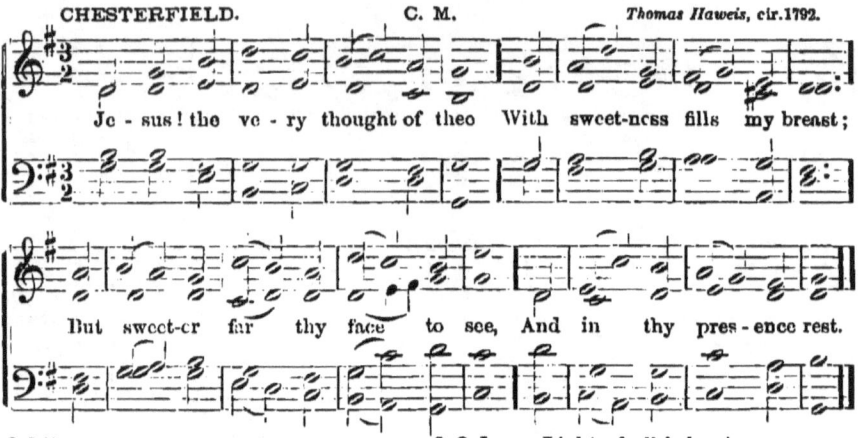

CHESTERFIELD. C. M.   *Thomas Haweis, cir.1792.*

Jesus! the very thought of thee With sweetness fills my breast;
But sweeter far thy face to see, And in thy presence rest.

385.   *"Jesu! dulcis Memoria."*   (731.)

1 JESUS! the very thought of thee
With sweetness fills my breast;
But sweeter far thy face to see,
And in thy presence rest.

2 Nor voice can sing, nor heart can frame,
Nor can the memory find,
A sweeter sound than thy blest name,
O Saviour of mankind!

3 O Hope of every contrite heart!
O Joy of all the meek!
To those who fall, how kind thou art!
How good to those who seek!

4 But what to those who find? Ah! this
Nor tongue nor pen can show:
The love of Jesus,—what it is,
None but his loved ones know.

5 Jesus! our only joy be thou!
As thou our prize wilt be;
Jesus! be thou our glory now,
And through eternity!
     Lat., *Bernard, of Clairvaux*, 1140.
        Tr., *Edward Caswall*, 1849.

386.   *"Jesu, Rex admirabilis!"*   (732.)

1 O JESUS! King most wonderful,
Thou Conqueror renowned;
Thou sweetness most ineffable,
In whom all joys are found!

2 When once thou visitest the heart,
Then truth begins to shine;
Then earthly vanities depart;
Then kindles love divine.

3 O Jesus, Light of all below!
Thou Fount of life and fire!
Surpassing all the joys we know,
All that we can desire,—

4 May every heart confess thy name,
And ever thee adore;
And, seeking thee, itself inflame
To seek thee more and more.

5 Thee may our tongues for ever bless;
Thee may we love alone;
And ever in our lives express
The image of thine own.
     Lat., *Bernard, of Clairvaux*, 1140.
        Tr., *Edward Caswall*, 1849.

387.   *"Jesu, Decus angelicum!"*   (733.)

1 O JESUS! thou the Beauty art,
Of angel worlds above;
Thy name is music to the heart,
Enchanting it with love.

2 O my sweet Jesus! hear the sighs
Which unto thee I send;
To thee mine inmost spirit cries,
My being's Hope and End.

3 Stay with us, Lord! and with thy light
Illume the soul's abyss;
Scatter the darkness of our night,
And fill the world with bliss.

4 O Jesus, spotless Virgin-Flower!
Our life and joy! to thee
Be praise, beatitude and power,
Through all eternity!
     Lat., *Bernard, of Clairvaux*, 1140.
        Tr., *Edward Caswall*, 1849.

THE LORD'S SUPPER. 139

MESSIAH. (BRADFORD.)   C. M.   *George Frederick Händel, 1741.*

How sweet and aw-ful is the place, With Christ with-in the doors,

While ev-er-last-ing love dis-plays The choic-est of her stores!

388.   *The Feast of divine Love.*   (734.)

1 How sweet and awful is the place,
With Christ within the doors,
While everlasting love displays
The choicest of her stores!

2 While all our hearts, and all our songs,
Join to admire the feast;
Each of us cry, with thankful tongues,—
"Lord! why was I a guest?"

3 "Why was I made to hear thy voice,
And enter while there 's room,
When thousands make a wretched choice,
And rather starve than come?"

4 'T was the same love that spread the feast,
That sweetly forced us in ;
Else we had still refused to taste,
And perished in our sin.

5 Pity the nations, O our God!
Constrain the earth to come;
Send thy victorious word abroad,
And bring the strangers home.

6 We long to see thy churches full,
That all the chosen race
May, with one voice, and heart, and soul,
Sing thy redeeming grace.
                             Isaac Watts, 1707.

389.   *The new Covenant sealed.*   (735.)

1 "The promise of my Father's love
Shall stand for ever good!"—
He said, and gave his soul to death,
And sealed the grace with blood.

2 To this dear covenant of thy word,
I set my worthless name;
I seal th' engagement to my Lord,
And make my humble claim.

3 Thy light, and strength, and pard'ning
And glory shall be mine;   [grace,
My life and soul, my heart and flesh,
And all my powers are thine.

4 I call that legacy my own,
Which Jesus did bequeath;
'T was purchased with a dying groan,
And ratified in death.

5 Sweet is the mem'ry of his name,
Who blessed us in his will,
And, to his testament of love,
Made his own life the seal.
                             Isaac Watts, 1707.

390.   *Christ, our Righteousness.*   (745.)

1 For ever here my rest shall be,
Close to thy bleeding side;
This all my hope, and all my plea,—
For me the Saviour died.

2 My dying Saviour, and my God!
Fountain for guilt and sin!
Sprinkle me ever with thy blood!
And cleanse and keep me clean.

3 Th' atonement of thy blood apply,
Till faith to sight improve,
Till hope shall in fruition die,
And all my soul be love.
                            Charles Wesley, 1740.

COMMEMORATION.

SWANWICK. C. M. J. Lucas, 17—.

Here at thy ta-ble, Lord! we meet, To feed on food di-vine; Thy bo-dy is the bread we eat, Thy pre-cious blood the wine, Thy pre-cious blood the wine.

391. *The Body and Blood of Christ.* (737.)

1 Here at thy table, Lord! we meet,
   To feed on food divine;
Thy body is the bread we eat,
   Thy precious blood the wine.

2 He, that prepares this rich repast,
   Himself comes down, and dies;
And then invites us thus to feast
   Upon the sacrifice.

3 Sure, there was never love so free,
   Dear Saviour! so divine;
Well thou may'st claim that heart of me,
   Which owes so much to thine.

4 Yes, thou shalt surely have my heart,
   My soul, my strength, my all;
With life itself I'll freely part,
   My Jesus! at thy call.
                    Samuel Stennett, 1787.

392. *Love unto Death.* (738.)

1 How condescending and how kind,
   Was God's eternal Son!
Our misery reached his heavenly mind,
   And pity brought him down.

2 When justice, by our sins provoked,
   Drew forth its dreadful sword,
He gave his soul up to the stroke,
   Without a murm'ring word.

3 He sunk beneath our heavy woes,
   To raise us to his throne;
There's ne'er a gift his hand bestows,
   But cost his heart a groan.

4 This was compassion, like a God,
   That, when the Saviour knew—
The price of pardon was his blood,
   His pity ne'er withdrew.

5 Now, though he reigns exalted high,
   His love is still as great;
Well he remembers Calvary,
   Nor lets his saints forget.

6 Here, let our hearts begin to melt,
   While we his death record,
And, with our joy for pardoned guilt,
   Mourn that we pierced the Lord.
                    Isaac Watts, 1707.

393. *Remembering Christ.* (739.)

1 If human kindness meets return,
   And owns the grateful tie;
If tender thoughts within us burn,
   To feel a friend is nigh;—

2 Oh! shall not warmer accents tell
   The gratitude we owe
To him, who died, our fears to quell—
   Our more than orphan's woe?

3 While yet his anguished soul surveyed
   Those pangs he would not flee,
What love his latest words displayed,—
   "Meet, and rememb'r me!"

4 Remember thee!—thy death, thy shame,
   Our sinful hearts to share!—
O mem'ry! leave no other name
   But his recorded there.
                    Gerard T. Noel, 1813.

THE LORD'S SUPPER

CHESTER. C. M. *Thomas Hastings*, 1828.

Come, let us lift our voices high, High as our joys a-rise, And join the songs a-bove the sky, Where pleas-ure nev-er dies, Where pleas-ure nev-er dies.

394. *The triumphal Feast.* (740.)

1 Come, let us lift our voices high,
 High as our joys arise,
 And join the songs above the sky,
 Where pleasure never dies.

2 Jesus, the Lord, that bled and died,
 And conquered when he fell;
 That rose again, and reigns supreme
 O'er heaven, and earth, and hell;

3 Jesus, the Lord, invites us here,
 To his triumphal feast;
 And brings immortal blessings down
 For each redeemed guest.

4 Victorious Lord! what can we pay
 For favors so divine?
 We would devote our hearts away,
 To be for ever thine.

5 We give thee, Lord! our highest praise—
 The tribute of our tongues;
 But themes, so infinite as these,
 Exceed our noblest songs.
  Isaac Watts, 1707, a.

395. *The peerless Name.* (747.)

1 Jesus! the name I love so well,
 The name I love to hear!
 No saint on earth his worth can tell,
 No heart conceive how dear.

2 It bids my trembling soul rejoice,
 And dries each rising tear;
 It tells me, in a still small voice,
 To trust and not to fear.

3 This name shall shed its fragrance still
 Along the thorny road;
 Shall sweetly smooth the rugged hill,
 That leads me up to God.

4 And there with all the blood-bought
 From sin and sorrow free, [throng,
 I'll sing the new eternal song
 Of Jesus' love to me.
  Frederick Whitfield, 1859.

396. *Lasting Remembrance of Christ.* (748.)

1 Jesus! thy love shall we forget,
 And never bring to mind
 The grace, that paid our hopeless debt,
 And bade us pardon find?

2 Shall we thy life of grief forget,
 Thy fasting and thy prayer;
 Thy locks with mountain vapors wet,
 To save us from despair?

3 Gethsemane can we forget,—
 Thy struggling agony,
 When night lay dark on Olivet,
 And none to watch with thee?

4 Life's brightest joys we may forget,
 Our kindred cease to love;
 But he, who paid our hopeless debt,
 Our constancy shall prove.

5 Our sorrows and our sins were laid,
 On thee, alone on thee:
 Thy precious blood our ransom paid—
 Thine all the glory be!
  William Mitchell, 1831.

ASPIRATION.

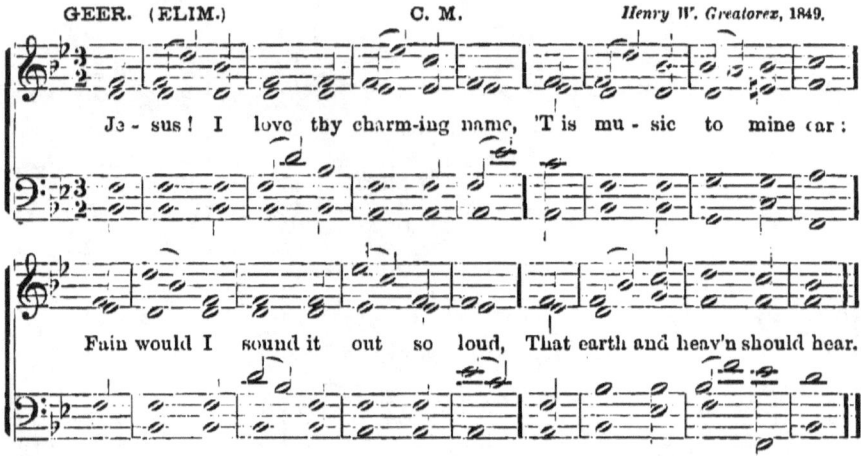

GEER. (ELIM.) C. M. Henry W. Greatorex, 1849.

Jesus! I love thy charming name, 'T is music to mine ear;
Fain would I sound it out so loud, That earth and heav'n should hear.

397. *Christ precious.* (749.)

1 Jesus! I love thy charming name,
'T is music to mine ear ;
Fain would I sound it out so loud,
That earth and heaven should hear.

2 Yes, thou art precious to my soul,
My Transport and my Trust ;
Jewels to thee are gaudy toys,
And gold is sordid dust.

3 All my capacious powers can wish
In thee doth richly meet :
Nor to mine eyes is life so dear,
Nor friendship half so sweet.

4 Thy grace still dwells upon my heart,
And sheds its fragrance there ;
The noblest balm of all its wounds,
The cordial of its care.

5 I 'll speak the honors of thy name,
With my last lab'ring breath ;
Then, speechless, clasp thee in mine arms,
The antidote of death.
Philip Doddridge, 1740.

398. *The Name of Jesus.* (746.)

1 How sweet the name of Jesus sounds,
In a believer's ear !
It soothes his sorrows, heals his wounds,
And drives away his fear.

2 It makes the wounded spirit whole,
And calms the troubled breast ;
'T is manna to the hungry soul,
And, to the weary, rest.

3 Jesus !—my Shepherd, Husband, Friend !
My Prophet, Priest, and King !
My Lord, my Life, my Way, my End !
Accept the praise I bring.

4 Weak is the effort of my heart,
And cold my warmest thought ;
But, when I see thee as thou art,
I 'll praise thee as I ought.

5 Till then, I would thy love proclaim,
With every fleeting breath ;
And may the music of thy name
Refresh my soul in death.
John Newton, 1779.

399. *The dearest Name.* (751.)

1 There is a name I love to hear,
I love to sing its worth ;
It sounds like music in mine ear,
The sweetest name on earth.

2 It tells me of a Saviour's love,
Who died to set me free :
It tells me of his precious blood,
The sinner's perfect plea.

3 It tells me what my Father hath
In store for every day,
And, though I tread a darksome path,
Yields sunshine all the way.

4 It tells of One, whose loving heart
Can feel my deepest woe,
Who in each sorrow bears a part,
That none can bear below.
Frederick Whitfield, 1859.

LOVE. 143

MONSON. C. M. Samuel R. Brown. Arr. Thomas Hastings, 1836.

Je-sus! these eyes have nev-er seen That ra-diant form of thine;
The veil of sense hangs dark be-tween Thy bless-ed face and mine.

400. *Love to the unseen Jesus.* (732.)

1 JESUS! these eyes have never seen
That radiant form of thine;
The veil of sense hangs dark between
Thy blessèd face and mine.

2 I see thee not, I hear thee not,
Yet art thou oft with me;
And earth hath ne'er so dear a spot,
As where I meet with thee.

3 Like some bright dream that comes un-
When slumbers o'er me roll, [sought
Thine image ever fills my thought,
And charms my ravished soul.

4 Yet, though I have not seen, and still
Must rest in faith alone,
I love thee, dearest Lord!—and will,
Unseen, but not unknown.

5 When death these mortal eyes shall seal,
And still this throbbing heart,
The rending veil shall thee reveal,
All glorious as thou art!
Ray Palmer, 1859.

401. *The great Melchisedec.* (753.)

1 THOU dear Redeemer, dying Lamb!
I love to hear of thee;
No music like thy charming name
Is half so sweet to me.

2 Oh! let me ever hear thy voice
In mercy to me speak;
And in my Priest, will I rejoice,
My great Melchisedec!

3 My Jesus shall be still my theme,
While in this world I stay;
I'll sing my Jesus' lovely name,
When all things else decay.

4 When I appear in yonder cloud,
With all thy favored throng,
Then will I sing more sweet, more loud,
And Christ shall be my song.
John Cennick, 1743.

402. *God All in All.* (755.)

1 MY GOD, my Portion, and my Love!
My everlasting All!
I've none but thee in heaven above,
Or on this earthly ball.

2 In vain the bright, the burning sun
Scatters his feeble light:
'T is thy sweet beams create my noon;
If thou withdraw,—'t is night.

3 How vain a toy is glittering wealth,
If once compared to thee!
Or what's my safety, or my health,
Or all my friends, to me?

4 Were I possessor of the earth,
And called the stars my own,—
Without thy graces and thyself,
I were a wretch undone.

5 Let others stretch their arms like seas,
And grasp in all the shore;
Grant me the visits of thy face,
And I desire no more.
Isaac Watts. 1707.

144 ASPIRATION.

YORK. Scotch Psalter. 1615.

My God! the Spring of all my joys, The Life of my de-lights, The Glo-ry of my bright-est days, And Com-fort of my nights!

403. *God, the Believer's Sun.* (758.)

1 My God! the Spring of all my joys,
  The Life of my delights,
  The Glory of my brightest days,
  And Comfort of my nights!

2 In darkest shades, if he appear,
  My dawning is begun;
  He is my soul's sweet Morning Star,
  And he my rising Sun.

3 The opening heavens around me shine,
  With beams of sacred bliss,
  While Jesus shows his heart is mine,
  And whispers—I am his.

4 My soul would leave this heavy clay,
  At that transporting word;
  Run up with joy the shining way,
  T' embrace my dearest Lord.

5 Fearless of hell and ghastly death,
  I'd break through every foe:
  The wings of love, and arms of faith,
  Should bear me conqueror through.
  Isaac Watts, 1707.

404. *Clinging to Christ.* (759.)

1 To whom, my Saviour! shall I go,
  If I depart from thee?
  My Guide through all this vale of woe,
  And more than all to me.

2 The world reject thy gentle reign,
  And pay thy death with scorn;
  Oh! they could plat thy crown again,
  And sharpen every thorn.

3 But I have felt thy dying love
  Breathe gently through my heart,
  To whisper hope of joys above;
  And can we ever part?

4 Ah! no; with thee, I'll walk below
  My journey to the grave:
  To whom, my Saviour! shall I go,
  When only thou canst save?
  Anon., 1825.

405. *Panting for more Love to Christ.* (761.)

1 Thou lovely Source of true delight,
  Whom I unseen adore!
  Unveil thy beauties to my sight;
  That I may love thee more.

2 Thy glory o'er creation shines;
  But, in thy sacred word,
  I read, in fairer, brighter lines,
  My bleeding, dying Lord.

3 'T is here, whene'er my comforts droop,
  And sins and sorrows rise,
  Thy love, with cheerful beams of hope,
  My fainting heart supplies.

4 But, ah! too soon the pleasing scene
  Is clouded o'er with pain;
  My gloomy fears rise dark between,
  And I again complain.

5 Jesus, my Lord, my life, my light!
  Oh! come with blissful ray;
  Break radiant through the shades of night,
  And chase my fears away.
  Anne Steele, 1760.

LOVE. 145

ARIEL. C. P. M. Lowell Mason, 1836.

406. *The matchless Worth of Jesus.* (776.)

1 OH! COULD I speak the matchless worth,
  Oh! could I sound the glories forth,
    Which in my Saviour shine!
  I'd soar, and touch the heavenly strings,
  And vie with Gabriel, while he sings
    In notes almost divine.

2 I'd sing the precious blood he spilt,
  My ransom from the dreadful guilt
    Of sin and wrath divine:
  I'd sing his glorious righteousness,
  In which all-perfect, heavenly dress
    My soul shall ever shine.

3 I'd sing the characters he bears,
  And all the forms of love he wears,
    Exalted on his throne:
  In loftiest songs of sweetest praise,
  I would, to everlasting days,
    Make all his glories known.

4 Well, the delightful day will come,
  When he, dear Lord! will bring me home,
    And I shall see his face:
  There, with my Saviour, brother, friend,
  A blessed eternity I'll spend,
    Triumphant in his grace.

Samuel Medley, 1789.

407. *Thirsting for Christ.* (777.)

1 O LOVE divine! how sweet thou art!
  When shall I find my willing heart
    All taken up by thee?
  I thirst, and faint, and die to prove
  The greatness of redeeming love,
    The love of Christ to me.

2 Stronger his love than death or hell;
  Its riches are unsearchable;
    The first-born sons of light
  Desire in vain its depths to see;
  They cannot reach the mystery,
    The length, and breadth, and height.

3 God only knows the love of God;
  Oh! that it now were shed abroad
    In this poor stony heart!
  For love I sigh; for love I pine;
  This only portion, Lord! be mine;—
    Be mine this better part!

4 Oh! that I could for ever sit,
  With Mary, at the Master's feet!
    Be this my happy choice;
  My only care, delight, and bliss,
  My joy, my heaven on earth be this,
    To hear the Bridegroom's voice!

Charles Wesley, 1740.

ASPIRATION.

BLENDON. L. M. Felice Giardini, cir. 1760.

Je-sus! and shall it ev-er be, A mor-tal man a-shamed of thee?
Ashamed of thee, whom angels praise, Whose glories shine thro' end-less days!

408. *Not ashamed of Christ.* (764.)

1 JESUS! and shall it ever be,
 A mortal man ashamed of thee?
 Ashamed of thee, whom angels praise,
 Whose glories shine through endless days!

2 Ashamed of Jesus! sooner far
 Let evening blush to own a star;
 He sheds the beams of light divine,
 O'er this benighted soul of mine.

3 Ashamed of Jesus! just as soon
 Let midnight be ashamed of noon;
 'T is midnight with my soul, till he,
 Bright Morning Star, bid darkness flee.

4 Ashamed of Jesus! that dear Friend,
 On whom my hopes of heaven depend!
 No; when I blush, be this my shame,
 That I no more revere his name.

5 Ashamed of Jesus! yes, I may,
 When I've no guilt to wash away,
 No tear to wipe, no good to crave,
 No fears to quell, no soul to save.

6 Till then,—nor is my boasting vain,—
 Till then, I boast a Saviour slain:
 And, Oh! may this my glory be,
 That Christ is not ashamed of me.
  Joseph Grigg, 1765.
  Altered by *Benjamin Francis,* 1787.

409. *Longing to be with Christ.* (765.)

1 WHEN, at this distance, Lord! we trace
 The various glories of thy face,
 What transport pours o'er all our breast,
 And charms our cares and woes to rest!

2 Away, ye dreams of mortal joy!
 Raptures divine my thoughts employ;
 I see the King of glory shine;
 I feel his love, and call him mine.

3 Yet still, our elevated eyes
 To nobler visions long to rise;
 That grand assembly would we join,
 Where all thy saints around thee shine.
  Philip Doddridge, 1740.

410. *Communion with Christ.* (770.)

1 OH! THAT I could for ever dwell,
 With Mary, at my Saviour's feet,
 And view the form I love so well,
 And all his tender words repeat:—

2 The world shut out from all my soul,
 And heaven brought in with all its bliss!—
 Oh! is there aught, from pole to pole,
 One moment, to compare with this?

3 This is the hidden life I prize,—
 A life of penitential love;
 When most my follies I despise,
 And raise my highest thoughts above:

4 When all I am, I clearly see,
 And freely own, with deepest shame;
 When the Redeemer's love to me
 Kindles within a deathless flame.

5 Thus would I live, till nature fail,
 And all my former sins forsake;
 Then rise to God, within the veil,
 And of eternal joys partake.
  Andrew Reed, 1825.

LOVE.

411. *The Loving-Kindness of Christ.* (767.)

1 Awake, my soul! in joyful lays,
And sing thy great Redeemer's praise;
He justly claims a song from me,
His loving-kindness is so free.

2 He saw me ruined in the fall,
Yet loved me, notwithstanding all,
And saved me from my lost estate;
His loving-kindness is so great.

3 Through mighty hosts of cruel foes,
Where earth and hell my way opposo,
He safely leads my soul along,
His loving-kindness is so strong.

4 Often I feel my sinful heart
Prone from my Jesus to depart;
And, though I oft have him forgot,
His loving-kindness changes not.

5 So, when I pass death's gloomy vale:
And life, and mortal powers shall fail;
Oh! may my last expiring breath
His loving-kindness sing in death!

6 Then shall I mount and soar away
To the bright world of endless day;
Then shall I sing, with sweet surprise
His loving-kindness in the skies!
Samuel Medley. 1787.

412. *The Presence of the Saviour.* (772.)

1 Lord! what a heaven of saving grace
Shines through the beauties of thy face,
And lights our passions to a flame!
Lord! how we love thy charming name.

2 When I can say,—"My God is mine!"
When I can feel thy glories shine,
I tread the world beneath my feet,
And all that earth calls good and great.

3 While such a scene of sacred joys
Our raptured eyes and souls employs,
Here we could sit and gaze away
A long, and everlasting day.

4 Well, we shall quickly pass the night,
To the fair coasts of perfect light;
Then shall our joyful senses rove
O'er the dear object of our love.
Isaac Watts, 1707.

413. *All-engrossing Love.* (769.)

1 Jesus! my heart within me burns,
To tell thee all its conscious love;
And from earth's low delight it turns,
To taste a joy like that above.

2 Though oft these lips my love have told,
They still the story would repeat;
To me the rapture ne'er grows old,
That thrills me, bending at thy feet.

3 I breathe my words into thine ear;
I seem to fix mine eyes on thine;
And, sure that thou dost wait to hear,
I dare in faith to call thee mine.

4 Reign thou sole Sovereign of my heart;
My all I yield to thy control;
Oh! let me never from thee part,
Thou best Beloved of my soul!
Ray Palmer, 1869.

ASPIRATION.

BRADEN. S. M. *William B. Bradbury*, 1844.

My God, my Life, my Love! To thee, to thee I call;
I can-not live, if thou re-move, For thou art All in all.

414. *God All, and in All.* (783.)

1 My God, my Life, my Love!
 To thee, to thee I call ;
 I cannot live, if thou remove,
 For thou art All in all.

2 Thy shining grace can cheer
 This dungeon where I dwell ;
 'T is paradise when thou art here ;
 If thou depart, 't is hell.

3 To thee, and thee alone,
 The angels owe their bliss ;
 They sit around thy gracious throne,
 And dwell where Jesus is.

4 Not all the harps above
 Can make a heavenly place,
 If God his residence remove,
 Or but conceal his face.

5 Nor earth, nor all the sky,
 Can one delight afford ;
 No, not a drop of real joy,
 Without thy presence, Lord !

6 Thou art the sea of love,
 Where all my pleasures roll,
 The circle where my passions move,
 And centre of my soul.
   Isaac Watts, 1707.

415. *Jesus, All in All.* (784.)

1 My Lord, my God, my Love !
 To thee, to thee I call ;
 Oh! come to me from heaven above,
 And be my God, my All.

2 Oh! when wilt thou be mine,
 Sweet Lover of my soul !
 My Jesus dear, my King divine!
 Come, o'er my heart to rule.

3 Oh! come, and fix thy throne
 Within my very heart ;
 Oh! make it burn for thee alone,
 And from me ne'er depart.

4 Begone ye, from my mind,
 Vain, childish, earthly toys!
 In Jesus, only, do I find
 True pleasures, solid joys.
   Anon., 1849.

416. *Living and dying to Jesus.* (785.)

1 Jesus! I live to thee,
 The lovliest and best ;
 My life in thee, thy life in me,
 In thy blest love I rest.

2 Jesus! I die to thee,
 Whenever death shall come ;
 To die in thee is life to me,
 In my eternal home.

3 Whether to live or die,
 I know not which is best ;
 To live in thee is bliss to me,
 To die is endless rest.

4 Living or dying, Lord !
 I ask but to be thine ;
 My life in thee, thy life in me,
 Makes heaven for ever mine.
   Henry Harbaugh, 1850.

LOVE.

417. *Love to Jesus attested.* (790.)

1 Hark! my soul! it is the Lord;
'T is thy Saviour; hear his word;
Jesus speaks, and speaks to thee,—
"Say, poor sinner! lovest thou me?

2 "I delivered thee, when bound,
And, when wounded, healed thy wound;
Sought thee wandering, set thee right,
Turned thy darkness into light.

3 "Can a woman's tender care
Cease towards the child she bare?
Yes, she may forgetful be,
Yet will I remember thee.

4 "Mine is an unchanging love,
Higher than the heights above;
Deeper than the depths beneath,—
Free and faithful, strong as death.

5 "Thou shalt see my glory soon,
When the work of grace is done;
Partner of my throne shalt be;—
Say, poor sinner! lovest thou me?"

6 Lord! it is my chief complaint,
That my love is weak and faint;
Yet I love thee, and adore,—
Oh! for grace to love thee more!

William Cowper, 1772.

418. *The Lesson of Love.* (791.)

1 Saviour! teach me, day by day,
Love's sweet lesson to obey;
Sweeter lesson cannot be,—
Loving him who first loved me.

2 With a child-like heart of love,
At thy bidding may I move;
Prompt to serve and follow thee,
Loving him who first loved me.

3 Teach me all thy steps to trace,
Strong to follow in thy grace;
Learning how to love from thee,
Loving him who first loved me.

4 Thus may I rejoice to show,
That I feel the love I owe;
Singing, till thy face I see,
Of his love who first loved me.

Anon. 1854.

419. *Immanuel's Name.* (793.)

1 Sweeter sounds than music knows
Charm me in Immanuel's name;
All her hopes my spirit owes
To his birth, and cross, and shame.

2 Did the Lord a man become,
That he might the law fulfill,
Bleed and suffer in my room?—
And canst thou, my tongue! be still?

3 No, I must my praises bring,
Though they worthless are, and weak;
For, should I refuse to sing,
Sure the very stones would speak.

4 O my Saviour, Shield, and Sun,
Shepherd, Brother, Lord, and Friend,
Every precious name in one!
I will love thee without end.

John Newton, 1779.

150 ASPIRATION.

HOTHAM.   7s. 8 LINES.   Martin Madan, 1776.

Jesus, Lover of my soul! Let me to thy bosom fly, While the nearer waters roll, While the tempest still is high; Hide me, O my Saviour! hide, Till the storm of life is past; Safe into the haven guide; Oh! receive my soul at last, Oh! receive my soul at last.

420.   *The sure Refuge.*   (799.)

1 JESUS, Lover of my soul!
  Let me to thy bosom fly,
While the nearer waters roll,
  While the tempest still is high;
Hide me, O my Saviour! hide,
  Till the storm of life is past;
Safe into the haven guide:
  Oh! receive my soul at last.

2 Other refuge have I none,
  Hangs my helpless soul on thee:
Leave, ah! leave me not alone,
  Still support and comfort me:
All my trust on thee is stayed,
  All my help from thee I bring;
Cover my defenceless head,
  With the shadow of thy wing.

3 Thou, O Christ! art all I want;
  More than all in thee I find;
Raise the fallen, cheer the faint.
  Heal the sick, and lead the blind:
Just and holy is thy name;
  I am all unrighteousness;
False and full of sin I am,
  Thou art full of truth and grace.

4 Plenteous grace with thee is found,
  Grace to cover all my sin;
Let the healing streams abound,
  Make and keep me pure within.
Thou of life the Fountain art,
  Freely let me take of thee:
Spring thou up within my heart,
  Rise to all eternity.
               Charles Wesley, 1740.

421.   *All Events in God's Hands.*   (800.)

1 SOVEREIGN Ruler of the skies,
  Ever gracious, ever wise!
All my times are in thy hand,
  All events at thy command:—

2 Times of sickness, times of health;
  Times of penury and wealth;
Times of trial and of grief;
  Times of triumph and relief;—

3 Times the tempter's power to prove;
  Times to taste a Saviour's love;
All must come, and last, and end,
  As shall please my heavenly Friend.

4 O thou Gracious, Wise, and Just!
  In thy hands my life I trust:
Have I somewhat dearer still?—
  I resign it to thy will.
               John Ryland, 1777.

FAITH.

Let sinners take their course, And choose the road to death;
But, in the worship of my God, I'll spend my daily breath.

422.   PSALM 55.   (805.)

1 LET sinners take their course,
  And choose the road to death;
  But, in the worship of my God,
  I'll spend my daily breath.

2 My thoughts address his throne,
  When morning brings the light,
  I seek his blessing every noon,
  And pay my vows at night.

3 Thou wilt regard my cries,
  O my eternal God!
  While sinners perish in surprise,
  Beneath thine angry rod,

4 Because they dwell at ease,
  And no sad changes feel,
  They neither fear, nor trust thy name,
  Nor learn to do thy will.

5 But I, with all my cares,
  Will lean upon the Lord;
  I'll cast my burden on his arm,
  And rest upon his word.

6 His arm shall well sustain
  The children of his love;
  The ground, on which their safety stands,
  No earthly power can move.
  Isaac Watts, 1719.

423.   PSALM 31.   (810.)

1 MY SPIRIT on thy care,
  Blest Saviour! I recline;
  Thou wilt not leave me to despair,
  For thou art Love divine.

2 In thee I place my trust,
  On thee I calmly rest;
  I know thee good, I know thee just,
  And count thy choice the best.

3 Whate'er events betide,
  Thy will they all perform;
  Safe in thy breast my head I hide,
  Nor fear the coming storm.

4 Let good or ill befall,
  It must be good for me;
  Secure of having thee in all,
  Of having all in thee.
  Henry Francis Lyte, 1834.

424.   *Jesus, our Trust.*   (811.)

1 O SAVIOUR! who didst come
  By water and by blood;
  Confessed on earth, adored in heaven,
  Eternal Son of God!

2 Jesus, our Life and Hope,
  To endless years the same!
  We plead thy gracious promises,
  And rest upon thy name.

3 By faith in thee we live,
  By faith in thee we stand,
  By thee we vanquish sin and death,
  And gain the heavenly land.

4 O Lord! increase our faith;
  Our fearful spirits calm:
  Sustain us through this mortal strife,
  Then give the victor's palm.
  Anon., 1865.

ASPIRATION.

QUITO.   L. M.   William Horsley, 1774–1858.

Thou only Sovereign of my heart, My Refuge, my almighty Friend! And can my soul from thee depart, On whom alone my hopes depend? On whom alone my hopes depend?

425.   *Life and Safety in Christ alone.*   (815.)

1 Thou only Sovereign of my heart,
    My Refuge, my almighty Friend!
And can my soul from thee depart,
    On whom alone my hopes depend?

2 Whither, ah! whither shall I go,
    A wretched wanderer from my Lord?
Can this dark world of sin and woe
    One glimpse of happiness afford?

3 Eternal life thy words impart,
    On these my fainting spirit lives;
Here sweeter comforts cheer my heart,
    Than all the round of nature gives.

4 Let earth's alluring joys combine,
    While thou art near, in vain they call;
One smile, one blissful smile of thine,—
    My dearest Lord! outweighs them all.

5 Thy name my inmost powers adore;
    Thou art my Life, my Joy, my Care;
Depart from thee! 't is death, — 't is
'T is endless ruin, deep despair! [more;

6 Low at thy feet my soul would lie;
    Here safety dwells, and peace divine;
Still let me live beneath thine eye,
    For life, eternal life is thine.
                Anne Steele, 1760.

426.   *The great Advocate.*   (819.)

1 Look up, my soul! with cheerful eye;
    See where the great Redeemer stands,
The glorious Advocate on high,
    With precious incense in his hands!

2 He sweetens every humble groan;
    He recommends each broken prayer;
Recline thy hope on him alone,
    Whose power and love forbid despair.

3 Teach my weak heart, O gracious Lord!
    With stronger faith to call thee mine;
Bid me pronounce the blissful word,
    "My Father God!" with joy divine.
                Anne Steele, 1760.

427.   *Christ, the Life of the Soul.*   (820.)

1 When sins and fears prevailing rise,
    And fainting hope almost expires,
Jesus! to thee I lift mine eyes,
    To thee I breathe my soul's desires.

2 Art thou not mine, my living Lord?
    And can my hope, my comfort die,
Fixed on thine everlasting word,— [sky?
    That word which built the earth and

3 If my immortal Saviour lives,
    Then my immortal life is sure;
His word a firm foundation gives;
    Here let me build, and rest secure.

4 Here let my faith unshaken dwell:
    Immovable the promise stands;
Nor all the powers of earth or hell
    Can e'er dissolve the sacred bands.

5 Here, O my soul! thy trust repose;
    If Jesus is for ever mine,
Not death itself, that last of foes,
    Shall break a union so divine.
                Anne Steele, 1760.

FAITH. 153

MEDFIELD. C. M. *William Mather*, 1790.

My Shepherd will supply my need, Jehovah is his name;
In pastures fresh he makes me feed, Beside the living stream.

428. PSALM 23. (823.)

1 My SHEPHERD will supply my need,
  Jehovah is his name;
  In pastures fresh he makes me feed,
  Beside the living stream.

2 He brings my wandering spirit back,
  When I forsake his ways;
  And leads me, for his mercy's sake,
  In paths of truth and grace.

3 When I walk through the shades of death,
  Thy presence is my stay;
  A word of thy supporting breath
  Drives all my fears away.

4 Thy hand, in spite of all my foes,
  Doth still my table spread;
  My cup with blessings overflows,
  Thine oil anoints my head.

5 The sure provisions of my God
  Attend me all my days;
  Oh! may thy house be mine abode,
  And all my work be praise!

6 There would I find a settled rest,
  While others go and come,
  No more a stranger or a guest,
  But like a child at home.
  Isaac Watts, 1719.

429. *The Power of Faith.* (827.)

1 FAITH adds new charms to earthly bliss,
  And saves me from its snares;
  Its aid, in every duty, brings,
  And softens all my cares.

2 The wounded conscience knows its power,
  The healing balm to give;
  That balm the saddest heart can cheer,
  And make the dying live.

3 Wide it unveils celestial worlds.
  Where deathless pleasures reign;
  And bids me seek my portion there,
  Nor bids me seek in vain;—

4 Shows me the precious promise, sealed
  With the Redeemer's blood;
  And helps my feeble hope to rest
  Upon a faithful God.

5 There, there unshaken would I rest,
  Till this vile body dies;
  And then, on faith's triumphant wings,
  At once to glory rise.
  Daniel Turner, 1787.

430. PSALM 125. (831.)

1 UNSHAKEN as the sacred hill,
  And fixed as mountains be,
  Firm as a rock the soul shall rest,
  That leans, O Lord! on thee.

2 Not walls, nor hills, could guard so well
  Old Salem's happy ground,
  As those eternal arms of love,
  That every saint surround.

3 Deal gently, Lord! with souls sincere,
  And lead them safely on
  To the bright gates of paradise,
  Where Christ, their Lord, is gone.
  Isaac Watts, 1707.

154 ASPIRATION.

STEPHENS. (NAYLAND.) C. M. William Jones, 1780.

Oh! could our thoughts and wish-es fly, A-bove these gloom-y shades,
To those bright worlds, be-yond the sky, Which sor-row ne'er in-vades!

431. *Pleasures unseen.* (832.)

1 Oh! could our thoughts and wishes fly,
  Above these gloomy shades,
To those bright worlds, beyond the sky,
  Which sorrow ne'er invades!—

2 There joys, unseen by mortal eyes,
  Or reason's feeble ray,
In ever-blooming prospect rise,
  Unconscious of decay.

3 Lord! send a beam of light divine,
  To guide our upward aim;
With one reviving touch of thine,
  Our languid hearts inflame.

4 Then shall, on faith's sublimest wing,
  Our ardent wishes rise   [spring,
To those bright scenes, where pleasures
  Immortal, in the skies.
                    Anne Steele, 1760.

432. *Delight in God.* (829.)

1 O Lord! I would delight in thee,
  And on thy care depend;
To thee in every trouble flee,
  My best, my only Friend!

2 When all created streams are dried,
  Thy fullness is the same;
May I with this be satisfied,
  And glory in thy name.

3 No good in creatures can be found,
  But may be found in thee;
I must have all things, and abound,
  While God is God to me.

4 Oh! that I had a stronger faith,
  To look within the veil,
To credit what my Saviour saith,
  Whose word can never fail.

5 He that has made my heaven secure,
  Will here all good provide;
While Christ is rich, can I be poor?
  What can I want beside?

6 O Lord! I cast my care on thee;
  I triumph and adore;
Henceforth my great concern shall be,
  To love and praise thee more.
                    John Ryland, 1787.

433. *Mercies and Thanks.* (828.)

1 How can I sink with such a prop
  As my eternal God,
Who bears the earth's huge pillars up,
  And spreads the heavens abroad?

2 How can I die, while Jesus lives,
  Who rose and left the dead?
Pardon and grace my soul receives
  From my exalted Head.

3 All that I am, and all I have,
  Shall be for ever thine;
Whate'er my duty bids me give,
  My cheerful hands resign.

4 Yet, if I might make some reserve,
  And duty did not call,
I love my God with zeal so great,
  That I should give him all.
                    Isaac Watts, 1709.

HOPE.

MAITLAND. C. M. —Allen. Western Melody.

Must Jesus bear the cross, alone, And all the world go free?
No, there's a cross for every one, And there's a cross for me....

434. *The Cross and the Crown.* (838.)

1 Must Jesus bear the cross alone,
  And all the world go free?
  No, there's a cross for every one,
  And there's a cross for me.

2 How happy are the saints above,
  Who once went mourning here!
  But now they taste unmingled love,
  And joy without a tear.

3 This consecrated cross I'll bear,
  Till death shall set me free,
  And then go home my crown to wear,
  For there's a crown for me.

4 Upon the crystal pavement, down
  At Jesus' piercèd feet,
  Joyful, I'll cast my golden crown,
  And his dear name repeat.

5 And palms shall wave, and harps shall ring
  Beneath heaven's arches high;
  The Lord, that lives, the ransomed sing,
  That lives no more to die.

6 Oh! precious cross! Oh! glorious crown!
  Oh! resurrection day!
  Ye angels! from the skies come down,
  And bear my soul away.

  vs. 1–3., *G. N. Allen,* 1849, a.

435. *The Example of the Saints.* (845.)

1 Rise, O my soul! pursue the path,
  By ancient worthies trod;
  Aspiring, view those holy men,
  Who lived and walked with God.

2 Though dead, they speak in reason's ear,
  And in example live;
  Their faith, and hope, and mighty deeds,
  Still fresh instruction give.

3 'T was through the Lamb's most precious blood
  They conquered every foe;
  And, to his power and matchless grace,
  Their crowns and honors owe.

4 Lord! may I ever keep in view
  The patterns thou hast given;
  And ne'er forsake the blessèd path
  Which led them safe to heaven.

  John Needham, 1768.

436. *Assurance of Hope.* (835.)

1 When I can read my title clear,
  To mansions in the skies,
  I bid farewell to every fear,
  And wipe my weeping eyes.

2 Should earth against my soul engage,
  And hellish darts be hurled,
  Then I can smile at Satan's rage,
  And face a frowning world.

3 Let cares like a wild deluge come,
  And storms of sorrow fall;
  May I but safely reach my home,
  My God, my heaven, my all:

4 There shall I bathe my weary soul
  In seas of heavenly rest,
  And not a wave of trouble roll
  Across my peaceful breast.

  Isaac Watts, 1707.

ASPIRATION.

MIGDOL. L. M. Lowell Mason, 1840.

Stand up, my soul! shake off thy fears, And gird the gos-pel ar-mor on,
March to the gates of end-less joy, Where thy great Cap-tain Sa-viour's gone.

437. *The Christian Warfare.* (847.)

1 STAND up, my soul! shake off thy fears,
And gird the gospel armor on,
March to the gates of endless joy, [gone.
Where thy great Captain Saviour's

2 Hell and thy sins resist thy course,
But hell and sin are vanquished foes,
Thy Jesus nailed them to the cross,
And sung the triumph when he rose.

3 What, though the prince of darkness rage,
And waste the fury of his spite?
Eternal chains confine him down
To fiery deeps, and endless night.

4 What, though thine inward lusts rebel?
'T is but a struggling gasp for life;
The weapons of victorious grace
Shall slay thy sins, and end the strife.

5 Then let my soul march boldly on,
Press forward to the heavenly gate,
There peace and joy eternal reign, [wait.
And glittering robes for conquerors

6 There shall I wear a starry crown,
And triumph in almighty grace,
While all the armies of the skies
Join in my glorious Leader's praise.
Isaac Watts, 1707.

438. *The Christian Race.* (848.)

1 AWAKE, our souls! away, our fears!
Let every trembling thought be gone;
Awake, and run the heavenly race,
And put a cheerful courage on.

2 True,—'t is a strait and thorny road,
And mortal spirits tire and faint;
But they forget the mighty God,
Who feeds the strength of every saint:

3 Thee, mighty God! whose matchless
Is ever new, and ever young, [power,
And firm endures while endless yea s
Their everlasting circles run.

4 From thee, the overflowing spring,
Our souls shall drink a fresh supply;
While such, as trust their native strength,
Shall melt away, and droop, and die.

5 Swift as an eagle cuts the air,
We 'll mount aloft to thine abode;
On wings of love, our souls shall fly,
Nor tire amidst the heavenly road.
Isaac Watts, 1707.

439. *Holiness and Grace.* (855.)

1 So LET our lips and lives express
The holy gospel, we profess;
So let our works and virtues shine,
To prove the doctrine all-divine.

2 Thus shall we best proclaim abroad
The honors of our Saviour God;
When the salvation reigns within,
And grace subdues the power of sin.

3 Religion bears our spirits up,
While we expect that blessed hope,—
The bright appearance of the Lord;—
And faith stands leaning on his word.
Isaac Watts, 1709.

HOPE. 157

GRATITUDE. L. M.
From *Ami Bost*:
Adapted by *Thomas Hastings*, 1837.

Who shall the Lord's e-lect condemn?—'T is God that jus-ti-fies their souls;
And mer-cy, like a might-y stream, O'er all their sins di-vine-ly rolls.

440. *Security of the Saints.* (851.)

1 Who shall the Lord's elect condemn?—
    'Tis God, that justifies their souls;
    And mercy, like a mighty stream,
    O'er all their sins divinely rolls.

2 Who shall adjudge the saints to hell!
    'Tis Christ that suffered in their stead,
    And, the salvation to fulfill,
    Behold him, rising from the dead!

3 He lives, he lives, and sits above,
    For ever interceding there;
    Who shall divide us from his love?
    Or what shall tempt us to despair?

4 Shall persecution or distress,
    Famine, or sword, or nakedness!
    He, that hath loved us, bears us through,
    And makes us more than conquerors too.

5 Faith hath an overcoming power,
    It triumphs in the dying hour:
    Christ is our life, our joy, our hope;
    Nor can we sink with such a prop.

6 Not all that men on earth can do,
    Nor powers on high, nor powers below,
    Shall cause his mercy to remove,
    Or wean our hearts from Christ our love.
        Isaac Watts, 1707.

441. *Hope in the Covenant.* (851.)

1 How oft have sin and Satan strove
    To rend my soul from thee, my God!
    But everlasting is thy love,
    And Jesus seals it with his blood.

2 The oath and promise of the Lord
    Join to confirm the wondrous grace;
    Eternal power performs the word,
    And fills all heaven with endless praise.

3 Amid temptations, sharp and long,
    My soul to this dear refuge flies;
    Hope is my anchor, firm and strong,
    While tempests blow, and billows rise.

4 The gospel bears my spirit up;
    A faithful and unchanging God
    Lays the foundation for my hope,
    In oaths, and promises, and blood.
        Isaac Watts, 1709.

442. *The Bread of Life.* (852.)

1 Away from earth my spirit turns,
    Away from every transient good;
    With strong desire my bosom burns,
    To feast on heaven's diviner food.

2 Thou, Saviour! art the living bread;
    Thou wilt my every want supply;
    By thee sustained, and cheered, and led,
    I'll press through dangers to the sky.

3 What, though temptations oft distress,
    And sin assails and breaks my peace?
    Thou wilt uphold, and save, and bless,
    And bid the storms of passion cease.

4 Then let me take thy gracious hand,
    And walk beside thee onward still;
    Till my glad feet shall safely stand,
    For ever firm, on Zion's hill.
        Ray Palmer, 1862.

158 ASPIRATION.

CHRISTMAS. C. M. From *George Frederick Handel*, 1685-1759.

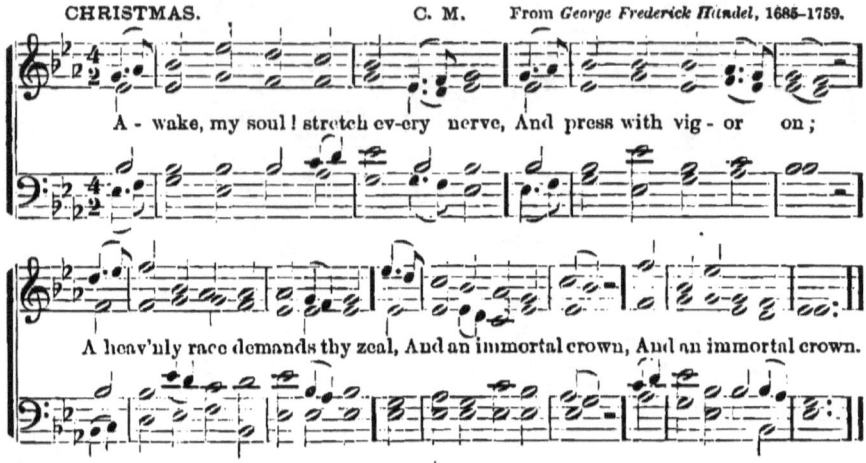

A-wake, my soul! stretch ev-ery nerve, And press with vig-or on;

A heav'nly race demands thy zeal, And an immortal crown, And an immortal crown.

---

443. *The Christian Race.* (841.)

1 Awake, my soul! stretch every nerve,
And press with vigor on;
A heavenly race demands thy zeal,
And an immortal crown.

2 A cloud of witnesses around
Hold thee in full survey;
Forget the steps already trod,
And onward urge thy way.

3 'T is God's all-animating voice,
That calls thee from on high;
'T is his own hand presents the prize,
To thine aspiring eye.

4 Blest Saviour! introduced by thee,
Have I my race begun;
And, crowned with victory at thy feet,
I'll lay my honors down.
Philip Doddridge, 1740.

444. *Victory through the Lamb.* (844.)

1 Give me the wings of faith, to rise
Within the veil, and see
The saints above,—how great their joys,
How bright their glories be.

2 Once they were mourning here below,
And wet their couch with tears;
They wrestled hard, as we do now,
With sins, and doubts, and fears.

3 I ask them, whence their victory came?
They, with united breath,
Ascribe their conquest to the Lamb,—
Their triumph to his death.

4 They marked the footsteps that he trod;
His zeal inspired their breast;
And, following their incarnate God,
Possess the promised rest.

5 Our glorious Leader claims our praise,
For his own pattern given,
While the long cloud of witnesses
Show the same path to heaven.
Isaac Watts, 1709.

445. *The blissful Hope of Heaven.* (837.)

1 My soul, triumphant in the Lord,
Shall tell its joys abroad,
And march with holy vigor on,
Supported by its God.

2 Through all the winding maze of life
His hand hath been my guide;
And, in that long-experienced care,
My heart shall still confide.

3 His grace through all the desert flows,
An unexhausted stream:
That grace, on Zion's sacred mount,
Shall be my endless theme.

4 Beyond the choicest joys of earth
These distant courts I love;
But, Oh! I burn with strong desire
To view thy house above.

5 Mingled with all the shining band,
My soul would there adore;—
A pillar in thy temple fixed,
To be removed no more.
Philip Doddridge, 1740.

HOPE. 159

MADISON.   8s. 8 LINES.   *Sylvanus B. Pond*, 1841.

To Jesus, the Crown of my hope, My soul is in haste to be gone; Oh! bear me, ye cherubim! up, And waft me away to his throne: My Saviour! whom absent I love, Whom not having seen, I adore, Whose name is exalted above All glory, dominion and power;

446.   *Longing to be with Jesus.*   (856.)

1 To Jesus, the Crown of my hope,
    My soul is in haste to be gone;
  Oh! bear me, ye cherubim! up,
    And waft me away to his throne:
  My Saviour! whom absent I love,
    Whom, not having seen, I adore,
  Whose name is exalted above
    All glory, dominion, and power;

2 Dissolve thou these bands that detain
    My soul from her portion in thee;
  Ah! strike off this adamant chain,
    And make me eternally free!
  When that happy era begins,
    When arrayed in thy glories I shine,
  Nor grieve any more by my sins
    The bosom on which I recline:

3 Oh! then shall the veil be removed,
    And round me thy brightness be pour'd;
  I shall meet him whom absent I loved,
    I shall see whom unseen I adored;
  And then, never more shall the fears,
    The trials, temptations, and woes,
  Which darken this valley of tears,
    Intrude on my blissful repose.
          William Cowper, 1800.

447.   *Panting for Heaven.*   (857.)

1 Ye angels! who stand round the throne,
    And view my Immanuel's face,—
  In rapturous songs make him known,
    Tune all your soft harps to his praise:
  He formed you the spirits you are,
    So happy, so noble, so good;
  When others sunk down in despair,
    Confirmed by his power, you stood.

2 Ye saints! who stand nearer than they,
    And cast your bright crowns at his feet,
  His grace and his glory display,
    And all his rich mercy relate;
  He snatched you from hell and the grave,
    He ransomed from death and despair:
  For you he was mighty to save,
    Almighty to bring you safe there.

3 Oh! when will the period appear
    When I shall unite in your song?
  I'm weary of lingering here,
    And I to your Saviour belong;
  I want—Oh! I want to be there,
    Where sorrow and sin bid adieu;
  Your joy and your friendship to share,
    To wonder, and worship with you.
          Maria De Fleury, 1806.

160 ASPIRATION.

DENNIS. S. M. From *Hans G. Nägeli*, 1773–1836. Adapted by *Lowell Mason*, 1849.

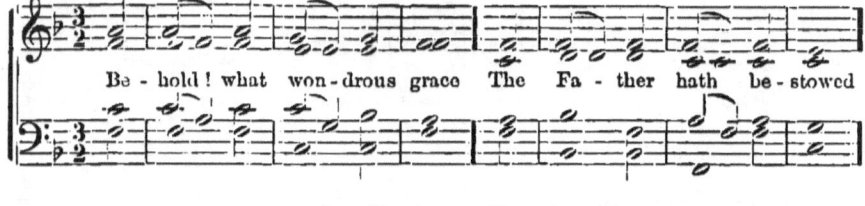

Be - hold ! what won - drous grace The Fa - ther hath be - stowed

On sin - ners of a mor - tal race, To call them sons of God !

448. *Adoption.* (858.)

1 BEHOLD ! what wondrous grace
The Father hath bestowed
On sinners of a mortal race,
To call them sons of God !

2 'T is no surprising thing,
That we should be unknown ;
The Jewish world knew not their King,
God's everlasting Son.

3 Nor doth it yet appear
How great we must be made ;
But, when we see our Saviour here,
We shall be like our Head.

4 A hope so much divine
May trials well endure,
May purge our souls from sense and sin,
As Christ, the Lord, is pure.

5 If, in my Father's love,
I share a filial part,
Send down thy Spirit like a dove,
To rest upon my heart.

6 We would no longer lie
Like slaves beneath the throne ;
My faith shall — " Abba, Father !" — cry,
And thou the kindred own.
Isaac Watts, 1707.

449. *One with Christ.* (865.)

1 MY SAVIOUR ! I am thine
By everlasting bands ;
My name, my heart, I would resign,
My soul is in thy hands.

2 To thee I still would cleave,
With ever-growing zeal ;
Let millions tempt me Christ to leave,
They never shall prevail.

3 His Spirit shall unite
My soul, to him, my Head ;
Shall form me to his image bright,
And teach his path to tread.

4 Death may my soul divide
From this abode of clay;
But love shall keep me near his side,
Through all the gloomy way.

5 Since Christ and we are one,
What should remain to fear ?
If he in heaven hath fixed his throne,
He 'll fix his members there.
Philip Doddridge, 1740.

450. *Christ unseen and beloved.* (866.)

1 NOT with our mortal eyes
Have we beheld the Lord ;
Yet we rejoice to hear his name,
And love him in his word.

2 On earth we want the sight
Of our Redeemer's face ;
Yet, Lord ! our inmost thoughts delight
To dwell upon thy grace.

3 And, when we taste thy love,
Our joys divinely grow
Unspeakable, like those above,
And heaven begins below.
Isaac Watts, 1709.

DIVINE FELLOWSHIP.

THATCHER. S. M. From *George Frederick Handel*, 1732.

Your harps, ye trembling saints! Down from the willows take;
Loud to the praise of love divine. Bid every string awake.

451. *Trust in God.* (831.)

1 Your harps, ye trembling saints!
  Down from the willows take!
  Loud to the praise of love divine,
  Bid every string awake.

2 Though in a foreign land,
  We are not far from home;
  And, nearer to our house above,
  We every moment come.

3 His grace will, to the end,
  Stronger and brighter shine;
  Nor present things, nor things to come,
  Shall quench the spark divine.

4 When we in darkness walk,
  Nor feel the heavenly flame;
  Then is the time to trust our God,
  And rest upon his name.

5 Soon shall our doubts and fears
  Subside at his control;
  His loving kindness shall break through
  The midnight of the soul.

6 Blest is the man, O God!
  That stays himself on thee:—
  Who wait for thy salvation, Lord!
  Shall thy salvation see.

Augustus M. Toplady, 1772.

452. *Singing along the Way.* (839.)

1 Now let our voices join
  To raise a sacred song;
  Ye pilgrims! in Jehovah's ways,
  With music pass along.

2 See!—flowers of paradise,
  In rich profusion, spring;
  The sun of glory gilds the path,
  And dear companions sing.

3 See! Salem's golden spires,
  In beauteous prospect, rise;
  And brighter crowns than mortals wear,
  Which sparkle through the skies.

4 All honor to his name,
  Who drew the shining trace,—
  To him, who leads the wanderers on,
  And cheers them with his grace.

Philip Doddridge, 1740.

453. *No Rest, but in God.* (869.)

1 My SPIRIT longs for thee
  To dwell within my breast;
  Although unworthy, Lord! I be
  Of so divine a Guest.

2 Of so divine a Guest
  Unworthy though I be,
  Yet hath my panting heart no rest,
  Until it come to thee.

3 Until it come to thee,
  In vain I look around;
  In all that I can hear or see,
  No rest is to be found.

4 No rest is to be found,
  But in thy bleeding love:
  Oh! let my ardent wish be crowned,
  And send it from above.

John Byrom, 1814, a.

ASPIRATION.

HEATH. C. M. *Lowell Mason, 1835.*

As pants the hart for cool-ing streams, When heat-ed in the chase,
So pants my soul, O Lord! for thee, And thy re-fresh-ing grace.

454. PSALM 42. (870.)

1 As PANTS the hart for cooling streams,
 When heated in the chase,
 So pants my soul, O Lord! for thee,
 And thy refreshing grace.

2 For thee, the Lord, the living Lord,
 My thirsty soul doth pine;
 Oh! when shall I behold thy face,
 Thou Majesty divine!

3 I sigh to think of happier days,
 When thou, O Lord! wert nigh;
 When every heart was tuned to praise,
 And none so blessed as I.

4 Why restless, why cast down, my soul?
 Trust God, and thou shalt sing
 His praise again, and find him still
 Thy health's eternal spring.
  Nahum Tate, 1696.
  Altered by *Henry Francis Lyte*, 1834.

455. *The Hope of Heaven.* (873.)

1 MY THOUGHTS surmount these lower skies,
 And look within the veil;
 There springs of endless pleasure rise,
 The waters never fail.

2 There I behold, with sweet delight,
 The blessed Three in One;
 And strong affections fix my sight
 On God's incarnate Son.

3 His promise stands for ever firm,
 His grace shall ne'er depart,
 He binds my name upon his arm,
 And seals it on his heart.

4 I would not be a stranger still
 To that celestial place,
 Where I for ever hope to dwell
 Near my Redeemer's face.
  Isaac Watts, 1709.

456. *The beatific Vision.* (875.)

1 FROM thee, my God! my joys shall rise,
 And run eternal rounds,
 Beyond the limits of the skies,
 And all created bounds.

2 The holy triumphs of my soul
 Shall death itself outbrave,
 Leave dull mortality behind,
 And fly beyond the grave.

3 There, where my blessed Jesus reigns,
 In heaven's unmeasured space,
 I'll spend a long eternity
 In pleasure and in praise.

4 Millions of years my wondering eyes
 Shall o'er thy beauties rove,
 And endless ages I'll adore
 The glories of thy love.

5 Sweet Jesus! every smile of thine
 Shall fresh endearments bring,
 And thousand tastes of new delight
 From all thy graces spring.

6 Haste, my beloved! fetch my soul
 Up to thy blessed abode,—
 Fly, for my spirit longs to see
 My Saviour and my God.
  Isaac Watts, 1707.

DIVINE FELLOWSHIP.

ROCHESTER.   C. M.   *Aaron Williams' Coll., cir. 1760.*

God, my Support-er and my Hope, My Help, for-ev-er near! Thine arm of mer-cy held me up, When sink-ing in des-pair.

457.   PSALM 73.   (879.)

1 GOD, my Supporter and my Hope,
  My Help for ever near !
  Thine arm of mercy held me up,
  When sinking in despair.

2 Thy counsels, Lord ! shall guide my feet,
  Through this dark wilderness :
  Thy hand conduct me near thy seat,
  To dwell before thy face.

3 Were I in heaven without my God,
  'T would be no joy to me ;
  And, whilst this earth is my abode,
  I long for none but thee.

4 What, if the springs of life were broke,
  And flesh and heart should faint?
  God is my soul's eternal Rock,
  The Strength of every saint.

5 But to draw near to thee, my God !
  Shall be my sweet employ :
  My tongue shall sound thy works abroad,
  And tell the world my joy.
                Isaac Watts, 1719.

458.   *Retirement.*   (871.)

1 FAR from the world, O Lord ! I flee,
  From strife and tumult far ;
  From scenes, where Satan wages still
  His most successful war.

2 The calm retreat, the silent shade,
  With prayer and praise agree ;
  And seem, by thy sweet bounty, made
  For those who follow thee.

3 There, if thy Spirit touch the soul,
  And grace her mean abode,
  Oh ! with what peace, and joy, and love,
  She communes with her God !

4 There, like the nightingale, she pours
  Her solitary lays ;
  Nor asks a witness of her song,
  Nor thirsts for human praise.

5 Author and Guardian of my life !
  Sweet Source of light divine,
  And,—all harmonious names in one,—
  My Saviour ! thou art mine !
                William Cowper, 1772.

459.   *Longing for Christ.*   (876.)

1 OH ! could I find from day to day,
  A nearness to my God ;
  Then should my hours glide sweet away,
  And live upon thy word.

2 Lord ! I desire with thee to live,
  Anew from day to day,
  In joys the world can never give,
  Nor ever take away.

3 O Jesus ! come and rule my heart,
  And I 'll be wholly thine ;
  And never, never more depart ;
  For thou art wholly mine.

4 Thus, till my last expiring breath,
  Thy goodness I 'll adore ;
  And, when my flesh dissolves in death,
  My soul shall love thee more.
                Benjamin Cleveland, 1790.

164 ASPIRATION.

SWEET HOUR.   L. M. 8 LINES.   *William B. Bradbury, 1861.*

Sweet hour of pray'r! sweet hour of pray'r! That calls me from a world of care,
And bids me, at my Father's throne, Make all my wants and wishes known;
D. C.—And oft escaped the tempter's snare, By thy return, sweet hour of pray'r!
In sea-sons of dis-tress and grief, My soul has oft-en found re-lief,

460.   *Sweet Hour of Prayer.*   (882.)

1 SWEET hour of prayer! sweet hour of prayer!
That calls me from a world of care,
And bids me, at my Father's throne,
Make all my wants and wishes known:
In seasons of distress and grief,
My soul has often found relief,
And oft escaped the tempter's snare,
By thy return, sweet hour of prayer!

2 Sweet hour of prayer! sweet hour of prayer!
Thy wings shall my petition bear,
To him, whose truth and faithfulness
Engage the waiting soul to bless:
And, since he bids me seek his face,
Believe his word, and trust in grace,
I'll cast on him my every care,
And wait for thee, sweet hour of prayer!

3 Sweet hour of prayer! sweet hour of prayer!
May I thy consolations share,
Till, from Mount Pisgah's lofty height,
I view my home, and take my flight:
This robe of flesh I'll drop, and rise,
To seize the everlasting prize;
And shout, while passing through the air,
Farewell, farewell, sweet hour of prayer!
Miss Fanny Crosby, 1849.

461.   *The Hour of Prayer.*   (884.)

1 MY GOD! is any hour so sweet,
From blush of morn to evening star,
As that which calls me to thy feet—
The hour of prayer. the hour of prayer?

2 Blest is that tranquil hour of morn,
And blest that solemn hour of eve,
When, on the wings of prayer up-borne,
The world I leave,—the world I leave.

3 Then is my strength by thee renewed;
Then are my sins by thee forgiven;
Then dost thou cheer my solitude
With hopes of heaven,—with hopes of heaven.

4 No words can tell what sweet relief,
Here for my every want I find;
What strength for warfare, balm for grief,
What peace of mind! what peace of mind!

5 Hushed is each doubt; gone, every fear;
My spirit seems in heaven to stay;
And ev'n the penitential tear
Is wiped away,—is wiped away.

6 Lord! till I reach yon blissful shore,
No privilege so dear shall be,
As thus my inmost soul to pour
In prayer to thee,—in prayer to thee.
Charlotte Elliott, 1851.

DIVINE FELLOWSHIP.

EVENING HYMN. L. M. *Thomas Tallis*, cir. 1567. Altered.

My God! permit me not to be A stranger to my self and thee;
A-midst a thousand thoughts I rove, For-get-ful of my high-est love.

462. *Retirement and Meditation.* (887.)

1 My God! permit me not to be
A stranger to myself and thee;
Amidst a thousand thoughts I rove,
Forgetful of my highest love.

2 Why should my passions mix with earth,
And thus debase my heavenly birth?
Why should I cleave to things below,
And let my God, my Saviour, go?

3 Call me away from flesh and sense;
One sovereign word can draw me thence;
I would obey the voice divine,
And all inferior joys resign.

4 Be earth, with all her scenes, withdrawn,
Let noise and vanity be gone;
In secret silence of the mind,
My heaven, and there my God, I find.
Isaac Watts, 1709.

463. *The Presence of Christ in Heaven.* (888.)

1 Oh! for a sweet, inspiring ray,
To animate our feeble strains,
From the bright realms of endless day,—
The blissful realms, where Jesus reigns!

2 There, low before his glorious throne,
Adoring saints and angels fall;
And, with delightful worship, own
His smile their bliss, their heaven, their all.

3 Immortal glories crown his head,
While tuneful hallelujahs rise,
And love, and joy, and triumph spread
Through all th' assemblies of the skies.

4 He smiles,—and seraphs tune their songs
To boundless rapture, while they gaze;
Ten thousand, thousand joyful tongues
Resound his everlasting praise.

5 There, all the favorites of the Lamb
Shall join at last the heavenly choir:
Oh! may the joy-inspiring theme,
Awake our faith and warm desire.

6 Dear Saviour! let thy Spirit seal
Our interest in that blissful place;
Till death remove this mortal veil,
And we behold thy lovely face.
Anne Steele, 1760.

464. *Vision of the great God.* (890.)

1 Oh! might I once mount up, and see
The glories of th' eternal skies,
What little things these worlds would be!
How despicable to mine eyes!

2 Had I a glance of thee, my God!
Kingdoms and men would vanish soon,
Vanish, as though I saw them not,
As a dim candle dies at noon.

3 Then they might fight, and rage, and rave;
I should perceive the noise, no more
Than we can hear a shaking leaf,
While rattling thunders round us roar.

4 Great All in all, eternal King!
Let me but view thy lovely face,
And all my powers shall bow, and sing
Thine endless grandeur and thy grace.
Isaac Watts, 1707.

ASPIRATION.

SPANISH HYMN.   7s. 6 or 8 lines.   Spanish Melody.

Pleasant are thy courts above, In the land of light and love;
Pleasant are thy courts below, In this land of sin and woe;
D. C.—For the bright-ness of thy face, For thy full-ness, God of grace!

Oh! my spi-rit longs and faints For the con-verse of thy saints,

465.   PSALM 84.   (895.)

1 Pleasant are thy courts above,
In the land of light and love;
Pleasant are thy courts below,
In this land of sin and woe:
Oh! my spirit longs and faints
For the converse of thy saints,
For the brightness of thy face,
For thy fullness, God of grace!

2 Happy birds, that sing and fly
Round thine altars, O Most High!
Happier souls, that find a rest
In a heavenly Father's breast!
Like the wandering dove, that found
No repose on earth around,
They can to their ark repair,
And enjoy it ever there.

3 Happy souls! their praises flow,
Even in this vale of woe;
Waters in the desert rise,
Manna feeds them from the skies;
On they go from strength to strength,
Till they reach thy throne at length;
At thy feet adoring fall,
Who hast led them safe through all.

4 Lord! be mine this prize to win,
Guide me through a world of sin;
Keep me by thy saving grace,
Give me at thy side a place;

Sun and Shield alike thou art;
Guide and guard my erring heart;
Grace and glory flow from thee,
Shower, Oh! shower them, Lord! on me.
Henry Francis Lyte, 1834.

466.   Christ to live, and Gain to die.   (896.)

1 Christ, of all my hopes the Ground,—
Christ, the Spring of all my joy!
Still in thee may I be found,
Still for thee my powers employ;
Fountain of o'erflowing grace!
Freely from thy fullness give;
Till I close my earthly race,
May I prove it "Christ to live!"

2 When I touch the blessèd shore,
Back the closing waves shall roll;
Death's dark stream shall never more
Part from thee my ravished soul:
Thus,—Oh! thus, an entrance give
To the land of cloudless sky;
Having known it "Christ to live,"
Let me know it, "gain to die."

3 Gain, to part from all my grief;
Gain, to bid my sins farewell;
Gain, of all my gains the chief,
Ever with the Lord to dwell:
This thy people's portion, Lord!
Peace on earth, and bliss on high;
This their ever-sure reward,
"Christ to live, and gain to die!"
Ralph Wardlaw, 1817.

DIVINE FELLOWSHIP. 167

467. *Rejoicing in Hope.* (909.)

1 CHILDREN of the heavenly King!
As ye journey, sweetly sing;
Sing your Saviour's worthy praise,
Glorious in his works and ways.

2 We are traveling home to God,
In the way the fathers trod;
They are happy now, and we
Soon their happiness shall see.

3 Shout, ye little flock and blest!
You on Jesus' throne shall rest;
There, your seat is now prepared,—
There's your kingdom and reward.

4 Fear not, brethren! joyful stand
On the borders of your land;
Jesus Christ, your Father's Son,
Bids you undismayed go on.

5 Lord! obediently we go,
Gladly leaving all below;
Only thou our Leader be,
And we still will follow thee.
John Cennick, 1742.

468. PSALM 23. (901.)

1 To THY pastures fair and large,
Heavenly Shepherd! lead thy charge;
And my couch, with tenderest care,
Midst the springing grass prepare.

2 When I faint with summer's heat,
Thou shalt guide my weary feet
To the streams that, still and slow,
Through the verdant meadow flow.

3 Safe the dreary vale I tread,
By the shades of death o'erspread,
By thy rod and staff supplied,—
This my guard, and that my guide.

4 Constant, to my latest end,
Thou my footsteps shalt attend;
And shalt bid thy hallowed dome
Yield me an eternal home.
James Merrick, 1765, a.

469. *Leaning on Christ's Arm.* (902.)

1 JESUS, merciful and mild!
Lead me as a helpless child;
On no other arm but thine,
Would my weary soul recline.

2 Thou canst fit me, by thy grace,
For the heavenly dwelling-place;
All thy promises are sure,
Ever shall thy love endure.

3 Then what more could I desire,
How to greater bliss aspire?
All I need, in thee I see,
Thou art All in all to me.

4 Jesus, Saviour all divine!
Hast thou made me truly thine?
Hast thou bought me by thy blood?
Reconciled my heart to God?

5 Hearken to my tender prayer,
Let me thine own image bear;
Let me love thee more and more,
Till I reach heaven's blissful shore.
Thomas Hastings, 1858.

ASPIRATION.

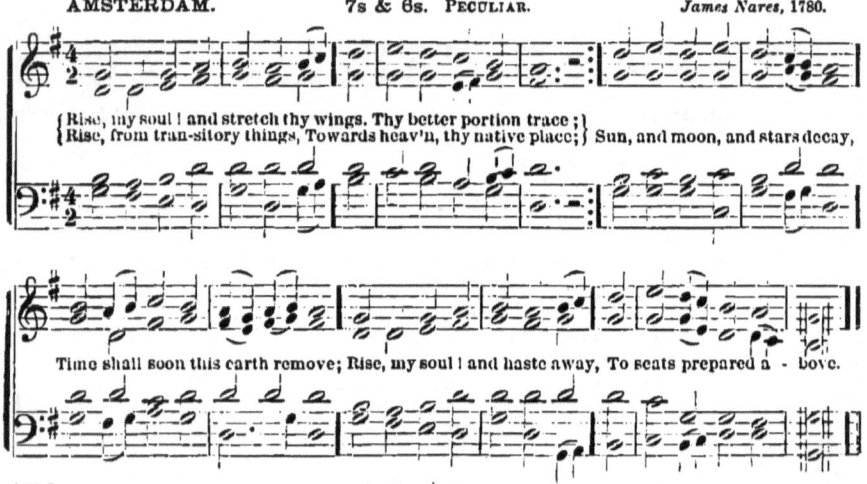

AMSTERDAM. 7s & 6s. PECULIAR. James Nares, 1780.

{ Rise, my soul! and stretch thy wings. Thy better portion trace;
Rise, from transitory things, Towards heav'n, thy native place; } Sun, and moon, and stars decay, Time shall soon this earth remove; Rise, my soul! and haste away, To seats prepared a-bove.

470. *Pilgrim's Song.* (907.)

1 Rise, my soul! and stretch thy wings,
   Thy better portion trace;
Rise, from transitory things,
   Towards heaven, thy native place;
Sun, and moon, and stars decay,
   Time shall soon this earth remove;
Rise, my soul! and haste away,
   To seats prepared above.

2 Rivers to the ocean run,
   Nor stay in all their course;
Fire ascending seeks the sun;
   Both speed them to their source:
So a soul, that's born of God,
   Pants to view his glorious face;
Upward tends to his abode,
   To rest in his embrace.

3 Cease, ye pilgrims! cease to mourn,
   Press onward to the prize;
Soon our Saviour will return,
   Triumphant in the skies:
Yet a season,—and you know,
   Happy entrance will be given,
All our sorrows left below,
   And earth exchanged for heaven.
                   Robert Seagrave, 1748, a.

471. *"Christ and him crucified."* (908.)

1 Vain, delusive world! adieu!
   With all of creature good;
Only Jesus I pursue,
   Who bought me with his blood:
All thy pleasures I forego;
   All thy pomps, thy wealth and pride;
Only Jesus will I know,
   And Jesus, crucified.

2 Other knowledge I disdain;
   'Tis all but vanity:
Christ, the Lamb of God, was slain;—
   He tasted death for me:
Me to save from endless woe,
   Christ, th' atoning Victim died:
Only Jesus will I know,
   And Jesus, crucified.

3 Him to know is life and peace,
   And pleasure without end;
This is all my happiness,
   On Jesus to depend;
Daily in his grace to grow,
   Ever in his faith abide;
Only Jesus will I know,
   And Jesus, crucified.

4 Him, in all my works, I seek,
   Who hung upon the tree:
Only of his love I speak,
   Who freely died for me:
While I sojourn here below,
   Nothing will I seek beside:
Only Jesus will I know,
   And Jesus, crucified.
                   Charles Wesley, 1742, a.

DIVINE FELLOWSHIP.

BETHANY. 6s & 4s. *Lowell Mason*, 1859.

Nearer, my God! to thee: Nearer to thee; Ev'n tho' it be a cross That raiseth me,

Still all my song shall be, Nearer, my God! to thee, Nearer, my God! to thee, Nearer to thee.

472.   *Nearer to God.*   (911.)

1 NEARER, my God! to thee,—
  Nearer to thee;
Ev'n though it be a cross
  That raiseth me,
Still all my song shall be,
Nearer, my God! to thee,—
  Nearer to thee.

2 Though like the wanderer,
  The sun gone down,
Darkness be over me,
  My rest a stone,
Yet, in my dreams, I'd be
Nearer, my God! to thee,—
  Nearer to thee.

3 There let the way appear,
  Steps unto heaven;
All that thou send'st to me,
  In mercy given;
Angels to beckon me
Nearer, my God! to thee,—
  Nearer to thee.

4 Then, with my waking thoughts
  Bright with thy praise,
Out of my stony griefs
  Bethel I'll raise;
So by my woes to be
Nearer, my God! to thee,—
  Nearer to thee.

5 Or if, on joyful wing,
  Cleaving the sky,

Sun, moon and stars forgot,
  Upward I fly,
Still all my song shall be,
Nearer, my God! to thee,—
  Nearer to thee.
Mrs. Sarah Flower Adams, 1841.

473.   *Closer with God.*   (912.)

1 SAVIOUR! I follow on,
  Guided by thee,
Seeing not yet the hand
  That leadeth me;
Hushed be my heart and still,
Fear I no further ill,
Only to meet thy will
  My will shall be.

2 Riven the rock for me,
  Thirst to relieve;
Manna from heaven falls
  Fresh every eve;
Never a want severe
Causeth my eye a tear,
But thou dost whisper near,
  "Only believe."

3 Saviour! I long to walk
  Closer with thee;
Led by thy guiding hand
  Ever to be;
Constantly near thy side,
Quickened and purified,
Living for him who died
  Freely for me!
Charles S. Robinson, 1862.

ASPIRATION.

OLIPHANT. 8s, 7s & 4. Lowell Mason, 1832.

Guide me, O thou great Jehovah! Pilgrim thro' this barren land;
I am weak, but thou art mighty............ Hold me with thy powerful hand;
Bread of heav-en! Bread of heav-en! Feed me now and ev-er-more.

474. *God, the Pilgrim's Guide.* (913.)

1 GUIDE me, O thou great Jehovah!
  Pilgrim through this barren land;
  I am weak, but thou art mighty;
  Hold me with thy powerful hand:
    Bread of heaven!
  Feed me now and evermore.

2 Open now the crystal fountain,
  Whence the healing streams do flow;
  Let the fiery cloudy pillar
  Lead me all my journey through:
    Strong Deliverer!
  Be thou still my Strength and Shield.

3 When I tread the verge of Jordan,
  Bid my anxious fears subside;
  Death of deaths, and hell's destruction!
  Land me safe on Canaan's side:
    Songs of praises,
  I will ever give to thee.
  William Williams, 1774.

475. *Jesus, the great Deliverer.* (914.)

1 JESUS, Lord of life and glory!
  Bend from heaven thy gracious ear;
  While our waiting souls adore thee,
  Friend of helpless sinners! hear;
    By thy mercy,
  Oh! deliver us, good Lord!

2 Taught by thine unerring Spirit,
  Boldly we draw nigh to God,
  Only in thy spotless merit,
  Only through thy precious blood:
    By thy mercy,
  Oh! deliver us, good Lord!

3 From the depth of nature's blindness,
  From the hardening power of sin,
  From all malice and unkindness,
  From the pride that lurks within,
    By thy mercy,
  Oh! deliver us, good Lord!

4 When temptation sorely presses,
  In the day of Satan's power,
  In our times of deep distresses,
  In each dark and trying hour,
    By thy mercy,
  Oh! deliver us, good Lord!
  James J. Cummins, 1849.

476. *Triune Guidance.* (915.)

1 LEAD us, heavenly Father! lead us
  O'er the world's tempestuous sea;
  Guard us, guide us, keep us, feed us,
  For we have no help but thee;
  Yet possessing every blessing,
  If our God our Father be.

2 Saviour! breathe forgiveness o'er us;
  All our weakness thou dost know;
  Thou didst tread this earth before us;
  Thou didst feel its keenest woe;
  Lone and dreary, faint and weary,
  Through the desert thou didst go.

3 Spirit of our God! descending,
  Fill our hearts with heavenly joy;
  Love with every passion blending,
  Pleasure that can never cloy;
  Thus provided, pardoned, guided,
  Nothing can our peace destroy.
  James Edmeston, 1820.

DIVINE GRACE.

SEYMOUR. 7s. From *Carl Maria von Weber*, 1825.

Come, my soul! thy suit prepare; Jesus loves to answer prayer;
He himself has bid thee pray, Therefore will not say thee nay.

477. *"Ask, and ye shall receive."* (916.)

1 Come, my soul! thy suit prepare;
  Jesus loves to answer prayer;
  He himself has bid thee pray,
  Therefore will not say thee nay.

2 Thou art coming to a King,
  Large petitions with thee bring;
  For his grace and power are such,
  None can ever ask too much.

3 With my burden I begin,
  Lord! remove this load of sin;
  Let thy blood, for sinners spilt,
  Set my conscience free from guilt.

4 Lord! I come to thee for rest,
  Take possession of my breast;
  There thy blood-bought right maintain,
  And without a rival reign.

5 While I am a pilgrim here,
  Let thy love my spirit cheer;
  As my Guide, my Guard, my Friend,
  Lead me to my journey's end.

6 Show me what I have to do,
  Every hour my strength renew;
  Let me live a life of faith.
  Let me die thy people's death.
  John Newton, 1779.

478. *The Mercy-Seat.* (917.)

1 Lord! I cannot let thee go,
  Till a blessing thou bestow;
  Do not turn away thy face,
  Mine's an urgent, pressing case.

2 Once a sinner, near despair,
  Sought thy mercy-seat by prayer,
  Mercy heard and set him free;
  Lord! that mercy came to me.

3 Thou hast helped in every need;
  This emboldens me to plead;
  After so much mercy past,
  Canst thou let me sink at last?

4 No; I must maintain my hold;
  'T is thy goodness makes me bold;
  I can no denial take,
  When I plead for Jesus' sake.
  John Newton, 1779.

479. *The Image of God.* (918.)

1 Father of eternal grace!
  Glorify thyself in me;
  Meekly beaming in my face,
  May the world thine image see.

2 Happy only in thy love,
  Poor, unfriended, or unknown;
  Fix my thoughts on things above,
  Stay my heart on thee alone.

3 Humble, holy, all-resigned
  To thy will, thy will be done!—
  Give me, Lord! the perfect mind
  Of thy well-beloved Son.

4 Counting gain and glory loss,
  May I tread the path he trod;
  Die with Jesus on the cross,
  Rise with him, to thee, my God!
  James Montgomery, 1808.

ASPIRATION.

KENTUCKY. (IOWA.) S. M. Aaron Chapin, 1822.

A charge to keep I have, A God to glo-ri-fy;
A nev-er-dy-ing soul to save, And fit it for the sky.

480. *The Christian's Life-Work.* (922.)

1 A charge to keep I have,
   A God to glorify;
   A never-dying soul to save,
   And fit it for the sky:—

2 To serve the present age,
   My calling to fulfill,—
   Oh! may it all my powers engage,
   To do my Master's will.

3 Arm me with jealous care,
   As in thy sight to live;
   And, Oh! thy servant, Lord! prepare
   A strict account to give.

4 Help me to watch and pray,
   And on thyself rely;
   Assured, if I my trust betray,
   I shall for ever die.
                    Charles Wesley, 1762.

481. *The Throne of Grace.* (923.)

1 Behold the throne of grace!
   The promise calls me near;
   There Jesus shows a smiling face,
   And waits to answer prayer.

2 That rich atoning blood,
   Which sprinkled round I see,
   Provides, for those who come to God,
   An all-prevailing plea.

3 My soul! ask what thou wilt;
   Thou canst not be too bold;
   Since his own blood for thee he spilt,
   What else can he withhold?

4 Thine image, Lord! bestow,
   Thy presence and thy love;
   I ask to serve thee here below,
   And reign with thee above.

5 Teach me to live by faith;
   Conform my will to thine;
   Let me victorious be in death,
   And then in glory shine.
                    John Newton, 1779.

482. *The Lord's Prayer.* (924.)

1 Our heavenly Father! hear
   The prayer we offer now;—
   "Thy name be hallowed far and near!
   To thee all nations bow!

2 "Thy kingdom come!—thy will
   On earth be done in love,
   As saints and seraphim fulfill
   Thy perfect law above!

3 "Our daily bread supply,
   While, by thy word, we live;
   The guilt of our iniquity
   Forgive, as we forgive.

4 "From dark temptation's power,—
   From Satan's wiles defend;
   Deliver in the evil hour,
   And guide us to the end.

5 "Thine, then, for ever be
   Glory and power divine!
   The sceptre, throne, and majesty
   Of heaven and earth are thine."
                    James Montgomery, 1825.

DIVINE GRACE.

SEASONS. L. M. From *Ignace Pleyel*, 1757-1831.

O thou, to whose all-searching sight, The darkness shineth as the light!

Search, prove my heart; it pants for thee; Oh! burst these bonds, and set it free.

483. *The Believer's Support.* (927.)

1 O THOU, to whose all-searching sight
The darkness shineth as the light!
Search, prove my heart; it pants for thee;
Oh! burst these bonds, and set it free.

2 Wash out its stains, refine its dross;
Nail my affections to the cross;
Hallow each thought; let all within
Be clean, as thou, my Lord! art clean.

3 If in this darksome wild I stray,
Be thou my Light, be thou my Way;
No foes, no violence I fear,
No fraud, while thou, my God, art near.

4 When rising floods my soul o'erflow,
When sinks my heart in waves of woe,
Jesus! thy timely aid impart,
And raise my head and cheer my heart.

5 Saviour! where'er thy steps I see,
Dauntless, untired, I follow thee;
Oh! let thy hand support me still,
And lead me to thy holy hill.

From Ger. of *Gerhard Tersteegen*, 1731.
Tr., *John Wesley*, 1739.

484. *"Ask what thou wilt!"* (931.)

1 AND dost thou say, "Ask what thou wilt?"
Lord! I would seize the golden hour;
I pray to be released from guilt,
And freed from sin and Satan's power.

2 More of thy presence, Lord! impart;
More of thine image let me bear;
Erect thy throne within my heart,
And reign without a rival there.

3 Give me to read my pardon sealed,
And from thy joy to draw my strength;
To have thy boundless love revealed,
In all its height and breadth and length.

4 Grant these requests;— I ask no more,
But to thy care the rest resign;
Sick, or in health, or rich, or poor,
All shall be well, if thou art mine.

John Newton, 1779.

485. *Coming to the Mercy-Seat.* (932.)

1 WHAT various hindrances we meet
In coming to a mercy-seat!
Yet who, that knows the worth of prayer,
But wishes to be often there?

2 Prayer makes the darkened cloud withdraw;
Prayer climbs the ladder Jacob saw;
Gives exercise to faith and love;
Brings every blessing from above.

3 Restraining prayer, we cease to fight;
Prayer makes the Christian's armor bright;
And Satan trembles when he sees
The weakest saint upon his knees.

4 Have you no words? ah! think again;
Words flow apace, when you complain,
And fill your fellow-creature's ear
With the sad tale of all your care.

5 Were half the breath, thus vainly spent,
To heaven in supplication sent,
Your cheerful song would oftener be,
"Hear what the Lord has done for me!"

William Cowper, 1772.

174 ASPIRATION.

BYEFIELD. C. M. *Thomas Hastings,* 1840.

Prayer is the soul's sincere desire, Uttered or unexpressed;

The motion of a hidden fire, That trembles in the breast.

486. *Prayer.* (933.)

1 PRAYER is the soul's sincere desire,
   Uttered or unexpressed;
   The motion of a hidden fire,
   That trembles in the breast.

2 Prayer is the burden of a sigh,
   The falling of a tear,
   The upward glancing of an eye,
   When none but God is near.

3 Prayer is the simplest form of speech,
   That infant lips can try;
   Prayer, the sublimest strains that reach
   The Majesty on high.

4 Prayer is the Christian's vital breath,
   The Christian's native air:
   His watchword at the gates of death;
   He enters heaven with prayer.

5 Prayer is the contrite sinner's voice,
   Returning from his ways;
   While angels in their songs rejoice,
   And cry—"Behold he prays!"

6 O thou, by whom we come to God,—
   The Life, the Truth, the Way!
   The path of prayer thyself hast trod;
   Lord! teach us how to pray.
   James Montgomery, 1819.

487. *A clean Heart.* (936.)

1 OH! FOR a heart to praise my God,—
   A heart from sin set free;
   A heart that always feels thy blood
   So freely spilt for me!

2 A heart resigned, submissive, meek,
   My dear Redeemer's throne;
   Where only Christ is heard to speak,
   Where Jesus reigns alone!—

3 An humble, lowly, contrite heart,
   Believing, true, and clean,
   Which neither life nor death can part
   From him that dwells within!—

4 A heart in every thought renewed,
   And filled with love divine;
   Perfect, and right, and pure, and good;
   A copy, Lord! of thine.

5 Thy nature, gracious Lord! impart;
   Come quickly from above;
   Write thy new name upon my heart,—
   Thy new, best name of love.
   Charles Wesley, 1742.

488. PSALM 119. (937.)

1 OH! THAT thy statutes every hour
   Might dwell upon my mind:
   Thence I derive a quickening power,
   And daily peace I find.

2 To meditate thy precepts, Lord!
   Shall be my sweet employ;
   My soul shall ne'er forget thy word;—
   Thy word is all my joy.

3 How would I run in thy commands,
   If thou my heart discharge
   From sin and Satan's hateful chains,
   And set my feet at large!
   Isaac Watts, 1719.

DIVINE GRACE.

BROWN. C. M. *William B. Bradbury, 1840.*

Thou art my Por-tion, O my God! Soon as I know thy way,
My heart makes haste t' o-bey thy word, And suf-fers no de-lay.

489.   PSALM 119.   (942.)

1 Thou art my Portion, O my God!
  Soon as I know thy way,
  My heart makes haste t' obey thy word,
  And suffers no delay.

2 I choose the path of heavenly truth,
  And glory in my choice ;
  Not all the riches of the earth
  Could make me so rejoice.

3 The testimonies of thy grace
  I set before my eyes ;
  Thence I derive my daily strength,
  And there my comfort lies.

4 If once I wander from thy path,
  I think upon my ways,
  Then turn my feet to thy commands,
  And trust thy pardoning grace.

5 Now I am thine, for ever thine,
  Oh ! save thy servant, Lord !
  Thou art my Shield, my Hiding-Place,
  My hope is in thy word.

6 Thou hast inclined this heart of mine
  Thy statutes to fulfill ;
  And thus, till mortal life shall end,
  Would I perform thy will.
  Isaac Watts, 1719.

490.   "Thy Will be done."   (943.)

1 Lord ! as to thy dear cross we flee,
  And plead to be forgiven,
  So let thy life our pattern be,
  And form our souls for heaven.

2 Help us, through good report and ill,
  Our daily cross to bear ;
  Like thee, to do our Father's will,
  Our brethren's griefs to share.

3 Let grace our selfishness expel,
  Our earthliness refine ;
  And kindness in our bosoms dwell
  As free and true as thine.

4 If joy shall at thy bidding fly,
  And grief 's dark day come on,
  We, in our turn, would meekly cry,
  "Father ! thy will be done ! "
  John H. Gurney, 1838.

491.   *Purity of Heart and Life.*   (944.)

1 Oh ! may my heart, by grace renewed,
  Be my Redeemer's throne ;
  And be my stubborn will subdued,
  His government to own.

2 Let deep repentance, faith, and love,
  Be joined with godly fear ;
  And all my conversation prove
  My heart to be sincere.

3 Preserve me from the snares of sin,
  Through my remaining days ;
  And in me let each virtue shine
  To my Redeemer's praise.

4 Let lively hope my soul inspire ;
  Let warm affections rise ;
  And may I wait with strong desire,
  To mount above the skies !
  John Fawcett, 1782.

TRIBULATION.

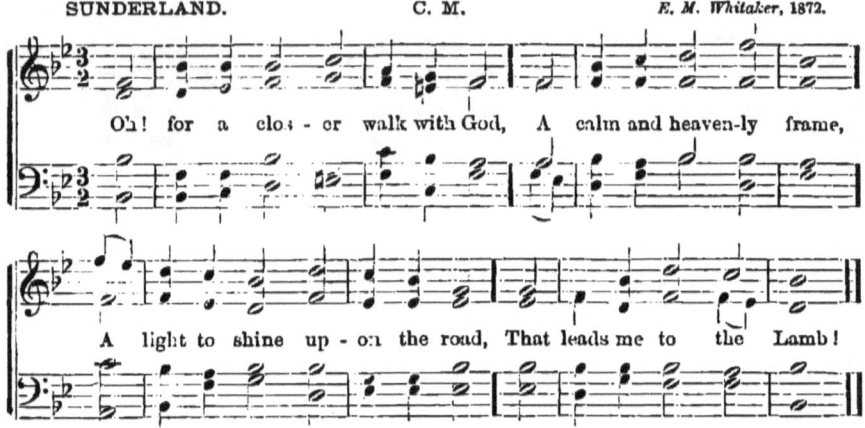

SUNDERLAND. C. M.   E. M. Whitaker, 1872.

Oh! for a clos-er walk with God, A calm and heaven-ly frame, A light to shine up-on the road, That leads me to the Lamb!

492.   *Walking with God.*   (945.)

1 Oh! for a closer walk with God,
   A calm and heavenly frame,
   A light, to shine upon the road,
   That leads me to the Lamb!

2 Where is the blessedness I knew
   When first I saw the Lord?
   Where is the soul-refreshing view
   Of Jesus, and his word?

3 What peaceful hours I once enjoyed!
   How sweet their memory still!
   But they have left an aching void,
   The world can never fill.

4 Return, O holy Dove! return,
   Sweet Messenger of rest!
   I hate the sins that made thee mourn,
   And drove thee from my breast.

5 The dearest idol I have known,
   Whate'er that idol be,
   Help me to tear it from thy throne,
   And worship only thee.

6 So shall my walk be close with God,
   Calm and serene my frame;
   So purer light shall mark the road
   That leads me to the Lamb.
                    William Cowper, 1772.

493.   *Past Joys recalled.*   (948.)

1 Sweet was the time, when first I felt
   The Saviour's pardoning blood,
   Applied to cleanse my soul from guilt,
   And bring me home to God.

2 Soon as the morn the light revealed,
   His praises tuned my tongue;
   And, when the evening shade prevailed,
   His love was all my song.

3 In prayer, my soul drew near the Lord,
   And saw his glory shine;
   And, when I read his holy word,
   I called each promise mine.

4 But now, when evening shade prevails,
   My soul in darkness mourns;
   And, when the morn the light reveals,
   No light to me returns.

5 Rise, Saviour!—help me to prevail,
   And make my soul thy care;
   I know thy mercy cannot fail,—
   Let me that mercy share.
                   John Newton, 1779: v. 5, a.

494.   PSALM 90.   (947.)

1 Return, O God of love! return;
   Earth is a tiresome place:
   How long shall we, thy children, mourn
   Our absence from thy face?

2 Let heaven succeed our painful years,
   Let sin and sorrow cease;
   And, in proportion to our tears,
   So make our joys increase.

3 Thy wonders to thy servants show,
   Make thine own work complete;
   Then shall our souls thy glory know,
   And own thy love was great.
                        Isaac Watts, 1719.

SPIRITUAL TROUBLE.

DUNDEE. (FRENCH.) C. M. *Andre Hart's* "Psalter," 1615.

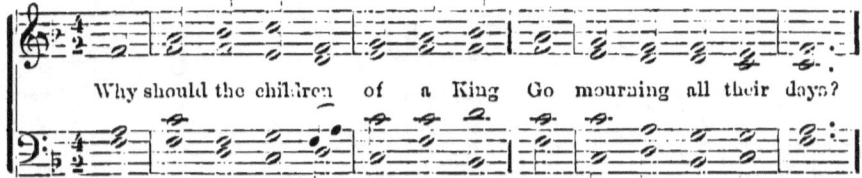

Why should the children of a King Go mourning all their days?

Great Comforter! descend, and bring Some tokens of thy grace.

495. *The witnessing and sealing Spirit.* (954.)

1 WHY should the children of a King
  Go mourning all their days?
  Great Comforter! descend, and bring
  Some tokens of thy grace.

2 Dost thou not dwell in all the saints,
  And seal the heirs of heaven?
  When wilt thou banish my complaints,
  And show my sins forgiven?

3 Assure my conscience of her part
  In the Redeemer's blood;
  And bear thy witness with my heart,
  That I am born of God.

4 Thou art the Earnest of his love,
  The Pledge of joys to come:
  And thy soft wings, celestial Dove!
  Will safe convey me home.
  Isaac Watts, 1709.

496. *Repentance at the Cross.* (955.)

1 OH! if my soul were formed for woe,
  How would I vent my sighs?
  Repentance should like rivers flow,
  From both my streaming eyes.

2 'T was for my sins, my dearest Lord
  Hung on the cursed tree,
  And groaned away a dying life
  For thee, my soul! for thee.

3 Oh! how I hate those lusts of mine,
  That crucified my God,— [flesh
  Those sins, that pierced and nailed his
  Fast to the fatal wood!

4 Yes, my Redeemer! they shall die,
  My heart has so decreed,
  Nor will I spare the guilty things
  That made my Saviour bleed.

5 Whilst with a melting broken heart,
  My murdered Lord I view,
  I'll raise revenge against my sins,
  And slay the murderers too.
  Isaac Watts, 1707.

497. *Love to the Creatures.* (956.)

1 How vain are all things here below,
  How false, and yet how fair!
  Each pleasure hath its poison too,
  And every sweet a snare.

2 The brightest things below the sky
  Give but a flattering light;
  We should suspect some danger nigh,
  Where we possess delight.

3 Our dearest joys, and nearest friends,
  The partners of our blood,
  How they divide our wavering minds,
  And leave but half for God!

4 The fondness of a creature's love,—
  How strong it strikes the sense!
  Thither the warm affections move,
  Nor can we call them thence.

5 Dear Saviour! let thy beauties be
  My soul's eternal food;
  And grace command my heart away
  From all created good.
  Isaac Watts, 1707.

TRIBULATION.

SHOEL. L. M. *Thomas Shoel,* 1810.

Sweet peace of conscience, heavenly guest! Come, fix thy mansion in my breast;
Dispel my doubts, my fears control, And heal the anguish of my soul.

498. *A good Conscience.—* (963.)

1 Sweet peace of conscience, heavenly guest!
Come, fix thy mansion in my breast;
Dispel my doubts, my fears control,
And heal the anguish of my soul.

2 Come, smiling hope, and joy sincere!
Come, make your constant dwelling here;
Still let your presence cheer my heart,
Nor sin compel you to depart.

3 Thou God of hope and peace divine!
Oh! make these sacred pleasures mine;
Forgive my sins, my fears remove,
And send the tokens of thy love.

4 Then should mine eyes, without a tear,
See death with all his terrors near;
My heart should then in death rejoice,
And raptures tune my faltering voice.

Ottiwell Heginbotham, 1768.

499. *The inconstant Heart.* (970.)

1 Ah! wretched, vile, ungrateful heart!
That can from Jesus thus depart;
Thus, fond of trifles, vainly rove,
Forgetful of a Saviour's love!

2 In vain I charge my thoughts to stay,
And chide each vanity away;
There's naught beneath a power divine,
That can this roving heart confine.

3 Jesus! to thee I would return,
At thy dear feet, repentant, mourn;
There let me view thy pardoning love,
And never from thy sight remove.

4 Oh! let thy love, with sweet control,
Bind all the passions of my soul;
Bid every vanity depart,
And dwell for ever in my heart.

Anne Steele, 1760.

500. *An interceding Saviour.* (971.)

1 O Thou, the contrite sinner's Friend,
Who loving, lov'st them to the end!
On this alone my hopes depend,
  That thou wilt plead for me,—for me.

2 When, weary in the Christian race,
Far off appears my resting-place,
And fainting I mistrust thy grace,
  Then, Saviour! plead for me,—for me.

3 When I have erred, and gone astray,
Afar from thine and wisdom's way,
And see no glimmering guiding ray,
  Still, Saviour! plead for me,—for me.

4 When Satan, by my sins made bold,
Strives from thy cross to loose my hold,
Then, with thy pitying arms, enfold,
  And plead, Oh! plead for me,—for me.

5 And, when my dying hour draws near,
Darkened with anguish, guilt, and fear,
Then to my fainting sight appear,
  Pleading in heaven for me,—for me.

6 When the full light of heavenly day
Reveals my sins in dread array,
Say, thou hast washed them all away;
  Oh! say, thou plead'st for me,—for me.

Charlotte Elliott, 1837.

SPIRITUAL TROUBLE. 179

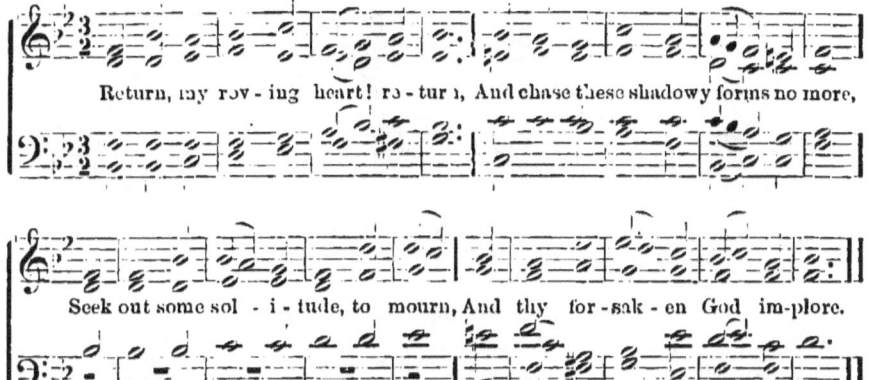

GERMANY. L. M. From *Ludwig van Beethoven*, 1770–1827.

Return, my rov-ing heart! re-turn, And chase these shadowy forms no more,
Seek out some sol-i-tude, to mourn, And thy for-sak-en God im-plore.

501. *Communing with the Heart.* (967.)

1 RETURN, my roving heart! return, [more,
  And chase these shadowy forms no
Seek out some solitude, to mourn,
  And thy forsaken God implore.

2 And thou, my God! whose piercing eye
  Distinct surveys each deep recess,
In these abstracted hours draw nigh,
  And with thy presence fill the place.

3 Through all the mazes of my heart,
  My search let heavenly wisdom guide,
And still its radiant beams impart,
  Till all be searched and purified.

4 Then, with the visits of thy love,
  Vouchsafe my inmost soul to cheer;
Till every grace shall join to prove,
  That God has fixed his dwelling there.
    Philip Doddridge, 1740.

502. *The Spirit's gracious Return.* (969.)

1 AND will th' offended God again
  Return and dwell with sinful men?
Will he, within this bosom, raise
  A living temple to his praise?

2 The joyful news transports my breast;
  All hail! I cry, thou heavenly Guest!
Lift up your heads, ye powers within!
  And let the King of glory in.

3 Enter with all thy heavenly train;
  Here live, and here for ever reign;
Thy sceptre o'er my passions sway;
  Let love command, and I'll obey.

4 Reason and conscience shall submit,
  And pay their homage at thy feet;
To thee I'll consecrate my heart,
  And bid each rival thence depart.
    Samuel Stennett, 1787.

503. *Believing against Hope.* (972.)

1 AWAY, my unbelieving fear!
  Fear shall in me no more have place;
My Saviour doth not yet appear;
  He hides the brightness of his face:
But shall I, therefore, let him go,
  And basely to the tempter yield?
No, in the strength of Jesus, no;
  I never will give up my shield.

2 Although the vine its fruit deny,
  Although the olive yield no oil,
The withering fig-tree droop and die,
  The field elude the tiller's toil,
The empty stall no herd afford,
  And perish all the bleating race,—
Yet will I triumph in the Lord,—
  The God of my salvation praise.

3 In hope, believing against hope,
  Jesus my Lord and God I claim;
Jesus, my Strength, shall lift me up;
  Salvation is in Jesus' name:
To me he soon shall bring it nigh;
  My soul shall then outstrip the wind,
On wings of love mount up on high,
  And leave the world and sin behind.
    Charles Wesley, 1742.

TRIBULATION.

OLNEY. S. M.   *Lowell Mason.* 1830.

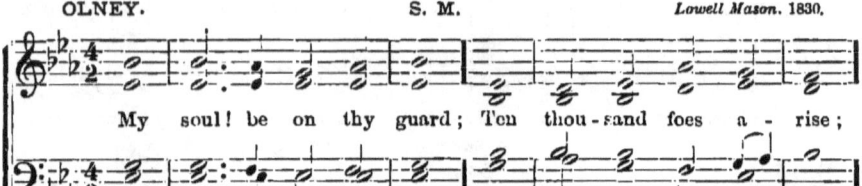

My soul! be on thy guard; Ten thou-sand foes a-rise;

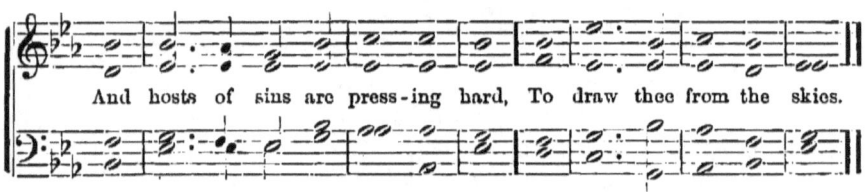

And hosts of sins are press-ing hard, To draw thee from the skies.

504.   *Watch and pray.*   (960.)

1 My soul! be on thy guard;
    Ten thousand foes arise;
  And hosts of sins are pressing hard,
    To draw thee from the skies.

2 Oh! watch, and fight, and pray;
    The battle ne'er give o'er;
  Renew it boldly every day,
    And help divine implore.

3 Ne'er think the victory won,
    Nor once at ease sit down;
  Thy arduous work will not be done,
    Till thou obtain the crown.

4 Fight on, my soul! till death
    Shall bring thee to thy God;
  He'll take thee, at thy parting breath,
    Up to his blest abode.
                George Heath, 1806.

505.   Psalm 25.   (961.)

1 Mine eyes and my desire
    Are ever to the Lord;
  I love to plead his promises,
    And rest upon his word.

2 Turn, turn thee to my soul,
    Bring thy salvation near;
  When will thy hand release my feet
    Out of the deadly snare?

3 When shall the sovereign grace
    Of my forgiving God
  Restore me, from those dangerous ways,
    My wandering feet have trod?

4 With every morning's light,
    My sorrow new begins;
  Look on my anguish and my pain,
    And pardon all my sins.

5 Oh! keep my soul from death,
    Nor put my hope to shame;
  For I have placed my only trust
    In my Redeemer's name.

6 With humble faith I wait
    To see thy face again;
  Of Ismel it shall ne'er be said,
    "He sought the Lord in vain."
                Isaac Watts, 1719.

506.   *Backslidings lamented.*   (962.)

1 O Jesus, full of grace!
    To thee I make my moan;
  Let me again behold thy face;
    Call home thy banished one.

2 Again my pardon seal,
    Again my soul restore,
  And freely my backslidings heal,
    And bid me sin no more.

3 Wilt thou not bid me rise?
    Speak, and my soul shall live;
  Forgive,— my gasping spirit cries,—
    Abundantly forgive.

4 Thine utmost mercy show;
    Say to my drooping soul,—
  "In peace and full assurance go;
    Thy faith hath made thee whole."
                Charles Wesley, 1756.

AFFLICTIONS. 181

GREENVILLE. 8s & 7s. 6 or 8 LINES.
From *Jean Jacques Rousseau*, 1750.
Adapted by *J. B. Cramer*.

Gen-tly, Lord! Oh! gen-tly lead us Thro' this lone-ly vale of tears;
Thro' the changes thou'st de-creed us. Till our last great change appears.
D.C. Let thy good-ness nev-er fail us, Lead us in thy per-fect way.

When temp-ta-tion's darts as-sail us, When in de-vious paths we stray,

507. *Pilgrimage.* (983.)

1 GENTLY, Lord! Oh! gently lead us
  Through this lonely vale of tears;
  Through the changes thou 'st decreed us,
  Till our last great change appears.

2 When temptation's darts assail us,
  When in devious paths we stray,
  Let thy goodness never fail us,
  Lead us in thy perfect way.

3 In the hour of pain and anguish,
  In the hour when death draws near,
  Suffer not our hearts to languish,
  Suffer not our souls to fear.

4 And, when mortal life is ended,
  Bid us on thy bosom rest,
  Till, by angel bands attended,
  We awake among the blest.
  Thomas Hastings, 1831.

508. *Onward and upward.* (982.)

1 TAKE, my soul! thy full salvation,
  Rise, o'er sin, and fear, and care;
  Joy to find, in every station,
  Something still to do or bear:
  Think what Spirit dwells within thee;
  What a Father's smile is thine·
  What a Saviour died to win thee!
  Child of heaven, shouldst thou repine?

2 Haste, then, on from grace to glory,
  Armed by faith, and winged by prayer!
  Heaven's eternal day 's before thee,
  God's own hand shall guide thee there:

Soon shall close thine earthly mission,
  Swift shall pass thy pilgrim days,
Hope soon change to glad fruition,
  Faith to sight, and prayer to praise.
  Henry Francis Lyte, 1829.

509. *Sorrow turned to Joy.* (985.)

1 O MY SOUL! what means this sadness?
  Wherefore art thou thus cast down?
  Let thy griefs be turned to gladness,
  Bid thy restless fears begone;
    Look to Jesus,
  And rejoice in his dear name.

2 Though ten thousand ills beset thee,
  From without and from within,
  Jesus saith, he 'll ne'er forget thee,
  But will save from hell and sin:
    He is faithful
  To perform his gracious word.

3 Though distresses now attend thee,
  And thou tread'st the thorny road;
  His right hand shall still defend thee;
  Soon he 'll bring thee home to God;
    Therefore praise him,—
  Praise the great Redeemer's name.

4 Oh! that I could now adore him,
  Like the heavenly hosts above,
  Who for ever bow before him,
  And unceasing sing his love!
    Happy songsters!
  When shall I your chorus join?
  John Fawcett, 1782.

TRIBULATION.

PORTUGUESE HYMN. 11s. Attributed to *John Reading*, 1760.

How firm a foun-da-tion, ye saints of the Lord! Is laid for your faith, in his ex-cel-lent word! What more can he say, than to you he hath said, You, who un-to Je-sus for ref-uge have fled? You, who un-to Je-sus for ref-uge have fled?

510. *The Promises of Christ.* (990.)

1 How firm a foundation, ye saints of the Lord!
Is laid for your faith, in his excellent word! [hath said,
What more can he say, than to you he
You, who unto Jesus for refuge have fled?

2 "Fear not, I am with thee, Oh! be not dismayed;
I, I am thy God, and will still give thee aid; [thee to stand,
I'll strengthen thee, help thee, and cause
Upheld by my righteous, omnipotent hand.

3 When, through the deep waters, I call thee to go,
The rivers of woe shall not thee overflow;
For I will be with thee, thy trouble to bless,
And sanctify to thee thy deepest distress.

4 When through fiery trials thy pathway shall lie, [ply;
My grace, all-sufficient, shall be thy sup-
The flame shall not hurt thee; I only design [refine.
Thy dross to consume, and thy gold to

5 E'en down to old age, all my people shall prove
My sovereign, eternal, unchangeable love:
And, when hoary hairs shall their temples adorn, [be borne.
Like lambs they shall still in my bosom

6 The soul that on Jesus hath leaned for repose,
I will not, I will not desert to his foes;
That soul, though all hell should endeavor to shake, [sake."
I'll never,—no, never,—no, never for-
K———, 1787.

511. *The Home above.* (991.)

1 My rest is in heaven, my rest is not here,
Then why should I murmur when trials appear?
Be hushed, my dark spirit! the worst that can come, [thee home.
But shortens thy journey, and hastens

2 It is not for me to be seeking my bliss,
And building my hopes in a region like this;
I ask not my portion, I seek not my rest,
Till I find them, O Lord! in thy sheltering breast.

Henry Francis Lyte, 1833.

AFFLICTIONS. 183

HORTON. 7s *Xavier Schnyder von Wartensee*, 1786.

Cast thy bur-den on the Lord, On-ly lean up-on his word;
Thou wilt soon have cause to bless His e-ter-nal faith-ful-ness.

512. *God's Faithfulness.* (998.)

1 Cast thy burden on the Lord,
Only lean upon his word;
Thou wilt soon have cause to bless
His eternal faithfulness.

2 He sustains thee by his hand,
He enables thee to stand;
Those, whom Jesus once hath loved,
From his grace are never moved.

3 Heaven and earth may pass away,
God's free grace shall not decay;
He hath promised to fulfill
All the pleasure of his will.

4 Jesus! Guardian of thy flock,
Be thyself our constant Rock;
Make us, by thy powerful hand,
Strong as Sion's mountain stand.
Rowland Hill, 1783.

513. *The Christian Soldier cheered.* (1001.)

1 Much in sorrow, oft in woe,
Onward, Christians! onward go;
Fight the fight; and, worn with strife,
Steep with tears the bread of life.

2 Onward, Christians! onward go;
Join the war, and face the foe;
Faint not:—much doth yet remain;
Dreary is the long campaign.

3 Shrink not, Christians! will ye yield?
Will ye quit the painful field?
Will ye flee in danger's hour?
Know ye not your Captain's power?

4 Let your drooping hearts be glad;
March, in heavenly armor clad;
Fight, nor think the battle long;
Victory soon shall tune your song.

5 Let not sorrow dim your eye;
Soon shall every tear be dry;
Let not woe your course impede;
Great your strength, if great your need.

6 Onward, then; to battle move;
More than conquerors ye shall prove;
Though opposed by many a foe,
Christian soldiers! onward go.
First 10 lines, *Henry Kirke White*, 1806.
Completed by *Fanny Fuller Maitland*, 1827.

514. *All-sufficient Grace.* (1000.)

1 Wait, my soul! upon the Lord,
To his gracious promise flee,
Laying hold upon his word,—
"As thy days thy strength shall be."

2 If the sorrows of thy case
Seem peculiar still to thee,
God has promised needful grace;
"As thy days thy strength shall be."

3 Days of trial, days of grief,
In succession thou mayest see;
This is still thy sweet relief,—
"As thy days thy strength shall be."

4 Rock of ages! I'm secure,
With thy promise, full and free,
Faithful, positive, and sure,—
"As thy days thy strength shall be."
William F. Lloyd, 1835.

184   TRIBULATION.

OLIVET.   6s & 4s.   *Lowell Mason*, 1831.

My faith looks up to thee, Thou Lamb of Calvary, Saviour divine! Now hear me while I pray, Take all my guilt away, Oh! let me from this day, Be wholly thine!

515.   *Looking to Jesus.*   (1004.)

1 My FAITH looks up to thee,
    Thou Lamb of Calvary,
      Saviour divine !
   Now hear me while I pray,
   Take all my guilt away,
   Oh ! let me, from this day,
      Be wholly thine !

2 May thy rich grace impart
   Strength to my fainting heart;
      My zeal inspire;
   As thou hast died for me,
   Oh ! may my love to thee
   Pure, warm, and changeless be,
      A living fire !

3 While life's dark maze I tread,
   And griefs around me spread,
      Be thou my Guide;
   Bid darkness turn to day,
   Wipe sorrow's tears away,
   Nor let me ever stray
      From thee aside.

4 When ends life's transient dream,
   When death's cold, sullen stream
      Shall o'er me roll,
   Blest Saviour ! then, in love,
   Fear and distrust remove;
   Oh ! bear me safe above,
      A ransomed soul !

Ray Palmer, 1830.

516.   *Jesus, All in All.*   (1005.)

1 JESUS ! thy name I love,
   All other names above,
      Jesus, my Lord !
   Oh ! thou art all to me;
   Nothing to please I see,
   Nothing apart from thee,
      Jesus, my Lord !

2 Thou, blesséd Son of God !
   Hast bought me with thy blood,
      Jesus, my Lord !
   Oh ! how great is thy love,
   All other loves above,—
   Love that I daily prove,
      Jesus, my Lord !

3 When unto thee I flee,
   Thou wilt my Refuge be,
      Jesus, my Lord !
   What need I now to fear ?
   What earthly grief or care ?
   Since thou art ever near,
      Jesus, my Lord !

4 Soon thou wilt come again;
   I shall be happy then,
      Jesus, my Lord !
   Then thine own face I'll see,
   Then I shall like thee be,
   Then evermore with thee,
      Jesus, my Lord !

Anon., 1851.

AFFLICTIONS.

AGATHA.   Gs. 8 LINES.   From *Carl Maria Von Weber*, 1820.

My Jesus! as thou wilt! Oh! may thy will be mine; Into thy hand of love I would my all resign; Thro' sorrow, or thro' joy, Conduct me as thine own, And help me still to say— My Lord! thy will be done.

517.   *"Mein Jesu! wie Du willst!"*   (1006.)

1 My Jesus! as thou wilt!
   Oh! may thy will be mine;
Into thy hand of love
   I would my all resign;
Through sorrow, or through joy,
   Conduct me as thine own,
And help me still to say,—
   My Lord! thy will be done!

2 My Jesus! as thou wilt!
   Though seen through many a tear,
Let not my star of hope
   Grow dim or disappear:
Since thou on earth hast wept,
   And sorrowed oft alone,
If I must weep with thee,
   My Lord! thy will be done!

3 My Jesus! as thou wilt!
   If loved ones must depart,
Suffer not sorrow's flood
   To overwhelm my heart:
For they are blest with thee;
   Their race and conflict won;
Let me but follow them;
   My Lord! thy will be done!

4 My Jesus! as thou wilt!
   All shall be well for me;
Each changing future scene
   I gladly trust with thee;
Straight to my home above
   I travel calmly on,
And sing, in life or death,—
   My Lord! thy will be done!

Ger., *Benjamin Schmolke*, 1716.
Tr., *Jane Borthwick*, 1854.

518.   *Thy Way, not mine.*   (1007.)

1 Thy way, not mine, O Lord!
   However dark it be!
Lead me by thine own hand;
   Choose out the path for me;
I dare not choose my lot;
   I would not, if I might;
Choose thou for me, my God!
   So shall I walk aright.

2 Choose thou for me my friends,
   My sickness or my health;
Choose thou my cares for me,
   My poverty or wealth:
Not mine,—not mine,—the choice,
   In things or great or small;
Be thou my Guide, my Strength,
   My Wisdom, and my All.

Horatius Bonar, 1857.

TRIBULATION.

LEIGHTON. S. M. *Henry W. Greatorex*, 1849.

My soul! repeat his praise, Whose mercies are so great;
Whose anger is so slow to rise, So ready to abate.

519. PSALM 103. (1014.)

1 My soul! repeat his praise,
  Whose mercies are so great;
  Whose anger is so slow to rise,
  So ready to abate.

2 God will not always chide;
  And, when his strokes are felt,
  His strokes are fewer than our crimes,
  And lighter than our guilt.

3 High as the heavens are raised
  Above the ground we tread,
  So far the riches of his grace
  Our highest thoughts exceed.

4 His power subdues our sins,
  And his forgiving love,
  Far as the east is from the west,
  Doth all our guilt remove.

Isaac Watts, 1719.

520. *God's Hand in Sorrow.* (1018.)

1 It is thy hand, my God!
  My sorrow comes from thee;
  I bow beneath thy chastening rod,
  'T is love that bruises me.

2 I would not murmur, Lord!
  Before thee I am dumb; [word,
  Lest I should breathe one murm'ring
  To thee for help I come.

3 My God! thy name is Love;
  A Father's hand is thine;
  With tearful eyes I look above,
  And cry, "Thy will be mine!"

4 I know thy will is right,
  Though it may seem severe;
  Thy path is still unsullied light,
  Though dark it may appear,

5 Jesus for me hath died;
  Thy Son thou didst not spare;
  His pierced hands, his bleeding side,
  Thy love for me declare.

6 Here my poor heart can rest;
  My God! it cleaves to thee;
  Thy will is love; thine end is blest;
  All work for good to me.

James George Deck, 1843.

521. *Burdens cast on God.* (1020.)

1 How gentle God's commands!
  How kind his precepts are!—
  "Come, cast your burdens on the Lord,
  And trust his constant care."

2 While Providence supports,
  Let saints securely dwell;
  That hand, which bears all nature up,
  Shall guide his children well.

3 Why should this anxious load
  Press down your weary mind?
  Haste to your heavenly Father's throne,
  And sweet refreshment find.

4 His goodness stands approved,
  Down to the present day:
  I'll drop my burden at his feet,
  And bear his song away.

Philip Doddridge, 1740.

AFFLICTIONS.

DENNIS. S. M.
From *Hans G. Nägeli*, 1773–1836.
Adapted by *Lowell Mason*, 1849.

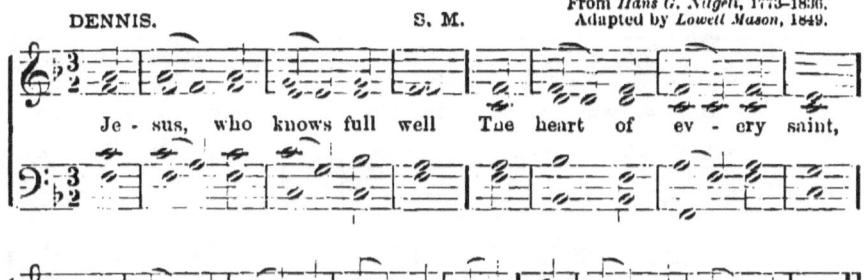

Je-sus, who knows full well The heart of ev-ery saint,

In-vites us, all our grief to tell, To pray and nev-er faint.

522. *Importunity.* (1023.)

1 JESUS, who knows full well
  The heart of every saint,
Invites us, all our grief to tell,
  To pray and never faint.

2 He bows his gracious ear,—
  We never plead in vain;
Then let us wait till he appear,
  And pray, and pray again.

3 Jesus, the Lord, will hear
  His chosen when they cry;
Yes, though he may awhile forbear
  He 'll help them from on high.

4 Then let us earnest cry,
  And never faint in prayer;
He sees, he hears, and, from on high,
  Will make our cause his care.
    John Newton, 1779, a.

523. *"Befiehl du deine Wege."* (1021.)

1 COMMIT thou all thy griefs
  And ways into his hands,
To his sure truth and tender care,
  Who earth and heaven commands.

2 Give to the winds thy fears!
  Hope, and be undismayed;
God hears thy sighs and counts thy tears,
  God shall lift up thy head.

3 Through waves, and clouds, and storms,
  He gently clears thy way;
Wait thou his time; so shall this night
  Soon end in joyous day.

4 What, though thou rulest not?
  Yet heaven, and earth and hell,
Proclaim,—God sitteth on the throne,
  And ruleth all things well.

5 Leave to his sovereign sway
  To choose, and to command;
So shalt thou wondering own, his way
  How wise, how strong his hand!
    Ger., *Paul Gerhardt*, 1666.
    Tr., *John Wesley*, 1739.

524. *The Cross and Crown.* (1022.)

1 OH! WHAT, if we are Christ's,
  Is earthly shame or loss?
Bright shall the crown of glory be,
  When we have borne the cross.

2 Keen was the trial once,
  Bitter the cup of woe,
When martyred saints, baptized in blood,
  Christ's sufferings shared below.

3 Bright is their glory now,
  Boundless their joy above,
Where, on the bosom of their God,
  They rest in perfect love.

4 Lord! may that grace be ours,
  Like them, in faith, to bear
All that of sorrow, grief, or pain
  May be our portion here.

5 Enough, if thou at last
  The word of blessing give,
And let us rest beneath thy feet,
  Where saints and angels live.
    Henry W. Baker, 1852.

TRIBULATION.

NAOMI. C. M. Lowell Mason, 1836.

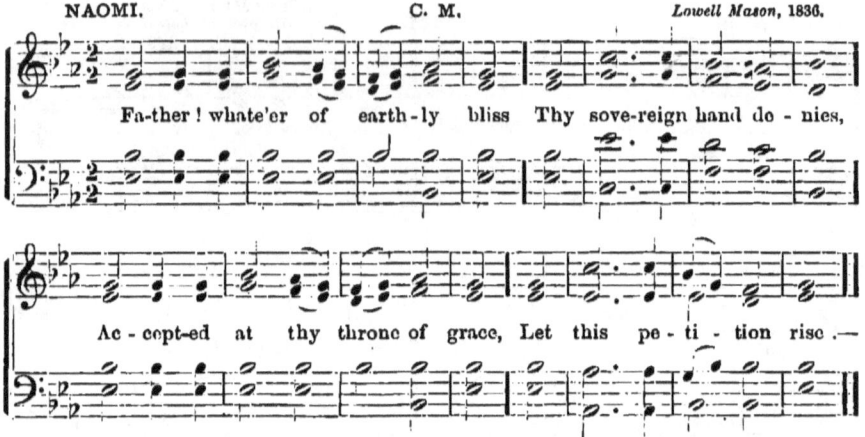

Fa-ther! whate'er of earth-ly bliss Thy sove-reign hand de-nies, Ac-cept-ed at thy throne of grace, Let this pe-ti-tion rise.—

525. *Resignation.* (1026.)

1 FATHER! whate'er of earthly bliss
    Thy sovereign hand denies,
  Accepted at thy throne of grace,
    Let this petition rise :—

2 "Give me a calm, a thankful heart,
    From every murmur free ;
  The blessings of thy grace impart,
    And let me live to thee.

3 Let the sweet hope, that thou art mine,
    My path of life attend ;
  Thy presence through my journey shine,
    And bless its happy end."
            Anne Steele, 1760.

526. *Submission.* (1029.)

1 O LORD! my best desire fulfill,
    And help me to resign
  Life, health, and comfort to thy will,
    And make thy pleasure mine.

2 Why should I shrink at thy command,
    Whose love forbids my fears?
  Or tremble at the gracious hand
    That wipes away my tears?

3 No! let me rather freely yield
    What most I prize to thee,
  Who never hast a good withheld,
    Or wilt withhold, from me.

4 Thy favor, all my journey through,
    Thou art engaged to grant :
  What else I want, or think I do,
    'T is better still to want.

5 Wisdom and mercy guide my way ;
    Shall I resist them both ?
  A poor blind creature of a day,
    And crushed before the moth !

6 But, ah ! my inmost spirit cries,—
    Still bind me to thy sway ;
  Else the next cloud, that veils my skies,
    Drives all these thoughts away.
            William Cowper, 1772.

527. *Submission to Affliction.* (1031.)

1 NAKED as from the earth we came,
    And crept to life at first,
  We to the earth return again,
    And mingle with our dust.

2 The dear delights we here enjoy,
    And fondly call our own,
  Are but short favors borrowed now,
    To be repaid anon.

3 'T is God that lifts our comforts high,
    Or sinks them in the grave ;
  He gives, and — blessed be his name !—
    He takes but what he gave.

4 Peace, all our angry passions ! then ;
    Let each rebellious sigh
  Be silent, at his sovereign will,
    And every murmur die.

5 If smiling mercy crown our lives
    Its praises shall be spread ;
  And we 'll adore the justice too,
    That strikes our comforts dead.
            Isaac Watts, 1707.

AFFLICTIONS.

BRATTLE STREET. C. M. 8 LINES. From *Ignace Pleyel*, 1757-1831.

When languor and disease invade, This trembling house of clay, 'T is sweet to look beyond the flesh,...... And long to fly away; Sweet to look inward, and attend The whispers of his love; Sweet to look upward, to the place Where Jesus pleads above.

528. *Consolations in Illness.* (1032.)

1 When languor and disease invade
  This trembling house of clay,
'T is sweet to look beyond the flesh,
  And long to fly away;
Sweet to look inward, and attend
  The whispers of his love;
Sweet to look upward, to the place
  Where Jesus pleads above.

2 Sweet to reflect, how grace divine
  My sins on Jesus laid;
Sweet to remember, that his blood
  My debt of sufferings paid;
Sweet on his righteousness to stand,
  Which saves from second death,
Sweet to experience, day by day,
  His Spirit's quickening breath.

3 Sweet, in the confidence of faith,
  To trust his firm decrees;
Sweet to lie passive in his hands,
  And know no will but his:
If such the sweetness of the stream,
  What must the Fountain be,
Where saints and angels draw their bliss
  Immediately from thee?

Augustus M. Toplady, 1778.

529. *Rest in the divine Will.* (1033.)

1 Whilst thee I seek, protecting Power!
  Be my vain wishes stilled;
And may this consecrated hour
  With better hopes be filled!
Thy love the power of thought bestowed;
  To thee my thoughts would soar;
Thy mercy o'er my life has flowed;
  That mercy I adore.

2 In each event of life, how clear
  Thy ruling hand I see!
Each blessing to my soul more dear!
  Because conferred by thee:
In every joy that crowns my days,
  In every pain I bear,
My heart shall find delight in praise,
  Or seek relief in prayer.

3 When gladness wings the favored hour,
  Thy love my thoughts shall fill;
Resigned, when storms of sorrow lower,
  My soul shall meet thy will:
My lifted eye, without a tear,
  The gathering storm shall see;
My steadfast heart shall know no fear;
  That heart will rest on thee.

Helen Maria Williams, 1786.

TRIBULATION.

BARBY. C. M. *William Tansur, 1735.*

O thou, from whom all good-ness flows! I lift my heart to thee;
In all my sor-rows, con-flicts, woes, Dear Lord! re-mem-ber me.

530. *"Remember me."* (1040.)

1 O THOU, from whom all goodness flows!
   I lift my heart to thee;
   In all my sorrows, conflicts, woes,
   Dear Lord! remember me.

2 When, groaning, on my burdened heart
   My sins lie heavily,
   My pardon speak, new peace impart,
   In love, remember me.

3 If on my face, for thy dear name,
   Shame and reproaches be,
   All hail reproach, and welcome shame,
   If thou remember me!

4 The hour is near — consigned to death,
   I own the just decree;
   Saviour! with my last parting breath,
   I'll cry — "Remember me!"
   Thomas Haweis, 1792.

531. *The Believer's Portion.* (1041.)

1 IF CHRIST is mine, then all is mine,
   And more than angels know;
   Both present things and things to come,
   And grace and glory too.

2 If he is mine, I need not fear
   The rage of earth and hell;
   He will support my feeble frame,
   And all their power repel.

3 If he is mine, let friends forsake,
   And earthly comforts flee:
   He, the Dispenser of all good,
   Is more than these to me.

4 If he is mine, I'll fearless pass
   Through death's tremendous vale;
   He'll be my comfort and my stay,
   When heart and flesh shall fail.

5 Let Jesus tell me, he is mine;
   I nothing want beside:
   My soul shall at the Fountain live,
   When all the streams are dried.
   Benjamin Beddome, 1776.

532. PSALM 27. (1037.)

1 SOON as I heard my Father say, —
   "Ye children! seek my grace;"
   My heart replied without delay, —
   "I'll seek my Father's face."

2 Let not thy face be hid from me,
   Nor frown my soul away;
   God of my life! I fly to thee,
   In a distressing day.

3 Should friends and kindred near and dear,
   Leave me to want, or die,
   My God would make my life his care,
   And all my need supply.

4 My fainting flesh had died with grief,
   Had not my soul believed,
   To see thy grace provide relief;
   Nor was my hope deceived.

5 Wait on the Lord, ye trembling saints!
   And keep your courage up:
   He'll raise your spirit when it faints,
   And far exceed your hope.
   Isaac Watts, 1719.

AFFLICTIONS.

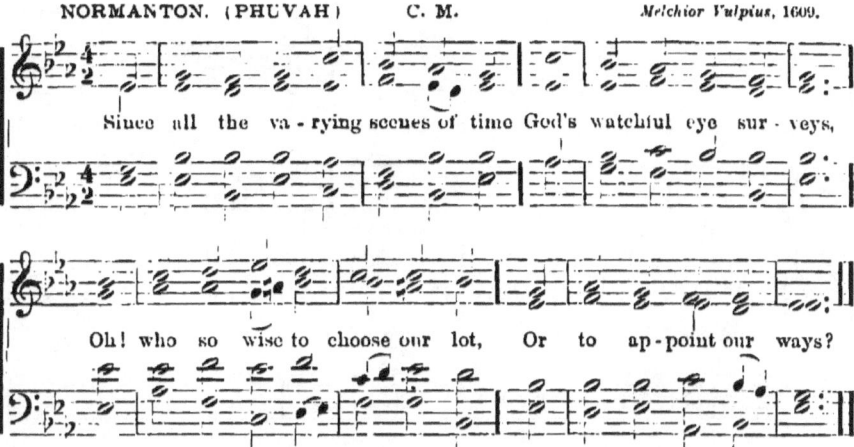

NORMANTON. (PHUVAH)   C. M.   *Melchior Vulpius*, 1609.

Since all the va-rying scenes of time God's watchful eye sur-veys,

Oh! who so wise to choose our lot, Or to ap-point our ways?

533.   *Confidence in God's Government.*   (1046.)

1 Since all the varying scenes of time
    God's watchful eye surveys,
Oh! who so wise to choose our lot,
    Or to appoint our ways?

2 Good, when he gives—supremely good;
    Nor less, when he denies:
E'en crosses, from his sovereign hand,
    Are blessings in disguise.

3 Why should we doubt a Father's love,
    So constant and so kind?
To his unerring gracious will,
    Be every wish resigned.

4 In thy fair book of life divine,
    My God! inscribe my name;
There let it fill some humble place,
    Beneath my Lord, the Lamb!
                        James Hervey, 1745, a.

534.   *Light shining out of Darkness.*   (1043.)

1 God moves in a mysterious way,
    His wonders to perform;
He plants his footsteps in the sea,
    And rides upon the storm.

2 Deep in unfathomable mines
    Of never-failing skill,
He treasures up his bright designs,
    And works his sovereign will.

3 Ye fearful saints! fresh courage take;
    The clouds, ye so much dread,
Are big with mercy, and shall break
    In blessings on your head.

4 Judge not the Lord by feeble sense,
    But trust him for his grace;
Behind a frowning providence,
    He hides a smiling face.

5 His purposes will ripen fast,
    Unfolding every hour;
The bud may have a bitter taste,
    But sweet will be the flower.

6 Blind unbelief is sure to err,
    And scan his work in vain;
God is his own interpreter,
    And he will make it plain.
                        William Cowper, 1772.

535.   *Comfort for the Mourner.*   (1051.)

1 O Thou, who driest the mourner's tear!
    How dark this world would be,
If, when deceived and wounded here,
    We could not fly to thee!

2 The friends, who in our sunshine live,
    When winter comes, are flown;
And he, who has but tears to give,
    Must weep those tears alone.

3 Oh! who would bear life's stormy doom,
    Did not thy wing of love   [gloom,
Come, brightly wafting, through the
    Our peace-branch from above?

4 Then sorrow, touched by thee, grows
    With more than rapture's ray; [bright,
As darkness shows us worlds of light
    We never saw by day.
                        Thomas Moore, 1816.

TRIBULATION.

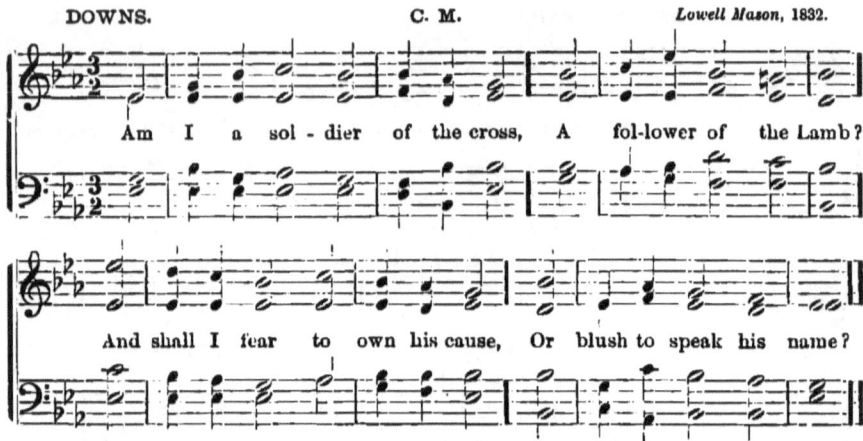

Am I a sol-dier of the cross, A fol-lower of the Lamb?
And shall I fear to own his cause, Or blush to speak his name?

536. *Holy Fortitude.* (1052.)

1 Am I a soldier of the cross,
A follower of the Lamb?
And shall I fear to own his cause,
Or blush to speak his name?

2 Must I be carried to the skies,
On flowery beds of ease?
While others fought to win the prize,
And sailed through bloody seas?

3 Are there no foes for me to face?
Must I not stem the flood?
Is this vile world a friend to grace,
To help me on to God?

4 Sure, I must fight, if I would reign;
Increase my courage, Lord!
I'll bear the toil, endure the pain,
Supported by thy word.

5 Thy saints in all this glorious war,
Shall conquer, though they die;
They see the triumph from afar,
And seize it with their eye.

6 When that illustrious day shall rise,
And all thine armies shine
In robes of victory through the skies,
The glory shall be thine.
Isaac Watts, 1723.

537. *Refuge and Strength in God.* (1034.)

1 My God! 't is to thy mercy-seat,
My soul for shelter flies;
'T is here I find a safe retreat,
When storms and tempests rise!

2 My cheerful hope can never die,
If thou, my God! art near;
Thy grace can raise my comforts high,
And banish every fear.

3 My great Protector, and my Lord!
Thy constant aid impart;
And let thy kind, thy gracious word
Sustain my trembling heart.

4 Oh! never let my soul remove
From this divine retreat;
Still let me trust thy power and love,
And dwell beneath thy feet.
Anne Steele, 1760.

538. *The Peace of God.* (1054.)

1 We bless thee for thy peace, O God!
Deep as the soundless sea,
Which falls like sunshine on the road
Of those who trust in thee;—

2 That peace which suffers and is strong,
Trusts where it cannot see,
Deems not the trial way too long,
But leaves the end with thee;—

3 That peace which flows serene and deep,
A river in the soul,
Whose banks a living verdure keep;—
God's sunshine o'er the whole.

4 Such, Father! give our hearts such peace,
Whate'er the outward be,
Till all life's discipline shall cease,
And we go home to thee.
Anon., 1862.

AFFLICTIONS.

RETREAT.   L. M.   *Thomas Hastings, 1832.*

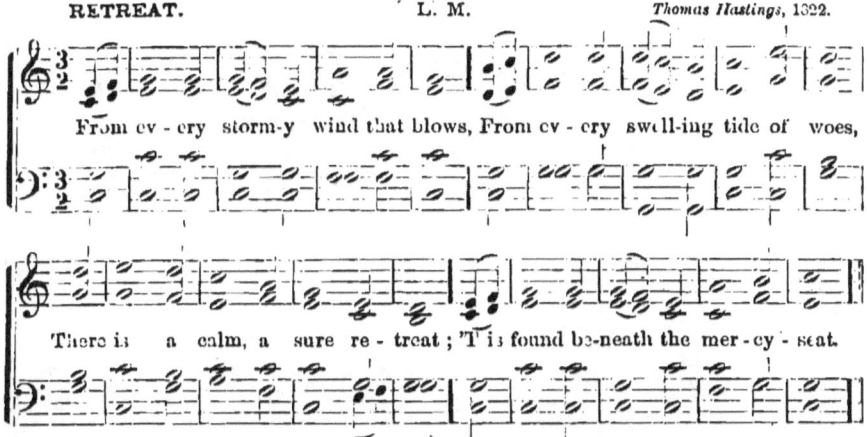

From ev-ery storm-y wind that blows, From ev-ery swell-ing tide of woes, There is a calm, a sure re-treat; 'T is found be-neath the mer-cy - seat.

539.   *The Mercy-Seat.*   (1055.)

1 From every stormy wind that blows,
From every swelling tide of woes,
There is a calm, a sure retreat; –
'T is found beneath the mercy-seat.

2 There is a place where Jesus sheds
The oil of gladness on our heads, –
A place, than all besides. more sweet ;
It is the blood-bought mercy-seat.

3 There is a spot where spirits blend,
Where friend holds fellowship with friend;
Though sundered far, by faith they meet
Around one common mercy-seat.

4 There, there, on eagle wings we soar,
And time, and sense seem all no more ;
And heaven comes down our souls to greet,
And glory crowns the mercy-seat!

5 Oh! may my hand forget her skill,
My tongue be silent, cold, and still,
This bounding heart forget to beat,
If I forget the mercy-seat!

Hugh Stowell, 1827.

540.   *"Thy Will be done."*   (1058.)

1 My God and Father! while I stray
Far from my home, in life's rough way,
Oh! teach me, from my heart, to say, –
"Thy will be done, – thy will be done!"

2 What, though in lonely grief I sigh
For friends beloved, no longer nigh?
Submissive still would I reply,
"Thy will be done, – thy will be done!"

3 If thou should'st call me to resign
What most I prize, – it ne'er was mine ,
I only yield thee what was thine : –
"Thy will be done, – thy will be done!"

4 If but my fainting heart be blessed
With thy sweet Spirit for its guest,
My God! to thee I leave the rest ; –
"Thy will be done, – thy will be done!"

5 Renew my will, from day to day ;
Blend it with thine, and take away
All that now makes it hard to say, –
"Thy will be done, – thy will be done!"

6 Then, when on earth I breathe no more
The prayer, oft mixed with tears before,
I 'll sing upon a happier shore, –
"Thy will be done, – thy will be done!"

Charlotte Elliott, 1834.

541.   *The Darkness of Providence.*   (1059.)

1 Lord! we adore thy vast designs,
Th' obscure abyss of providence ;
Too deep to sound with mortal lines,
Too dark to view with feeble sense.

2 Now thou arrayest thine awful face
In angry frowns, without a smile :
We, through the cloud, believe thy grace,
Secure of thy compassion still.

3 Dear Father! if thy lifted rod
Resolve to scourge us here below,
Still we must lean upon our God ;
Thine arm shall bear us safely through.

Isaac Watts, 1707.

TRIBULATION

WARD. L. M. Scotch. Arr. by *Lowell Mason*, 1830.

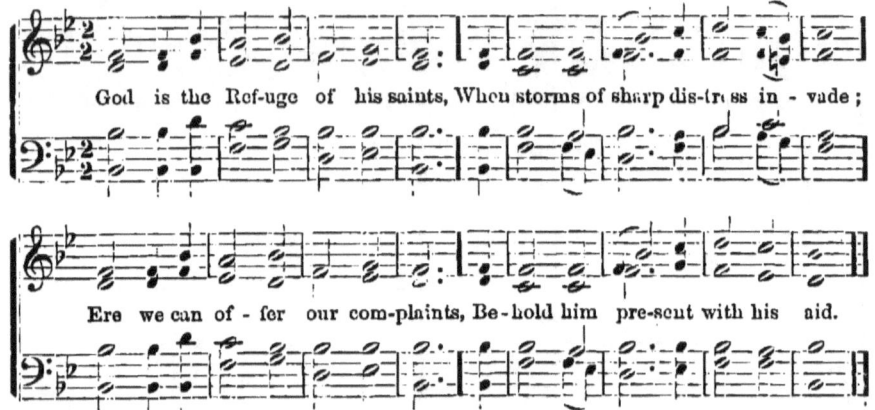

God is the Refuge of his saints, When storms of sharp distress invade; Ere we can offer our complaints, Behold him present with his aid.

542. PSALM 46. (1061.)

1 GOD is the Refuge of his saints,
  When storms of sharp distress invade;
  Ere we can offer our complaints,
  Behold him present with his aid.

2 Let mountains, from their seats be hurled,
  Down to the deep, and buried there;
  Convulsions shake the solid world;—
  Our faith shall never yield to fear.

3 Loud may the troubled ocean roar,—
  In sacred peace our souls abide,
  While every nation, every shore,
  Trembles, and dreads the swelling tide.

4 There is a stream, whose gentle flow
  Supplies the city of our God;
  Life, love, and joy still gliding through,
  And watering our divine abode:—

5 That sacred stream,—thy holy word,—
  That all our raging fear controls:
  Sweet peace thy promises afford,
  And give new strength to fainting souls.

6 Zion enjoys her monarch's love,
  Secure against a threatening hour;
  Nor can her firm foundations move,
  Built on his truth, and armed with power.

Isaac Watts, 1719.

543. *Strength for every Trial.* (1062.)

1 HAST thou within a care so deep,
  It chases from thine eyelids sleep?
  To thy Redeemer take that care,
  And change anxiety to prayer.

2 Hast thou a hope, with which thy heart
  Would almost feel it death to part?
  Entreat thy God that hope to crown,
  Or give thee strength to lay it down.

3 Hast thou a friend, whose image dear
  May prove an idol worshiped here?
  Implore the Lord, that naught may be
  A shade between himself and thee.

4 Whate'er the care that breaks thy rest,
  Whate'er the wish that swells thy breast,
  Spread before God that wish, that care,
  And change anxiety to prayer.

Anon., 1851.

544. *The Wisdom of God.* (1063.)

1 WAIT, O my soul! thy Maker's will;
  Tumultuous passions! all be still;
  Nor let a murmuring thought arise;
  His ways are just, his counsels wise.

2 He in the thickest darkness dwells;
  Performs his work, the cause conceals;
  And, though his footsteps are unknown
  Judgment and truth support his throne.

3 In heaven and earth, in air and seas,
  He executes his wise decrees;
  And by his saints it stands confessed,
  That what he does is ever best.

4 Then, O my soul! submissive wait,
  With reverence bow before his seat;
  And, midst the terrors of his rod,
  Trust in a wise and gracious God.

Benjamin Beddome, 1778.

SELF-EXAMINATION.

APPLETON. L. M. Adapted from *William Boyce*, 1710-1779.

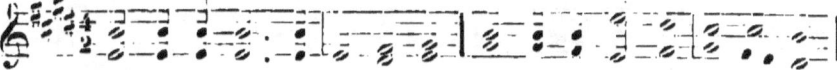

Hap-py the man, whose cautious feet, Shun the broad way that sinners go;
Who hates the place where atheists meet, And fears to talk as scoffers do.

545. PSALM 1. (1070.)

1 HAPPY the man, whose cautious feet
Shun the broad way that sinners go ;
Who hates the place where atheists meet,
And fears to talk as scoffers do.

2 He loves t' employ his morning light
Among the statutes of the Lord,
And spends the wakeful hours of night,
With pleasure pondering o'er the word.

3 He, like a plant by gentle streams,
Shall flourish in immortal green ;
And heaven will shine, with kindest beams,
On every work his hands begin.

4 But sinners find their counsels crossed ;
As chaff before the tempest flies,
So shall their hopes be blown and lost,
When the last trumpet shakes the skies.
Isaac Watts, 1719.

546. PSALM 26. (1070.)

1 JUDGE me, O Lord! and prove my ways,
And try my reins, and try my heart ;
My faith upon thy promise stays,
Nor from thy law my feet depart.

2 I hate to walk, I hate to sit,
With men of vanity and lies ;
The scoffer and the hypocrite
Are the abhorrence of mine eyes,

3 Amongst thy saints will I appear,
With hands well washed in innocence :
But, when I stand before thy bar,
The blood of Christ is my defence.

4 I love thy habitation, Lord !—
The temple where thine honors dwell ;
There shall I hear thy holy word,
And there thy works of wonder tell.

5 Let not my soul be joined at last
With men of treachery and blood,
Since I my days on earth have passed
Among the saints, and near my God.
Isaac Watts, 1719.

547. PSALM 139. (1072.)

1 LORD! thou hast searched and seen me through ;
Thine eye commands, with piercing view,
My rising and my resting hours,
My heart and flesh, with all their powers.

2 My thoughts, before they are my own,
Are to my God distinctly known ;
He knows the words I mean to speak,
Ere from my opening lips they break.

3 Within thy circling power I stand ;
On every side I find thy hand ;
Awake, asleep, at home, abroad,
I am surrounded still with God.

4 Amazing knowledge, vast and great !
What large extent ! what lofty height !
My soul, with all the powers I boast,
Is in the boundless prospect lost.

5 Oh! may these thoughts possess my breast,
Where'er I rove, where'er I rest ;
Nor let my weaker passions dare
Consent to sin, for God is there.
Isaac Watts, 1719.

SELF-EXAMINATION.

HAMBURG.   L. M.   Gregorian. Adapted by Lowell Mason, 1825.

Sure, the blest Com-fort-er is nigh; 'T is he sus-tains my faint-ing heart;
Else would my hopes for ev - er die, And ev-ery cheer-ing ray de - part.

548.   *The Witness of the Spirit.*   (1073.)

1 Sure, the blest Comforter is nigh;
   'T is he sustains my fainting heart;
  Else would my hopes for ever die,
   And every cheering ray depart.

2 When some kind promise glads my soul,
   Do I not find his healing voice
  The tempest of my fears control,
   And bid my drooping powers rejoice?

3 Whene'er, to call the Saviour mine,
   With ardent wish my heart aspires;
  Can it be less than power divine,
   Which animates these strong desires?

4 What less than thine almighty word
   Can raise my heart from earth and dust;
  And bid me cleave to thee, my Lord!
   My Life, my Treasure, and my Trust?

5 And, when my cheerful hope can say,—
   I love my God and taste his grace,
  Lord! is it not thy blissful ray, [peace?
   Which brings this dawn of sacred

6 Let thy kind Spirit in my heart
   For ever dwell, O God of love!
  And light and heavenly peace impart,
   Sweet Earnest of the joys above.
           Anne Steele, 1760.

549.   Psalm 15.   (1078.)

1 Who shall ascend thy heavenly place,
   Great God! and dwell before thy face?
  The man that minds religion now,
   And humbly walks with God below:

2 Whose hands are pure, whose heart is
   clean.   [mean:
  Whose lips still speak the things they
   No slanders dwell upon his tongue;
  He hates to do his neighbor wrong.

3 He loves his enemies, and prays
   For those that curse him to his face;
  And doth to all men still the same
   That he would hope or wish from them.

4 Yet, when his holiest works are done,
   His soul depends on grace alone;
  This is the man thy face shall see,
   And dwell for ever, Lord! with thee.
           Isaac Watts, 1719.

550.   *Almost a Saint.*   (1075.)

1 Broad is the road that leads to death,
   And thousands walk together there;
  But wisdom shows a narrower path,
   With here and there a traveler.

2 "Deny thyself and take thy cross,"—
   Is the Redeemer's great command:
  Nature must count her gold but dross,
   If she would gain this heavenly land.

3 The fearful soul, that tires and faints,
   And walks the ways of God no more,
  Is but esteemed almost a saint,
   And makes his own destruction sure.

4 Lord! let not all my hopes be vain;
   Create my heart entirely new,
  Which hypocrites could ne'er attain:—
   Which false apostates never knew.
           Isaac Watts, 1719.

SELF-EXAMINATION.

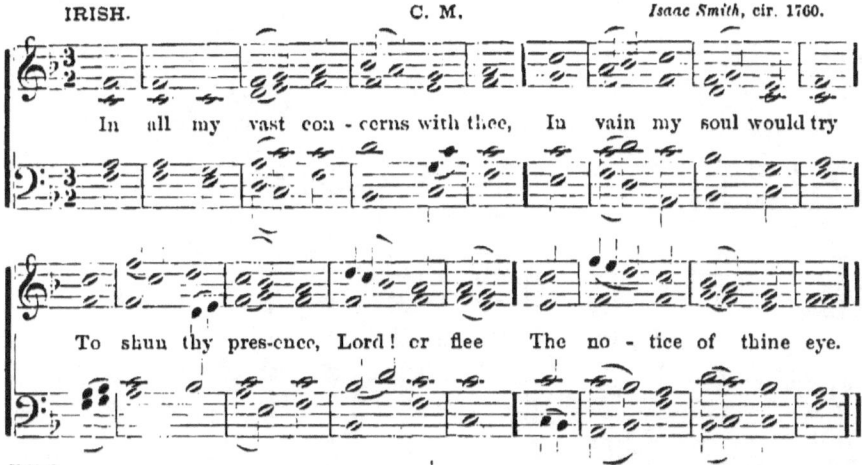

IRISH. C. M. Isaac Smith, cir. 1760.

In all my vast concerns with thee, In vain my soul would try
To shun thy presence, Lord! or flee The notice of thine eye.

551. PSALM 139. (1079.)

1 IN ALL my vast concerns with thee,
In vain my soul would try
To shun thy presence, Lord! or flee
The notice of thine eye.

2 Thine all-surrounding sight surveys
My rising and my rest,
My public walks, my private ways,
And secrets of my breast.

3 My thoughts lie open to the Lord,
Before they 're formed within ;
And ere my lips pronounce the word,
He knows the sense I mean.

4 Oh! wondrous knowledge, deep and high !
Where can a creature hide !
Within thy circling arms I lie,
Beset on every side.

5 So let thy grace surround me still,
And like a bulwark prove,
To guard my soul from every ill,
Secured by sovereign love.
Isaac Watts, 1719.

552. PSALM 139. (1080.)

1 LORD ! where shall guilty souls retire,
Forgotten and unknown ?
In hell they meet thy dreadful fire,
In heaven thy glorious throne.

2 Should I suppress my vital breath
T' escape the wrath divine,
Thy voice would break the bars of death,
And make the grave resign.

3 If, winged with beams of morning light,
I fly beyond the west,
Thy hand, which must support my flight,
Would soon betray my rest.

4 If, o'er my sins I think to draw
The curtains of the night,
Those flaming eyes, that guard thy law,
Would turn the shades to light.

5 The beams of noon, the midnight hour,
Are both alike to thee ;
Oh ! may I ne'er provoke that power,
From which I cannot flee!
Isaac Watts, 1719.

553. *The Searcher of Hearts.* (1081.)

1 GOD is a spirit, just and wise ;
He sees our inmost mind ;
In vain to heaven we raise our cries,
And leave our hearts behind.

2 Nothing but truth before his throne
With honor can appear ;
The painted hypocrites are known
Through the disguise they wear.

3 Their lifted eyes salute the skies ;
Their bending knees the ground ;
But God abhors the sacrifice,
Where not the heart is found.

4 Lord! search my thoughts, and try my
And make my soul sincere ; [ways,
Then shall I stand before thy face,
And find acceptance there.
Isaac Watts, 1709.

SELF-EXAMINATION.

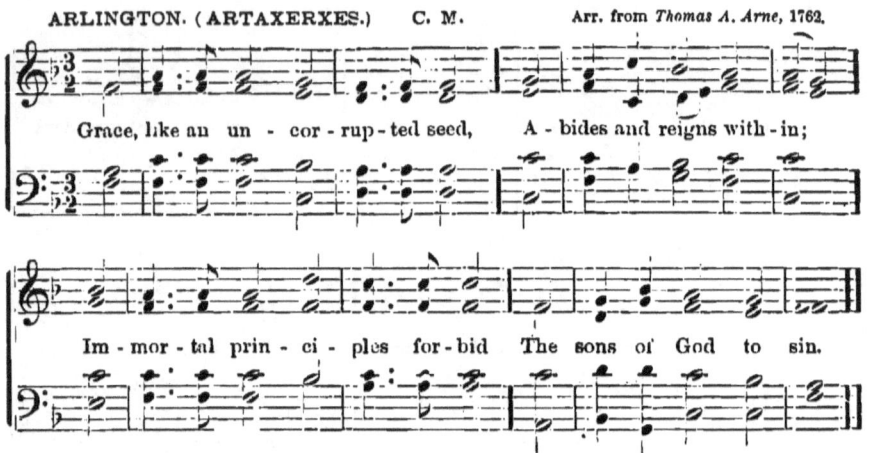

ARLINGTON. (ARTAXERXES.)　C. M.　Arr. from *Thomas A. Arne*, 1762.

Grace, like an uncorrupted seed, Abides and reigns within;
Immortal principles forbid The sons of God to sin.

554.　*The Marks of true Piety.*　(1086.)

1 GRACE, like an uncorrupted seed,
　Abides and reigns within;
Immortal principles forbid
　The sons of God to sin.

2 Not, by the terrors of a slave,
　Do they perform his will,
But, with the noblest powers they have,
　His sweet commands fulfill.

3 They find access, at every hour,
　To God within the veil;
Hence they derive a quickening power,
　And joys that never fail.

4 O happy souls! O glorious state
　Of overflowing grace!
To dwell so near their Father's seat,
　And see his lovely face.

5 Lord! I address thy heavenly throne;
　Call me a child of thine;
Send down the Spirit of thy Son,
　To form my heart divine.

6 There shed thy choicest love abroad,
　And make my comforts strong:
Then shall I say, My Father God!
　With an unwavering tongue.
　　　　　　　　　　Isaac Watts, 1709.

555.　*The Contrite Heart.*　(1083.)

1 THE Lord will happiness divine
　On contrite hearts bestow;
Then tell me, gracious God! is mine
　A contrite heart or no?

2 I hear, but seem to hear in vain,
　Insensible as steel;
If aught is felt, 't is only pain,
　To find I cannot feel.

3 My best desires are faint and few,
　I fain would strive for more;
But, when I cry, "My strength renew!"
　Seem weaker than before.

4 Thy saints are comforted, I know,
　And love thy house of prayer;
I therefore go where others go,
　But find no comfort there.

5 Oh! make this heart rejoice or ache;—
　Decide this doubt for me;
And, if it be not broken, break;
　And heal it, if it be.
　　　　　　　　　　William Cowper, 1772.

556.　*The Witness of the Spirit.*　(1084.)

1 COME, Holy Ghost! my soul inspire;
　This one great gift impart,—
What most I need, and most desire,
　An humble, holy heart.

2 Bear witness, I am born again,
　My many sins forgiven;
Nor let a gloomy doubt remain,
　To cloud my hope of heaven.

3 More of myself grant I may know,
　From sin's deceit be free,
In all the Christian graces grow,
　And live alone to thee.
　　　　　　　　　　Anon., 1825.

THE CHURCH.

ST. GEORGE. (BRAY.)   C. M.   Altered from *Nicolaus Hermann*, 1544.

Lo! what a glorious sight appears, To our believing eyes! The earth and sea are passed away, And the old rolling skies, And the old rolling skies.

557. *The Glory of Christ's Kingdom.* (1103.)

1 Lo! what a glorious sight appears,
   To our believing eyes!
The earth and sea are passed away,
   And the old rolling skies.

2 From the third heaven where God resides,
   That holy, happy place,
The new Jerusalem comes down,
   Adorned with shining grace.

3 Attending angels shout for joy,
   And the bright armies sing,
"Mortals! behold the sacred seat
   Of your descending King.

4 The God of glory down to men
   Removes his blest abode,
Men, the dear objects of his grace,
   And he the loving God.

5 His own soft hands shall wipe the tears
   From every weeping eye,   [fears
And pains, and groans, and griefs, and
   And death itself shall die."

6 How long, dear Saviour! Oh! how long
   Shall this bright hour delay?
Fly swifter round, ye wheels of time!
   And bring the welcome day,
                Isaac Watts, 1707.

558. *The Church immovable.* (1107.)

1 Oh! where are kings and empires now,
   Of old that went and came?
But, Lord! thy church is praying yet,
   A thousand years the same.

2 We mark her goodly battlements,
   And her foundations strong;
We hear within the solemn voice
   Of her unending song.

3 For, not like kingdoms of the world,
   Thy holy church, O God!   [ing her,
Though earthquake shocks are threaten-
   And tempests are abroad;

4 Unshaken as eternal hills,
   Immovable she stands,
A mountain that shall fill the earth,
   A house not made by hands.
             Arthur Cleveland Coxe, 1839, a.

559.   Psalm 118.   (1105.)

1 Behold the sure foundation stone,
   Which God in Zion lays,
To build our heavenly hopes upon,
   And his eternal praise.

2 Chosen of God, to sinners dear;
   And saints adore his name:—
They trust their whole salvation here,
   Nor shall they suffer shame.

3 The foolish builders, scribe and priest,
   Reject it with disdain;
Yet on this rock the church shall rest,
   And envy rage in vain.

4 What, though the gates of hell withstood?
   Yet must this building rise:
'T is thine own work, almighty God!
   And wondrous in our eyes.
                Isaac Watts, 1719.

CHURCH RELATIONS.

SHIRLAND. S. M. Samuel Stanley, cir. 1800.

I love thy king-dom, Lord! The house of thine a-bode,
The church, our blest Re-deem-er saved With his own pre-cious blood.

560. PSALM 137. (1094.)

1 I LOVE thy kingdom, Lord!
　The house of thine abode,
The church, our blest Redeemer saved
　With his own precious blood.

2 I love thy church, O God!
　Her walls before thee stand,
Dear as the apple of thine eye,
　And graven on thy hand.

3 For her my tears shall fall,
　For her my prayers ascend ;
To her my cares and toils be given,
　Till toils and cares shall end.

4 Beyond my highest joy
　I prize her heavenly ways,
Her sweet communion, solemn vows,
　Her hymns of love and praise.

5 Jesus, thou Friend divine,
　Our Saviour and our King!
Thy hand, from every snare and foe
　Shall great deliverance bring.

6 Sure as thy truth shall last,
　To Zion shall be given
The brightest glories earth can yield,
　And brighter bliss of heaven.
　　　　　　Timothy Dwight, 1800.

561. PSALM 48. (1095.)

1 FAR as thy name is known,
　The world declares thy praise ;
Thy saints, O Lord! before thy throne
　Their songs of honor raise.

2 With joy let Judah stand
　On Zion's chosen hill,
Proclaim the wonders of thy hand,
　And counsels of thy will.

3 Let strangers walk around
　The city where we dwell,
Compass and view thy holy ground,
　And mark the building well ;

4 The orders of thy house,
　The worship of thy court,
The cheerful songs, the solemn vows ;
　And make a fair report.

5 How decent, and how wise!
　How glorious to behold!
Beyond the pomp that charms the eyes,
　And rites adorned with gold.

6 The God we worship now
　Will guide us, till we die ;
Will be our God, while here below ;
　And ours above the sky.
　　　　　　Isaac Watts, 1719.

562. PSALM 117. (1096.)

1 THY name, almighty Lord!
　Shall sound through distant lands ;
Great is thy grace, and sure thy word ; —
　Thy truth for ever stands.

2 Far be thine honor spread,
　And long thy praise endure,
Till morning light, and evening shade
　Shall be exchanged no more.
　　　　　　Isaac Watts, 1719.

THE CHURCH. 201

PILESGROVE. L. M. *Nahum Mitchell*, 1812.

Great God, whose u-ni-ver-sal sway The known and unknown worlds o-bey! Now give the king-dom to thy Son; Ex-tend his power, ex-alt his throne.

563. PSALM 72. (1100.)

1 Great God, whose universal sway
The known and unknown worlds obey!
Now give the kingdom to thy Son;
Extend his power, exalt his throne.

2 Thy sceptre well becomes his hands,
All heaven submits to his commands;
His justice shall avenge the poor,
And pride and rage prevail no more.

3 As rain on meadows newly mown,
So shall he send his influence down;
His grace, on fainting souls, distills,
Like heavenly dew, on thirsty hills.

4 The heathen lands, that lie beneath
The shades of overspreading death,
Revive at his first dawning light,
And deserts blossom at the sight.

5 The saints shall flourish in his days,
Dressed in the robes of joy and praise;
Peace, like a river, from his throne,
Shall flow to nations yet unknown.
Isaac Watts, 1719.

564. PSALM 72. (1101.)

1 JESUS shall reign where'er the sun
Does his successive journeys run;
His kingdom stretch from shore to shore,
Till moons shall wax and wane no more.

2 For him shall endless prayer be made,
And praises throng to crown his head;
His name, like sweet perfume, shall rise
With every morning sacrifice.

3 People and realms of every tongue
Dwell on his love, with sweetest song;
And infant voices shall proclaim
Their early blessings on his name.

4 Blessings abound where'er he reigns;
The prisoner leaps to lose his chains;
The weary find eternal rest,
And all the sons of want are blessed.

5 Let every creature rise, and bring
Peculiar honors to our King;
Angels descend with songs again,
And earth repeat the long Amen.
Isaac Watts, 1719.

565. *The Glory of the Church.* (1102.)

1 TRIUMPHANT Zion! lift thy head
From dust, and darkness, and the dead;
Though humbled long, awake at length,
And gird thee with thy Saviour's strength.

2 Put all thy beauteous garments on,
And let thy various charms be known;
The world thy glories shall confess,
Decked in the robes of righteousness.

3 No more shall foes unclean invade,
And fill thy hallowed walls with dread;
No more shall hell's insulting host,
Their vict'ry and thy sorrows boast.

4 God, from on high, thy groans will hear;
His hand thy ruins shall repair;
Nor will thy watchful Monarch cease
To guard thee in eternal peace.
Philip Doddridge, 1740.

CHURCH RELATIONS.

WEBB. (GOODWIN.)   7s & 6s. 8 LINES.   *George James Webb,* 1837.

Hail to the Lord's Anoin-ted, Great David's greater Son! Hail, in the time ap-poin-ted,
D. C.—To take a-way transgres-sion.

FINE.   *D. S.*

His reign on earth be-gun! He comes to break oppres-sion, To set the cap-tive free,
And rule in e-qui-ty.

---

566.   PSALM 72.   (1109.)

1 Hail to the Lord's Anointed,
    Great David's greater Son!
Hail, in the time appointed,
    His reign on earth begun!
He comes to break oppression,
    To set the captive free,
To take away transgression,
    And rule in equity.

2 He comes, with succor speedy,
    To those who suffer wrong;
To help the poor and needy,
    And bid the weak be strong;
To give them songs for sighing,
    Their darkness turn to light,
Whose souls, condemned and dying,
    Were precious in his sight.

3 He shall come down, like showers
    Upon the fruitful earth,
And love, joy, hope, like flowers,
    Spring in his path to birth:
Before him on the mountains,
    Shall peace, the herald, go;
And righteousness, in fountains,
    From hill to valley flow.

4 For him shall prayer unceasing
    And daily vows ascend;
His kingdom still increasing,—
    A kingdom without end:

The tide of time shall never
    His cov'nant remove;
His name shall stand for ever;
    That name to us is — Love.
James Montgomery, 1822.

567.   *The Triumph of the Gospel.*   (1110.)

1 Now be the gospel banner,
    In every land, unfurled;
And be the shout,— "Hosanna!"—
    Reëchoed through the world:
Till every isle and nation,
    Till every tribe and tongue,
Receive the great salvation,
    And join the happy throng.

2 What, though th' embattled legions
    Of earth and hell combine?
His power, throughout their regions,
    Shall soon resplendent shine:
Ride on, O Lord! victorious,
    Immanuel, Prince of peace!
Thy triumph shall be glorious,—
    Thine empire still increase.

3 Yes,— thou shalt reign for ever,
    O Jesus, King of kings!
Thy light, thy love, thy favor,
    Each ransomed captive sings:
The isles for thee are waiting,
    The deserts learn thy praise,
The hills and valleys greeting,
    The song responsive raise.
Thomas Hastings, 1830.

THE CHURCH.

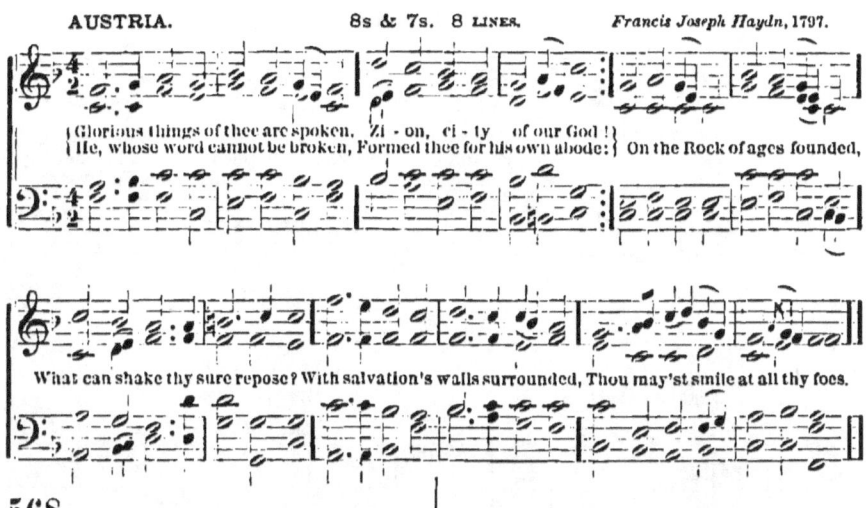

568. *The Glory of the Church.* (1116.)

1 GLORIOUS things of thee are spoken,
  Zion, city of our God!
He, whose word cannot be broken,
  Formed thee for his own abode:
On the Rock of ages founded,
  What can shake thy sure repose?
With salvation's walls surrounded,
  Thou mayest smile at all thy foes.

2 See! the streams of living waters,
  Springing from eternal love,
Well supply thy sons and daughters,
  And all fear of want remove:
Who can faint, while such a river
  Ever flows their thirst t'assuage?—
Grace, which, like the Lord, the Giver,
  Never fails from age to age.

3 Round each habitation hovering,
  See the cloud and fire appear,
For a glory and a covering,
  Showing that the Lord is near!
Thus deriving, from their banner,
  Light by night, and shade by day,
Safe they feed upon the manna
  Which he gives them when they pray.
                            John Newton, 1779.

569. *Zion's Glory.* (1117.)

1 ZION is Jehovah's dwelling;
  There the King of kings appears;
Hers is glory, far excelling
  All the worlding sees, or hears:

Zion's walls are everlasting,
  Formed through endless years to shine;
Strength and beauty, never-wasting,
  Show their origin divine.

2 Zion claims peculiar honor;
  High distinction marks her lot;
Light eternal shines upon her;
  Her's a sun, that faileth not:
Zion's city hath foundations;
  God himself has raised her walls;
She survives the wreck of nations;
  Zion stands, whatever falls.

3 Happy they who, now discerning
  Zion's glory, thither move!
Earth, with all its honors, spurning,
  Zion is the place they love:
There the Lord, his face disclosing,
  Fills his people's hearts with joy;
While, from all their toils reposing,
  Bliss is theirs without alloy.

4 Brethren! let the prospect cheer us;
  Fair the lot that's cast for us:
When we call, our God will hear us;
  Happy who are favored thus!
Let the timid fear no longer:
  What though earth and hell oppose?
He who pleads our cause is stronger,
  Stronger far, than all our foes.
                            Thomas Kelly, 1804.

CHURCH RELATIONS.

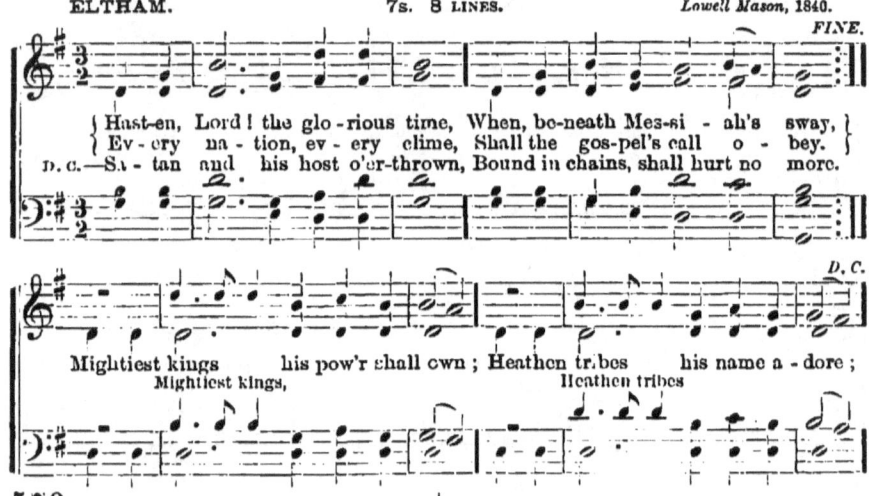

ELTHAM. 7s. 8 LINES. Lowell Mason, 1840.

Hasten, Lord! the glorious time, When, beneath Messiah's sway,
Every nation, every clime, Shall the gospel's call obey.
D. C.—Satan and his host o'erthrown, Bound in chains, shall hurt no more.
Mightiest kings his pow'r shall own; Heathen tribes his name adore;

570. PSALM 72. (1118.)

1 HASTEN, Lord! the glorious time,
When, beneath Messiah's sway,
Every nation, every clime,
Shall the gospel's call obey.

2 Mightiest kings his power shall own,
Heathen tribes his name adore;
Satan and his host, o'erthrown,
Bound in chains, shall hurt no more.

3 Then shall wars and tumults cease;
Then be banished grief and pain;
Righteousness, and joy, and peace,
Undisturbed shall ever reign.

4 Bless we, then, our gracious Lord;
Ever praise his glorious name;
All his mighty acts record;
All his wondrous love proclaim.
Harriet Auber, 1829.

571. *Triumphs of the Gospel.* (1119.)

1 Who are these, that come from far,
Led by Jacob's rising star?
Strangers now to Zion come,
There to seek a peaceful home.

2 Lo! they gather like a cloud,
Or as doves their windows crowd:
Zion wonders at the sight,—
Zion feels a strange delight.

3 Zion now no more shall sigh,
God will raise her glory high;
He will send a large increase,—
He will give his people peace.

4 Sons of Zion! sing aloud;
See her sun, without a cloud!
God will make her joy complete;
Zion's sun shall never set.
Thomas Kelly, (?) 1835.

572. *The Song of Jubilee.* (1120.)

1 HARK!—the song of jubilee,
Loud as mighty thunders roar,—
Or the fullness of the sea,
When it breaks upon the shore;—
"Hallelujah! for the Lord
God omnipotent shall reign!"
Hallelujah! let the word
Echo round the earth and main.

2 Hallelujah!—hark!—the sound,
From the depths unto the skies,
Wakes, above, beneath, around,
All creation's harmonies:
See Jehovah's banners furled!
Sheathed his sword! he speaks—'t is done,
And the kingdoms of this world
Are the kingdoms of his Son.

3 He shall reign from pole to pole
With illimitable sway;
He shall reign, when, like a scroll,
Yonder heavens have passed away;
Then the end;—beneath his rod,
Man's last enemy shall fall;
Hallelujah!—Christ in God,
God in Christ, is all in all.
James Montgomery, 1819.

MINISTRY.

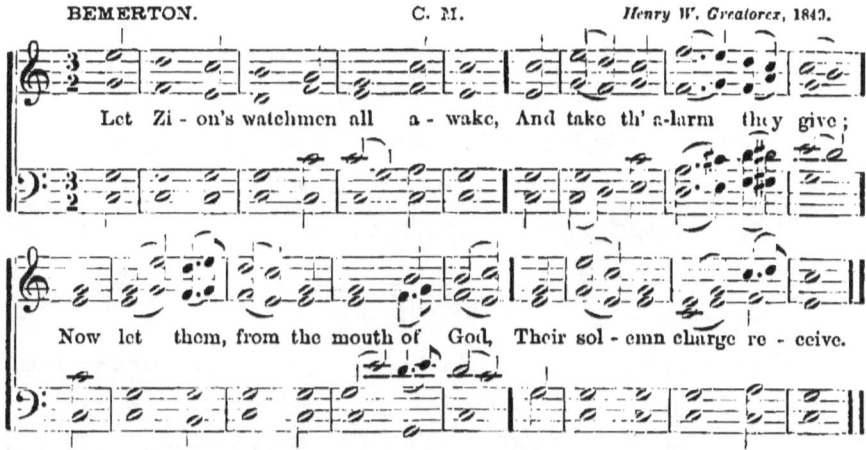

BEMERTON. C. M. Henry W. Greatorex, 1849.

Let Zi-on's watchmen all a-wake, And take th' a-larm they give;
Now let them, from the mouth of God, Their sol-emn charge re-ceive.

573. *The Pastor's Charge.* (1130.)

1 Let Zion's watchmen all awake,
  And take th' alarm they give ;
  Now let them from the mouth of God,
  Their solemn charge receive.

2 'T is not a cause of small import
  The pastor's care demands ;
  But what might fill an angel's heart,
  And filled a Saviour's hands.

3 They watch for souls, for which the Lord
  Did heavenly bliss forego ; —
  For souls, which must for ever live
  In raptures, or in woe.

4 All to the great tribunal haste,
  Th' account to render there ;
  And shouldst thou strictly mark our faults,
  Lord ! how should we appear ?

5 May they that Jesus, whom they preach,
  Their own Redeemer, see ;
  And watch thou daily o'er their souls,
  That they may watch for thee.
                        Philip Doddridge, 1736.

574. *A faithful Ministry.* (1131.)

1 Jesus ! the word of mercy give,
  And let it swiftly run ;
  Let all who preach the word believe,
  And put salvation on.

2 Jesus ! let all thy servants shine
  Illustrious as the sun ;
  And, bright with borrowed rays divine,
  Their glorious circuit run.

3 Beyond the reach of mortals, spread
  Their light where'er they go ;
  And heavenly influences shed
  On all the world below.

4 As giants may they run their race,
  Exulting in their might ;
  As burning luminaries, chase
  The gloom of error's night.

5 As the bright Sun of righteousness,
  Their healing wings display ;
  And let their lustre still increase
  Unto the perfect day.
                        Charles Wesley, 1762, a.

575. *The Preacher's Theme.* (1134.)

1 Christ and his cross is all our theme ;
  The mysteries that we speak
  Are scandal in the Jews' esteem,
  And folly to the Greek.

2 But souls, enlightened from above,
  With joy receive the word ;
  They see what wisdom, power, and love,
  Shine in their dying Lord.

3 The vital savor of his name
  Restores their fainting breath ;
  But unbelief perverts the same
  To guilt, despair, and death.

4 Till God diffuse his graces down,
  Like showers of heavenly rain,
  In vain Apollos sows the ground,
  And Paul may plant in vain.
                        Isaac Watts, 1709.

CHURCH RELATIONS.

ORLAND. L. M. William Arnold, 1768-1832.

Fa-ther of mer-cies! in thy house, Smile on our hom-age, and our vows;
While, with a grate-ful heart, we share These pledg-es of our Sav-iour's care.

576. *The Ordination of a Minister.* (1121.)

1 FATHER of mercies! in thy house,
Smile on our homage, and our vows;
While, with a grateful heart, we share
These pledges of our Saviour's care.

2 The Saviour, when to heaven he rose,
In splendid triumph o'er his foes,
Scattered his gifts on men below,
And wide his royal bounties flow.

3 Hence sprung th' apostles' honored name,
Sacred beyond heroic fame;
In lowlier forms, to bless our eyes,
Pastors from hence, and teachers rise.

4 So shall the bright succession run,
Through the last courses of the sun;
While unborn churches, by their care,
Shall rise and flourish, large and fair.

5 Jesus, our Lord, their hearts shall know,
The Spring, whence all these blessings flow,
Pastors and people shout his praise,
Through the long round of endless days.
Philip Doddridge, 1745.

577. *Prayer for Ministers.* (1122.)

1 FATHER of mercies! bow thine ear,
Attentive to our earnest prayer:
We plead for those who plead for thee,
Successful pleaders may they be!

2 How great their work, how vast their charge!
Do thou their anxious souls enlarge;
To them thy sacred truth reveal,
Suppress their fear, inflame their zeal.

3 Teach them aright to sow the seed;
Teach them thy chosen flock to feed,
Teach them immortal souls to gain,
Nor let them labor, Lord! in vain.

4 Let thronging multitudes around
Hear from their lips the joyful sound,
In humble strains thy grace adore,
And feel thy new-creating power.
Benjamin Beddome, 1787.

578. *The Preacher's Commission.* (1124.)

1 "Go, preach my gospel," saith the Lord,
"Bid the whole earth my grace receive;
He shall be saved that trusts my word,
He shall be damned that won't believe.

2 I'll make your great commission known;
And ye shall prove my gospel true,
By all the works that I have done,
By all the wonders ye shall do.

3 Go, heal the sick; go, raise the dead;
Go, cast out devils in my name;
Nor let my prophets be afraid,
Tho' Greeks reproach, and Jews blaspheme.

4 Teach all the nations my commands,
I'm with you till the world shall end;
All power is trusted to my hands,
I can destroy, and I defend."

5 He spake; and light shone round his head;
On a bright cloud to heaven he rode:
They, to the farthest nation, spread
The grace of their ascended God.
Isaac Watts, 1709.

THE MINISTRY.

ANVERN. L. M. German. Adapted by *Lowell Mason*, 1840.

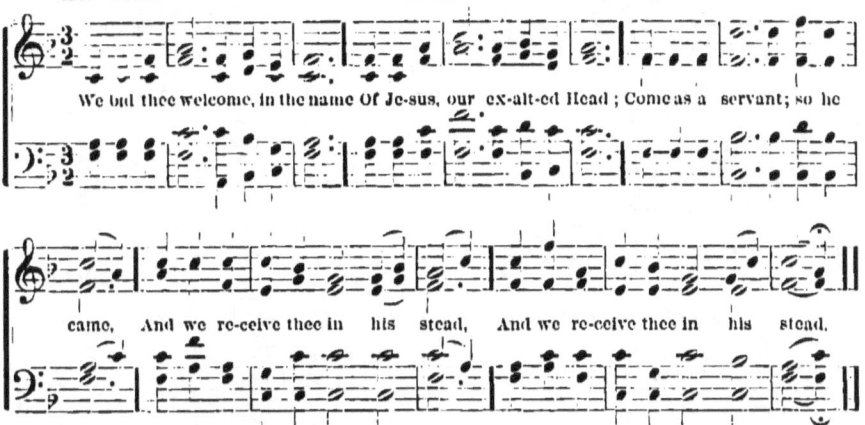

We bid thee welcome, in the name Of Jesus, our exalted Head; Come as a servant; so he came, And we receive thee in his stead, And we receive thee in his stead.

579. *Welcome to a Pastor.* (1127.)

1 WE BID thee welcome, in the name
   Of Jesus, our exalted Head;
  Come as a servant; so he came,
   And we receive thee in his stead.

2 Come as a shepherd: guard and keep
   This fold from hell, and earth, and sin;
  Nourish the lambs, and feed the sheep,
   The wounded heal, the lost bring in.

3 Come as a teacher, sent from God,
   Charged his whole counsel to declare;
  Lift o'er our ranks the prophet's rod,
   While we uphold thy hands with prayer.

4 Come as a messenger of peace,
   Filled with the Spirit, fired with love;
  Live to behold our large increase,
   And die to meet us all above.
          James Montgomery, 1825.

580. *The Installation of a Pastor.* (1128.)

1 SPIRIT of peace and holiness!
  This new-created union bless;
  Bind each to each in ties of love,
  And ratify our work above.

2 Saviour, who carest for thy sheep!
  The shepherd of thy people keep;
  Guide him in every doubtful way,
  Nor let his feet from duty stray.

3 Gird thou his heart with strength divine:
  Let Christ through all his conduct shine;
  Faithful in all things may he be,
  Dead to the world, alive to thee.

4 O Thou, whose love doth never fail!
  Breathe on this dry and thirsty vale;
  And may it, from this hour, appear,
  That thy reviving power is here.

5 Lord of the Sabbath! unto thee
  Our spirits rise in harmony;
  Accept our praise, our sins remove,
  And fit us for thy courts above.
          Samuel F. Smith, 1843.

581. *A Meeting of Ministers.* (1125.)

1 POUR out thy Spirit from on high;
   Lord! thine assembled servants bless;
  Graces and gifts to each supply.
   And clothe thy priests with righteous- [ness.

2 Within thy temple, when we stand,
   To teach the truth as taught by thee,
  Saviour! like stars in thy right hand,
   The angels of the churches be!

3 Wisdom and zeal, and faith impart,
   Firmness with meekness from above,
  To bear thy people on our heart,   [love:
   And love the souls whom thou dost

4 To watch and pray, and never faint:
   By day and night, strict guard to keep;
  To warn the sinner, cheer the saint,
   Nourish thy lambs, and feed thy sheep.

5 Then, when our work is finished here,
   In humble hope, our charge resign;
  When the chief Shepherd shall appear,
   O God! may they and we be thine.
          James Montgomery, 1825.

CHURCH RELATIONS.

LUTHER. S. M. *Thomas Hastings*, 1835.

How beauteous are their feet, Who stand on Zion's hill! Who bring sal-va-tion on their tongues, And words of peace reveal! And words of peace re-veal!

582. *The Heralds of Christ.* (1139.)

1 How beauteous are their feet,
  Who stand on Zion's hill!
Who bring salvation on their tongues,
  And words of peace reveal!

2 How charming is their voice!
  How sweet the tidings are!—
"Zion! behold thy Saviour King,
  He reigns and triumphs here!"

3 How happy are our ears,
  That hear this joyful sound,
Which kings and prophets waited for,
  And sought, but never found!

4 How blessed are our eyes,
  That see this heavenly light!
Prophets and kings desired it long,
  But died without the sight.

5 The watchmen join their voice,
  And tuneful notes employ;
Jerusalem breaks forth in songs,
  And deserts learn the joy.

6 The Lord makes bare his arm,
  Through all the earth abroad;
Let every nation now behold
  Their Saviour and their God.
                    Isaac Watts, 1707.

583. *Ordination of Missionaries.* (1140.)

1 YE messengers of Christ!
  His sovereign voice obey;
Arise, and follow where he leads,
  And peace attend your way.

2 The Master, whom you serve,
  Will needful strength bestow;
Depending on his promised aid,
  With sacred courage go.

3 Mountains shall sink to plains,
  And hell in vain oppose;
The cause is God's, and must prevail
  In spite of all his foes.

4 Go, spread a Saviour's fame;
  And tell his matchless grace
To the most guilty and depraved
  Of Adam's numerous race.
                    Mrs. Voke, 1806.

584. *Vigilance.* (1141.)

1 YE SERVANTS of the Lord!
  Each in his office wait,
Observant of his heavenly word,
  And watchful at his gate.

2 Let all your lamps be bright,
  And trim the golden flame;
Gird up your loins as in his sight,
  For awful is his name.

3 Watch! 't is your Lord's command;
  And, while we speak, he's near:
Mark the first signal of his hand,
  And ready all appear.

4 Oh! happy servant he,
  In such a posture found!
He shall his Lord with rapture see,
  And be with honor crowned.
                    Philip Doddridge, 1740.

BAPTISM.

COLCHESTER. C. M. From *Aaron Williams'* Coll., cir. 1760.

Behold! what con-de-scend-ing love Jesus on earth dis-plays!
To babes and sucklings, he ex-tends The rich-es of his grace.

585. *Children blessed by Jesus.* (1142.)

1 BEHOLD! what condescending love
Jesus on earth displays!
To babes and sucklings, he extends
The riches of his grace.

2 He still the ancient promise keeps,
To our forefathers given;
Young children in his arms he takes,
And calls them heirs of heaven.

3 Forbid them not, whom Jesus calls,
Nor dare the claim resist,
Since his own lips to us declare—
Of such will heaven consist.

4 With flowing tears, and thankful hearts,
We give them up to thee;
Receive them, Lord! into thine arms,—
Thine may they ever be.
John Peacock, 1806, a.

586. *The Saviour blessing Children.* (1143.)

1 WHEN Jesus left his Father's throne,
He chose an humble birth;
Like us, unhonored and unknown,
He came to dwell on earth.

2 Like him, may we be found below,
In wisdom's path of peace;
Like him, in grace and knowledge, grow,
As years and strength increase.

3 Sweet were his words, and kind his look,
When mothers round him pressed;
Their infants, in his arms, he took,
And on his bosom blessed.

4 When Jesus into Salem rode,
The children sang around; [strewed
For joy, they plucked the palms, and
Their garments on the ground.

5 Hosanna our glad voices raise,
Hosanna to our King!
Should we forget our Saviour's praise,
The stones themselves would sing.

6 For we have learned to love his name;
That name, divinely sweet,
May every pulse through life proclaim,
And our last breath repeat.
James Montgomery, 1825.

587. *Christ receiving Children.* (1145.)

1 SEE Israel's gentle Shepherd stand,
With all-engaging charms!
Hark! how he calls the tender lambs,
And folds them in his arms!

2 "Permit them to approach," he cries,
"Nor scorn their humble name;
For 't was to bless such souls as these,
The Lord of angels came."

3 We bring them, Lord! in thankful hands,
And yield them up to thee;
Joyful that we ourselves are thine,—
Thine let our offspring be.

4 Ye little flock! with pleasure hear,—
Ye children! seek his face;
And fly, with transport, to receive
The blessings of his grace.
Philip Doddridge, 1740.

CHURCH RELATIONS.

HEBRON. L. M. *Lowell Mason,* 1830.

Lord! I am thine, en-tire-ly thine, Purchased and saved by blood di-vine;
With full consent thine I would be, And own thy sovereign right in me.

588. *Self-Dedication to God.* (1160.)

1 LORD! I am thine, entirely thine,
  Purchased and saved by blood divine;
  With full consent thine I would be,
  And own thy sovereign right in me.

2 Grant one poor sinner more a place,
  Among the children of thy grace;
  A wretched sinner, lost to God,
  But ransomed by Immanuel's blood.

3 Thine would I live, thine would I die,
  Be thine through all eternity;
  The vow is past beyond repeal;
  Now will I set the solemn seal.

4 Here, at that cross, where flows the blood
  That bought my guilty soul for God,
  Thee my new Master now I call,
  And consecrate to thee my all.

5 Do thou assist a feeble worm,
  The great engagement to perform;
  Thy grace can full assistance lend,
  And on that grace I dare depend.
  Samuel Davies, 1769.

589. *The Day of Espousals.* (1157.)

1 OH! happy day! that fixed my choice
  On thee, my Saviour and my God!
  Well may this glowing heart rejoice,
  And tell its raptures all abroad.

2 O happy bond! that seals my vows
  To him who merits all my love!
  Let cheerful anthems fill his house,
  While to that sacred shrine I move.

3 'T is done; the great transaction 's done;
  I am my Lord's, and he is mine;
  He drew me, and I followed on,
  Charmed to confess the voice divine.

4 Now rest, my long divided heart!
  Fixed on this blissful centre, rest;
  With ashes who would grudge to part,
  When called on angels' bread to feast?

5 High Heaven, that heard the solemn vow,
  That vow renewed shall daily hear,
  Till, in life's latest hour, I bow,
  And bless in death a bond so dear.
  Philip Doddridge, 1740.

590. *Converts welcomed.* (1158.)

1 COME in, thou blessed of the Lord!
  Enter in Jesus' precious name;
  We welcome thee, with one accord,
  And trust the Saviour does the same.

2 Those joys, which earth cannot afford,
  We'll seek in fellowship to prove,
  Joined in one spirit to our Lord,
  Together bound by mutual love.

3 And, while we pass this vale of tears,
  We'll make our joys and sorrows known;
  We'll share each other's hopes and fears,
  And count a brother's case our own.

4 Once more, our welcome we repeat;
  Receive assurance of our love;
  Oh! may we all together meet,
  Around the throne of God above.
  Thomas Kelly, 1812.

ENTERING INTO COVENANT.

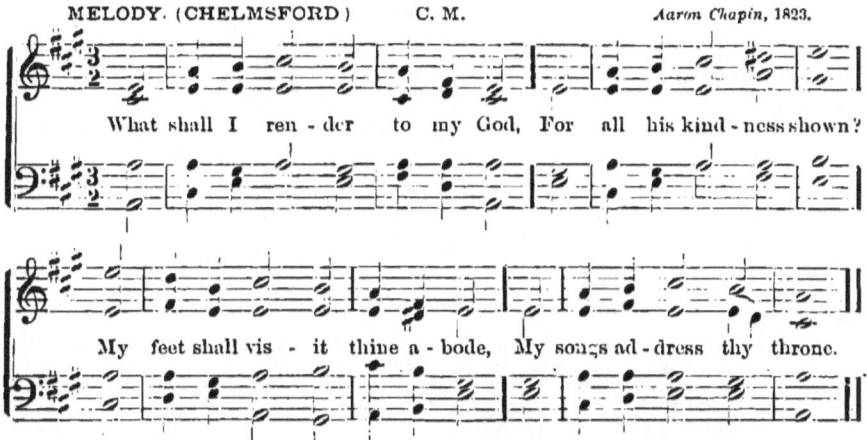

MELODY. (CHELMSFORD.) C. M. — Aaron Chapin, 1823.

What shall I render to my God, For all his kindness shown? My feet shall visit thine abode, My songs address thy throne.

591. PSALM 116. (1162.)

1 WHAT shall I render to my God,
  For all his kindness shown?
 My feet shall visit thine abode,
  My songs address thy throne.

2 Among the saints that fill thy house,
  My offerings shall be paid:
 There shall my zeal perform the vows,
  My soul in anguish made.

3 How much is mercy thy delight,
  Thou ever-blessed God!
 How dear thy servants in thy sight!
  How precious is their blood!

4 How happy all thy servants are!
  How great thy grace to me!
 My life, which thou hast made thy care,
  Lord! I devote to thee.

5 Now I am thine, for ever thine,
  Nor shall my purpose move;
 Thy hand hath loosed my bonds of pain,
  And bound me with thy love.

6 Here in thy courts I leave my vow,
  And thy rich grace record;
 Witness, ye saints! who hear me now,
  If I forsake the Lord.
          Isaac Watts, 1719.

592. *"Hinder me not."* (1165.)

1 IN all my Lord's appointed ways,
  My journey I'll pursue;
 "Hinder me not"—ye much-loved saints!
  For I must go with you.

2 Through floods and flames, if Jesus leads,
  I'll follow where he goes;
 "Hinder me not!"—shall be my cry,
  Though earth and hell oppose.

3 Through duty, and through trials too,
  I'll go at his command;
 "Hinder me not," for I am bound
  To my Immanuel's land.

4 And, when my Saviour calls me home,
  Still this my cry shall be,—
 "Hinder me not,"—come, welcome, death!
  I'll gladly go with thee.
          John Ryland, 1773.

593. *Covenant Vows.* (1164.)

1 WITNESS, ye men and angels! now,
  Before the Lord we speak;
 To him we make our solemn vow,
  A vow we dare not break;—

2 That, long as life itself shall last,
  Ourselves to Christ we yield;
 Nor from his cause will we depart,
  Or ever quit the field.

3 We trust not in our native strength,
  But on his grace rely,
 That, with returning wants, the Lord
  Will all our need supply.

4 Oh! guide our doubtful feet aright,
  And keep us in thy ways;
 And, while we turn our vows to prayers,
  Turn thou our prayers to praise.
          Benjamin Beddome, 1790.

CHURCH RELATIONS.

WOODSTOCK. C. M. *Deodatus Dutton, Jr.*, 1829.

How sweet, how heavenly is the sight, When those, that love the Lord, In one an-oth-er's peace de-light, And so ful-fill his word!—

594. *Brotherly Love.* (1171.)

1 How sweet, how heavenly is the sight,
When those, that love the Lord,
In one another's peace delight,
And so fulfill his word!—

2 When each can feel his brother's sigh,
And with him bear a part;
When sorrow flows from eye to eye,
And joy from heart to heart:—

3 When, free from envy, scorn, and pride,
Our wishes all above,
Each can his brother's failings hide,
And show his brother's love:—

4 When love, in one delightful stream,
Through every bosom flows;
When union sweet, and dear esteem,
In every action glows.

5 Love is the golden chain, that binds
The happy souls above;
And he 's an heir of heaven that finds
His bosom glow with love.
Joseph Swain, 1792.

595. *Saints all of one Family.* (1172.)

1 Come, let us join our friends above,
That have obtained the prize,
And, on the eagle wings of love,
To joy celestial rise.

2 Let saints below in concert sing
With those to glory gone;
For all the servants of our King
In earth and heaven are one.

3 One family, we dwell in him,—
One church above, beneath;
Though now divided by the stream,—
The narrow stream of death.

4 One army of the living God,
To his command we bow;
Part of the host have crossed the flood,
And part are crossing now.

5 Ev'n now to their eternal home
Some happy spirits fly;
And we are to the margin come,
And soon expect to die.

6 Dear Saviour! be our constant Guide;
Then, when the word is given,
Bid Jordan's narrow stream divide,
And land us safe in heaven.
Charles Wesley, 1759, a.

596. *Saints all of one Spirit.* (1173.)

1 Blessed be the dear, uniting love,
That will not let us part;
Our bodies may far off remove;
We still are one in heart.

2 Joined in one spirit to our Head,
Where he appoints we go;
We still in Jesus' footsteps tread,
And show his praise below.

3 Oh! may we ever walk in him,
And nothing know beside!
Nothing desire, nothing esteem,
But Jesus crucified!
Charles Wesley, 1742.

FELLOWSHIP.

Sweet the time, exceeding sweet, When the saints together meet, When the Saviour is the theme, When they joy to sing of him!

597. *The Sweetness of Christian Fellowship.* (1174.)

1 SWEET the time, exceeding sweet,
When the saints together meet,
When the Saviour is the theme,
When they joy to sing of him!

2 Sing we then eternal love,
Such as did the Father move;
He beheld the world undone, —
Loved the world, and gave his Son.

3 Sing the Son's amazing love;
How he left the realms above,
Took our nature and our place,
Lived and died to save our race.

4 Sing we, too, the Spirit's love;
With our wretched hearts he strove,
Took the things of Christ, and showed
How to reach his blest abode.

5 Sweet the place, exceeding sweet,
Where the saints in glory meet;
Where the Saviour's still the theme,
Where they see and sing of him.
George Burder, 1779, v. 4, a.

598. *Christian Union and Love.* (1175.)

1 JESUS, Lord! we look to thee,
Let us in thy name agree;
Show thyself the Prince of peace,
Bid all strife for ever cease.

2 By thy reconciling love,
Every stumbling-block remove;
Each to each unite, endear;
Come, and spread thy banner here.

3 Make us one in heart and mind,
Courteous, pitiful, and kind,
Lowly, meek, in thought and word,
Wholly like our blessed Lord.

4 Let us each for others care,
Each his brother's burden bear,
To thy church a pattern give,
Showing how believers live.

5 Let us, then, with joy remove
To thy family above;
On the wings of angels fly,
Showing how believers die.
Charles Wesley, 1749, a.

599. *Cleaving to God's People.* (1176.)

1 PEOPLE of the living God!
I have sought the world around,
Paths of sin and sorrow trod,
Peace and comfort nowhere found.

2 Now to you my spirit turns,—
Turns, a fugitive unblessed;
Brethren! where your altar burns,
Oh! receive me into rest!

3 Lonely I no longer roam,
Like the cloud, the wind, the wave;
Where you dwell shall be my home,
Where you die shall be my grave;

4 Mine the God whom you adore,
Your Redeemer shall be mine;
Earth can fill my soul no more,
Every idol I resign.
James Montgomery, 1825.

CHURCH RELATIONS.

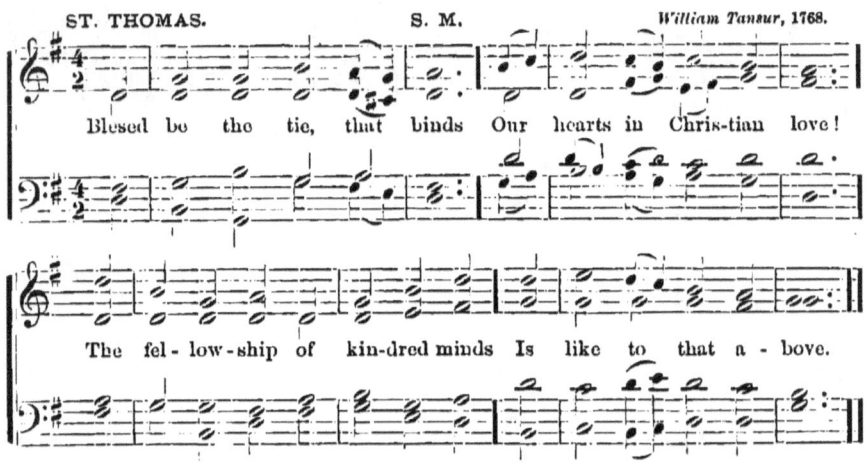

600. *Love to the Brethren.* (1177.)

1 BLESSED be the tie, that binds
  Our hearts in Christian love!
  The fellowship of kindred minds
  Is like to that above.

2 Before our Father's throne,
  We pour our ardent prayers;
  Our fears, our hopes, our aims are one,
  Our comforts and our cares.

3 We share our mutual woes;
  Our mutual burdens bear;
  And often for each other flows
  The sympathizing tear.

4 When we asunder part,
  It gives us inward pain:
  But we shall still be joined in heart,
  And hope to meet again.

5 This glorious hope revives
  Our courage by the way;
  While each in expectation lives,
  And longs to see the day.

6 From sorrow, toil, and pain,
  And sin we shall be free;
  And perfect love and friendship reign
  Through all eternity.
  John Fawcett, 1772.

601. PSALM 133. (1178.)

1 BLESSED are the sons of peace,
  Whose hearts and hopes are one;
  Whose kind designs to serve and please
  Through all their actions run.

2 Blessed is the pious house
  Where zeal and friendship meet;
  Their songs of praise, their mingled vows,
  Make their communion sweet.

3 Thus, when, on Aaron's head,
  They poured the rich perfume,
  The oil through all his raiment spread,
  And pleasure filled the room.

4 Thus, on the heavenly hills,
  The saints are blessed above,
  Where joy, like morning dew, distills,
  And all the air is love.
  Isaac Watts, 1719.

602. *Communion of Saints.* (1179.)

1 LET party names no more
  The Christian world o'erspread;
  Gentile and Jew, and bond and free,
  Are one in Christ, their Head.

2 Among the saints on earth,
  Let mutual love be found:
  Heirs of the same inheritance,
  With mutual blessings crowned.

3 Let envy, child of hell!
  Be banished far away:
  Those should in strictest friendship dwell,
  Who the same Lord obey.

4 Thus will the church below
  Resemble that above;
  Where streams of endless pleasure flow,
  And every heart is love.
  Benjamin Beddome, 1769.

FELLOWSHIP.

WARE. L. M. George Kingsley, 1838.

O Lord! how joyful 't is to see The brethren join in love to thee!
On thee alone their heart relies; Their only strength thy grace supplies.

603. *"Oh! quam juvat fratres, Deus!"* (1183.)

1 O Lord! how joyful 't is to see
 The brethren join in love to thee!
 On thee alone their heart relies;
 Their only strength thy grace supplies.

2 How sweet, within thy holy place,
 With one accord to sing thy grace,
 Besieging thine attentive ear
 With all the force of fervent prayer.

3 Oh! may we love the house of God,
 Of peace and joy the blest abode!
 Oh! may no angry strife destroy
 That sacred peace, that holy joy!

4 The world without may rage, but we
 Will only cling more close to thee,
 With hearts to thee more wholly given,
 More weaned from earth, more fixed on heaven.

5 Lord! show'r upon us, from above,
 The sacred gift of mutual love;
 Each other's wants may we supply,
 And reign together in the sky.
  Lat., *Santolius Victorinus,* 1660.
   Tr., *John Chandler,* 1837.

604. *Christian Friendship.* (1184.)

1 How blest the sacred tie, that binds,
 In union sweet, according minds!
 How swift the heavenly course they run,
 Whose hearts, whose faith, whose hopes are one!

2 To each the soul of each how dear!
 What jealous love, what holy fear!
 How doth the generous flame within
 Refine from earth, and cleanse from sin!

3 Their streaming eyes together flow
 For human guilt and mortal woe;
 Their ardent prayers together rise,
 Like mingling flames in sacrifice.

4 Together oft they seek the place
 Where God reveals his awful face;
 How high, how strong, their raptures swell,
 There 's none but kindred souls can tell.

5 Nor shall the glowing flame expire,
 When nature droops her sickening fire;
 Then shall they meet in realms above,
 A heaven of joy, a heaven of love.
  Mrs. Anna L. Barbauld, 1797.

605. *Brotherly Love.* (1182.)

1 Now, by the love of Christ, my God,
 His sharp distress, his sore complaints,
 By his last groans, his dying blood,
 I charge my soul to love the saints.

2 Clamor, and wrath, and war be gone;
 Envy and spite for ever cease;
 Let bitter words no more be known
 Amongst the saints, the sons of peace.

3 The Spirit, like a peaceful dove,
 Flies from the realms of noise and strife;
 Why should we vex and grieve his love,
 Who seals our souls to heavenly life?

4 Tender and kind be all our thoughts,
 Through all our lives let mercy run:
 So God forgives our numerous faults,
 For the dear sake of Christ, his Son.
  Isaac Watts, 1709, line 1st. a.

CHURCH RELATIONS.

CAPTIVITY. L. M. *William B. Bradbury, 1847.*

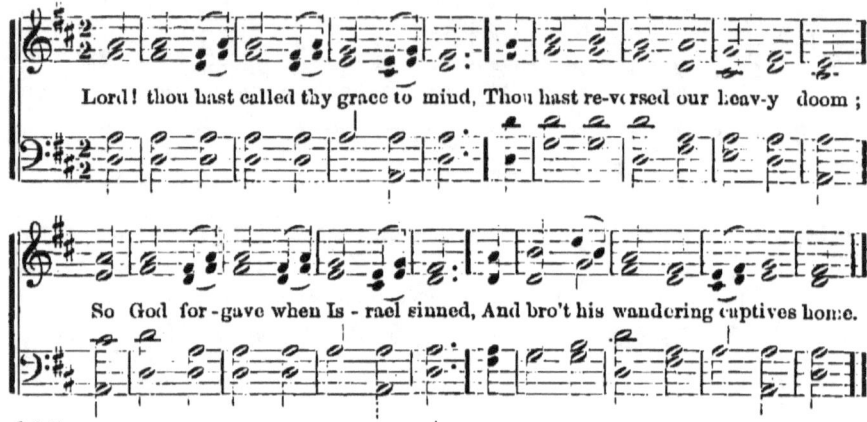

Lord! thou hast called thy grace to mind, Thou hast reversed our heavy doom;
So God forgave when Israel sinned, And bro't his wandering captives home.

606. PSALM 85. (1191.)

1 Lord! thou hast called thy grace to mind,
  Thou hast reversed our heavy doom;
  So God forgave when Israel sinned,
  And bro't his wandering captives home.

2 Thou hast begun to set us free,
  And made thy fiercest wrath abate;
  Now let our hearts be turned to thee,
  And thy salvation be complete.

3 Revive our dying graces, Lord!
  And let thy saints in thee rejoice;
  Make known thy truth, fulfill thy word;
  We wait for praise to tune our voice.

4 We wait to hear what God will say;
  He 'll speak, and give his people peace;
  But let them run no more astray;
  Lest his returning wrath increase.
  Isaac Watts, 1719.

607. PSALM 80. (1187.)

1 Great Shepherd of thine Israel!
  Who didst between the cherubs dwell,
  And led the tribes, thy chosen sheep,
  Safe through the desert and the deep;

2 Thy church is in the desert now:
  Shine from on high and guide us through;
  Turn us to thee, thy love restore;
  We shall be saved, and sigh no more.

3 Great God, whom heavenly hosts obey.
  How long shall we lament, and pray,
  And wait in vain thy kind return?
  How long shall thy fierce anger burn?

4 Instead of wine and cheerful bread,
  Thy saints with their own tears are fed;
  Turn us to thee, thy love restore;
  We shall be saved, and sigh no more.

5 Hast thou not planted, with thy hands,
  A lovely vine in these fair lands?
  But now, dear Lord! look down, and see
  Thy mourning vine, that lovely tree!

6 Return, almighty God! return,
  Nor let thy bleeding vineyard mourn;
  Turn us to thee, thy love restore;
  We shall be saved and sigh no more.
  Isaac Watts, 1719.

608. The Vision of the dry Bones. (1188.)

1 Look down, O Lord! with pitying eye;
  See Adam's race in ruin lie;
  Sin spreads its trophies o'er the ground,
  And scatters slaughtered heaps around.

2 And can these mouldering corpses live?
  And can these perished bones revive?
  That, mighty God! to thee is known;
  That wondrous work is all thine own.

3 Thy ministers are sent in vain
  To prophesy upon the slain;
  In vain they call, in vain they cry,
  Till thine almighty aid is nigh.

4 But, if thy Spirit deign to breathe,
  Life spreads through all the realms of death;
  Dry bones obey thy powerful voice;
  They move, they waken, they rejoice.
  Philip Doddridge, 1740.

REVIVAL.

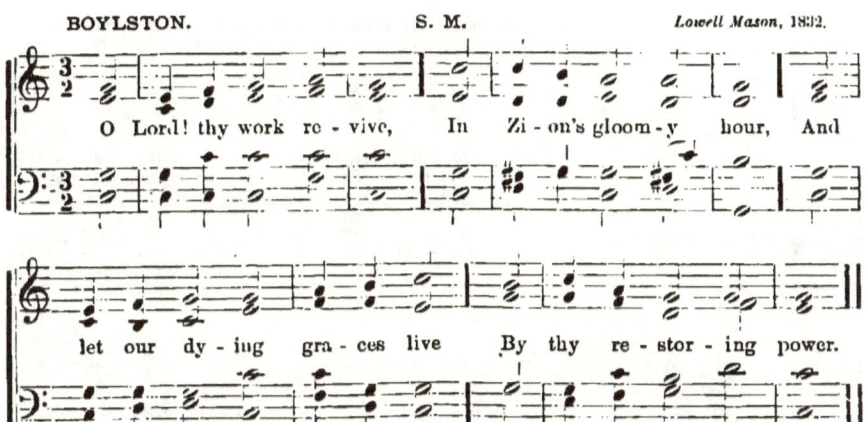

BOYLSTON. S. M. *Lowell Mason, 1832.*

O Lord! thy work re-vive, In Zi-on's gloom-y hour, And let our dy-ing gra-ces live By thy re-stor-ing power.

609. *Prayer for a Revival.* (1196.)

1 O Lord! thy work revive,
   In Zion's gloomy hour,
And let our dying graces live
   By thy restoring power.

2 Oh! let thy chosen few
   Awake to earnest prayer;
Their covenant again renew,
   And walk in filial fear.

3 Thy Spirit then will speak
   Through lips of humble clay,
Till hearts of adamant shall break,
   Till rebels shall obey.

4 Now lend thy gracious ear:
   Now listen to our cry;
Oh! come and bring salvation near;
   Our souls on thee rely.

Mrs. Phœbe H. Brown, 1831.

610. *A Revival sought.* (1195.)

1 Revive thy work, O Lord!
   Thy mighty arm make bare;
Speak, with the voice that wakes the dead,
   And make thy people hear.

2 Revive thy work, O Lord!
   Disturb this sleep of death;
Quicken the smouldering embers now,
   By thine almighty breath.

3 Revive thy work, O Lord!
   Exalt thy precious name;
And, by the Holy Ghost, our love
   For thee and thine inflame.

4 Revive thy work, O Lord!
   And give refreshing showers;
The glory shall be all thine own,
   The blessing, Lord! be ours.

Albert Midlane, 1861.

611. *Longing for a Revival.* (1197.)

1 Oh! for the happy hour
   When God will hear our cry;
And send, with a reviving power,
   His Spirit from on high!

2 We meet, we sing, we pray,
   We listen to the word,
In vain; we see no cheering ray,
   No cheering voice is heard.

3 Our prayers are faint and dull,
   And languid all our songs;
Where once with joy our hearts were full,
   And rapture tuned our tongues.

4 While many seek thy house,
   How few, around thy board,
Meet to recount their solemn vows,
   And bless thee as their Lord!

5 Thou, thou alone canst give
   Thy gospel sure success;
Canst bid the dying sinner live
   Anew in holiness.

6 Come, then, with power divine,
   Spirit of life and love!
Then shall our people all be thine,
   Our church, like that above.

George W. Bethune, 1843.

CHURCH RELATIONS.

GREENVILLE. 8s & 7s. 8 lines. From *Jean Jacques Rousseau*, 1750. Adapted by *J. B. Cramer*.

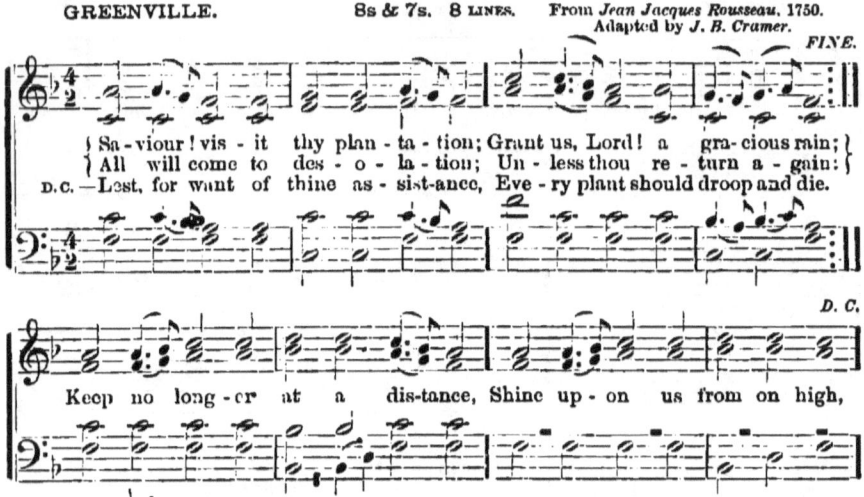

Saviour! visit thy plantation; Grant us, Lord! a gracious rain;
All will come to desolation; Unless thou return again:
D.C.—Lest, for want of thine assistance, Every plant should droop and die.

Keep no longer at a distance, Shine upon us from on high,

---

612. *A spiritual Drought.* (1198.)

1 SAVIOUR! visit thy plantation;
Grant us, Lord! a gracious rain;
All will come to desolation,
Unless thou return again:
Keep no longer at a distance,
Shine upon us from on high,
Lest, for want of thine assistance,
Every plant should droop and die.

2 Surely, once thy garden flourished;
Every part looked gay and green;
Then thy word our spirits nourished:
Happy seasons we have seen!
But a drought has since succeeded,
And a sad decline we see;
Lord! thy help is greatly needed;
Help can only come from thee.

3 Some, in whom we once delighted,
We shall meet no more below:
Some, alas! we fear, are blighted,
Scarce a single leaf they show:
Dearest Saviour! hasten hither,
Thou canst make them bloom again;
Oh! permit them not to wither,
Let not all our hopes be vain.

4 Let our mutual love be fervent;
Make us prevalent in prayers;
Let each one, esteemed thy servant,
Shun the world's bewitching snares:

Break the tempter's fatal power,
Turn the stony heart to flesh,
And begin, from this good hour,
To revive thy work afresh.
John Newton, 1779.

613. *Comfort for the Church.* (1199.)

1 HEAR what God, the Lord, hath spoken;
O my people, faint and few,
Comfortless, afflicted, broken!
Fair abodes I build for you;
Themes of heartfelt tribulation
Shall no more perplex your ways;
You shall name your walls "Salvation,"
And your gates shall all be "Praise."

2 There, like streams that feed the garden,
Pleasures without end shall flow;
For the Lord, your faith rewarding,
All his bounty shall bestow:
Still in undisturbed possession,
Peace and righteousness shall reign;
Never shall you feel oppression,
Hear the voice of war again.

3 Ye, no more your suns descending,
Waning moons no more shall see,
But, your griefs for ever ending,
Find eternal noon in me:
God shall rise, and shining o'er you,
Change to day the gloom of night;
He, the Lord, shall be your Glory,
God, your everlasting Light.
William Cowper, 1772.

REVIVAL.

ZERAH. C. M. Lowell Mason, 1837.

Let Zi-on and her sons rejoice, Behold the promised hour! Her God hath heard her mourning voice, And comes t' exalt his power; Her God hath heard her mourning voice, And comes t' exalt his power.

614. PSALM 102. (1202.)

1 Let Zion and her sons rejoice;
 Behold the promised hour!
 Her God hath heard her mourning voice,
 And comes t' exalt his power.

2 Her dust and ruins, that remain,
 Are precious in our eyes;
 Those ruins shall be built again,
 And all that dust shall rise.

3 The Lord will raise Jerusalem,
 And stand in glory there;
 Nations shall bow before his name,
 And kings attend with fear.

4 He sits a sovereign on his throne,
 With pity in his eyes;
 He hears the dying prisoners groan,
 And sees their sighs arise.

5 He frees the souls condemned to death,
 And, when his saints complain,
 It sha' n't be said, that praying breath
 Was ever spent in vain.

6 This shall be known, when we are dead,
 And left on long record,
 That ages yet unborn may read,
 And trust, and praise the Lord.
 Isaac Watts, 1719.

615. PSALM 126. (1203.)

1 Ye servants of the living God!
 Let praise your hearts employ;
 And, as you tread the heavenly road,
 Lift up the voice of joy.

2 Have they not reason to rejoice,
 Whose sins have been forgiven;—
 Called by a gracious Father's voice
 To be the heirs of heaven?

3 How do the captive's transports flow,
 When rescued from his chains!
 And how must sinners joy to know
 Their great Deliverer reigns!

4 Oh! grant us, Lord! to feel and own
 The power of love divine,
 The blood that doth for sin atone,
 The grace which makes us thine.
 William H. Bathurst, 1830.

616. *A Revival sought.* (1204.)

1 Blest Jesus! come thou gently down,
 And fill this hallowed place;
 Oh! make thy glorious goings known,
 Diffuse around thy grace.

2 Shine, dearest Lord! from realms of day,
 Disperse the gloom of night;
 Chase all our clouds and doubts away,
 And turn the shades to light.

3 Revive, O God! desponding saints,
 Who languish, droop and sigh;
 Refresh the soul that tires and faints,
 Fill mourning hearts with joy.

4 Make known thy power, victorious King!
 Subdue each stubborn will;
 Then sovereign grace we'll join to sing
 On Zion's sacred hill.
 Anon., 1850.

CHURCH RELATIONS.

MORNING STAR. 7s. 8 LINES. Lowell Mason, 1830.

Watchman! tell us of the night, What its signs of promise are;—Traveler! o'er yon mountain's height, See that glo-ry-beam-ing star!—Watchman! does its beau-teous ray Aught of joy or hope foretell?—Traveler! yes; it brings the day, Promised day of Is-ra-el!—

617.   *The Glory-beaming Star.*   (1211.)

1 WATCHMAN! tell us of the night!
  What its signs of promise are;—
  Traveler! o'er yon mountain's height,
  See that glory-beaming star!—
  Watchman! does its beauteous ray
  Aught of joy or hope foretell?—
  Traveler! yes; it brings the day,
  Promised day of Israel!—

2 Watchman! tell us of the night;
  Higher yet that star ascends;—
  Traveler! blessedness and light,
  Peace and truth, its course portends;—
  Watchman! will its beams alone
  Gild the spot that gave them birth?—
  Traveler! ages are its own;
  See, it bursts o'er all the earth!—

3 Watchman! tell us of the night,
  For the morning seems to dawn;—
  Traveler! darkness takes its flight,
  Doubt and terror are withdrawn;—
  Watchmen! let thy wanderings cease;
  Hie thee to thy quiet home!—
  Traveler! lo! the Prince of peace,
  Lo! the Son of God, is come!—

  John Bowring, 1825.

618.   *Home Missions.*   (1212.)

1 SOLDIERS of the cross! arise;
  Gird you with your armor bright;
  Mighty are your enemies,
  Hard the battle ye must fight;
  O'er a faithless fallen world,
  Raise your banner to the sky,
  Let it float there, wide unfurled,
  Bear it onward, lift it high.

2 Mid the homes of want and woe,
  Strangers to the living word,
  Let the Saviour's herald go,
  Let the voice of hope be heard;
  To the weary and the worn,
  Tell of realms where sorrows cease;
  To the outcast and forlorn,
  Speak of mercy, grace, and peace.

3 Guard the helpless, seek the strayed,
  Comfort troubles, banish grief;
  With the Spirit's sword arrayed,
  Scatter sin and unbelief;
  Be the banner still unfurled,
  Bear it bravely still abroad,
  Till the kingdoms of the world
  Are the kingdoms of the Lord.

  William Walsham How, 1854.

MISSIONS.

RHINE. H. M.   *Thomas Hastings,* 1836.

All hail! in-car-nate God! The wondrous things, foretold Of thee, in sa-cred writ, With joy our eyes behold: Still does thine arm new trophies wear, And monuments of glo-ry rear.

619.   *The Great Conqueror.*   (1215.)

1 ALL hail! incarnate God!
   The wondrous things, foretold
   Of thee, in sacred writ,
     With joy our eyes behold:
  Still does thine arm new trophies wear,
  And monuments of glory rear.

2 Oh! haste, victorious Prince!
   That glorious, happy day,
   When souls, like drops of dew,
     Shall own thy gentle sway;
  Oh! may it bless our longing eyes,
  And bear our shouts beyond the skies!

3 All hail! triumphant Lord!
   Eternal be thy reign;
   Behold the nations sue
     To wear thy gentle chain:
  When earth and time are known no more,
  Thy throne shall stand for ever sure.
                    Elizabeth Scott, 1763.

620.   PSALM 45.   (1216.)

1 GIRD on thy conquering sword,
   Ascend thy shining car,
   And march, almighty Lord!
     To wage thy holy war:
  Before his wheels, in glad surprise,
  Ye valleys! rise; and sink, ye hills!

2 Before thine awful face
   Millions of foes shall fall,
   The captives of thy grace,—
     That grace which conquers all:
  The world shall know, great King of kings!
  What wondrous things thine arm can do.

3 Here, to my willing soul,
   Bend thy triumphant way;
   Here every foe control,
     And all thy power display:
  My heart, thy throne, blest Jesus! see,
  Bows low to thee, to thee alone.
                    Philip Doddridge, 1736.

621.   *Prayer for the Spirit.*   (1217.)

1 O THOU that hearest prayer!
   Attend our humble cry;
   And let thy servants share
     Thy blessing from on high:
  We plead the promise of thy word;
  Grant us thy Holy Spirit, Lord!

2 If earthly parents hear
   Their children when they cry;
   If they, with love sincere,
     Their children's wants supply;
  Much more wilt thou thy love display,
  And answer when thy children pray.

3 Our Heavenly Father, thou;—
   We. children of thy grace:
   Oh! let thy Spirit now
     Descend, and fill the place:
  That all may feel the heavenly flame,
  And all unite to praise thy name.

4 Oh! send thy Spirit down
   On all the nations, Lord!
   With great success to crown
     The preaching of thy word,
  That heathen lands may own thy sway,
  And cast their idol-gods away.
                    John Burton, 1824.

CHURCH RELATIONS.

SURREY. L. M. —— *Costello*, cir. 1810.

In-dulgent Sovereign of the skies! And wilt thou bow thy gracious ear? While feeble mortals raise their cries, Wilt thou, the great Je-ho-vah, hear? Wilt thou, the great Je-ho-vah, hear?

622. *Pleading for the Perishing.* (1223.)

1 INDULGENT Sovereign of the skies!
   And wilt thou bow thy gracious ear?
   While feeble mortals raise their cries,
   Wilt thou, the great Jehovah, hear?

2 How shall thy servants give thee rest,
   Till Zion's mouldering walls thou raise?
   Till thine own power shall stand con-
   And make Jerusalem a praise? [fessed,

3 Look down, O God! with pitying eye,
   And view the desolation round;
   See, what wide realms in darkness lie,
   And hurl their idols to the ground.

4 Loud let the gospel trumpet blow,
   And call the nations from afar;
   Let all the isles their Saviour know,
   And earth's remotest ends draw near.

5 On all our souls let grace descend,
   Like heavenly dew, in copious showers;
   That we may call our God our Friend,
   That we may hail salvation ours.
   Philip Doddridge, 1740.

623. *The Glory of the latter Day.* (1219.)

1 ARISE, arise; with joy survey
   The glory of the latter day;
   Already is the dawn begun
   Which marks at hand the rising sun.

2 "Behold the way!" ye heralds! cry;
   Spare not, but lift your voices high;
   Convey the sound from pole to pole,
   Glad tidings to the captive soul.

3 Behold the way to Zion's hill,
   Where Israel's God delights to dwell!
   He fixes there his lofty throne,
   And calls the sacred place his own.

4 The north gives up; the south no more
   Keeps back her consecrated store;
   From east to west the message runs,
   And either India yields her sons.

5 Auspicious dawn! thy rising ray
   With joy we view, and hail the day:
   Great Sun of righteousness! arise,
   And fill the world with glad surprise.
   Thomas Kelly, 1809, a.

624. *For a missionary Meeting.* (1220.)

1 ASSEMBLED at thy great command,
   Before thy face, dread King! we stand:
   The voice that marshaled every star,
   Has called thy people from afar.

2 We meet, through distant lands, to spread
   The truth, for which the martyrs bled;
   Along the line, to either pole,
   The thunder of thy praise to roll.

3 Our prayers assist, accept our praise,
   Our hopes revive, our courage raise,
   Our counsels aid; and, Oh! impart
   The single eye, the faithful heart.

4 Forth with thy chosen heralds come,
   Recall the wandering spirits home;
   From Zion's mount send forth the sound,
   To spread the spacious world around.
   William B. Collyer, 1812.

MISSIONS. 223

MISSIONARY CHANT.   L. M.   Charles Zeuner, 1832.

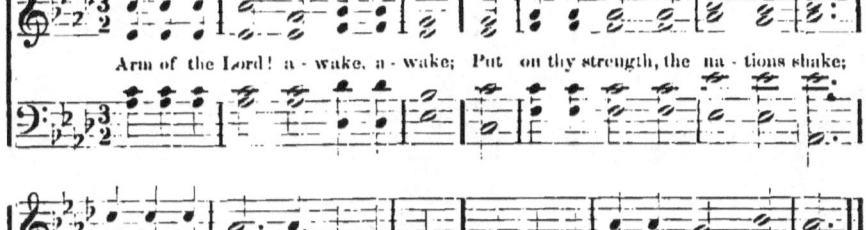

Arm of the Lord! a-wake, a-wake; Put on thy strength, the na-tions shake;
And let the world, a-dor-ing, see Triumphs of mer-cy, wrought by thee.

625. *The universal Reign of Christ.* (1228.)

1 ARM of the Lord! awake, awake;
  Put on thy strength, the nations shake;
  And let the world, adoring, see
  Triumphs of mercy, wrought by thee.

2 Say to the heathen, from thy throne,
  "I am Jehovah God alone!"
  Thy voice their idols shall confound,
  And cast their altars to the ground.

3 No more let human blood be spilt,
  Vain sacrifice for human guilt;
  But to each conscience be applied
  The blood, that flowed from Jesus' side.

4 Almighty God! thy grace proclaim,
  In every clime, of every name,
  Till adverse powers before thee fall,
  And crown the Saviour - Lord of all.
  William Shrubsole, 1776.

626. *The coming Reign of Christ.* (1229.)

1 ASCEND thy throne, almighty King!
  And spread thy glories all abroad;
  Let thine own arm salvation bring,
  And be thou known the gracious God.

2 Let millions bow before thy seat;
  Let humble mourners seek thy face;
  Bring daring rebels to thy feet,
  Subdued by thy victorious grace.

3 Oh! let the kingdoms of the world
  Become the kingdoms of the Lord;
  Let saints and angels praise thy name,
  Be thou thro' heaven and earth adored.
  Benjamin Beddome, 1778.

627. *Christ's coming to Reign.* (1224.)

1 JESUS! thy church, with longing eyes,
  For thine expected coming waits;
  When will the promised light arise,
  And glory beam from Zion's gates?

2 E'en now, when tempests round us fall,
  And wintry clouds o'ercast the sky,
  Thy words with pleasure we recall,
  And deem that our redemption's nigh.

3 Oh! come and reign o'er every land;
  Let Satan from his throne be hurled,
  All nations bow to thy command,
  And grace revive a dying world.

4 Teach us, in watchfulness and prayer,
  To wait for the appointed hour;
  And fit us, by thy grace, to share
  The triumphs of thy conquering power.
  William H. Bathurst, 1831.

628. *The Time to favor Zion.* (1225.)

1 SOVEREIGN of worlds! display thy power;
  Be this thy Zion's favored hour;
  Oh! bid the morning star arise;
  Oh! point the heathen to the skies.

2 Set up thy throne where Satan reigns,
  In western wilds and eastern plains;
  Far let the gospel's sound be known;
  Make thou the universe thine own.

3 Speak, and the world shall hear thy voice;
  Speak, and the desert shall rejoice:
  Dispel the gloom of heathen night;
  Bid every nation hail the light.
  B. H. Draper, 1816.

CHURCH RELATIONS.

YARMOUTH. 7s & 6s. 8 lines. Lowell Mason, 1835.

Stand up, stand up for Jesus, Ye soldiers of the cross! Lift high his royal banner, It must not suffer loss; From victory unto victory, His army shall he lead, Till every foe is vanquished, Till every foe is vanquished, And Christ is Lord indeed.

629. *Good Soldiers.* (1240.)

1 STAND up, stand up for Jesus,
  Ye soldiers of the cross!
  Lift high his royal banner,
  It must not suffer loss:
  From victory unto victory
  His army shall he lead,
  Till every foe is vanquished,
  And Christ is Lord indeed.

2 Stand up, stand up for Jesus,
  The trumpet call obey;
  Forth to the mighty conflict,
  In this his glorious day:
  Ye that are men! now serve him,
  Against unnumbered foes;
  Your courage rise with danger,
  And strength to strength oppose.

3 Stand up, stand up for Jesus;
  Stand in his strength alone;
  The arm of flesh will fail you;
  Ye dare not trust your own:
  Put on the gospel armor,
  And, watching unto prayer,
  Where duty calls, or danger,
  Be never wanting there.

4 Stand up, stand up for Jesus;
  The strife will not be long;
  This day, the noise of battle,—
  The next, the victor's song:
  To him that overcometh,
  A crown of life shall be;
  He, with the King of glory,
  Shall reign eternally!
                    George Duffield. 1858.

630. PSALM 14. (1241.)

1 OH! that the Lord's salvation
  Were out of Zion come,
  To heal his ancient nation,
  To lead his outcasts home!
  How long the holy city
  Shall heathen feet profane?
  Return, O Lord! in pity,
  Rebuild her walls again.

2 Let fall thy rod of terror,
  Thy saving grace impart;
  Roll back the veil of error,
  Release the fettered heart:
  Let Israel, home returning,
  Their lost Messiah see;
  Give oil of joy for mourning,
  And bind thy church to thee.
                Henry Francis Lyte. 1834.

MISSIONS.

631. *Salvation for all the World.* (1242.)

1 From Greenland's icy mountains,
  From India's coral strand,
Where Afric's sunny fountains
  Roll down their golden sand,—
From many an ancient river,
  From many a palmy plain,
They call us to deliver
  Their land from error's chain.

2 What, though the spicy breezes
  Blow soft o'er Ceylon's isle ;
Though every prospect pleases,
  And only man is vile ?
In vain with lavish kindness
  The gifts of God are strown ;
The heathen, in his blindness,
  Bows down to wood and stone !

3 Can we, whose souls are lighted
  With wisdom from on high,—
Can we, to men benighted,
  The lamp of life deny ?
Salvation, Oh ! salvation !—
  The joyful sound proclaim,
Till each remotest nation
  Has learned Messiah's name.

4 Waft, waft, ye winds ! his story,
  And you, ye waters ! roll,
Till, like a sea of glory,
  It spreads from pole to pole ;
Till, o'er our ransomed nature,
  The Lamb, for sinners slain,
Redeemer, King, Creator,
  In bliss returns to reign !
              Reginald Heber, 1819.

632. *The universal Hallelujah.* (1244.)

1 When shall the voice of singing
  Flow joyfully along,
When hill and valley, ringing
  With one triumphant song,
Proclaim the contest ended,
  And him, who once was slain,
A second time descended,
  In righteousness to reign ?

2 Then, from the craggy mountains,
  The sacred shout shall fly ;
And shady vales and fountains
  Shall echo the reply :
High tower and lowly dwelling
  Shall send the hymn around,
All hallelujah swelling
  In one continued sound.
              James Edmeston, 1822.

CHURCH RELATIONS.

BROOMSGROVE.   C. M.   *Thomas Williams' Coll., cir. 1768.*

Shine, mighty God! on Zi-on shine, With beams of heav'nly grace; Reveal thy pow'r thro' all our coasts, And show thy smiling face, And show thy smiling face.

633.   PSALM 67.   (1232.)

1 Shine, mighty God! on Zion shine
 With beams of heavenly grace;
 Reveal thy power through all our coasts,
 And show thy smiling face.

2 When shall thy name, from shore to shore,
 Sound all the earth abroad,
 And distant nations know and love
 Their Saviour and their God?

3 Sing to the Lord, ye distant lands!
 Sing loud with solemn voice;
 Let every tongue exalt his praise,
 And every heart rejoice.

4 Earth shall obey her Maker's will,
 And yield a full increase;
 Our God will crown his chosen land,
 With fruitfulness and peace.

5 God, the Redeemer, scatters round
 His choicest favors here,
 While the creation's utmost bound
 Shall see, adore, and fear.
                       Isaac Watts, 1719, a.

634.   *The Diffusion of the Gospel.*   (1235.)

1 Great God! the nations of the earth
 Are by creation thine;
 And, in thy works, by all beheld,
 Thy radiant glories shine.

2 But, Lord! thy greater love has sent
 Thy gospel to mankind,
 Unveiling what rich stores of grace
 Are treasured in thy mind.

3 Lord! when shall these glad tidings
 The spacious earth around, [spread
 Till every tribe and every soul,
 Shall hear the joyful sound!

4 Oh! when shall Afric's sable sons
 Enjoy the heavenly word,
 And vassals, long enslaved, become
 The freedmen of the Lord?

5 When shall th' untutored India tribes,
 A dark, bewildered race,
 Sit down at our Immanuel's feet,
 And learn and feel his grace!

6 Smile! Lord, on each divine attempt
 To spread the gospel's rays;
 And build, on sin's demolished throne,
 The temples of thy praise.
                      Thomas Gibbons, 1769.

635.   *The Gospel Heralds.*   (1237.)

1 Go, and the Saviour's grace proclaim,
 Ye favored men of God!
 Go, publish, through Immanuel's name,
 Salvation bought with blood.

2 He, who has called you to the war,
 Will recompense your pains;
 Before Messiah's conquering car,
 Shall mountains sink to plains.

3 Shrink not, though earth and hell oppose,
 But plead your Master's cause;
 Assured that e'en your mightiest foes
 Shall bow before his cross.
                       Thomas Morell. 1818.

MISSIONS.

TAMWORTH. 8s, 7s & 4. Scotch Melody. Adapted by Charles Lockhart, cir. 1790.

(O'er the gloomy hills of darkness, Cheered by no celestial ray,)
(Sun of righteousness! a-rising, Bring the bright, the glorious day;)
Send the gospel, send the gospel, To the earth's remotest bound.

636. *Success of the Gospel.* (1247.)

1 O'er the gloomy hills of darkness,
   Cheered by no celestial ray,
   Sun of righteousness! arising,
   Bring the bright, the glorious day;
     Send the gospel,
   To the earth's remotest bound.

2 Kingdoms wide that sit in darkness,—
   Grant them, Lord! the glorious light;
   And, from eastern coast to western,
   May the morning chase the night;
     And redemption,
   Freely purchased, win the day.

3 Fly abroad, thou mighty gospel!
   Win and conquer, never cease;
   May thy lasting, wide dominions,
   Multiply and still increase;
     Sway thy sceptre,
   Saviour! all the world around.
        William Williams, 1772, a.

637. *Light for the Gentiles.* (1248.)

1 O'er the realms of pagan darkness,
   Let the eye of pity gaze;
   See the kindreds of the people,
   Lost in sin's bewildering maze; -
     Darkness brooding
   On the face of all the earth!

2 Light of them that sit in darkness!
   Rise and shine, thy blessings bring;
   Light, to lighten all the Gentiles!
   Rise with healing in thy wing:
     To thy brightness,
   Let all kings and nations come.

3 May the heathen, now adoring
   Idol-gods of wood and stone,
   Come, and, worshiping before him,
   Serve the living God alone:
     Let thy glory
   Fill the earth, as floods the sea.

4 Thou, to whom all power is given!
   Speak the word; at thy command,
   Let the company of preachers
   Spread thy name from land to land:
     Lord! be with them,
   Alway to the end of time.
        Thomas Cotterill, 1819.

638. *Dawning of the latter Day.* (1251.)

1 Yes, we trust, the day is breaking;
   Joyful times are near at hand;
   God, the mighty God, is speaking
   By his word in every land;
     Mark his progress!
   Darkness flies, at his command.

2 While the foe becomes more daring,
   While he enters like a flood,
   God, the Saviour, is preparing
   Means to spread his truth abroad:
     Every language
   Soon shall tell the love of God.

3 God of Jacob, high and glorious!
   Let thy people see thy hand;
   Let the gospel be victorious,
   Through the world, in every land;
     Let the idols
   Perish, Lord! at thy command.
        Thomas Kelly, 1809.

CHURCH RELATIONS.

WATCHMAN. S. M. James Leach, 1789.

O Lord, our God! a-rise; The cause of truth main-tain;
And wide, o'er all the peo-pled world, Ex-tend her bless-ed reign.

639. *The universal Reign of Christ.* (1256.)

1 O Lord, our God! arise;
  The cause of truth maintain;
  And wide, o'er all the peopled world,
  Extend her blessèd reign.

2 Thou Prince of life! arise,
  Nor let thy glory cease;
  Far spread the conquests of thy grace,
  And bless the earth with peace.

3 Thou Holy Ghost! arise:
  Expand thy quickening wing,
  And o'er a dark and ruined world
  Let light and order spring.

4 All on the earth! arise;
  To God, the Saviour, sing;
  From shore to shore, from earth to heaven,
  Let echoing anthems ring!
  Ralph Wardlaw, 1803.

640. *Christ's Coming.* (1259.)

1 Come, Lord! and tarry not;
  Bring the long-looked-for day;
  Oh! why these years of waiting here,
  These ages of delay?

2 Come, for thy saints still wait;
  Daily ascends their sigh;
  The Spirit and the Bride say, Come!
  Dost thou not hear the cry?

3 Come, and make all things new,
  Build up this ruined earth,
  Restore our faded paradise,—
  Creation's second birth.

4 Come and begin thy reign
  Of everlasting peace;
  Come, take the kingdom to thyself,
  Great King of righteousness!
  Horatius Bonar, 1857.

641. *The Panoply of God.* (1260.)

1 Soldiers of Christ! arise,
  And put your armor on,—
  Strong, in the strength which God sup- [plies,
  Through his eternal Son:—

2 Strong, in the Lord of hosts,
  And in his mighty power;
  Who in the strength of Jesus trusts,
  Is more than conqueror.

3 Stand, then, in his great might,
  With all his strength endued;
  And take, to arm you for the fight,
  The panoply of God:—

4 That, having all things done,
  And all your conflicts past,
  You may o'ercome through Christ alone,
  And stand entire at last.

5 From strength to strength go on;
  Wrestle, and fight, and pray;
  Tread all the powers of darkness down,
  And win the well-fought day.

6 Still let the Spirit cry,
  In all his soldiers, "Come,"
  Till Christ, the Lord, descends from high,
  And takes the conquerors home.
  Charles Wesley, 1749.

WORKING AND GIVING.

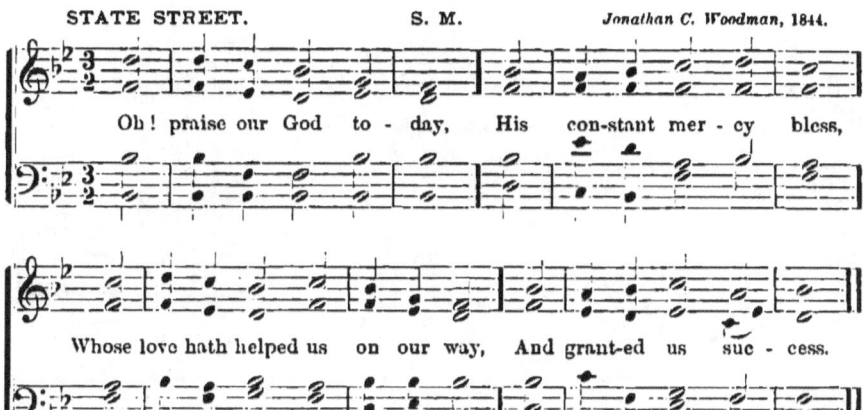

STATE STREET. S. M.   *Jonathan C. Woodman, 1844.*

Oh! praise our God to-day, His constant mercy bless, Whose love hath helped us on our way, And grant-ed us suc-cess.

642.   *The Law of Love.*   (1263.)

1 Oh! PRAISE our God to-day,
  His constant mercy bless,
Whose love hath helped us on our way,
  And granted us success.

2 His arm the strength imparts
  Our daily toil to bear;
His grace alone inspires our hearts,
  Each other's load to share.

3 Oh! happiest work below,
  Earnest of joy above,
To sweeten many a cup of woe,
  By deeds of holy love!

4 Lord! may it be our choice
  This blessed rule to keep,
"Rejoice with them that do rejoice,
  And weep with them that weep."

5 God of the widow! hear;
  Our work of mercy bless;
God of the fatherless! be near,
  And grant us good success.
                   Henry W. Baker, 1852.

643.   *Doing Good.*   (1264.)

1 WE GIVE thee but thine own,
  Whate'er the gift may be:
All that we have is thine alone,
  A trust, O Lord! from thee.

2 To comfort and to bless,
  To find a balm for woe,
To tend the lone and fatherless
  Is angels' work below.

3 The captive to release,
  To God the lost to bring,
To teach the way of life and peace,
  It is a Christ-like thing.

4 And we believe thy word,
  Though dim our faith may be:
Whate'er for thine we do, O Lord,
  We do it unto thee.
                   William Walsham How, 1854.

644.   *Contributions.*   (1265.)

1 THY bounties, gracious Lord!
  With gratitude we own;
We bless thy providential grace,
  Which showers its blessings down.

2 With joy the people bring
  Their offerings round thy throne;
With thankful souls, behold! we pay
  A tribute of thine own.

3 Let a Redeemer's blood
  Diffuse its virtues wide;
Hallow and cleanse our every gift,
  And all our follies hide.

4 Oh! may this sacrifice
  To thee, the Lord, ascend,
An odor of a sweet perfume,
  Presented by his hand.

5 Well pleased our God shall view
  The products of his grace;
And, in a plentiful reward,
  Fulfill his promises.
                   Elizabeth Scott, 1806.

CHURCH RELATIONS.

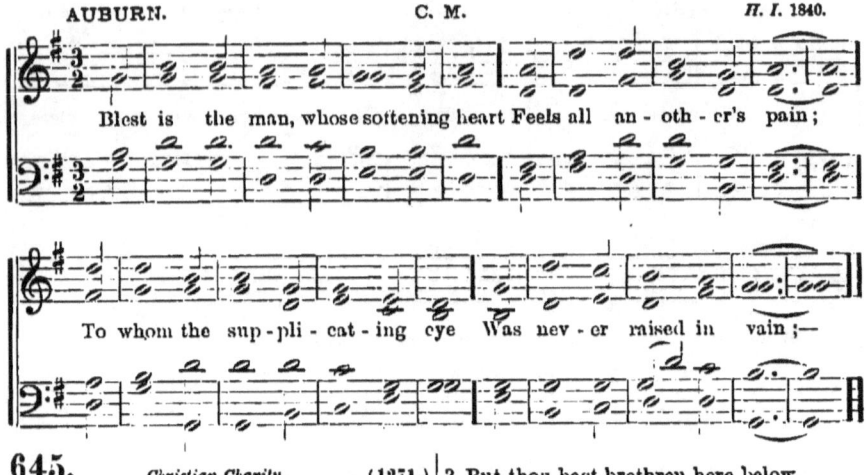

AUBURN. C. M. H. I. 1840.

Blest is the man, whose softening heart Feels all an-oth-er's pain;
To whom the sup-pli-cat-ing eye Was nev-er raised in vain;—

645. *Christian Charity.* (1271.)

1 BLEST is the man, whose softening heart
    Feels all another's pain;
  To whom the supplicating eye
    Was never raised in vain;—

2 Whose breast expands with generous
    A stranger's woes to feel, [warmth,
  And bleeds in pity o'er the wound
    He wants the power to heal.

3 He spreads his kind supporting arms
    To every child of grief;
  His secret bounty largely flows,
    And brings unasked relief.

4 To gentle offices of love,
    His feet are never slow;
  He views, through mercy's melting eye,
    A brother in a foe.

5 Peace, from the bosom of his God,
    The Lord to him will give;
  And, when he kneels before the throne,
    His trembling soul shall live.
                Mrs. Anna L. Barbauld, 1772.

646. *Christ relieved in his Saints.* (1269.)

1 JESUS, my Lord! how rich thy grace!
    Thy bounties—how complete!
  How shall I count the matchless sum?
    How pay the mighty debt?

2 High on a throne of radiant light,
    Dost thou exalted shine;
  What can my poverty bestow,
    When all the worlds are thine.

3 But thou hast brethren here below,
    The partners of thy grace,
  And wilt confess their humble names
    Before thy Father's face.

4 In them may'st thou be clothed, and fed,
    And visited, and cheered;
  And, in their accents of distress,
    My Saviour's voice be heard.
                Philip Doddridge, 1740.

647. *The good Samaritan.* (1266.)

1 FATHER of mercies! send thy grace,
    All-powerful from above,
  To form, in our obedient souls,
    The image of thy love.

2 Oh! may our sympathizing breasts
    That generous pleasure know,
  Kindly to share in others' joy,
    And weep for others' woe.

3 When the most helpless sons of grief,
    In low distress, are laid,
  Soft be our hearts their pains to feel,
    And swift our hands to aid.

4 So Jesus looked on dying men,
    When throned above the skies;
  And midst th' embraces of his God,
    He felt compassion rise.

5 On wings of love, the Saviour flew,
    To raise us from the ground;
  And made the richest of his blood
    A balm for every wound.
                Philip Doddridge, 1740.

WORKING AND GIVING.

ALFRETON. L. M. *William Beastall.*

O Lord of heaven, and earth, and sea! To thee all praise and glo-ry be;
How shall we show our love to thee, Who giv-est all—who giv-est all?

648. *Giving to God.* (1272.)

1 O Lord of heaven, and earth, and sea!
  To thee all praise and glory be;
  How shall we show our love to thee,
  Who givest all—who givest all?

2 The golden sunshine, vernal air,
  Sweet flowers and fruit thy love declare;
  When harvests ripen, thou art there,
  Who givest all—who givest all.

3 For peaceful homes and healthful days,
  For all the blessings earth displays,
  We owe thee thankfulness and praise,
  Who givest all—who givest all.

4 For souls redeemed, for sins forgiven,
  For means of grace and hopes of heaven,
  What can to thee, O Lord! be given,
  Who givest all—who givest all.

5 We lose what on ourselves we spend,
  We have, as treasures without end,
  Whatever, Lord! to thee we lend,
  Who givest all—who givest all?

6 Whatever, Lord! we lend to thee,
  Repaid a thousandfold will be;
  Then gladly will we give to thee,
  Who givest all—who givest all.
  Christopher Wordsworth, 1865.

649. PSALM 41. (1275.)

1 BLEST is the man whose heart doth move,
  And melt with pity, to the poor;
  Whose soul, by sympathizing love,
  Feels what his fellow saints endure.

2 His heart contrives, for their relief,
  More good than his own hands can do;
  He, in the time of general grief,
  Shall find the Lord has pity too.

3 His soul shall live secure on earth,
  With secret blessings on his head,
  When drought, and pestilence, and dearth
  Around him multiply their dead.

4 Or, if he languish on his couch,
  God will pronounce his sins forgiven,
  Will save him with a healing touch,
  Or take his willing soul to heaven.
  Isaac Watts, 1719.

650. *Jesus, the Model of Benevolence.* (1277.)

1 WHEN Jesus dwelt in mortal clay,
  What were his works from day to day,
  But miracles of power and grace,
  That spread salvation through our race?

2 Teach us, O Lord! to keep in view
  Thy pattern, and thy steps pursue:
  Let alms bestowed, let kindness done,
  Be witnessed by each rolling sun.

3 That man may last, but never lives,
  Who much receives, but nothing gives,
  Whom none can love, whom none can thank,
  Creation's blot, creation's blank:

4 But he, who marks, from day to day,
  In generous acts his radiant way,
  Treads the same path the Saviour trod,
  The path to glory and to God.
  Thomas Gibbons, 1784.

SPECIAL OCCASIONS.

PORTUGAL.   L. M.   *Thomas Thorley, 17—,*

Here, in thy name, e-ter-nal God! We build this earthly house for thee;
Oh! choose it for thy fixed a-bode, From ev-ery er-ror keep it free.

---

651.   *A House for God.*   (1285.)

1 Here, in thy name, eternal God!
    We build this earthly house for thee;
    Oh! choose it for thy fixed abode,
    From every error keep it free.

2 Here, when thy messengers proclaim
    The blessed gospel of thy Son,
    Still, by the power of his great name,
    Be mighty signs and wonders done.

3 When children's voices raise the song,—
    "Hosanna!"—to their heavenly King,
    Let heaven with earth the strain prolong;
    "Hosanna!"—let the angels sing.

4 But will, indeed, Jehovah deign
    Here to abide, no transient guest?
    Here will the world's Redeemer reign,
    And here the Holy Spirit rest?

5 That glory never hence depart!
    Yet choose not, Lord! this house alone;
    Thy kingdom come to every heart!
    In every bosom fix thy throne!
          James Montgomery, 1825, v. 1, a.

652.   *Laying a Corner-Stone.*   (1286.)

1 An earthly temple here we raise,
    Lord God, our Saviour! to thy praise;
    Oh! make thy gracious presence known,
    While now we lay its corner-stone.

2 Within the house thy servants rear
    Deign by thy Spirit to appear;
    On all its walls salvation write,
    From corner-stone to topmost height.

3 And, when this temple, "made with
    Upon its firm foundation stands, [hands,"
    Oh! may we all, with loving heart,
    In nobler building bear a part:

4 Where every polished stone shall be
    A human soul won back to thee;
    All resting upon Christ alone,—
    The chief and precious Corner-Stone.

5 So, when our toil is o'er at last,
    All labor in both temples passed,
    Oh! may it then by works be shown,
    That faith hath laid this corner-stone.
          Mrs. Catherine H. Johnson, 1866.

653.   *God's great Temple.*   (1287.)

1 The perfect world, by Adam trod,
    Was the first temple,—built by God;
    His fiat laid the corner-stone,
    And heaved its pillars, one by one.

2 He hung its starry roof on high—
    The broad, illimitable sky;
    He spread its pavement, green and bright,
    And curtained it with morning light.

3 The mountains in their places stood,
    The sea, the sky, and "all was good;"
    And, when its first pure praises rang,
    The "morning stars together sang."

4 Lord, 't is not ours to make the sea
    And earth and sky a house for thee;
    But, in thy sight, our offering stands,—
    An humbler temple "made with hands."
          Nathaniel P. Willis, 1826.

ERECTION OF CHURCHES.

CHIMES.   **C. M.**   *Lowell Mason, 1840.*

E-ter-nal Source of ev-ery good! Be-fore thy throne we bow,
And bless thee for thy gift, bestowed On pil-grims here be-low.

654.   *Dedication of a Church.*   (1288.)

1 ETERNAL Source of every good!
 Before thy throne we bow,
 And bless thee for thy gift, bestowed
 On pilgrims here below.

2 Our hearts and hands hast thou inclined
 To raise this house of prayer;
 Oh! may we seek, and ever find,
 Thy gracious presence here.

3 Long may thy heralds here proclaim
 The wonders of thy grace,
 And sinners, taught to fear thy name,
 Repenting, seek thy face.

4 Here may thy children sweetly feed
 On manna sent from heaven,
 Drink freely at the fountain-head,
 Whence living streams are given.

5 Here let our offspring, and their sons,
 Be of the Saviour blessed;
 And thus, while time its circuit runs,
 Find here a settled rest.

6 To the eternal, sacred Three,
 The great mysterious One,
 Now may this house devoted be,—
 To thee, and thee alone.
                    Benjamin Beddome, 1790.

655.   *The House of God.*   (1289.)

1 O THOU, whose own vast temple stands,
 Built over earth and sea!
 Accept the walls that human hands
 Have raised to worship thee.

2 Lord! from thine inmost glory send,
 Within these walls t' abide,
 The peace that dwelleth without end,
 Serenely by thy side!

3 May erring minds, that worship here,
 Be taught the better way;
 And they who mourn, and they who fear,
 Be strengthened as they pray.

4 May faith grow firm, and love grow warm,
 And pure devotion rise,   [storm
 While, round these hallowed walls, the
 Of earth-born passion dies.
                    William C. Bryant, 1835.

656.   *A new House of Worship.*   (1290.)

1 GOD of the universe! to thee
 This sacred house we rear,
 And now, with songs and bended knee,
 Invoke thy presence here.

2 Long may this echoing dome resound
 The praises of thy name,
 These hallowed walls to all around
 The Triune God proclaim.

3 Here let thy love, thy presence dwell;
 Thy glory here make known;
 Thy people's home, Oh! come and fill,
 And seal it as thine own.

4 And, when the last long Sabbath morn
 Upon the just shall rise,
 May all who own thee here be borne
 To mansions in the skies.
                    Miss Mary O——, 1841.

NUREMBERG. 7s. Johann Rudolph Ahle, 1664.

Praise to God, immortal praise, For the love that crowns our days;
Bounteous Source of every joy! Let thy praise our tongues employ.

657. *Thanksgivings.* (1291.)

1 PRAISE to God, immortal praise,
   For the love that crowns our days;
   Bounteous Source of every joy!
   Let thy praise our tongues employ.

2 For the flocks that roam the plain,
   Yellow sheaves of ripened grain,
   Clouds that drop their fattening dews,
   Suns that temperate warmth diffuse;—

3 All that spring, with bounteous hand,
   Scatters o'er the smiling land,
   All that liberal autumn pours
   From her rich o'erflowing stores;—

4 Lord! for these our souls shall raise
   Grateful vows, and solemn praise;
   And, when every blessing 's flown,
   Love thee for thyself alone.
      Mrs. Anna L. Barbauld, 1772.

658. PSALM 107. (1292.)

1 THANK and praise Jehovah's name;
    For his mercies, firm and sure,
   From eternity the same,
    To eternity endure.

2 Let the ransomed thus rejoice,
    Gathered out of every land,
   As the people of his choice,
    Plucked from the destroyer's hand.

3 To a pleasant land he brings,
    Where the vine and olive grow,
   Where, from flowery hills, the springs
    Through luxuriant valleys flow.

4 He, with health, renews their frame,
   Lengthens out their numbered days:
   Let them glorify his name,
   With the sacrifice of praise.

5 Oh! that men would praise the Lord,
   For his goodness to their race;
   For the wonders of his word,
   And the riches of his grace!
      James Montgomery, 1822.

659. *Our native Land.* (1293.)

1 SWELL the anthem, raise the song;
   Praises to our God belong;
   Saints and angels! join to sing,
   Praise to heav'n's almighty King.

2 Blessings, from his liberal hand,
   Pour around this happy land;
   Let our hearts, beneath his sway,
   Hail the bright triumphant day.

3 Now to thee our joys ascend,
   Thou hast been our heavenly Friend;
   Guarded by thy mighty power,
   Peace and freedom bless our shore.

4 Here, beneath a virtuous sway,
   Lawful rulers we obey;
   Here, we feel no tyrant's rod,
   Here, we own and worship God.

5 Hark! the voice of nature sings
   Praises to the King of kings;
   Let us join the choral song,
   And the heavenly notes prolong.
      Nathan Strong, 1799.

FESTIVALS.

AMERICA. 6s & 4s. Adapted by *Henry Carey*, obit. 1743.

My country! 't is of thee, Sweet land of liberty, Of thee I sing; Land, where my fathers died! Land of the pilgrims' pride! From every mountain side, Let freedom ring!

660. *Native Country.* (1297.)

1 My country! 't is of thee,
Sweet land of liberty,
  Of thee I sing;
Land, where my fathers died!
Land of the pilgrims' pride!
From every mountain side,
  Let freedom ring!

2 My native country! thee,—
Land of the noble, free,—
  Thy name — I love;
I love thy rocks and rills,
Thy woods and templed hills:
My heart with rapture thrills
  Like that above.

3 Let music swell the breeze,
And ring, from all the trees,
  Sweet freedom's song:
Let mortal tongues awake;
Let all that breathe partake;
Let rocks their silence break,—
  The sound prolong.

4 Our fathers' God! to thee,
Author of liberty,
  To thee we sing:
Long may our land be bright,
With freedom's holy light;
Protect us, by thy might,
  Great God, our King!

Samuel F. Smith, 1832.

661. *Our Native Land.* (1299.)

1 God bless our native land!
Firm may she ever stand,
  Through storm and night;
When the wild tempests rave,
Ruler of winds and wave!
Do thou our country save,
  By thy great might.

2 For her our prayer shall rise,
To God, above the skies;
  On him we wait;
Thou, who art ever nigh,
Guardian with watchful eye!
To thee aloud we cry,—
  God save the State!

John S. Dwight, 1844.

662. *Thanks for the Harvest.* (1301.)

1 The God of harvest praise;
In loud thanksgivings, raise
  Hand, heart, and voice!
The valleys laugh and sing;
Forests and mountains ring;
The plains their tribute bring;
  The streams rejoice.

2 Yea, bless his holy name,
And joyous thanks proclaim
  Through all the earth;
To glory in your lot
Is comely; but be not
God's benefits forgot
  Amidst your mirth.

3 The God of harvest praise;
Hands, hearts, and voices raise,
  With one accord;
From field to garner throng,
Bearing your sheaves along,
And, in your harvest song,
  Bless ye the Lord.

James Montgomery, 1853.

SPECIAL OCCASIONS.

ABRIDGE. C. M. *Isaac Smith, 1770.*

Lord! while for all mankind we pray, Of every clime and coast,
Oh! hear us for our native land,— The land we love the most.

663. *Prayer for our Country.* (1304.)

1 Lord! while for all mankind we pray,
   Of every clime and coast,
   Oh! hear us for our native land,—
   The land we love the most.

2 Oh! guard our shore from every foe,
   With peace our borders bless,
   With prosperous times our cities crown,
   Our fields with plenteousness.

3 Unite us in the sacred love
   Of knowledge, truth and thee;
   And let our hills and valleys shout
   The songs of liberty.

4 Here may religion, pure and mild,
   Smile on our Sabbath hours;
   And piety and virtue bless
   The home of us and ours.

5 Lord of the nations! thus to thee
   Our country we commend;
   Be thou her Refuge and her Trust,
   Her everlasting Friend.
   John Reynell Wreford, 1837.

664. *For a Temperance Meeting.* (1305.)

1 'T is thine alone, almighty Name!
   To raise the dead to life,
   The lost inebriate to reclaim
   From passion's fearful strife.

2 What ruin hath intemperance wrought!
   How widely roll its waves!
   How many myriads hath it brought
   To fill dishonored graves!

3 And see, O Lord! what numbers still
   Are maddened by the bowl,
   Led captive at the tyrant's will,
   In bondage, heart and soul!

4 Stretch forth thy hand, O God, our King!
   And break the galling chain;
   Deliverance to the captive bring,
   And end th' usurper's reign.

5 The cause of Temperance is thine own;
   Our plans and efforts bless;
   We trust, O Lord! in thee alone
   To crown them with success.
   Edwin F. Hatfield, 1872.

665. *A Christian Marriage.* (1306.)

1 Since Jesus freely did appear
   To grace a marriage feast;
   O Lord! we ask thy presence here,
   To make a wedding guest.

2 Upon the bridal pair look down,
   Who now have plighted hands;
   Their union with thy favor crown,
   And bless the nuptial bands.

3 With gifts of grace their hearts endow,
   Of all rich dowries best;
   Their substance bless; and peace bestow,
   To sweeten all the rest.

4 In purest love their souls unite,
   That they, with Christian care,
   May make domestic burdens light,
   By taking mutual share.
   John Berridge, 1775, v. 4, a.

FAST DAYS.

666. *A Day of Fasting and Prayer.* (1310.)

1 See, gracious God! before thy throne,
  Thy mourning people bend!
  'T is on thy sovereign grace alone,
  Our humble hopes depend.

2 Tremendous judgments, from thy hand,
  Thy dreadful power display:
  Yet mercy spares this guilty land,
  And still we live to pray.

3 Great God! why is our country spared,
  Ungrateful as we are?
  Oh! be thine awful warnings heard,
  While mercy cries "Forbear!"

4 How changed, alas! are truths divine,
  For error, guilt, and shame!
  What impious numbers, bold in sin,
  Disgrace the Christian name!

5 Oh! turn us, turn us, mighty Lord!
  By thy resistless grace;
  Then shall our hearts obey thy word,
  And humbly seek thy face.
  Anne Steele, 1756.

667. *"Solemne nos Jejunii."* (1311.)

1 Once more the solemn season calls,
  A holy fast to keep;
  And now, within the temple walls,
  Let priest and people weep.

2 Yet all in vain the sound of woe,
  To reach the Father's ear,
  If from the heart it does not flow,
  To prove our grief sincere.

3 Vain, vain, in ashes though we mourn,
  Our garments rend in twain,
  Unless the smitten heart is torn
  With penitential pain.

4 Then let us cry to God betimes,
  Nor let his anger flow;
  Lest, mindful of our numerous crimes,
  It deal the threatened blow.

5 O Father, righteous Judge, and God!
  Thy wrath be slow to burn;
  Thou givest time to mark the rod,—
  Give also hearts to turn.
  Lat. *Charles Coffin*, 1700.
  Tr., *William Mercer*, 1864.

668. Psalm 60. (1312.)

1 Lord! thou hast scourged our guilty land!
  Behold thy people mourn!
  Shall vengeance ever guide thy hand?
  And mercy ne'er return?

2 Beneath the terrors of thine eye,
  Earth's haughty towers decay;
  Thy frowning mantle spreads the sky,
  And mortals melt away.

3 Our Zion trembles at thy stroke,
  And dreads thy lifted hand;
  Oh! heal the people thou hast broke,
  And save the sinking land.

4 Exalt thy banner in the field,
  For those that fear thy name;
  From barbarous hosts our nation shield,
  And put our foes to shame.
  Joel Barlow, 1786.

SPECIAL OCCASIONS.

BREWER. L. M. English Melody.

E-ter-nal Source of ev-ery joy! Well may thy praise our lips em-ploy,
While, in thy tem-ple, we ap-pear, Whose goodness crowns the circling year.

669. *The Year crowned with Goodness.* (1320.)

1 Eternal Source of every joy!
Well may thy praise our lips employ,
While, in thy temple, we appear,
Whose goodness crowns the circling year.

2 While, as the wheels of nature roll,
Thy hand supports the steady pole;
The sun is taught by thee to rise,
And darkness, when to veil the skies.

3 The flowery spring, at thy command,
Embalms the air and paints the land;
The summer rays, with vigor, shine
To raise the corn, and cheer the vine.

4 Thy hand, in autumn, richly pours,
Through all our coasts, redundant stores;
And winters, softened by thy care,
No more a face of horror wear.

5 Seasons, and months, and weeks, and days,
Demand successive songs of praise;
Still be the cheerful homage paid,
With opening light and evening shade.
Philip Doddridge, 1740.

670. *The New Year.* (1322.)

1 Great God! we sing thy mighty hand,
By which supported still we stand;
The opening year thy mercy shows;
That mercy crowns it till it close.

2 By day, by night, at home, abroad,
Still are we guarded by our God;
By his incessant bounty fed,
By his unerring counsel led.

3 With grateful hearts the past we own;
The future—all to us unknown—
We to thy guardian care commit,
And peaceful leave before thy feet.

4 In scenes exalted, or depressed,
Be thou our joy, and thou our rest;
Thy goodness all our hopes shall raise,
Adored, through all our changing days.

5 When death shall interrupt these songs,
And seal, in silence, mortal tongues,
Our Helper, God, in whom we trust,
In better worlds our souls shall boast.
Philip Doddridge, 1740.

671. *The New Year.* (1323.)

1 My Helper, God! I bless his name;
The same his power, his grace the same;
The tokens of his friendly care
Open, and crown, and close the year.

2 Amidst ten thousand snares I stand,
Supported by his guardian hand;
And see, when I survey my ways,
Ten thousand monuments of praise.

3 Thus far his arm hath led me on,
Thus far I make his mercy known;
And, while I tread this desert land,
New mercies shall new songs demand.

4 My grateful soul, on Jordan's shore,
Shall raise one sacred pillar more;
Then bear, in his bright courts above,
Inscriptions of immortal love.
Philip Doddridge, 1740.

THE YEAR.

672. *The Spring of the Year.* (1760.)

1 While beauty clothes the fertile vale,
  And blossoms on the spray,
  And fragrance breathes in every gale,
  How sweet the vernal day!

2 And, hark! the feathered warblers sing!
  'T is nature's cheerful voice;
  Soft music hails the lovely spring,
  And woods and fields rejoice.

3 How kind the influence of the skies!
  These showers, with blessings fraught,
  Bid verdure, beauty, fragrance, rise,
  And fix the roving thought.

4 Oh! let my wondering heart confess,
  With gratitude and love,
  The bounteous hand that deigns to bless,
  The garden, field, and grove.

5 That hand, in this hard heart of mine,
  Can make each virtue live;
  And kindly showers of grace divine,
  Life, beauty, fragrance give.

6 O God of nature, God of grace!
  Thy heavenly gifts impart,
  And bid sweet meditation trace
  Spring blooming in my heart.
    Anne Steele, 1760.

673. *The New Year.* (1324.)

1 Now, gracious Lord! thine arm reveal,
  And make thy glory known;
  Now let us all thy presence feel,
  And soften hearts of stone.

2 From all the guilt of former sin
  May mercy set us free;
  And let the year we now begin
  Begin and end with thee.

3 Send down thy Spirit from above,
  That saints may love thee more,
  And sinners now may learn to love,
  Who never loved before.

4 And, when before thee we appear,
  In our eternal home,
  May growing numbers worship here,
  And praise thee in our room.
    John Newton, 1779.

674. *The Close of the Year.* (1332.)

1 Awake, ye saints! and raise your eyes,
  And raise your voices high;
  Awake, and praise that sovereign love,
  That shows salvation nigh.

2 On all the wings of time it flies,
  Each moment brings it near!
  Then welcome each declining day,
  Welcome each closing year!

3 Not many years their round shall run,
  Nor many mornings rise,
  Ere all its glories stand revealed
  To our admiring eyes.

4 Ye wheels of nature! speed your course;
  Ye mortal powers! decay;
  Fast as ye bring the night of death,
  Ye bring eternal day.
    Philip Doddridge, 1740.

THE YEAR.

BENEVENTO. 7s. 8 lines. Samuel Webbe, 1770.

1. While, with ceaseless course, the sun Hasted thro' the former year, Many souls their race have run,
   Never more to meet us here; Fixed in an eternal state, They have done with all below;
   D. S.—We a little longer wait, But how little none can know.

---

675. *The Beginning of the Year.* (1333.)

1 WHILE, with ceaseless course, the sun
　Hasted through the former year,
Many souls their race have run,
　Never more to meet us here;
Fixed in an eternal state,
　They have done with all below;
We a little longer wait,
　But how little, none can know.

2 As the wingèd arrow flies
　Speedily the mark to find;
As the lightning from the skies
　Darts, and leaves no trace behind;
Swiftly thus our fleeting days
　Bear us down life's rapid stream:
Upward, Lord! our spirits raise;
　All below is but a dream.

3 Thanks for mercies past receive;
　Pardon of our sins renew;
Teach us, henceforth, how to live
　With eternity in view;
Bless thy word to young and old;
　Fill us with a Saviour's love;
And, when life's short tale is told,
　May we dwell with thee above!

John Newton, 1779.

---

676. *The Close of the Year.* (1334.)

1 THOU who roll'st the year around,
　Crowned with mercies large and free,
Rich thy gifts to us abound,
　Warm our thanks shall rise to thee:
Kindly to our worship bow,
　While our grateful praises swell,
That, sustained by thee, we now
　Bid the parting year farewell.

2 All its numbered days are sped,
　All its busy scenes are o'er,
All its joys for ever fled,
　All its sorrows felt no more:
Mingled with th' eternal past,
　Its remembrance shall decay;
Yet to be revived at last
　At the solemn judgment-day.

3 All our follies, Lord! forgive;
　Cleanse each heart and make us thine;
Let thy grace within us live,
　As our future suns decline;
Then, when life's last ev' shall come,
　Happy spirits, let us fly
To our everlasting home,
　To our Father's house on high.

Ray Palmer, 1865.

DEATH. 241

LONDON, NEW. C. M. *Andre Hart's "Psalter," 1615.*

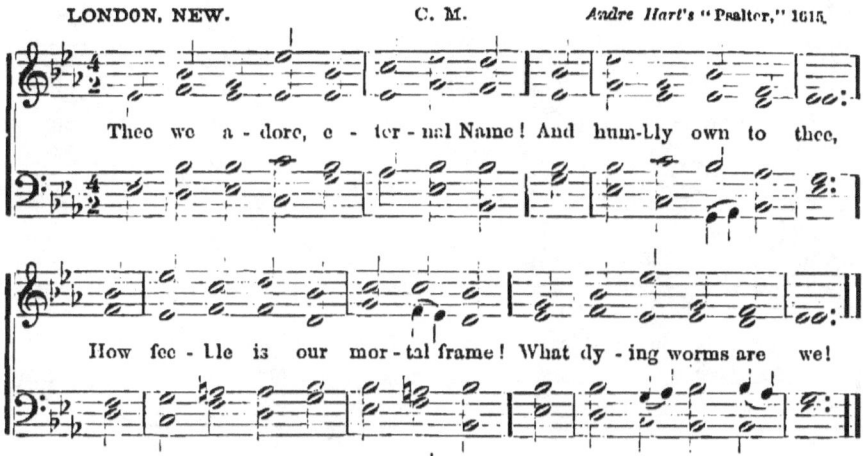

Thee we a-dore, e-ter-nal Name! And hum-bly own to thee, How fee-ble is our mor-tal frame! What dy-ing worms are we!

677. *Life, a brittle Thread.* (1335.)

1 THEE we adore, eternal Name!
  And humbly own to thee,
How feeble is our mortal frame!
  What dying worms are we!

2 The year rolls round, and steals away
  The breath that first it gave;
Whate'er we do, where'er we be,
  We're traveling to the grave.

3 Great God! on what a slender thread
  Hung everlasting things!
Th' eternal states of all the dead
  Upon life's feeble strings.

4 Infinite joy, or endless woe,
  Attends on every breath;
And yet how unconcerned we go
  Upon the brink of death!

5 Waken, O Lord! our drowsy sense,
  To walk this dangerous road;
And, if our souls are hurried hence,
  May they be found with God.
              Isaac Watts, 1707.

678. *Human Frailty.* (1339.)

1 LET others boast how strong they be,
  Nor death nor danger fear;
But we'll confess, O Lord! to thee,
  What feeble things we are.

2 Fresh as the grass our bodies stand,
  And flourish bright and gay;
A blasting wind sweeps o'er the land,
  And fades the grass away.

3 Our life contains a thousand springs,
  And dies if one be gone;
Strange that a harp of thousand strings
  Should keep in tune so long!

4 But 't is our God supports our frame,
  The God that built us first;
Salvation to th' almighty Name
  That reared us from the dust.
              Isaac Watts, 1707.

679. *The Shortness and Vanity of Life.* (1340.)

1 How short and hasty is our life!
  How vast our souls' affairs!
Yet senseless mortals vainly strive
  To lavish out their years.

2 Our days run thoughtlessly along,
  Without a moment's stay;
Just like a story, or a song,
  We pass our lives away.

3 God from on high invites us home,
  But we march heedless on,
And, ever hastening to the tomb,
  Stoop downward as we run.

4 How we deserve the deepest hell
  That slight the joys above!
What chains of vengeance should we feel,
  That break such cords of love.

5 Draw us, O God! with sovereign grace,
  And lift our thoughts on high,
That we may end this mortal race,
  And see salvation nigh.
              Isaac Watts, 1707.

CLOSE OF PROBATION.

BANGOR. C. M. *William Tansur's* Coll., 1735.

Hark! from the tombs a dole-ful sound! Mine ears! at-tend the cry;
"Ye liv-ing men! come, view the ground, Where you must shortly lie.

680. *The common Home.* (1341.)

1 Hark! from the tombs a doleful sound!
Mine ears! attend the cry;—
"Ye living men! come, view the ground,
Where you must shortly lie.

2 Princes! this clay must be your bed,
In spite of all your towers;
The tall, the wise, the reverend head
Must lie as low as ours."

3 Great God! is this our certain doom?
And are we still secure?—
Still walking downward to our tomb,
And yet prepared no more?

4 Grant us the powers of quickening grace
To fit our souls to fly:
Then, when we drop this dying flesh,
We'll rise above the sky.
Isaac Watts, 1707.

681. *The Bitterness of Death deplored.* (1342.)

1 When, bending o'er the brink of life,
My trembling soul shall stand,
Waiting to pass death's awful flood,
Great God! at thy command;—

2 When every long-loved scene of life
Stands ready to depart;
When the last sigh that shakes the frame,
Shall rend this bursting heart;—

3 O thou great Source of joy supreme,
Whose arm alone can save!—
Dispel the darkness, that surrounds
The entrance to the grave.

4 Lay thy supporting, gentle hand
Beneath my sinking head;
And let a beam of love divine
Illume my dying bed.

5 Leaning on thy dear faithful breast,
May I resign my breath,
And, in thy soft embraces, lose
"The bitterness of death."
William B. Collyer, 1812.

682. *Submission under Bereavement.* (1352.)

1 Peace!—'t is the Lord Jehovah's hand,
That blasts our joys in death,
Changes the visage once so dear,
And gathers back our breath.

2 'T is he,—the Potentate supreme
Of all the worlds above,—
Whose steady counsels wisely rule,
Nor from their purpose move.

3 'T is he, whose justice might demand
Our souls a sacrifice;
Yet scatters, with unwearied hand,
A thousand rich supplies.

4 Our covenant God and Father he,
In Christ, our bleeding Lord,
Whose grace can heal the bursting heart,
With one reviving word.

5 Silent I own Jehovah's name,
I kiss thy scourging hand;
And yield my comforts and my life
To thy supreme command.
Philip Doddridge, 1740.

DEATH.

MOUNT AUBURN. C. M. George Kingsley, 1838.

Be-hold the west-ern eve-ning light! It melts in deepen-ing gloom;
So calm-ly Chris-tians sink a-way. Des-cend-ing to the tomb.

683. *The Christian's Peace in Death.* (1347.)

1 BEHOLD the western evening light!
 It melts in deepening gloom;
 So calmly Christians sink away,
 Descending to the tomb.

2 The winds breathe low; the withering leaf
 Scarce whispers from the tree :
 So gently flows the parting breath,
 When good men cease to be.

3 How beautiful on all the hills
 The crimson light is shed !
 'T is like the peace the Christian gives
 To mourners round his bed.

4 How mildly on the wandering cloud
 The sunset beam is cast !
 'T is like the memory left behind,
 When loved ones breathe their last.

5 And now, above the dews of night,
 The yellow star appears ;
 So faith springs in the heart of those
 Whose eyes are bathed in tears.

6 But soon the morning's happier light
 Its glory shall restore ;
 And eyelids, that are sealed in death,
 Shall wake, to close no more.
 William B. O. Peabody, 1823.

684. *Dying on Pisgah's Top.* (1348.)

1 DEATH cannot make our souls afraid
 If God be with us there :
 We may walk through its darkest shade,
 And never yield to fear.

2 I could renounce my all below
 If my Creator bid,
 And run if I were called to go,
 And die as Moses did.

3 Might I but climb to Pisgah's top,
 And view the promised land,
 My flesh itself would long to drop,
 And pray for the command.

4 Clasped in my heavenly Father's arms,
 I would forget my breath,
 And lose my life among the charms
 Of so divine a death.
 Isaac Watts, 1707.

685. *Victory over Death.* (1349.)

1 OH ! FOR an overcoming faith
 To cheer my dying hours,
 To triumph o'er the monster, death,
 And all his frightful powers !

2 Joyful with all the strength I have,
 My quivering lips should sing,—
 Where is thy boasted victory, grave ?
 And where the monster's sting ?

3 If sin be pardoned I 'm secure,
 Death hath no sting beside ;
 The law gives sin its damning power,
 But Christ, my Ransom, died.

4 Now to the God of victory
 Immortal thanks be paid,
 Who makes us conquerors while we die,
 Through Christ, our living Head.
 Isaac Watts, 1707.

CLOSE OF PROBATION.

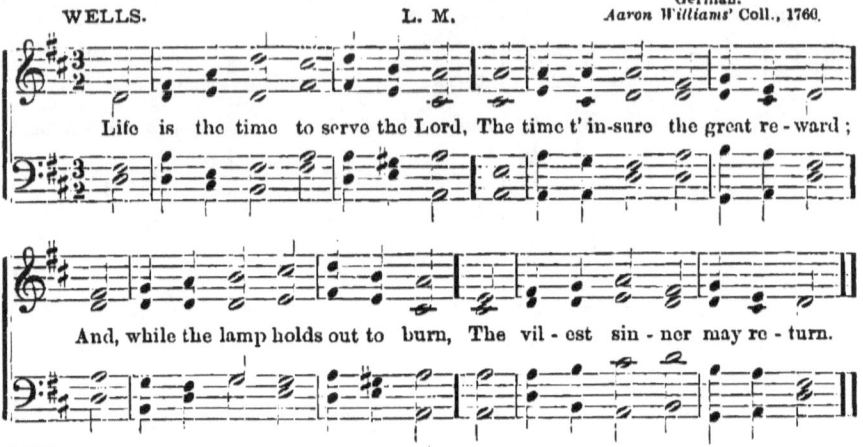

WELLS. L. M. German. Aaron Williams' Coll., 1760.

Life is the time to serve the Lord, The time t' insure the great reward;
And, while the lamp holds out to burn, The vilest sinner may return.

686. *Life, the Day of Grace and Hope.* (1353.)

1 LIFE is the time to serve the Lord,
  The time t' insure the great reward;
  And, while the lamp holds out to burn
  The vilest sinner may return.

2 Life is the hour, that God has given,
  T' escape from hell, and fly to heaven;
  The day of grace, and mortals may
  Secure the blessings of the day.

3 The living know that they must die,
  But all the dead forgotten lie;
  Their memory and their sense are gone,
  Alike unknowing and unknown.

4 Then, what my thoughts design to do,
  My hands! with all your might, pursue;
  Since no device, nor work, is found,
  Nor faith, nor hope beneath the ground.

5 There are no acts of pardon passed,
  In the cold grave to which we haste,
  But darkness, death, and long despair,
  Reign in eternal silence there.
  Isaac Watts, 1709.

687. *Death made easy.* (1361.)

1 WHY should we start and fear to die?
  What timorous worms we mortals are!
  Death is the gate of endless joy;
  And yet we dread to enter there.

2 The pains, the groans, and dying strife,
  Fright our approaching souls away;
  Still we shrink back again to life,
  Fond of our prison and our clay.

3 Oh! if my Lord would come and meet,
  My soul should stretch her wings in haste,
  Fly fearless through death's iron gate,
  Nor feel the terrors as she passed.

4 Jesus can make a dying bed
  Feel soft as downy pillows are,
  While on his breast I lean my head,
  And breathe my life out sweetly there.
  Isaac Watts, 1707.

688. PSALM 90. (1355.)

1 THROUGH every age, eternal God!
  Thou art our Rest, our safe Abode;
  High was thy throne, ere heaven was made,
  Or earth thy humble footstool laid.

2 Long hadst thou reigned, ere time began,
  Or dust was fashioned into man;
  And long thy kingdom shall endure,
  When earth and time shall be no more.

3 But man, weak man, is born to die,
  Made up of guilt and vanity;
  Thy dreadful sentence, Lord! was just,
  "Return, ye sinners! to your dust."

4 Death, like an overflowing stream,
  Sweeps us away; our life 's a dream;
  An empty tale; a morning flower,
  Cut down, and withered in an hour.

5 Teach us, O Lord! how frail is man;
  And kindly lengthen out our span,
  Till a wise care of piety
  Fit us to die, and dwell with thee.
  Isaac Watts, 1719.

DEATH. 245

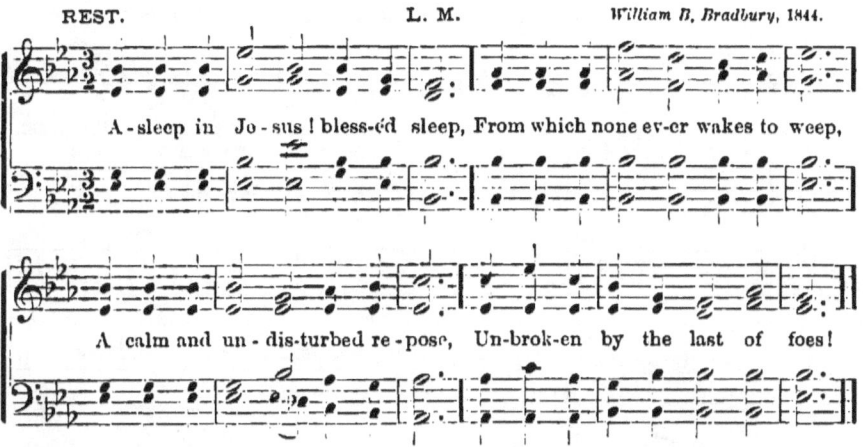

REST. L. M. *William B. Bradbury*, 1844.

A-sleep in Je-sus! bless-ed sleep, From which none ev-er wakes to weep,
A calm and un-dis-turbed re-pose, Un-brok-en by the last of foes!

689. *Asleep in Jesus.* (1362.)

1 ASLEEP in Jesus! blessed sleep,
From which none ever wakes to weep,
A calm and undisturbed repose,
Unbroken by the last of foes!

2 Asleep in Jesus! Oh! how sweet
To be for such a slumber meet,
With holy confidence to sing—
That death hath lost his venomed sting!

3 Asleep in Jesus! peaceful rest,
Whose waking is supremely blest;
No fear, no woe, shall dim that hour
That manifests the Saviour's power.

4 Asleep in Jesus! Oh! for me
May such a blissful refuge be!
Securely shall my ashes lie,
Waiting the summons from on high.

5 Asleep in Jesus! time nor space
Debars this precious hiding-place:
On Indian plains, or Lapland snows,
Believers find the same repose.

6 Asleep in Jesus! far from thee
Thy kindred and their graves may be;
But thine is still a blessed sleep,
From which none ever wakes to weep.
Mrs. Margaret Mackay, 1832.

690. *The Death of the Righteous.* (1359.)

1 How blest the righteous, when he dies,
When sinks a weary soul to rest!
How mildly beam the closing eyes!
How gently heaves th' expiring breast!

2 So fades a summer cloud away;
So sinks the gale, when storms are o'er;
So gently shuts the eye of day;
So dies a wave along the shore.

3 A holy quiet reigns around,
A calm which life nor death destroys:
And naught disturbs that peace profound,
Which his unfettered soul enjoys.

4 Farewell, conflicting hopes and fears,
Where lights and shades alternate dwell!
How bright th' unchanging morn appears!
Farewell, inconstant world! farewell!

5 Life's labor done, as sinks the clay,
Light from its load the spirit flies;
While heaven and earth combine to say,
"How blest the righteous when he dies!"
Mrs. Anna L. Barbauld, 1773.

691. PSALM 39. (1358.)

1 OH! LET me, heavenly Lord! extend
My view, to life's approaching end:
What are my days?—a span, their line:
And what my age, compared with thine?

2 Our life advancing to its close,
While scarce its earliest dawn it knows,
Swift, through an empty shade, we run,
And vanity and man are one.

3 God of my fathers! here, as they,
I walk, the pilgrim of a day;
A transient guest, thy works admire,
And instant to my home retire.
James Merrick, 1765.

CLOSE OF PROBATION.

SAUL. L. M. 4 or 6 LINES. From *George Frederick Handel*, 1740.

Unveil thy bo-som, faith-ful tomb! Take this new treasure to thy trust,
And give these sa-cred rel-ics' room, To seek a slum-ber in the dust;
And give these sa-cred rel-ics room, To seek a slumber in the dust.

692. *The Burial of a Believer.* (1365.)

1 UNVEIL thy bosom, faithful tomb!
 Take this new treasure to thy trust,
 And give these sacred relics room,
 To seek a slumber in the dust.

2 Nor pain, nor grief, nor anxious fear,
 Invade thy bounds; — no mortal woes
 Can reach the lovely sleeper here,
 And angels watch his soft repose.

3 So Jesus slept; — God's dying Son
 Passed through the grave, and blessed the bed!
 Rest here, fair saint! till, from his throne,
 The morning break, and pierce the shade.

4 Break from his throne, illustrious morn!
 Attend, O earth! his sovereign word;
 Restore thy trust a glorious form, —
 He must ascend to meet the Lord.
Isaac Watts, 1734.

693. *The Hour of Departure.* (1356.)

1 THE hour of my departure 's come;
 I hear the voice that calls me home;
 At last, O Lord! let trouble cease,
 And let thy servant die in peace.

2 The race appointed I have run,
 The combat 's o'er, the prize is won;
 And now my witness is on high,
 And now my record 's in the sky.

3 Not in mine innocence I trust;
 I bow before thee in the dust;
 And, through my Saviour's blood alone,
 I look for mercy at thy throne.

4 I leave the world without a tear,
 Save for the friends I held so dear;
 To heal their sorrows, Lord! descend,
 And to the friendless prove a Friend.

5 I come, I come, at thy command;
 I give my spirit to thy hand;
 Stretch forth thine everlasting arms,
 And shield me in the last alarms.

6 The hour of my departure 's come;
 I hear the voice that calls me home;
 Now, O my God! let trouble cease;
 Now let thy servant die in peace.
Michael Bruce, 1766.

DEATH.

694. *The Pilgrim's Song.* (1373.)

1 A few more years shall roll,
 A few more seasons come,
And we shall be with those, that rest
 Asleep within the tomb.

2 A few more storms shall beat
 On this wild, rocky shore,
And we shall be where tempests cease,
 And surges swell no more.

3 A few more struggles here,
 A few more partings o'er,
A few more toils, a few more tears,
 And we shall weep no more.

4 A few more Sabbaths here
 Shall cheer us on our way,
And we shall reach the endless rest,
 Th' eternal Sabbath-day.

5 'T is but a little while
 And he shall come again,
Who died that we might live, who lives
 That we with him may reign.

6 Then, O my Lord! prepare
 My soul for that glad day;
Oh! wash me in thy precious blood,
 And take my sins away.
  Horatius Bonar, 1856.

695. *Dying, not Death.* (1374.)

1 It is not death to die, —
 To leave this weary road,
And, midst the brotherhood on high,
 To be at home with God.

2 It is not death to close
 The eye long dimmed by tears,
And wake, in glorious repose
 To spend eternal years.

3 It is not death to fling
 Aside this sinful dust,
And rise, on strong exulting wing,
 To live among the just.

4 Jesus, thou Prince of life!
 Thy chosen cannot die;
Like thee, they conquer in the strife,
 To reign with thee on high.
  George W. Bethune, 1847.

696. *At Home in Heaven.* (1375.)

1 "For ever with the Lord!"
 Amen! so let it be;
Life from the dead is in that word;
 'T is immortality.

2 Here, in the body pent,
 Absent from him I roam,
Yet nightly pitch my moving tent
 A day's march nearer home.

3 "For ever with the Lord!"
 Father! if 't is thy will,
The promise of that faithful word
 Ev'n here to me fulfill.

4 So, when my latest breath
 Shall rend the veil in twain,
By death, I shall escape from death,
 And life eternal gain.
  James Montgomery, 1835.

CLOSE OF PROBATION.

FREDERICK. 11s. George Kingsley, 1838.

I would not live alway; I ask not to stay Where storm after storm rises dark o'er the way;

The few lurid mornings, that dawn on us here, Are enough for life's woes, full enough for its cheer.

697. *"I would not live alway."* (1378.)

1 I WOULD not live alway; I ask not to stay
Where storm after storm rises dark o'er
   the way; [here,
The few lurid mornings, that dawn on us
Are enough for life's woes, full enough for
   its cheer.

2 I would not live alway, thus fettered by
   sin, [in;
Temptation without and corruption with-
E'en the rapture of pardon is mingled
   with fears, [tent tears.
And the cup of thanksgiving with peni-

3 I would not live alway; no, welcome the
   tomb; [its gloom;
Since Jesus hath lain there, I dread not
There sweet be my rest, till he bid me
   arise, [skies.
To hail him in triumph descending the

4 Who, who would live alway, away from
   his God; [abode,
Away from yon heaven, that blissful
Where the rivers of pleasure flow o'er the
   bright plains, [reigns?
And the noontide of glory eternally

5 Where the saints of all ages in harmony
   meet,
Their Saviour and brethren transported
   to greet;

While the anthems of rapture unceasingly
   roll, [the soul.
And the smile of the Lord is the feast of
       William A. Muhlenberg, 1823.

698. *Gone to the Grave.* (1379.)

1 THOU art gone to the grave; but we will
   not deplore thee, [pass the tomb;
Though sorrows and darkness encom-
Thy Saviour has passed through its portal
   before thee, [through the gloom.
And the lamp of his love is thy guide

2 Thou art gone to the grave; we no longer
   behold thee, [by thy side:
Nor tread the rough paths of the world
But the wide arms of mercy are spread
   to enfold thee, [died.
And sinners may die, for the sinless hath

3 Thou art gone to the grave; and, its man-
   sion forsaking, [ered long;
Perchance thy weak spirit in fear ling-
But the mild rays of paradise beamed on
   thy waking, [the seraphim's song.
And the sound which thou heardst was

4 Thou art gone to the grave; but we will
   not deplore thee; [dian and Guide;
Whose God was thy Ransom, thy Guar-
He gave thee, he took thee, and he will
   restore thee; [has died.
And death has no sting, for the Saviour
       Reginald Heber, 1812.

DEATH.

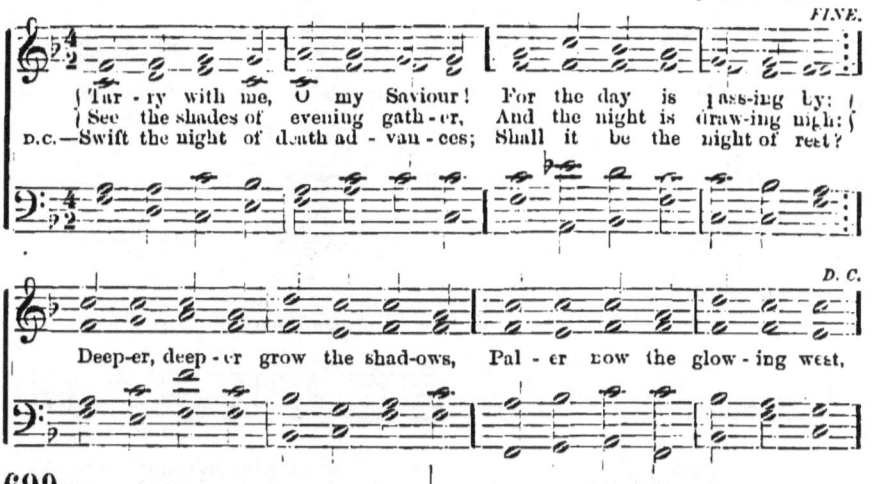

OTTO. 8s & 7s. 8 LINES. Henry K. Oliver, 1840.

Tar-ry with me, O my Saviour! For the day is passing by;
See the shades of evening gath-er, And the night is drawing nigh:
D.C.—Swift the night of death ad-vances; Shall it be the night of rest?

Deep-er, deep-er grow the shad-ows, Pal-er now the glow-ing west,

699. *The final Struggle.* (1384.)

1 TARRY with me, O my Saviour!
   For the day is passing by;
See! the shades of evening gather,
   And the night is drawing nigh;
Deeper, deeper grow the shadows,
   Paler now the glowing west,
Swift the night of death advances;
   Shall it be the night of rest?

2 Lonely seems the vale of shadow;
   Sinks my heart with troubled fear;
Give me faith for clearer vision,
   Speak thou, Lord! in words of cheer;
Let me hear thy voice behind me,
   Calming all these wild alarms;
Let me, underneath my weakness,
   Feel the everlasting arms.

3 Feeble, trembling, fainting, dying,
   Lord! I cast myself on thee;
Tarry with me through the darkness;
   While I sleep, still watch by me:
Tarry with me, O my Saviour!
   Lay my head upon thy breast
Till the morning: then awake me;—
   Morning of eternal rest!

   Mrs. Caroline [Sprague] Smith, 1856. a.

700. *The departing Saint.* (1385.)

1 HAPPY soul! thy days are ended,
   All thy mourning days below;
Go, by angel guards attended,
   To the sight of Jesus go!

Waiting to receive thy spirit,
   Lo! the Saviour stands above;
Shows the purchase of his merit,
   Reaches out the crown of love.

2 Struggle through thy latest passion
   To thy dear Redeemer's breast,
To his uttermost salvation,
   To his everlasting rest:
For the joy he sets before thee
   Bear a momentary pain;
Die, to live the life of glory;
   Suffer, with thy Lord to reign.

   Charles Wesley, 1749.

701. *The happy Dead.* (1386.)

1 THINK, O ye, who fondly languish
   O'er the grave of those you love!
While your bosoms throb with anguish,
   They are warbling hymns above:
While your silent steps are straying
   Lonely thro' night's deepening shade,
Glory's brightest beams are playing,
   Round the happy Christian's head.

2 Light and peace at once deriving
   From the hand of God most high,
In his glorious presence living,
   They shall never, never die:
Cease, then, mourner! cease to languish
   O'er the grave of those you love;
Pain, and death, and night, and anguish,
   Enter not the world above.

   William B. Collyer, 1812.

GLORIFICATION.

ALL SAINTS. (WAREHAM.) L. M. — William Knapp, 1766.

What sin-ners val-ue I re-sign; Lord! 'tis e-nough that thou art mine;
I shall be-hold thy bliss-ful face, And stand complete in right-eous-ness.

702. PSALM 17. (1389.)

1 WHAT sinners value I resign;
 Lord! 't is enough that thou art mine;
 I shall behold thy blissful face,
 And stand complete in righteousness.

2 This life's a dream—an empty show;
 But the bright world, to which I go,
 Hath joys substantial and sincere;
 When shall I wake, and find me there?

3 Oh! glorious hour!—Oh! blest abode!
 I shall be near and like my God;
 And flesh and sin no more control
 The sacred pleasures of the soul.

4 My flesh shall slumber in the ground,
 Till the last trumpet's joyful sound:
 Then burst the chains, with sweet surprise,
 And in my Saviour's image rise.
   Isaac Watts, 1719.

703. PSALM 88. (1390.)

1 SHALL man, O God of light and life!
  For ever moulder in the grave?
  Canst thou forget thy glorious work,
  Thy promise, and thy power to save?

2 In those dark silent realms of night,
  Shall peace and hope no more arise?
  No future morning light the tomb,
  Nor day-star gild the darksome skies?

3 Cease, cease, ye vain desponding fears!
  When Christ, our Lord, from darkness sprang,
  Death, the last foe, was captive led,
  And heaven with praise and wonder rang.

4 Faith sees the bright eternal doors
  Unfold, to make his children way;
  They shall be clothed with endless life,
  And shine in everlasting day.

5 The trump shall sound; the dust awake,
  From the cold tomb the slumberers rise,
  Through heaven, with joy, their myriads spring;
  And hail their Saviour and their King.
   Timothy Dwight, 1800.

704. *The Resurrection of the Just.* (1391.)

1 WE sing his love who once was slain,
  Who soon o'er death revived again,
  That all his saints, through him might have
  Eternal conquest o'er the grave.

2 The saints, who now in Jesus sleep,
  His own almighty power shall keep,
  Till dawns the bright illustrious day,
  When death itself shall die away.

3 How loud shall our glad voices sing,
  When Christ his risen saints shall bring
  From beds of dust, and silent clay,
  To realms of everlasting day!

4 When Jesus we in glory meet,
  Our utmost joys shall be complete;
  When landed on that heavenly shore,
  Death and the curse will be no more.

5 Hasten, dear Lord! the glorious day,
  And this delightful scene display:
  When all thy saints from death shall rise,
  Raptured in bliss beyond the skies.
   Rowland Hill, 1796.

RESURRECTION. 251

CHINA. C. M. Timothy Swan, 1800.

Why do we mourn departing friends, Or shake at death's alarms?
'T is but the voice that Jesus sends, To call them to his arms.

705. *The Death of Christian Friends.* (1392.)

1 WHY do we mourn departing friends,
Or shake at death's alarms?
'T is but the voice that Jesus sends,
To call them to his arms.

2 Are we not tending upward too,
As fast as time can move?
Nor would we wish the hours more slow,
To keep us from our love.

3 Why should we tremble to convey
Their bodies to the tomb?
There the dear flesh of Jesus lay,
And left a long perfume.

4 The graves of all his saints he blessed,
And softened every bed;
Where should the dying members rest,
But with their dying Head?

5 Thence he arose, ascending high,
And showed our feet the way;
Up to the Lord our flesh shall fly
At the great rising day.
Isaac Watts, 1707.

706. *The Saints ascending to Heaven.* (1393.)

1 As JESUS died, and rose again
Victorious from the dead,
So his disciples rise, and reign
With their triumphant Head.

2 The time draws nigh, when, from the clouds,
Christ shall with shouts descend;
And the last trumpet's awful voice
The heavens and earth shall rend.

3 Then they who live shall changéd be,
And they who sleep shall wake;
The graves shall yield their ancient charge,
And earth's foundations shake.

4 The saints of God, from death set free,
With joy shall mount on high;
The heavenly host, with praises loud,
Shall meet them in the sky.

5 Together to their Father's house,
With joyful hearts, they go;
And dwell for ever with the Lord,
Beyond the reach of woe.
Michael Bruce, 1768.

707. *The Death of a Child.* (1394.)

1 LIFE is a span — a fleeting hour;
How soon the vapor flies!
Man is a tender, transient flower,
That ev'n in blooming dies.

2 The once-loved form, now cold and dead,
Each mournful thought employs;
And nature weeps her comforts fled,
And withered all her joys.

3 Hope looks beyond the bounds of time,
When what we now deplore
Shall rise, in full immortal prime,
And bloom to fade no more.

4 Then cease, fond nature! cease thy tears;
Religion points on high;
There everlasting spring appears,
And joys that cannot die.
Anne Steele, 1760.

GLORIFICATION.

AVON. (MARTYRDOM.) C. M. *Hugh Wilson*, 17—.

That aw-ful day will sure-ly come, Th' ap-point-ed hour makes haste,
When I must stand be-fore my Judge, And pass the sol-emn test.

708. *The awful Day.* (1398.)

1 That awful day will surely come,
  Th' appointed hour makes haste.
 When I must stand before my Judge,
  And pass the solemn test.

2 Thou lovely Chief of all my joys!
  Thou Sovereign of my heart!
 How could I bear, to hear thy voice!
  Pronounce the sound,—"Depart?"

3 Oh! wretched state of deep despair—
  To see my God remove,
 And fix my doleful station, where
  I must not taste his love!

4 Jesus! I throw my arms around,
  And hang upon thy breast;
 Without one gracious smile from thee,
  My spirit cannot rest.

5 Oh! tell me that my worthless name
  Is graven on thy hands;
 Show me some promise in thy book,
  Where my salvation stands.
          Isaac Watts, 1707.

709. Psalm 50. (1399.)

1 The Lord, the Judge, before his throne,
  Bids the whole earth draw nigh,
 The nations near the rising sun,
  And near the western sky.

2 No more shall bold blasphemers say,—
  "Judgment will ne'er begin;"
 No more abuse his long delay
  To impudence and sin.

3 Throned on a cloud our God shall come,
  Bright flames prepare his way,
 Thunder and darkness, fire and storm,
  Lead on the dreadful day.

4 Heaven from above his call shall hear,
  Attending angels come,
 And earth and hell shall know, and fear
  His justice, and their doom.
          Isaac Watts, 1719.

710. *The Solemn Test.* (1400.)

1 When, rising from the bed of death,
  O'erwhelmed with guilt and fear,
 I see my Maker face to face,—
  Oh! how shall I appear?

2 If yet, while pardon may be found,
  And mercy may be sought,
 My heart with inward horror shrinks,
  And trembles at the thought;—

3 When thou, O Lord! shalt stand disclosed
  In majesty severe,
 And sit in judgment on my soul,
  Oh! how shall I appear?

4 Then, see the sorrows of my heart,
  Ere yet it be too late;
 My pardon speak, for Jesus' sake,
  And bid my fears abate.

5 For never shall my soul despair
  Her pardon to procure,
 Who knows thine only Son has died
  To make her pardon sure.
          Joseph Addison, 1712, v. 4, a.

THE JUDGMENT.

711. *The Day of Judgment.* (1403.)

1 Day of Judgment, day of wonders!
  Hark!—the trumpet's awful sound,
  Louder than a thousand thunders,
  Shakes the vast creation round;
    How the summons
  Will the sinner's heart confound!

2 See the Judge, our nature wearing,
  Clothed in majesty divine!
  You, who long for his appearing,
  Then shall say,—"This God is mine!"
    Gracious Saviour!
  Own me in that day for thine.

3 At his call, the dead awaken,
  Rise to life from earth and sea;
  All the powers of nature, shaken
  By his looks, prepare to flee:
    Careless sinner!
  What will then become of thee?

4 But to those who have confessed,
  Loved and served the Lord below,
  He will say, "Come near, ye blessed!
  See the kingdom I bestow!
    You for ever
  Shall my love and glory know."
         John Newton, 1774.

712. *Christ coming to Judgment.* (1404.)

1 Lo! he cometh countless trumpets
  Blow to raise the sleeping dead;
  Midst ten thousand saints and angels,
  See their great exalted Head:
    Hallelujah!
  Welcome, welcome, Son of God!

2 Full of joyful expectation,
  Saints! behold the Judge appear!
  Truth and justice go before him;
  Now the royal sentence hear:
    Hallelujah!
  Welcome, welcome, Judge divine!

3 "Come, ye blessed of my Father,
  Enter into life and joy;
  Banish all your fears and sorrows;
  Endless praise be your employ:"
    Hallelujah!
  Welcome, welcome to the skies!
         John Cennick, 1752.

713. *The Judgment-Trumpet.* (1405.)

1 Hark!— the judgment-trumpet sounding
  Rends the skies and shakes the poles;
  Lo! the day, with wrath abounding,
  Breaks upon astonished souls:
    Every creature
  Now the awful Judge beholds.

2 Jesus, Captain of Salvation,
  Leads his armies down the skies,
  Every kindred, tribe and nation,
  From the sleep of death, arise:
    Heaven's loud summons
  Fills the world with dread surprise.

3 Zion's King, his throne ascending,
  Calls his saints before his face;
  Crowns, with glory never-ending,
  All the children of his grace;
    Heaven shall echo;—
  Songs of triumph fill the place.
         Nathan S. S. Beman, 1832.

254 GLORIFICATION.

MONMOUTH. (JUDGMENT.)   L. M.   Joseph Klug's "Gesangbuch," 1535.

In robes of judgment, lo! he comes; Shakes the wide earth and cleaves the tombs; Before him burns devouring fire; The mountains melt, the seas retire, The mountains melt, the seas retire.

714.   PSALM 97.   (1408.)

1 IN ROBES of judgment, lo! he comes;
  Shakes the wide earth and cleaves the
  Before him burns devouring fire; [tombs;
  The mountains melt, the seas retire.

2 His enemies, with sore dismay,
  Fly from the sight, and shun the day;
  Then lift your heads, ye saints! on high,
  And sing, for your redemption 's nigh.
                        Isaac Watts, 1719.

715.   *Christ's coming to Judgment.*   (1409.)

1 THE Lord will come — the earth shall
                                  quake,
  The hills their fixed seat forsake;
  And, withering from the vault of night,
  The stars withdraw their feeble light.

2 The Lord will come, — but not the same
  As once in lowly form he came, —
  A silent lamb to slaughter led,
  The bruised, the suffering and the dead.

3 The Lord will come, — a dreadful form,
  With wreath of flame, and robe of storm,
  On cherub-wings, and wings of wind, —
  Appointed Judge of humankind.

4 Can this be he, who wont to stray
  A pilgrim on the world's highway, [pride?
  By power oppressed, and mocked by
  O God! is this the Crucified?

5 Go, tyrants! to the rocks complain,
  Go, seek the mountain's cleft in vain;
  But faith, victorious o'er the tomb,
  Shall sing for joy,—"The Lord is come!"
                        Reginald Heber, 1811.

716.   *The Day of Wrath.*   (1410.)

1 THAT day of wrath, that dreadful day,
  When heaven and earth shall pass away,
  What power shall be the sinner's stay?
  How shall he meet that dreadful day?

2 When, shriveling like a parched scroll,
  The flaming heavens together roll;
  When louder yet, and yet more dread,
  Swells the high trump that wakes the dead;

3 Oh! on that day, that wrathful day,
  When man to judgment wakes from clay,
  Be thou, O Christ! the sinner's stay,
  Though heaven and earth shall pass away.
              Lat., Thomas of Celano, 1230.
              Tr., Walter Scott, 1805.

717.   *The last great Day.*   (1411.)

1 THAT fearful day, that day of dread,
  When thou shalt judge the quick and
  O God! I shudder to foresee   [dead;
  The awful things which then shall be!

2 When thou shalt come, thine angels
                                  round,
  With legions, and with trumpet sound;
  O Saviour! grant me, in the air,
  With all thy saints, to meet thee there!

3 Weep, O my soul! ere that great day,
  When God shall shine, in plain array;
  Oh! weep thy sin, that thou may'st be
  In that severest judgment free!

4 O Christ! forgive, remit, protect,
  And set thy servant with th' elect;
  That I may hear the voice, that calls
  The righteous to thy heavenly halls!
              Lat., Theodore, cir. 820.
              Tr., John M. Neale, 1862.

HEAVEN.

BEULAH. (IVES.)   7s. 8 LINES.   Arr. by *Elam Ives, Jr.*, 1846.

What are these in bright ar-ray, This in-num-er-a-ble throng, Round the al-tar night and day, Hymning one tri-umph-ant song?—"Worthy is the Lamb once slain, Blessing, hon-or, glo-ry, pow'r, Wisdom, riches, to ob-tain, New do-min-ion, ev-ery hour!"

718.   *The Redeemed in Heaven.*   (1412.)

1 What are these in bright array,
    This innumerable throng,
Round the altar night and day,
    Hymning one triumphant song?—
"Worthy is the Lamb once slain,
    Blessing, honor, glory, power,
Wisdom, riches, to obtain,
    New dominion, every hour!"

2 These through fiery trials trod,—
    These from great affliction came;
Now before the throne of God,
    Sealed with his almighty name,
Clad in raiment pure and white,
    Victor palms in every hand,
Through their dear Redeemer's might,
    More than conquerors they stand.

3 Hunger, thirst, disease unknown,
    On immortal fruits they feed;
Them, the Lamb, amidst the throne,
    Shall to living fountains lead;
Joy and gladness banish sighs,
    Perfect love dispel all fear,
And, for ever from their eyes,
    God shall wipe away the tear.
        James Montgomery, 1825.

719.   *The Songs and Bliss of Heaven.*   (1414.)

1 High in yonder realms of light,
    Dwell the raptured saints above,
Far beyond our feeble sight,
    Happy in Immanuel's love:
Pilgrims in this vale of tears,
    Once they knew, like us below,
Gloomy doubts, distressing fears,
    Torturing pain, and heavy woe.

2 Mid the chorus of the skies,
    Mid th' angelic lyres above,
Hark! their songs melodious rise,
    Songs of praise to Jesus' love:
Happy spirits! ye are fled,
    Where no grief can entrance find;
Lulled to rest the aching head,
    Soothed the anguish of the mind.

3 All is tranquil and serene,
    Calm and undisturbed repose,
There no cloud can intervene,
    There no angry tempest blows:
Every tear is wiped away,
    Sighs no more shall heave the breast,
Night is lost in endless day,
    Sorrow, in eternal rest.
        Thomas Raffles, 1812, v. 1, a.

GLORIFICATION.

TAPPAN. C. M. George Kingsley, 1838.

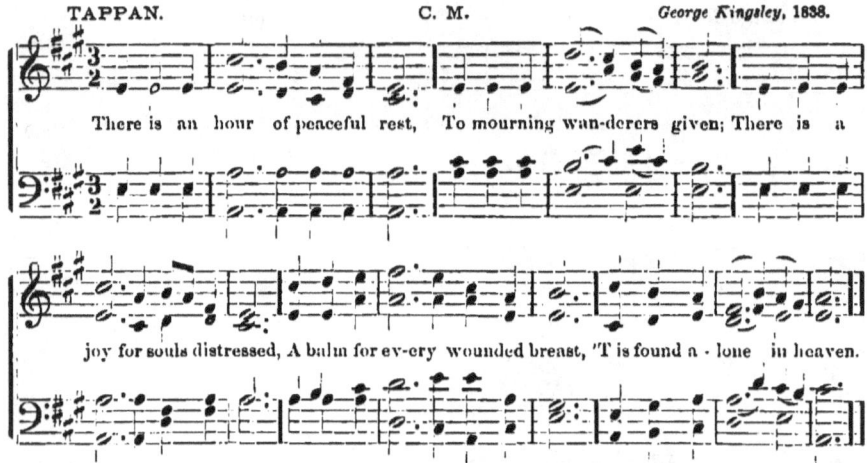

There is an hour of peaceful rest, To mourning wanderers given; There is a joy for souls distressed, A balm for every wounded breast, 'T is found alone in heaven.

720. *Heaven anticipated.* (1421.)

1 THERE is an hour of peaceful rest,
  To mourning wanderers given;
 There is a joy for souls distressed,
 A balm for every wounded breast,
  'T is found alone in heaven.

2 There is a home for weary souls,
  By sins and sorrows driven;
 When tossed on life's tempestuous shoals,
 Where storms arise and ocean rolls,
  And all is drear but heaven.

3 There, faith lifts up the tearless eye,
  The heart no longer riven,
 And views the tempest passing by,
 Sees evening shadows quickly fly,
  And all serene in heaven.

4 There, fragrant flowers immortal bloom,
  And joys supreme are given;
 There, rays divine disperse the gloom;—
 Beyond the dark and narrow tomb,
  Appears the dawn of heaven.
      William B. Tappan, 1829.

721. *The pious Dead.* (1426.)

1 HEAR what the voice from heaven pro-
  For all the pious dead;—   [claims
 Sweet is the savor of their names,
  And soft their sleeping bed.

2 They die in Jesus and are blessed;
  How kind their slumbers are!
 From sufferings and from sins released
  And freed from every snare.

3 Far from this world of toil and strife,
  They 're present with the Lord;
 The labors of their mortal life
  End in a large reward.
      Isaac Watts, 1707.

722. *Nothing like Heaven.* (1424.)

1 THIS world is poor, from shore to shore,
  And, like a baseless vision,
 Its lofty domes and brilliant ore,
 Its gems and crowns, are vain and poor;—
  There 's nothing rich but heaven.

2 Empires decay and nations die,
  Our hopes to winds are given;
 The vernal blooms in ruin lie,
 Death reigns o'er all beneath the sky:—
  There 's nothing sure but heaven.

3 Creation's mighty fabric all
  Shall be to atoms riven,—
 The skies consume, the planets fall,
 Convulsions rock this earthly ball;—
  There 's nothing firm but heaven.

4 A stranger, lonely here I roam,
  From place to place am driven;
 My friends are gone, and I 'm in gloom,
 This earth is all a dismal tomb;—
  I have no home but heaven.

5 The clouds disperse, the light appears,
  My sins are all forgiven,
 Triumphant grace hath quelled my fears;—
 Roll on, thou sun! fly swift, my years!
  I 'm on my way to heaven.
      David Nelson, 1832.

HEAVEN.

VARINA. C. M. 8 LINES. From *Christian Heinrich Rink*, 1770-1846.

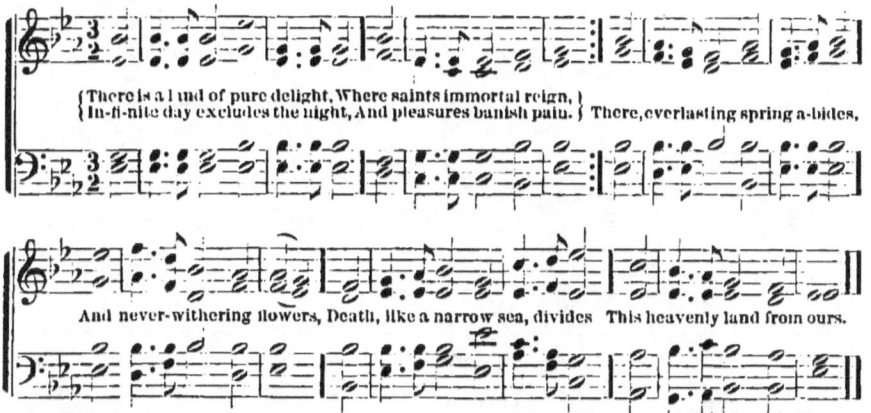

There is a land of pure delight, Where saints immortal reign, In-fi-nite day excludes the night, And pleasures banish pain. There, everlasting spring abides, And never-withering flowers, Death, like a narrow sea, divides This heavenly land from ours.

723. *The Land of endless Bliss.* (1427.)

1 THERE is a land of pure delight,
   Where saints immortal reign,
   Infinite day excludes the night,
   And pleasures banish pain.

2 There, everlasting spring abides,
   And never-withering flowers;
   Death, like a narrow sea, divides
   This heavenly land from ours.

3 Sweet fields, beyond the swelling flood,
   Stand dressed in living green;
   So to the Jews old Canaan stood,
   While Jordan rolled between.

4 But timorous mortals start and shrink
   To cross this narrow sea;
   And linger, shivering on the brink,
   And fear to launch away.

5 Oh! could we make our doubts remove,—
   These gloomy doubts that rise,—
   And see the Canaan that we love,
   With unbeclouded eyes;—

6 Could we but climb where Moses stood,
   And view the landscape o'er, [flood,
   Not Jordan's streams, nor death's cold
   Should fright us from the shore.
   Isaac Watts, 1707.

724. *The Martyrs glorified.* (1432.)

1 "THESE glorious minds, how bright they
   Whence all their white array? [shine,
   How came they to the happy seats
   Of everlasting day?"

2 From torturing pains to endless joys,
   On fiery wheels they rode; [white,
   And strangely washed their raiment
   In Jesus' dying blood.

3 Now they approach a spotless God,
   And bow before his throne;
   Their warbling harps, and sacred songs,
   Adore the Holy One.

4 The Lamb shall lead his heavenly flock
   Where living fountains rise;
   And love divine shall wipe away
   The sorrows of their eyes.
   Isaac Watts, 1707.

725. *The Joys unseen.* (1429.)

1 NOR eye has seen, nor ear has heard,
   Nor sense, nor reason known,
   What joys the Father has prepared,
   For those that love his Son.

2 But the good Spirit of the Lord
   Reveals a heaven to come:
   The beams of glory, in his word,
   Allure and guide us home.

3 Pure are the joys above the sky,
   And all the region peace;
   No wanton lips, nor envious eye,
   Can see or taste the bliss.

4 Those holy gates for ever bar
   Pollution, sin, and shame;
   None shall obtain admittance there
   But followers of the Lamb.
   Isaac Watts, 1709.

GLORIFICATION.

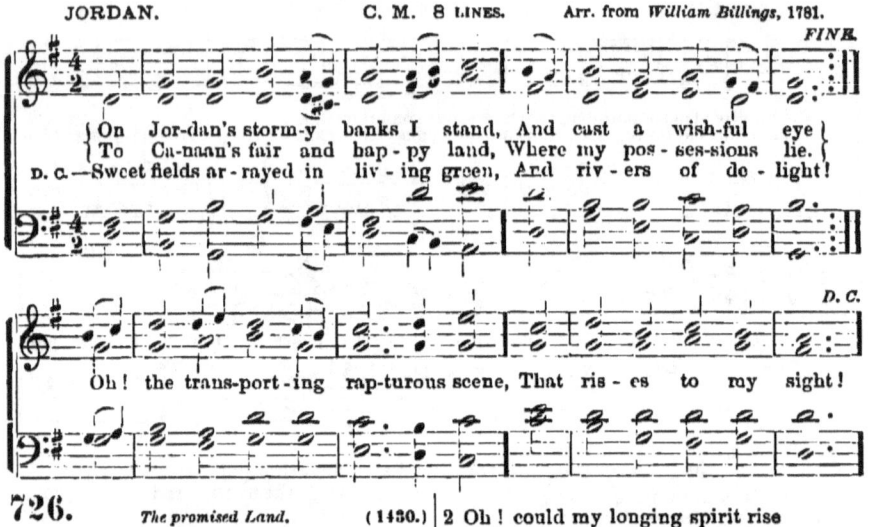

JORDAN. C. M. 8 LINES. Arr. from *William Billings*, 1781.

On Jordan's storm-y banks I stand, And cast a wish-ful eye
To Canaan's fair and hap-py land, Where my pos-ses-sions lie.
D. C.—Sweet fields ar-rayed in liv-ing green, And riv-ers of de-light!

Oh! the trans-port-ing rap-turous scene, That ris-es to my sight!

726. *The promised Land.* (1430.)

1 On Jordan's stormy banks I stand,
  And cast a wishful eye
To Canaan's fair and happy land,
  Where my possessions lie.

2 Oh! the transporting, rapturous scene,
  That rises to my sight!
Sweet fields arrayed in living green,
  And rivers of delight.

3 All o'er those wide-extended plains
  Shines one eternal day;
There God, the Son, for ever reigns,
  And scatters night away.

4 No chilling winds, or poisonous breath,
  Can reach that healthful shore;
Sickness and sorrow, pain and death,
  Are felt and feared no more.

5 When shall I reach that happy place,
  And be for ever blessed?
When shall I see my Father's face,
  And in his bosom rest?

6 Filled with delight, my raptured soul,
  Can here no longer stay;
Though Jordan's waves around me roll,
  Fearless I'd launch away,
      Samuel Stennett, 1787.

727. *Heaven unseen and immortal.* (1433.)

1 How far beyond our mortal sight
  The Lord of glory dwells!
A veil of interposing night
  His radiant face conceals.

2 Oh! could my longing spirit rise
  On strong, immortal wing,
And reach thy palace in the skies,
  My Saviour and my King!—

3 There, myriads worship at thy feet,
  And there—divine employ—
The triumphs of thy love repeat
  In songs of endless joy.

4 Thy presence beams eternal day,
  O'er all the blissful place;
Who would not drop this load of clay
  And die to see thy face?
      Anne Steele, 1760.

728. *The Moment after Death.* (1437.)

1 In vain my fancy strives to paint
  The moment after death,—
The glories that surround the saints,
  When yielding up their breath.

2 One gentle sigh their fetters breaks;
  We scarce can say,—"They're gone!"
Before the willing spirit takes
  Her mansion near the throne.

3 Thus much and this is all—we know;
  Saints are completely blest;
Have done with sin, and care, and woe,
  And with their Saviour rest.

4 On harps of gold, they praise his name,
  His face they always view;
Then let us followers be of them,
  That we may praise him too.
      John Newton, 1779.

HEAVEN.

729. *The new Jerusalem.* (1438.)

1 O MOTHER dear, Jerusalem!
 When shall I come to thee?
 When shall my sorrows have an end?
 Thy joys when shall I see?

2 O happy harbor of God's saints!
 O sweet and pleasant soil!
 In thee no sorrow may be found,
 No grief, no care, no toil.

3 Thy walls are made of precious stone,
 Thy bulwarks diamond-square;
 Thy gates are all of orient pearl;—
 O God! if I were there!

4 Oh! passing happy were my state,
 Might I be worthy found
 To wait upon my God and King
 His praises there to sound.

 F[rancis] B[aker,] 1616.
 Altered by David Dickson, 1649.

730. *The Worship of Earth and Heaven.* (1435.)

1 FATHER! I long, I faint, to see
 The place of thine abode;
 I'd leave thine earthly courts, and flee
 Up to thy seat, my God!

2 Here I behold thy distant face,
 And 't is a pleasing sight;
 But, to abide in thine embrace
 Is infinite delight.

3 I'd part with all the joys of sense,
 To gaze upon thy throne;
 Pleasure springs fresh for ever thence,
 Unspeakable, unknown.

4 There all the heavenly hosts are seen,
 In shining ranks they move,
 And drink immortal vigor in,
 With wonder and with love.

5 Then at thy feet, with awful fear,
 Th' adoring armies fall;
 With joy they shrink to nothing there,
 Before th' eternal All.

6 The more thy glories strike mine eyes,
 The humbler I shall lie;
 Thus, while I sink, my joys shall rise
 Immeasurably high.

 Isaac Watts, 1707.

731. *A blissful Death.* (1436.)

1 LORD! 't is an infinite delight,
 To see thy lovely face,
 To dwell whole ages in thy sight,
 And feel thy vital rays.

2 Thy love,— a sea without a shore,—
 Spreads life and joy abroad;
 Oh! 't is a heaven worth dying for,
 To see a smiling God!

3 Sweet was the journey to the skies,
 The wondrous prophet tried; [die;"
 "Come up the mount," says God, "and
 The prophet went — and died.

4 Softly his fainting head he lay
 Upon his Maker's breast;
 His Maker kissed his soul away,
 And laid his flesh to rest.

 Isaac Watts, 1705.

GLORIFICATION.

732. *The heavenly Home.* (1441.)

1 Sweet land of rest! for thee I sigh,
When will the moment come,
When I shall lay my armor by,
And dwell with Christ at home?

    Home, home, sweet, sweet home!
    And dwell with Christ at home.

2 On earth no tranquil joys I know,
No peaceful sheltering dome;
This world's a wilderness of woe,
This world is not my home.

3 To Jesus Christ I sought for rest,
He bade me cease to roam,
And fly for succor to his breast,
And he'd conduct me home.

4 Weary of wandering round and round
This vale of sin and gloom,
I long to quit th' unhallowed ground,
And dwell with Christ at home.

5 How long, dear Lord! wilt thou delay,
When will thy chariot come,
And fetch my waiting soul away
To heaven, my destined home?
G. M——, 1829.

733. *The Heavenly Jerusalem.* (1442.)

1 Jerusalem! my happy home,—
Name ever dear to me,—
When shall my labors have an end,
In joy, and peace, and thee?

2 When shall these eyes thy heaven-built walls
And pearly gates behold?
Thy bulwarks, with salvation strong,
And streets of shining gold?

3 Oh! when, thou city of my God!
Shall I thy courts ascend,—
Where congregations ne'er break up,
And Sabbaths have no end?

4 Why should I shrink at pain or woe,
Or feel, at death, dismay?
I've Canaan's goodly land in view,
And realms of endless day.

5 Apostles, martyrs, prophets, there,
Around my Saviour stand;
And soon my friends in Christ, below,
Will join the glorious band.

6 Jerusalem!—my happy home!
My soul still pants for thee;
Then shall my labors have an end,
When I thy joys shall see.
From F[rancis] B[aker,] 1616.
Anon., 1801.

734. *Paradise.* (1443.)

1 O paradise! O paradise!
Who doth not crave for rest?
Who would not seek the happy land,
Where they that loved are blest?

2 O paradise! O paradise!
'T is weary waiting here;
I long to be where Jesus is,
To feel, to see him near.

3 O paradise! O paradise!
I greatly long to see
The special place my dearest Lord
In love prepares for me.
Frederick W. Faber, 1849.

HEAVEN.

TRANQUILLITY. L. M. English Melody.—Marson.

Now let our souls, on wings sublime, Rise from the van-i-ties of time, Draw back the part-ing veil, and see The glo-ries of e-ter-ni-ty.

735. *The Dawn of Heaven.* (1444.)

1 Now let our souls, on wings sublime,
 Rise from the vanities of time,
 Draw back the parting veil, and see
 The glories of eternity.

2 Born by a new celestial birth,
 Why should we grovel here on earth?
 Why grasp at transitory toys,
 So near to heaven's eternal joys?

3 Shall aught beguile us on the road,
 While we are traveling back to God?
 For strangers into life we come,
 And dying is but going home.

4 Welcome, sweet hour of full discharge!
 That sets my longing soul at large,
 Unbinds my chains, breaks up my cell,
 And gives me with my God to dwell.

5 To dwell with God, to feel his love,
 Is the full heaven enjoyed above;
 And the sweet expectation now
 Is the young dawn of heaven below.
 Thomas Gibbons, 1762.

736. *"Better to depart."* (1445.)

1 While on the verge of life I stand,
 And view the scene on either hand,
 My spirit struggles with its clay,
 And longs to wing its flight away.

2 Where Jesus dwells my soul would be;
 It faints my much-loved Lord to see;
 Earth! twine no more about my heart,
 For 't is far better to depart.

3 Come, ye angelic envoys! come,
 And lead the willing pilgrim home:
 Ye know the way to Jesus' throne.—
 Source of my joys, and of your own.

4 That blessed interview, how sweet!
 To fall transported at his feet!
 Raised in his arms, to view his face,
 Through the full beamings of his grace!

5 Yet, with these prospects full in sight,
 I 'll wait thy signal for my flight;
 For, while thy service I pursue,
 I find my heaven begun below.
 Philip Doddridge, 1740.

737. *The Song of Heaven.* (1447.)

1 Hark! how the choral song of heaven
 Swells, full of peace and joy, above;
 Hark! how they strike their golden harps,
 And raise the tuneful notes of love.

2 No anxious care, nor thrilling grief,
 No deep despair, nor gloomy woe
 They feel, while high their lofty strains
 In noblest, sweetest concord flow.

3 When shall we join the heavenly host,
 Who sing Immanuel's praise on high,
 And leave behind our fears and doubts,
 To swell the chorus of the sky?

4 Oh! come, thou rapture-bringing morn!
 And usher in this joyful day;
 We long to see thy rising sun
 Drive all these clouds of grief away.
 R. S. M——, 1812.

GLORIFICATION.

PARADISE. 7s & 6s. 8 LINES. Frederick A. Weber.

O par-a-dise e-ter-nal! What bliss to en-ter thee,
And, once within thy por-tals, Se-cure for ev-er be! In thee no sin nor sor-row,
No pain nor death, is known; But pure glad life, en-dur-ing As heaven's benignant throne.

738. *The Paradise eternal.* (1450.)

1 O PARADISE eternal!
  What bliss to enter thee,
And, once within thy portals,
  Secure for ever be!
In thee no sin nor sorrow,
  No pain nor death, is known;
But pure glad life, enduring
  As heaven's benignant throne.

2 There all around shall love us,
  And we return their love;
One band of happy spirits,
  One family above:
There God shall be our portion,
  And we his jewels be;
And, gracing his bright mansions,
  His smile reflect and see.

3 So songs shall rise for ever,
  While all creation fair,
Still more and more revealed,
  Shall wake fresh praises there:
O paradise eternal!
  What joys in thee are known!
O God of mercy! guide us,
  Till all be felt our own.
          Thomas Davis, 1864.

739. *"Hic breve vivitur."* (1451.)

1 BRIEF life is here our portion;
  Brief sorrow, short-lived care;
The life, that knows no ending,
  The tearless life, is there:

O happy retribution!
  Short toil, eternal rest;
For mortals, and for sinners,
  A mansion with the blest!

2 There grief is turned to pleasure;
  Such pleasure, as below
No human voice can utter,
  No human heart can know:
And, after fleshly scandal,
  And, after this world's night,
And, after storm and whirlwind,
  Is calm, and joy, and light.

3 And there is David's fountain,
  And life in fullest glow;
And there the light is golden,
  And milk and honey flow;
The light, that hath no evening,
  The health, that hath no sore,
The life, that hath no ending,
  But lasteth evermore.

4 There Jesus shall embrace us,
  There Jesus be embraced,—
That spirit's food and sunshine,
  Whence earthly love is chased:
Yes! God, my King and Portion,
  In fullness of his grace,
We then shall see for ever,
  And worship face to face.
      Lat. Bernard de Morlaix, ab. 1150.
      Tr. John Mason Neale, 1851.

HEAVEN.

740. *"Urbs Syon aurea.* (1452.)

1 JERUSALEM, the golden,
  With milk and honey blest!
 Beneath thy contemplation
  Sink heart and voice oppressed:
 I know not, Oh! I know not
  What social joys are there,
 What radiancy of glory,
  What light beyond compare.

2 They stand, those halls of Zion,
  All jubilant with song,
 And bright with many an angel,
  And all the martyr throng;
 The Prince is ever in them,
  The daylight is serene;
 The pastures of the blessèd
  Are decked in glorious sheen.

3 There is the throne of David;
  And there, from care released,
 The song of them that triumph,
  The shout of them that feast:
 And they who, with their Leader,
  Have conquered in the fight,
 For ever and for ever
  Are clad in robes of white.

  Lat., *Bernard de Morlaix*, ab. 1150.
  Tr., *John Mason Neale*, 1851.

741. *"O bona Patria."* (1453.)

1 FOR thee, O dear, dear country!
  Mine eyes their vigils keep;
 For very love, beholding
  Thy happy name, they weep:
 The mention of thy glory
  Is unction to the breast,
 And medicine in sickness,
  And love, and life, and rest.

2 O one, O onely mansion!
  O paradise of joy!
 Where tears are ever banished,
  And smiles have no alloy;
 The cross is all thy splendor,
  The Crucified thy praise;
 His laud and benediction
  Thy ransomed people raise.

3 Jesus, the Gem of beauty,
  True God and Man, they sing;—
 The never-failing Garden,
  The ever-golden King;
 The Door, the Pledge, the Husband,
  The Guardian of his court;
 The Day-star of salvation,
  The Porter and the Port.

4 Thou hast no shore, fair ocean!
  Thou hast no time, bright day!
 Dear fountain of refreshment
  To pilgrims far away!
 Upon the Rock of ages,
  They raise thy holy tower;
 Thine is the victor's laurel,
  And thine the golden dower.

  Lat., *Bernard de Morlaix*, ab. 1150.
  Tr., *John Mason Neale*, 1851.

GLORIFICATION.

CHRISTINE. 7s & 6s. 8 LINES. S. P. W——, 1872.

Je-ru-sa-lem, the glo-rious! The glo-ry of th' e-lect,— O dear and fu-ture vis-ion,
D. S.—To thee my thoughts are kindled,

That ea-ger hearts ex-pect! Ev'n now by faith I see thee, Ev'n here thy walls dis-cern;
And strive, and pant, and yearn!

742. *"Urbs Syon inclyta, Gloria."* (1454.)

1 JERUSALEM, the glorious!
  The glory of th' elect,—
O dear and future vision,
  That eager hearts expect!
Ev'n now by faith I see thee,
  Ev'n here thy walls discern;
To thee my thoughts are kindled,
  And strive, and pant, and yearn!

2 Jerusalem the onely,
  That look'st from heaven below,
In thee is all my glory,
  In me is all my woe:
Jerusalem! exulting
  On that securest shore,
I hope thee, wish thee, sing thee,
  And love thee evermore!

3 O sweet and blessèd country!
  Shall I e'er see thy face?
O sweet and blessèd country!
  Shall I e'er win thy grace?—
Exult, O dust and ashes!
  The Lord shall be thy part;
His only, his for ever,
  Thou shalt be, and thou art!

Lat., *Bernard de Morlaix*, ab. 1150.
Tr. *John Mason Neale*, 1851.

743. *"Ermuntert euch, ihr Frommen."* (1455.)

1 REJOICE, all ye believers!
  And let your lights appear;
The evening is advancing,
  And darker night is near;
The Bridegroom is arising,
  And soon he draweth nigh;
Up! pray, and watch, and wrestle;
  At midnight comes the cry.

2 The watchers on the mountain
  Proclaim the Bridegroom near;
Go meet him as he cometh,
  With hallelujahs clear;
The marriage-feast is waiting,
  The gates wide open stand;
Up! up! ye heirs of glory!
  The Bridegroom is at hand.

3 Ye saints! who here in patience
  Your cross and sufferings bore,
Shall live and reign for ever,
  When sorrow is no more;
Around the throne of glory,
  The Lamb ye shall behold,
In triumph cast before him
  Your diadems of gold!

4 Our Hope and Expectation,
  O Jesus! now appear;
Arise, thou Sun so long'd for,
  O'er this benighted sphere:
With hearts and hands uplifted,
  We plead, O Lord! to see
The day of earth's redemption,
  That brings us unto thee!

Ger., *Laurentius Laurenti*, 1700.
Tr., *Jane Borthwick*, 1853.

HEAVEN.

744. *"No Sorrow there."* (1456.)

1 Oh! sing to me of heaven,
When I am called to die;
Sing songs of holy ecstasy,
To waft my soul on high:

There 'll be no sorrow there;
There 'll be no sorrow there;
In heaven above, where all is love,
There 'll be no sorrow there.

2 When cold and sluggish drops
Roll off my marble brow,
Break forth in songs of joyfulness,
Let heaven begin below.

3 When the last moments come,
Oh! watch my dying face,
To catch the bright seraphic gleam,
Which on each feature plays.

4 Then to my raptured ear
Let one sweet song be given;
Let music cheer me last on earth,
And greet me first in heaven!
Mrs. Mary S. B. Dana, 1850.

745. *A Home above.* (1457.)

1 I have a home above,
From sin and sorrow free;
A mansion, which eternal Love
Designed and formed for me.

2 My Father's gracious hand
Has built this sweet abode;
From everlasting it was planned,—
My dwelling-place with God.

3 My Saviour's precious blood
Has made my title sure;
He passed thro' death's dark raging flood,
To make my rest secure.

4 The Comforter has come,
The earnest has been given;
He leads me onward to the home,
Reserved for me in heaven.
Henry Bennett, 1851.

746. *Harping with their Harps.* (1458.)

1 Hark! hark the voice of praise
Around Jehovah's throne!
Songs of celestial joy they raise,
To mortal lips unknown.

2 In shining robes they stand
Upon the crystal sea;
The harps of God are in their hand,
And all is ecstasy.

3 Oh! for an angel's love,
A seraph's soaring wing,
To sing, with thousand saints above,
The triumphs of our King!

4 With pure and sinless heart,
His mercies to adore!
My God! to know thee as thou art,
Nor grieve thy Spirit more!

5 Blest hope!—a little while,
And we, amidst that throng
Shall live in our Redeemer's smile,
And swell the angels' song.
Anon., 1802. a.

266 GLORIFICATION.

SHINING SHORE. 8s & 7s. TROCHAIC. 8 lines. George F. Root, 1859.

My days are glid-ing swift-ly by, And I, a pil-grim stran-ger,
Would not de-tain them, as they fly, Those hours of toil and dan-ger;
D. C.—just be-fore, the shin-ing shore We may al-most dis-cov-er.

CHORUS.
For, Oh! we stand on Jordan's strand; Our friends are pass-ing o-ver; And,

747.   *Jordan's Strand.*   (1459.)

1 My days are gliding swiftly by,
   And I, a pilgrim stranger,
Would not detain them as they fly,
   Those hours of toil and danger:
       CHORUS.
For, Oh! we stand on Jordan's strand;
   Our friends are passing over;
And, just before, the shining shore
   We may almost discover.

2 We'll gird our loins, my brethren dear!
   Our heavenly home discerning;
Our absent Lord has left us word,—
   "Let every lamp be burning:"
CHORUS.—For, Oh! we stand, etc.

3 Should coming days be cold and dark,
   We need not cease our singing;
That perfect rest nought can molest,
   Where golden harps are ringing:
CHORUS.—For, Oh! we stand, etc.

4 Let sorrow's rudest tempest blow,
   Each cord on earth to sever;
Our King says,—"Come!"—and there's our home,
   For ever, Oh! for ever! [our home,
CHORUS.—For, Oh! we stand, etc.

David Nelson, 1835.

748.   *Wayfarers.*   (1460.)

1 WAYFARERS in the wilderness,
   By morn, and noon, and even,
Day after day, we journey on,
   With weary feet towards heaven:
       CHORUS.
O land above! O land of love!
   The glory shineth o'er thee;
O Christ, our King! in mercy bring
   Us thither, we implore thee!

2 By day the cloud before us goes,
   By night the cloud of fire,
To guide us o'er the trackless waste,
   To Canaan ever nigher:
CHORUS.—O land above! etc.

3 Each morning find we, as he said,
   The dew of daily manna;
And ever, when a foe appears,
   Confronts him Christ, our Banner:
CHORUS.—O land above! etc.

4 The sea was riven for our feet,
   And so shall be the river; [home,
And, by the King's highway brought
   We'll praise his name for ever:
CHORUS.—O land above! etc.

Alexander R. Thompson, 1869.

HEAVEN.

749. *Nearer Home.* (1461.)

1 ONE sweetly solemn thought
   Comes to me o'er and o'er ;
  I 'm nearer home to-day
   Than e'er I 've been before :

2 Nearer my Father's house,
   Where the blest mansions be ;
  Nearer the great white throne,
   Nearer the crystal sea :

3 Nearer the bound where we
   Must lay our burdens down ;
  Nearer to leave the cross,
   Nearer to gain the crown.

4 The waves of that deep sea
   Roll dark before my sight,
  But break, the other side,
   Upon a shore of light.

5 Oh ! if my mortal feet
   Have almost gained the brink,
  If I am nearer home
   To-day than e'en I think :

6 Father ! perfect my trust,
   That I may rest, in death,
  On Christ, my Lord, alone,
   And thus resign my breath.
             Phœbe Cary, 1852, a.

750. *The Heavenly Home.* (1462.)

1 THERE is a blessèd home
   Beyond this land of woe,
  Where trials never come,
   Nor tears of sorrow flow :

2 Where faith is lost in sight,
   And patient hope is crowned,
  And everlasting light
   Its glory throws around.

3 Oh ! joy all joys beyond,
   To see the Lamb who died,
  And count each sacred wound
   In hands, and feet, and side !

4 To give to him the praise
   Of every triumph won,
  And sing, through endless days,
   The great things he hath done !

5 Look up, ye saints of God !
   Nor fear to tread below
  The path, your Saviour trod,
   Of daily toil and woe.

6 Wait but a little while,
   In uncomplaining love ;
  His own most gracious smile
   Shall welcome you above.
             Henry W. Baker, 1862.

268   GLORIFICATION.

REST FOR THE WEARY.   8s & 7s.   J. W. Dadmun, 1860.

751.   *Rest for the Weary.*   (1463.)

1 IN THE Christian's home in glory,
    There remains a land of rest ;
There my Saviour's gone before me,
    To fulfill my soul's request.
      There is rest for the weary,
      There is rest for you,
      On the other side of Jordan,
      In the sweet fields of Eden,
      Where the tree of life is blooming,
      There is rest for you.

2 He is fitting up my mansion,
    Which eternally shall stand,
For my stay shall not be transient,
    In the holy, happy land.

3 Pain and sickness ne'er shall enter,
    Grief nor woe my lot shall share ;
But, in that celestial centre,
    I a crown of life shall wear.

4 Death itself shall then be vanquished,
    And his sting shall be withdrawn :
Shout for gladness, O ye ransomed !
    Hail with joy the rising morn.

5 Sing, Oh ! sing, ye heirs of glory !
    Shout your triumph as you go ;
Zion's gate will open for you,
    You shall find an entrance through.
                 William Hunter, 1857.

752.   *The Saints in Glory.*   (1464.)

1 HARK ! the sound of holy voices,
    Chanting at the crystal sea,—
Alleluia ! alleluia !
    Alleluia ! Lord ! to thee.

2 Multitude, which none can number,
    Like the stars in glory stand,
Clothed in white apparel, holding
    Palms of victory in their hands.

3 They have come from tribulation,
    And have washed their robes in blood,
Washed them in the blood of Jesus ;
    Tried they were, and firm they stood.

4 Gladly, Lord ! with thee they suffered ;
    Gladly, Lord ! with thee they died,
And, by death, to life immortal
    They were born and glorified.

5 Now they reign in heavenly glory,
    Now they walk in golden light,
Now they drink, as from a river,
    Holy bliss and infinite.

6 Love and peace they taste for ever,
    And all truth and knowledge see
In the beatific vision
    Of the blessed Trinity.
                Christopher Wordsworth, 1835.

1.   L. M.

Praise God, from whom all blessings flow;
Praise him all creatures here below!
Praise him above, ye heavenly host!
Praise Father, Son, and Holy Ghost.
Thomas Ken, 1697.

2.   L. M.

To God, the Father,—God, the Son,—
And God, the Spirit,— Three in One,
Be honor, praise, and glory given,
By all on earth, and all in heaven.
Isaac Watts, 1707.

3.   C. M.

To Father, Son, and Holy Ghost,
The God, whom we adore,
Be glory as it was, is now,
And shall be evermore.
Tate and Brady, 1696.

4.   C. M.

Let God,— the Father, and the Son,
And Spirit,— be adored,
Where there are works to make him known,
Or saints to love the Lord.
Isaac Watts, 1707.

5.   S. M.

To God,— the Father, Son,
And Spirit,— One in Three,
Be glory, as it was, is now,
And shall for ever be.
John Wesley, 1739.

6.   S. M.

Ye angels round the throne!
And saints that dwell below!
Worship the Father, love the Son,
And bless the Spirit too.
Isaac Watts, 1707.

7.   H. M.

To God the Father's throne
  Your highest honors raise;
Glory to God, the Son;
  To God, the Spirit, praise;
With all our powers, eternal King!
Thy name we sing, while faith adores.
Isaac Watts, 1709, a.

8.   6s & 4s.

To God,— the Father, Son,
And Spirit,— Three in One,
  All praise be given!
Crown him in every song;
To him your hearts belong;
Let all his praise prolong—
  On earth, in heaven.
E. F. H., 1843.

9.   7s.

Sing we, to our God above,
Praise eternal as his love;
Praise him,—all ye heavenly host!—
Father, Son and Holy Ghost.
Charles Wesley, 1739.

10.   7s & 6s.

Great God of earth and heaven!
  To thee our songs we raise;
To thee be glory given
  And everlasting praise:
We joyfully confess thee,
  Eternal Triune God!
We magnify, we bless thee,
  And spread thy praise abroad.
E. F. H., 1872.

11.   8s & 7s.   8 lines.

Praise the God of all creation;
  Praise the Father's boundless love;
Praise the Lamb, our Expiation;
  Priest and King enthroned above;
Praise the Fountain of salvation,
  Him, by whom our spirits live;
Undivided adoration
  To the one Jehovah give.
Josiah Conder, 1836.

12.   8s, 7s & 4.

Great Jehovah! we adore thee,
  God, the Father, God, the Son,
God, the Spirit, joined in glory
  On the same eternal throne;
    Endless praises
  To Jehovah, Three in One.
William Goode, 1811, a.

INDEX OF SUBJECTS.

Aaron, 601.
Abba, Father, 448.
Abrahamic Covenant, 585.
Absence from God, 425, 696.
Accepted Time, 283—285, 289, 290, 292, 293, 304.
Access to God, 250, 481, 522.
Adoption, 158, 448.
Adoration, 65—166.
  Father, 76—130.
  Son, 131—150.
  Spirit, 151—166.
  Trinity, 65—75.
Advent, First, 190—205.
  Second, 241, 706, 709, 711—715
Adversity, 507—544.
Advocate, 68, 250, 263, 316, 426
Afflictions, 507—544.
Alarm, 270, 331, 550, 679, 686.
All in All—See *Christ, God.*
Almost Christian, 550.
Alms, 642—650.
Angels, 24, 736.
Apostasy, 304, 492, 493, 499, 506.
Apostles' Commission, 576, 578.
Ascension of Christ, 230, 231, 234, 236, 238, 240, 244.
Ashamed of Christ, 355, 381, 408.
Aspiration, 397—491.
  For Divine Grace, 474—491.
  Of Faith, 420—433.
  Of Hope, 434—452.
  Of Love, 397—419.
Assurance of, 355, 436, 440, 451, 467, 495, 510, 548.
Atoning Sacrifice, 213—229.
  Completed, 241, 263, 297.
  Needed, 184—189.
  Sufficient, 277, 282, 288, 301, 305.
Attributes of God, 80, 84, 93.
Autumn, 657, 658, 662.
Backsliding, 304, 492, 493, 499, 506.
Baptism, 585—587.
Being of God, 169.
Believers—See *Saints.*
Benevolence, 642—644, 645—650.
  Of Christ, 210.
Bereavement, 507, 527, 533, 698.
Bible, 167—183.
Blindness, 333.
Blood of Christ — See *Atoning Sacrifice.*
Bondage of Sin, 187, 188, 303.
Book of Life, 533.

Bread of Life, 364, 375, 379, 380, 383, 391, 442.
Brevity of Life, 677, 679, 691, 707.
Broad Way, 550.
Brotherly Love, 6, 594—597.
Burdens—See *Afflictions.*
Burial, 658.
Calmness, 458, 462, 525.
Calvary, 214, 216.
Carnal Pleasure, 343.
Charity, 642—649.
Chastenings—See *Afflictions.*
Children, 585—587.
Choosing Christ, 281, 293, 489.
Christ:—
  Advent, First, 190—205.
    " Second, 241, 706, 709, 711—715.
  Advocate, 68, 250, 263, 316, 426.
  Agony, 214, 216, 396.
  All in All, 415, 466, 471, 516, 531.
  Ascension, 230, 231, 234.
  Atonement, 213—229, 362.
  Beauty, 134, 206, 256, 257, 405.
  Birth, 190—205.
  Blood—See *Atoning Sacrifice.*
  Bread of Life, 364, 375, 379, 380, 383, 391, 442.
  Captain, 437, 513, 713.
  Compassion—See *Love.*
  Condescension — See *Incarnation.*
  Conqueror, 234, 236, 244—246, 251, 394, 619, 620.
  Coronation, 147, 148, 245, 246, 261.
  Counsellor, 195.
  Cross of—See *Cross.*
  Crucified, 471, 575.
  Crucifixion, 215—217, 218—220, 222, 223, 227.
  Death of—See *Atoning Sacrifice.*
  Divinity, 131, 133, 135, 139, 141, 143, 198—200.
  Exaltation, 132, 145, 235, 264.
  Example, 209, 210, 216, 371.
  Excellency, 138, 139.
  Faithfulness of, 355, 509.
  Fountain, 221, 267, 466.
  Friend, 341, 475.
  Glory, 131—135, 137, 140, 144—146.
  Grace—See *Love.*
  Hiding Place, 315.
  Humanity, 203, 206—212.

Christ:—
  Humiliation, 196, 199, 234, 235, 252, 257.
  Immanuel, 136, 198.
  Incarnation, 190—205, 254.
  Intercession, 148, 230, 231, 242, 254, 255, 263, 362, 500.
  Judge, 262, 328, 331, 708—717.
  King, 146, 190, 195, 197, 202, 203, 205, 241, 242, 246, 247, 258, 262.
  Lamb of God, 137, 141, 149, 150, 213, 215, 221, 224, 259, 346, 718, 724.
  Light, 405—See *Sun.*
  Life, 206—212.
  Lord, our Righteousness, 185, 358.
  Love, 142, 220, 228, 234, 252, 255, 370, 396, 413.
  Loveliness, 136, 206, 208, 256, 383—387, 400, 409.
  Majesty, 131—150.
  Mediation, 255—See *Advocate.*
  Melchisedec, 401.
  Ministry, 206—212.
  Miracles, 207.
  Mission, 190, 191, 272.
  Name, 134, 142, 249, 253, 254, 395, 397—399, 401, 419, 425, 516.
  Nativity, 190—205.
  Obedience, 211.
  Offices of, 262, 398.
  Passover, 213—See *Lamb.*
  Patience of, 210, 211.
  Pearl of Great Price, 360.
  Physician, 333.
  Power of—See *Divinity.*
  Preciousness of, 395, 397—401, 403, 406.
  Presence of, 5, 60, 61, 368.
  Priest, 202, 211, 214, 244, 255, 262, 303.
  Prince of Glory, 227.
  " " Peace, 132, 133, 195, 567, 598, 617.
  Prophet, 202, 242, 262, 398.
  Ransom, 164, 223, 258.
  Redeemer—See *Atoning Sacrifice.*
  Refuge, 330, 420, 423.
  Resurrection, of, 18, 19, 230—240.
  Righteousness of, 185, 347, 358.

INDEX OF SUBJECTS. 271

Christ:—
  Rock of Ages, 363, 568.
  Sacrifice, Atoning, 213—229, 242, 254, 257, 260.
  Saviour—See *Atoning Sacrifice*.
  Second Coming of, 241, 706, 709, 711—715.
  Shepherd, 226, 380, 428, 468.
  Sufferings of, 214, 217—220, 222, 223, 377.
  Sun of Righteousness, 12, 62, 636, 637.
  Surety, 440.
  Sympathy of, 211, 218, 256.
  Teacher, 208, 210.
  Way, Truth, and Life, 212, 349.
  Wonderful, 195.
  Word of God, 193.
Christian:—
  Conflicts of, 492.
  Courage, 437, 618, 641.
  Death of, 683—685, 687, 693, 695, 699—701, 705, 721.
  Duties, 480, 549.
  Effort, 641—650.
  Encouragements—See *Tribulation*.
  Fellowship, 594—605.
  Graces—See *Faith, Hope, Love*.
  Love, 397—419.
  Peace, 498.
  Race, 438, 443.
  Warfare, 437, 504, 513, 536, 618, 629, 641.
Church:—
  557—572.
  Afflicted, 607, 611, 622.
  Beloved of God, 561.
  Beloved of Saints, 599.
  Erection, 651—656.
  Fellowship, 594—605.
  Glory of, 557—561, 565, 568, 569, 613.
  Increase of, 566, 567, 571, 640.
  Institutions of, 363—396, 585—587.
  Missions of, 566, 567, 571, 617—640
  Relations, 557—650.
  Revival of, 607—616.
  Security of, 558, 559.
  Union with, 589—593, 599.
  Unity of, 595, 596, 598, 600, 602.
Close of Probation, 677—701.
  Of Worship, 23, 36, 37, 43, 46, 64, 371.
City of God, 561, 568.
Comforter, 163, 164.
Coming of Christ—See *Advent*.
Commemoration, 363—396.
Commission, Apostolic, 573, 576, 578.
Communion with Christ, 368, 378, 407, 410, 412, 415, 416, 466.
  With God, 414, 457, 554.
  With Saints, 465, 594—605.
Compassion of Christ—See *Love of Christ*.
  Of God, 89, 108, 116, 296, 519.
  Of Saints, 645, 646, 649.
Completeness—See *All in All*

Condescension of Christ—See *Incarnation*.
Confession of Christ, 588—593, 599.
  Of Sin, 184, 306, 307, 310, 317, 340.
Confidence—See *Faith*.
Conflict with Sin, 492—506.
Conformity to Christ, 209, 210, 216, 371, 479, 487, 598.
Conqueror, Christ a, 234, 236, 240, 244—246, 248, 251, 394, 619, 620.
Conscience, 498.
Consecration of Property, 227, 354, 643, 644, 648, 650.
  Of Self, 338, 344, 345, 391—393, 433, 489, 588.
  Of Sanctuary, 651, 653—655.
Consolation, 507, 528.—See *Afflictions*.
Constancy, 433, 629.
Contentment, 352.—See *Resignation*.
Contributions, 643, 644, 648, 650.
Contrition, 184, 307, 310, 317, 324, 441.
Conversion, 332—362, 615.
Conversation, 6.
Conviction, 184.—See *Repentance*.
Coronation of Christ, 147, 245—247, 261.
Country, our, 659—661, 663.
Courage, 437, 536, 618, 641.
Covenant, entering into, 588—593.
  Of Grace, 109, 389, 440, 585.
Creation, First, 82, 93, 100, 122, 123.
  New—See *Regeneration*.
Creature Love, 497.
Cross, Bearing, 336, 434, 490, 524, 536.
  Glorying in the, 228, 369, 381.
  Power of the, 243, 334.
Crowns of Glory, 434, 435, 443, 437, 447, 452.
Crucifixion of Christ, 215, 216—220, 222—227.
  To the World, 227, 347.—See *Renunciation*.
Daily Duties, 3, 439, 480, 549.
  Worship, 1—14.
Darkness, Spiritual, 492—506.
Day of Grace, 285, 292, 686.
Death, Natural, 677—701.
  Of Friends, 607, 692, 698, 705.
  Of Saints, 683—685, 687, 690, 693, 695, 699—701, 705, 721, 731.
  Of the World, 343, 497.
Declensions, 492, 493, 611, 612.
Decrees, 86, 534, 544.
Dedication of Church, 651, 653—656.
  Of Self—See *Consecration*.
Delay, Danger of, 293.
Depravity, Native, 185, 186, 188, 608.
  Universal, 184—189, 226, 260, 608.
Despair, 708.
Devil, 437, 500.

Devotions, Daily, 1—14.
  Family, 594, 601, 604.
  Sabbath, 14—64.
Dismissions, 36, 37, 46, 64.
Distress, Spiritual, 492—506.
Doxologies, 46, 60, 63, 137, 562; and page 269.
Drought, Spiritual, 607, 608, 611, 612.
Duties, Daily, 3, 439, 480, 549.
Early Piety—See *Children, Youth*.
Earnest of the Spirit, 55, 495, 548.
Earnestness—See *Zeal*.
Earthly Pleasures—See *Renunciation*.
Ebenezer, 366.
Effort, Christian, 641—650.
Election, 86, 534, 544.
Erection of Churches, 651—656.
Espousals to Christ, 588—591.
Eternity, 331.—See *God*.
Evening, 4, 7, 9—12, 14.
  Of Lord's Day, 23, 25.
Evidences of Grace—See *Self-Examination*.
Exaltation of Christ, 132, 145, 235, 264.
Example of Christ, 209, 210, 216, 371.
  Of Christians, 435, 443, 444.
Expostulation, 269, 270, 274, 279, 284, 289—293, 298, 300, 304.
Faint-heartedness, 613.
Faith, Aspiration of, 420—433.
  Justification by, 340, 347, 352, 363.
  Power of, 424, 429, 440, 515.
  Prayer for, 432.
Faithfulness, of Christ, 355, 509.
  Of God, 88, 108, 175, 512.
Fall of Man—See *Depravity*.
Family Worship, 594, 601, 604.
Fast Days, 666—668.
Father, the Eternal, 76—130.
Feast, Gospel, 274, 277, 391.
  Sacramental, 363—396.
Fellowship, Aspiration for Divine, 453—473.
  Church, 594—605.
Festivals, 657—665.
Fidelity, 480, 481.
Forbearance, Christian, 210, 490, 605.
  Divine, 313, 325.
Forgiveness of Sin—See *Pardon*.
Foreign Missions, 567, 570, 578, 583, 617—640.
Formality, 54, 155, 546, 550.
Foundation of Hope, 263, 427, 441, 510.
Fountain of Blood, 187, 221.
  Of Living Water, 277, 278, 282, 284, 568.
Frailty of Man, 677, 678, 688, 707.
Friend of Sinners, 341, 475.
Friends, Burial of, 705.
  Glorified, 507, 595, 698, 745.
Fruits of Grace, 439, 479, 554.
Fullness of Grace, 277, 282, 288, 301, 305.
Funeral, 701, 705.
Future Retribution, 292, 708.
Gentleness, 490.

INDEX OF SUBJECTS.

Gethsemane, 214, 216, 396
Glorification, 702—752.
Glorified Saints, 447, 718, 719, 724, 728.
 Saviour, 435, 463, 726.
Glorying in the Cross, 223, 339, 381.
God:—
 All in all, 402, 414.
 Almighty, 81, 96, 99, 101.
 Attributes of, 80, 84, 93.
 Being of, 82, 169.
 Communion with, 414, 457, 458, 554.
 Compassion of, 69, 103, 116, 296, 519.
 Creator, 82, 94, 100, 122, 123.
 Decrees of, 81, 534, 544.
 Eternal, 97, 98.
 Faithfulness of, 88, 108, 175, 512.
 Father, 76—130.
 Forbearance of, 313, 325.
 Glory of, 66, 68, 71, 72, 100, 111, 119—122, 128.
 Goodness of, 80, 85—87, 102, 104, 110, 112, 133.
 Grace of, 85, 89, 116, 125, 127, 129.
 Guardian, 422, 428, 463.
 Guide, 428, 438, 474.
 Holiness of, 49.
 Incomprehensible, 80, 534, 544.
 Infinite, 81, 97, 96, 93.
 Judge, 710.
 Justice of, 93, 99.
 King—See *Sovereign*.
 Love of, 4, 72, 89, 92, 114, 115, 117, 118, 370.
 Majesty of, 81, 93, 96, 97, 131.
 Mercy of, 252, 296, 302.
 Omnipotent, 81, 99, 96, 101.
 Omnipresent, 547, 551, 552.
 Omniscient, 83, 103, 547, 551—553.
 Patience of, 313, 325.
 Pity of, 89, 108, 116, 296, 519.
 Presence of, 14, 15, 58, 59, 62.
 Providence of, 110, 521, 529.
 Purposes of, 86, 534, 544.
 Refuge, 422, 428, 468, 542.
 Shepherd, 428.
 Sovereign, 41, 76, 79, 84, 93, 95.
 Supreme, 74, 76, 96, 98, 421.
 Triune, 1, 18, 20, 65—75, 167.
 Truth of, 88, 89, 103, 109.
 Wisdom of, 81, 83, 100, 544.
 Works of, 81—84, 93, 96, 100, 103, 111, 113, 120—122, 124.
Good Works, 347, 549.
Gospel, Excellency of, 169, 170, 175, 177, 179—183.
 Feast, 274, 277, 301.
 Freeness of—See *Grace*.
 Fullness of, 277, 282, 288, 301, 305.
 Invitations of, 265—362.
 Message, 184, 269.
 Power of, 183, 257, 441, 620.
 Reception of, 332—362.
 Rejection of, 107, 207, 279, 289—293, 298.
 Spread of—See *Missions*.

Gospel:—
 Triumph of, 190, 557—572.—See *Missions*.
 Trumpet, 277, 303, 622.
Grace, Aspiration for Divine, 474—491.
 Converting, 151, 158, 161.
 Free, 189, 301.
 Justifying, 340, 347, 363.
 Quickening, 154—156.
 Renewing, 159, 160, 166.
 Restoring, 155, 157, 163, 164.
 Reviving, 152, 155, 156, 161, 162.—See *Revival*.
 Sanctifying, 154, 157—159, 161, 164—166.
 Sovereign, 187, 189, 260, 315.
Graces, Christian—See *Faith, Hope, Love*.
Gratitude, 60, 110, 126.
Grave, 597, 680, 686, 692, 698.
Grieving the Spirit, 291, 311.
Growth in Grace, 209, 459, 470, 474—491.
Guest, Divine, 289, 319.
Guidance, Divine, 428.
Guilt—See *Sin*.
Hallelujahs, 73, 78, 125, 128, 129.
Hardness of Heart, 309.
Harvest, Spiritual—See *Revival*.
 Temporal, 657, 658, 662.
Hearing the Word, 34, 177.
Heart, Clean, 487.
 Contrite, 487, 496, 553.
 Deceitful, 320, 499, 553.
 Hard, 309.
 New—See *Regeneration*.
 Searched, 151, 209, 483, 487, 501, 545—556.
 Surrendered, 329, 335, 336, 338, 339, 342, 343, 346, 349.
 Vile, 313, 319, 320, 479.
Heathen, Missions to, 617—640.
Heaven, 718—752.
 Anticipated, 187, 260, 315.—See *Heaven*.
 Blessedness of, 431, 720, 723, 727.
 Home, 445, 696, 720, 750, 751.
 Purity of, 725.
 Rest, 436, 511, 720, 726.
 Society of, 444, 447, 718, 724, 737, 752.
 Songs of, 447, 719, 727, 728, 746, 752.
 Worship of, 463, 730.
Heavens, Starry, 81—83, 100, 111.
Heirship of Saints, 436.
Hell, 704.
Heralds of the Gospel, 582.
Hiding Place, 315.
High Priest—See *Priesthood*.
Holiness of God, 49.
 Of Heaven, 725.
 Of Saints, 439, 483, 487.
Holy Scriptures, 167—183, 488, 489, 542.
Holy Spirit, 151—166.
 Absence of, 155.—See *Declensions*.
 Comforter, 163, 164.
 Descent of, 152, 156, 159, 162, 502, 608.
 Earnest of, 495, 548.

Holy Spirit:—
 Enlightening, 151, 153, 155, 158.
 Grieved, 291, 311.
 Influences of, 151—166.
 Inspirer, 154, 159, 162, 164, 167, 174.
 Invoked, 151—166.
 Refining, 370.
 Regenerating, 154, 160.
 Sanctifying, 154, 157—159, 161, 164—166.
 Striving, 286, 291, 311.
 Witness of, 55, 151, 153, 154, 156—158, 166, 495, 548, 556.
Home Missions, 618.
Hope, Aspiration of, 434—452.
 In Affliction, 528, 535, 750.
 In Darkness — See *Spiritual Trouble*.
 In Death, 683—685, 687, 690, 691, 693, 695, 699—701, 705, 721.
 Of Heaven—See *Heaven Anticipated*.
Hosannas, 72, 240, 257, 296.
House of God—See *Sanctuary*.
Household—See *Family*.
Humanity of Christ, 203, 206—212.
Humiliation of Christ, 196, 199, 204, 235, 252, 257.
 Days of, 666—668.
Humility, 479, 597.
Hypocrisy, 546, 550.
Image of God, 479, 481.
Immanuel, 126, 198.
Immortality, 695, 696, 702, 703.
Importunity, 44, 478, 522, 538.
Imputation, 213, 224.
Incarnation of Christ, 190—205.
Inconstancy, 320, 497, 499.
Indwelling Sin, 309, 320, 499, 553.
Infant Baptism, 585—587.
Infinity of God, 81, 96, 98.
Ingratitude, 313, 320.
Inspiration—See *Holy Scriptures*.
Installation, 576, 580, 582, 583.
Institutions of the Church, 363—396, 585—587.
Intercession of Christ, 148, 220, 231, 242, 254, 255, 263, 500.
Invitations of the Gospel, 265—305.
Invocation, 1—64.
Israel, 584.
Jehovah—See *God*.
Jerusalem, New, 355, 729, 733, 740, 742.
Jews, 584.
Joy of the Believer, 241, 297, 352, 411, 743.
Jubilee, 303, 572.
Judgment, the, 328, 331, 708—717.
Justice of God, 93, 99.
Justification, 340, 347, 363.
Kingdom of Christ—See *Royal Priesthood*.
 Prayer for, 557, 563, 570, 626, 640.
 Progress of, 557, 563, 566, 567, 571, 572, 625—627, 6 3, 634, 639.
Labor, Spiritual, 641—650.
Lamb of God—See *Christ*.
Latter Day, 623, 625, 632, 623, 638.
Law of God, 176, 180.

INDEX OF SUBJECTS.

Liberality—See *Charity.*
Life:—
   Brief, 677, 679, 691, 707.
   Frail, 677, 678, 688, 707.
Light of the World—See *Christ.*
Likeness to Christ—See *Conformity.*
Litany, 324.
Longing for Christ, 446, 459, 471, 476.
   For God, 453, 454, 464, 470, 472, 505.
   For Heaven, 431, 434, 443—447, 453, 456, 465, 466, 697.
Long-Suffering—See *Forbearance.*
Looking to Jesus, 473, 515.
Lord's Day, 14—31.
   Evening, 23, 25.
   Morning, 15—22, 24, 26—28, 29—31.
Lord's Prayer, 482.
Lord's Supper, 363—396.
Lord, our Righteousness, 185, 358.
Loss of all Things—See *Renunciation.*
   Of the Soul, 708.—See *Alarm.*
Lost State of Man.—See *Depravity.*
Love of Christ—See *Christ.*
   Of God—See *God.*
   Of Holy Spirit, 163, 548.
   To Christ, 397—419.
   To God, 402, 403, 414.
   To Saints, 6, 594—597.
   To the Church, 599.
Loving-Kindness, 411.
Lukewarmness, 54, 155, 546, 550.
Majesty of Christ, 131—150.
   Of God—See *God.*
Man, Fall of—See *Depravity.*
Marriage, 604, 665.
Martyrs, 435, 718, 719, 724, 752.
Mediation—See *Christ.*
Meditation, 9, 61, 462, 488.
Meekness, 479, 490.
Melchisedec, 401.
Mercy of God—See *God.*
Mercy-seat, 478, 486, 539.
Merits, Human, 347.
Message of the Gospel, 269.
Messiah, 570.
Millennium—See *Latter Day.*
Ministry, 573—584.
   Commission of, 576, 573, 578.
   Convocation of, 574, 581, 582, 584.
   Ordination of, 566, 576, 580, 583.
   Prayer for, 575, 577, 581.
Ministry of Christ, 206—212.
Miracle of Grace, 337.
Miracles of Christ, 207.
Mission of Christ, 190, 191, 272.
Missionaries, 583, 624, 635.
Missions, 617—640.
Morning and Evening, 1—13.
   Lord's Day, 15, 17—20, 21, 22, 24, 26, 27, 29—31.
Mortality—See *Death, Life.*
Mystery of Providence, 533, 534, 544.
Narrow Way, 550.
National, 659, 663.
Nativity of Christ, 190—205.
Nature and Revelation, 82, 169, 170, 179.
   Beauties of, 81, 82, 100.

Nearness to God, 5, 472, 473, 492.
Need of Salvation, 184—189.
New Birth—See *Regeneration.*
New Song, 141, 259.
New Year, 670, 671, 673, 675.
Now, 283, 284, 289, 290, 292, 293, 304.
Obedience, 41, 191, 290, 347, 489, 554.
Offers of Grace, 332—362.
Offices of Christ, 262, 398.
Old Age, 510, 699.
   Year, 674, 676.
Omnipotence—See *God.*
Omnipresence—See *God.*
Omniscience—See *God.*
Oneness with Christ, 449.
Opening of Worship—See *Invocation.*
Ordinances—See *Institutions.*
Ordinations—See *Ministry.*
Original Sin, 185, 186, 188, 608.
Panoply, 641.
Pardon, Found, 332—362.
   Offered, 266—305.
   Sought, 306—331.
Parents—See *Baptism.*
Parting, 36, 37, 46, 64, 371, 600.
Passover, 213.
Pastor, Installation of, 576, 580, 582, 583.
   Welcomed, 579.
Patience—See *Forbearance.*
Peace for the Troubled, 602.
   Of The Christian, 498.
Peace-Makers, 594, 598, 645.
Pearl of Great Price, 360.
Penitence—See *Repentance.*
Pentecost, 162.
Perseverance, 242, 440, 449.
Pilgrim Fathers, 660.
Pilgrimage of Man, 435, 452, 467, 470, 474, 477, 507, 694.
Pity of God—See *God.*
   To the Poor, 645, 646, 649.
Pleading for Mercy, 306—331.
Pleasures, Worldly—See *Renunciation.*
Poor, 645, 646, 649.
Praise to the Father, 76—130.
   To the Son, 131—150.
   To the Spirit, 151—166.
   To the Trinity, 65—75.
Prayer, 356, 460, 461, 477, 478, 481, 484—486, 522, 538, 543.
Prayer, Lord's, 482.
Preaching of the Gospel—See *Ministry.*
Preciousness of Christ—See *Christ.*
Predestination—See *Decrees.*
Priesthood, Royal, of Christ, 241—264.
Prince of Peace—See *Christ.*
Probation, Close of, 677—701.
Procrastination, 293.
Prodigal Son, 351, 357.
Profession, 589—593, 599.
Progress of Christ's Kingdom—See *Kingdom.*
Promised Land, 723, 726, 732, 734, 739, 741, 747, 748, 751.
Promises of God, 175, 181, 441, 510.
Prophet of God, 262, 398.

Providence—See *God.*
Punishment, Future, 292, 708.
Purity, 487, 491, 549.
Purposes of God—See *Decrees.*
Race, Christian, 438, 443.
Ransom, 164, 223, 258.
Reconciliation, 265—362.
Redeeming Love, 297.—See *Love of Christ.*
Redemption—See *Atoning Sacrifice.*
Refuge—See *Christ, God.*
Regeneration, Need of, 185, 188, 332.
   Sought, 151, 152, 165, 185, 487.
   Wrought, 151, 161, 183, 189, 556.
Rejoicing in God—See *Joy.*
Remembrance of Christ—See *Commemoration.*
Renunciation of the World, 336, 338, 342—344, 347, 348, 360, 361, 471.
Repentance, 184, 295, 300, 306, 307, 318, 326, 373, 496.
Resignation, 74, 421, 490, 517, 518, 520, 525, 526—529, 540, 544.
Resolves, 335, 336, 338, 339, 342, 343, 345—349, 354, 360, 361.
Rest for the Weary, 266, 268, 287, 288, 308, 315, 751.
Rest in Heaven, 511, 720, 726.—See *Heaven.*
Resurrection of Christ, 230—240.
Resurrection, the, 702—707.
Retirement—See *Meditation.*
Return to God, 325, 328—330, 494.
Revelation, 167—183.
Revival, 609—616.
Riches, 360.
Righteousness of Christ, 185, 347, 358.
   Robe of, 358.
Robe of Righteousness, 358.
Rock of Ages, 363, 568.
Room for All, 304.
Royal Priesthood of Christ, 241—264.
Sabbath—See *Lord's Day.*
Sabbath School—See *Children, Youth.*
Sacraments, 363—396, 585—587.
Sacrifice, Vicarious—See *Atoning Sacrifice.*
Safety of Believers, 558, 559.
Saint and Sinner, 545.
Saints:—
   Communion of, 465, 594—605.
   Death of—See *Death.*
   Security of, 558, 559.
   Union with Christ, 5, 449.
Salvation, 184—264.
Sanctification—See *Growth, Holy Spirit.*
Sanctuary, 32—64.
   Built, 651—656.
   Corner Stone laid, 651, 652.
   Dedication of, 651, 653—656.
   Loved, 15—17, 20, 28, 32—64, 546, 603.
Satan, 437, 500.
Scriptures—See *Holy Scriptures.*
Searching the Heart, 545—556.
Seasons, 669.
   Autumn, 657, 658, 662.

INDEX OF SUBJECTS.

Seasons:—
  Spring, 669, 672.
Second Birth—See *Regeneration*.
Security of Saints, 558, 559.
Seed-time and Harvest—See *Seasons*.
Self-Deception, 320, 499, 555.
  Dedication—See *Consecration*.
  Denial, 347, 348, 354, 536, 550.
  Examination, 545—556.
  Renunciation — See *Consecration*.
  Righteousness, 227, 347.
Shepherd—See *Christ, God*.
Showers of Grace, 321.
Sickness, 528.
Sin, Indwelling, 309, 320, 499, 555.
  Original, 185, 186, 188, 608.
Sincerity, 54, 556.
Sleep, 4, 5.
Soldier—See *Warfare*.
Son of God, 131—150.
Song, New, 141, 259.
Sorrow for Sin—See *Repentance*.
  For Trouble—See *Afflictions*.
Sovereignty of God—See *God*.
Special Occasions, 651—676.
Spirit of God—See *Holy Spirit*.
Spiritual Trouble, 492—506.
Spring, 669, 672.
Star of the East, 201, 205, 617.
Starry Heavens, 81—83, 100, 111.
Steadfastness, 437, 629.
Strength as our Days, 514, 530.
Submission—See *Resignation*.
Sufferings of Christ—See *Christ*.
Sun of Righteousness—See *Christ*.

Sunday Schools — See *Children, Youth*.
Supper, Lord's, 363—396.
Supremacy of God, 74, 76, 95, 98, 421.
Surety, 440.
Surrender, 329, 335, 336, 338, 339, 342, 343, 346, 349.
Sympathy—See *Christ, Pity*.
Table, Lord's, 363—396.
Teacher, the Great, 208, 210.
Te Deum, 65, 106.
Temperance, 439, 550, 664.
Temptation, 441, 442.
Tempter, 437, 500.
Thanksgiving, Days of, 657—659.
Throne of Grace, 481, 525.
Time—See *Death, Life, Year*.
To-Day, 283, 284, 289, 290, 292, 293, 304.
Tribulation, 492—544.
Trinity, 65—75.
Trust in Christ, 420, 423, 425, 427, 433.
  In God, 422, 430, 433, 451, 503, 523.
Truth of God—See *God*.
Trumpet, Gospel, 277, 303, 622.
  Judgment, 711—713
Unbelief—See *Alarm*.
Union of Saints with Christ, 5, 449.
  With each other, 594—605.
Unsearchableness of God, 80, 534, 544.
Vanity of Life—See *Life*.
  Of the World—See *Renunciation*.

Victory of Believers—See *Warfare*.
  Of Christ—See *Christ, a Conqueror*.
Vision of Dry Bones, 608.
Vows to God, 588, 589, 591—593, 599.
Waiting on God, 514.
Walking with God, 492.
Wanderings—See *Backsliding*.
Warfare, Christian, 437, 504, 513, 536, 618, 629, 641.
Warnings, 270, 290—292.
Watchfulness, 480, 504, 538, 584.
Watchmen, 573, 582, 617.
Waters of Life—See *Fountain*.
Way of Salvation—See *Salvation*.
Way to Zion, 276.
Way, Truth, and Life, 212, 349.
Weary, Rest for the, 266, 268, 287, 288, 308, 315, 751.
  Welcome to the, 265—268, 287, 301.
Wealth, Use of—See *Contributions*.
Witness—See *Holy Spirit*.
Word of God—See *Holy Scriptures*.
Working and Giving, 641—6.0.
World Renounced—See *Renunciation*.
Worship, Family, 504, 601, 604.
  Public—See *Lord's Day, Sanctuary*.
Year, and its Seasons, 669—676.
  Of Jubilee, 303, 572.
Yoke of Christ, 268, 287.
Youth, 176, 273, 585—587.
Zeal, 435, 437, 443, 480, 536, 646.
Zion, 204, 542, 569, 569, 571.

INDEX OF SCRIPTURE TEXTS.

GENESIS.
1 : 2 160
5 : 24 492
6 : 3 291
19 : 17 305
28 : 10—22 472
32 : 26 478

EXODUS.
25 : 22 539

DEUTERONOMY.
3 : 25 726
33 : 25 514
34 : 1 723

RUTH.
1 : 16 599

1st SAMUEL.
7 : 12 .... 365, 671

1st CHRONICLES.
29 : 10—13 127

2d CHRONICLES.
15 : 15 589

ESTHER.
4 : 16 281

JOB.
1 : 21 527
7 : 16 697
14 : 10 724
14 : 14 694
20 : 2 493

PSALMS.
1 545
5 49
8 121
14 630
15 549
17 702
18 95
19 .... 82, 169, 170
21 179
23 .... 428, 468
24 236
25 505
26 546
27 .... 51, 532
31 423
32 340
33 93
34 108
39 691
41 649
42 434
43 33
45 .... 206, 620
46 .... 251, 542
47 .... 238, 239
48 561
50 709
51 ..... 184, 306, 307, 317
55 422
60 668
63 53
66 112
67 633
68 237
72 ..... 563, 564, 566, 570
73 457
80 607
84 ...... 32, 58, 59, 465
85 606
88 .... 292, 703
89 .... 109, 177
90 .... 494, 688
92 26
93 57
95 .... 41, 101, 290
98 190
100 .... 76, 77, 79
102 614
103 .... 85, 89, 519
107 658
111 103
116 591
117 .... 63, 562
118 .... 147, 559
119 .... 176, 488, 489
122 .... 21, 48, 56
125 430
126 615
132 50
133 601
134 73
135 107
136 124
137 560
138 68
139 .... 547, 551, 552
141 6
145 ..... 80, 102, 104, 116
146 94
148 .. 78, 91, 122, 123, 125
150 .... 128, 129

PROVERBS.
8 : 17 273
11 : 24 650

ECCLESIASTES.
9 : 4—6, 10 686
12 : 7 692

CANTICLES.
1 : 7 380
2 : 4 367
2 : 16 403
3 : 2 382
4 : 16 612
5 : 10—16 256

ISAIAH.
7 : 14 419
9 : 6 195
12 : 4 96
33 : 17 750
35 : 8—10 467
40 : 9 112
40 : 28, 31 438
42 : 16 473
45 : 22 515
51 : 3 204
51 : 9 625
52 : 1, 2 565
52 : 7 582
53 : 4—6 226
55 : 1 ..... 265, 277, 295
60 : 1, 2 629
60 : 18 613
60 : 20 719
61 : 1—3 191
61 : 10 358
62 : 6, 7 622

JEREMIAH.
3 : 22 313
31 : 3 388
50 : 5 276

LAMENTATIONS.
3 : 23 4

EZEKIEL.
11 : 19 309
33 : 11 .... 298, 524
36 : 37 152
38 : 3 608

DANIEL.
2 : 44 558

HOSEA.
6 : 3 43
11 : 8 325
14 : 1 314

HABBAKKUK.
3 : 2 640

ZECHARIAH.
9 : 12 187
13 : 1 221

MATTHEW.
1 : 21 397
2 : 9, 10 205
6 : 9—13 482
5 : 10 540
7 : 7 477
10 : 40—42 590
11 : 28 .. 208, 268, 287, 288, 315
12 : 20 211
13 : 17 596

17 : 4, 8 .... 385, 409	4 : 24 553	**GALATIANS.**	**HEBREWS.**
19 : 14 587	6 : 51 442	4 : 6 27	1 : 3 143
21 : 22 484	6 : 68 .... 404, 425	5 : 22 556	1 : 6 146
25 : 6 743	11 : 25 608	5 : 24 498	4 : 9 .... 28, 751
25 : 13 584	13 : 9 396	6 : 14 .... 227, 228, 245, 369	4 : 14—16 ...... 211, 255
25 : 34 .... 711, 712	14 : 2 745		4 : 16 481
25 : 40 646	14 : 6 212	**EPHESIANS.**	6 : 17—19 441
25 : 41 708	14 : 19 427	1 : 13, 14 495	7 : 22 242
25 : 46 328	14 : 26 548	2 : 5 372	11 : 13 435
25 : 36—46 216	19 : 30 .... 215, 229	2 : 8 .... 352, 353, 372	11 : 14 742
25 : 41 504	21 : 17 417	3 : 15 595	12 : 1, 2 443
27 : 46 222		3 : 16 60	13 : 5 510
27 : 50—53 223	**ACTS.**	4 : 8 240	13 : 17 573
28 : 20 578	4 : 32 604	4 : 11, 12 576	13 : 20 46
	10 : 44 55	4 : 15 596	
MARK.	16 : 9 631	4 : 30—32 605	**1st PETER.**
8 : 38 408	17 : 24, 25 119	6 : 13 .... 629, 641	1 : 8 450
10 : 14 587	26 : 22 670	6 : 14 437	2 : 7 .... 397, 398, 406
13 : 37 480			3 : 7 485
14 : 24 374	**ROMANS.**	**PHILIPPIANS.**	5 : 7 .... 512, 521
14 : 36 517	1 : 16 186	1 : 21, 22 ...... 376, 466	
16 : 15 578	5 : 8 142	1 : 23 .... 446, 736	**2d PETER.**
	5 : 12 145	2 : 6 131	1 : 10 436
LUKE.	6 : 3 389	3 : 7—10 347	3 : 10 716
1 : 78 201	8 : 8 188	3 : 12—14 443	
2 : 8—14 .... 194, 196, 197, 202	8 : 14—16 495	4 : 4 241	**1st JOHN.**
2 : 32 636	12 : 5 600	4 : 13 424	3 : 1—3 448
4 : 18, 19 ...... 191, 308	13 : 11 ...... 451, 674, 749		4 : 8 118
9 : 23 .... 3, 336, 434, 550		**1st THESSALONIANS.**	4 : 19 .... 418, 516
10 : 30—37 647	**1st CORINTHIANS.**	4 : 14 689	4 : 21 594
10 : 38—42 9	1 : 22—24 254	4 : 17 696	
10 : 39 410	1 : 30 260		**REVELATION.**
10 : 42 407	2 : 2 .... 471, 575	**2d THESSALONIANS.**	1 : 18 132
11 : 13 621	2 : 9, 10 ...... 725, 736	1 : 7 715	3 : 11 524
12 : 35—38 584	2 : 16 479		3 : 20 280
14 : 16—23 388	3 : 6 575	**1st TIMOTHY.**	5 : 6—10 137
15 : 7, 10 ...... 351, 357	3 : 21—23 531	1 : 15 296	5 : 9 737
15 : 18 295	5 : 7 213	6 : 12 513	5 : 12 .... 133, 149, 150, 141
18 : 1 522	6 : 17 449		7 : 9 444
18 : 13 310	6 : 20 354	**2d TIMOTHY.**	7 : 13 .... 718, 724
19 : 41 373	11 : 24, 25 393	1 : 12 355	11 : 15 .... 572, 626
22 : 19 379	11 : 23—26 379		14 : 13 .... 600, 721
23 : 42 .... 316, 530	12 : 13 602	**TITUS.**	15 : 3, 4 259
24 : 29 .... 23, 699	15 : 55 685	2 : 10—13 439	19 : 12 .... 213, 247
24 : 34 233			21 : 2 733
	2d CORINTHIANS.		21 : 1—4 557
JOHN.	1 : 22 .... 166, 495		21 : 10 .... 729, 741
1 : 12, 13 189	2 : 15 575		21 : 23 463
1 : 29 346	4 : 18 431		21 : 27 725
3 : 3 .... 188, 189, 332	5 : 8 705		
3 : 17 .... 272, 296	6 : 2 283		

ALPHABETICAL INDEX OF TUNES.

|| Copyright tunes.

NAME.	METRE.	AUTHOR OR SOURCE.	PAGE.
ABRIDGE	C. M.	Isaac Smith, 1770. Har., Edward J. Hopkins, 1868	236
Agatha	6s, 8 lines	From Carl Maria Von Weber, 1820	185
(Ahira)	S. M.	(See "Leighton.")	186
Aletta	7s, 4 or 6 lines	William B. Bradbury, 1856	117
Alfreton	L. M.	William Beastall	231
All Saints	L. M.	William Knapp, 1760	250
America	6s & 4s	Henry Carey, obit, 1743	235
Amsterdam	7, 6, P.	James Nares, 1780	168
Angels	L. M.	Orlando Gibbons, 1623. Har., Wm. Henry Monk, 1861	34
Antioch	C. M.	From George Frederick Handel, 1684-1759. Adapted by Lowell Mason, 1836.	70
Anvern	L. M.	German. Adapted by Lowell Mason, 1840	207
Appleton	L. M.	From a Chant, by William Boyce, 1710-1779	195
Arcadia	C. M.	Thomas Hastings, 1839	100
Ariel	C. P. M.	Lowell Mason, 1836	145
Arlington	C. M.	From "Artaxerxes." Thomas A. Arne, 1762. Arr.	198
Armenia	C. M.	Sylvanus B. Pond, 1835	112
Arnheim	L. M.	Samuel Holyoke, 1785. Altered	76
||Auburn	C. M.	H. I——, 1846	230
Austria	8s & 7s, 6 or 8 l.	"Gott erhalte Franz den Kaiser." Francis Joseph Haydn, 1797	203
Autumn	8s & 7s, 8 lines	Spanish melody	121
Avon	C. M.	Hugh Wilson, 17—	252
Aznion	C. M.	Carl Gotthelf Gläser, 1828. Arr., Lowell Mason, 1839	42
BALERMA	C. M.	Spanish melody, 16th Century. Ad. by R. Simpson	58
Bangor	C. M.	Old Welsh melody. William Tansur's Coll., 1735	242
Barby	C. M.	William Tansur, 1735	190
Bartimeus	8s & 7s 4, or 6 l.	Daniel Read, 1804	120
Bavaria	8s & 7s, 4, 6, or 8 l.	German melody. "Plymouth Coll." 1855	78
Belmont	8s, 7s, & 4	Anon., 1830	96
Bemerton	C. M.	Henry W. Greatorex, 1849	52, 205
Benevento	7s, 8 lines	Samuel Webbe, cir. 1770	240
Bera	L. M.	John E. Gould, 1851	104
Bethany	6s & 4's	Lowell Mason. "Sabbath H. and T. Book," 1859	169
Bethesda	H. M.	Maurice Greene, obit, 1755	130
Bethlehem	C. M.	Spencer Madan, obit, 1813	129
Beulah	7s, 8 lines	Elam Ives, Jr., 1846	255
Blendon	L. M.	Felice Giardini, cir. 1760	146
Bonar	S. M., 8 lines	Lowell Mason, 1858	247
Boylston	S. M.	Lowell Mason, 1832	82, 217
Braden	C. M.	William B. Bradbury, 1844	148
(Bradford)	C. M.	(See "Messiah.")	139
Brattle Street	C. M., 8 lines	Ignace Pleyel, 1757-1831	189
(Bray)	S. M.	(See "St. George.")	199
Brewer	L. M.	English melody	238
Broomsgrove	C. M.	Thomas Williams' Coll., 1768	226
Brown	C. M.	William B. Bradbury, 1840	175
Byefield	C. M.	Thomas Hastings, 1840	174

ALPHABETICAL INDEX OF TUNES.

NAME.	METRE.	AUTHOR OR SOURCE.	PAGE.
CAMBRIDGE	C. M.	John Randall, 1790	40, 98
Captivity	L. M.	William B. Bradbury, 1847	216
(Chelmsford)	C. M.	See ("Melody.")	211
Chester	C. M.	Thomas Hastings, 1828	141
Chesterfield	C. M.	Thomas Haweis, cir. 1792	138
Chimes	C. M.	Lowell Mason 1840	233
China	C. M.	Timothy Swan, 1800	251
‖Christine	7s & 6s, 8 lines	S. P. W——, 1872	264
Christmas	C. M.	From George Frederick Handel, 1685-1759	71, 158
Clarendon	C. M.	Isaac Tucker, 1800	45
Colchester	C. M.	Aaron Williams' Coll., cir. 1760	21, 209
Conway	C. M.	English melody	91
Coronation	C. M.	Oliver Holden, 1793	90
Coventry	C. M.	English melody	80
Cowper	C. M.	Lowell Mason, 1830	81
DALSTON	S. P. M.	Aaron Williams, 1760	24
Darwell	H. M.	John Darwell, cir. 7750	88
Dedham	C. M.	William Gardiner, 1830	59
(Denfield)	C. M.	(See "Azmon.")	42
Dennis	S. M.	From Hans G. Nageli, 1773-1836. Adapted by Lowell Mason, 1849	160, 187
Detroit	S. M.	Eurotas P. Hastings, 1846	134
Devizes	C. M.	Isaac Tucker, 1800	65
Dover	S. M.	English melody	94
Downs	C. M.	Lowell Mason, 1832	192
Duke Street	L. M.	J. Hatton or William Reeve, cir. 1790	6
Dunbar	S. M.	E—— W. Dunbar, 1854. ("Sacred Melodies.")	265
Dundee	C. M.	Scotch Psalter (Andro Hart, Edinburgh, Printer), 1615	39, 177
(Dundee)	C. M.	(See "Windsor.")	114
(ELIM)	C. M.	(See "Geer.")	142
Ellenthorpe	L. M.	Francis Linley, cir. 1790	67
Eltham	7s, 8 lines	Lowell Mason, 1840	204
Ernan	L. M.	Lowell Mason, 1850	124
Evan	C. M.	Celtic melody, Arr., William Henry Havergal, 1849	69
Evening Hymn	L. M.	Thomas Tallis, Parker's Psalter, 1567. Abridged and altered	165
Even me	8, 7, 8, 7, 6, 7; or 8s & 7s, 6 lines	William B Bradbury, 1862. ("Golden Shower.")	115
Ewing	7s & 6s, 8 lines	Alexander Ewing, 1860	263
FEDERAL STREET	L. M.	Henry K. Oliver, 1832	57
(Florence)	C. M.	(See "Valentia.")	127
(Forest)	L. M.	(See "Rockbridge.")	68
(Fountain)	C. M.	(See "Cowper.")	81
Frederick	11s	George Kingsley, 1838. ("Sacred Choir.")	248
(French)	C. M.	(See "Dundee.")	39, 177
GANGES	C. P. M.	Old melody	119
Geer	C. M.	Henry W. Greatorex (Root and Sweetser's Coll.), 1849	142
Geneva	C. M.	John Cole, 1805	43
Germany	L. M.	From Ludwig van Beethoven, 1770-1827	179
Gethsemane	7s, 6 lines	Richard Redhead, 1853	79
Glasgow	C. M.	George F. Root (Root and Sweetser's Coll.), 1849	99
Golden Hill	S. M.	Aaron Chapin, cir. 1823	102
(Goodwin)	7s & 6s, 8 lines	(See "Webb.")	202
‖Gould	11s & 10s	S. P. W——, 1871	75
Gratitude	L. M.	Ami Bost (of Switzerland). Ad. by Thomas Hastings, 1837	157
Greenville	8s, 7s, & 4	Jean Jacques Rousseau, 1712-1778	181, 218
HADDAM	H. M.	English melody. Arr. Lowell Mason, 1822	29
Halle	7s	Francis Joseph Haydn, 1732-1809. Ad. by Hastings ("Church Melodies")	28
Hamburg	L. M.	First Gregorian Tone. Ad. by Lowell Mason, 1825	83, 196
Harwell	8, 7, 8, 7, 7, 7; or 8s & 7s, 6 or 8 l.	Lowell Mason, 1840	55
Harwich	H. M.	"Nun danket alle Gott" Johann Critger, 1649. Ad. by Lowell Mason, 1822	47
Heath	C. M.	Lowell Mason, 1835	162
Heber	C. M.	George Kingsley, 1838	77
Hebron	L. M.	Lowell Mason, 1830	135, 210
Hendon	7s	Cæsar Malan, 1830	20

ALPHABETICAL INDEX OF TUNES.

NAME.	METRE.	AUTHOR OR SOURCE.	PAGE.
Henry	C. M.	Sylvanus B. Pond, 1835	38
Holley	7s.	George Hews ("Handel and Haydn Coll."), 1835	9, 213
Hollingside	7s, 8 lines.	John B. Dykes ("Hymns Ancient and Modern"), 1861	116
Hope	6s & 4s. P	Theodore E. Perkins, 1858	123
Horton	7s.	From Xavier Schnyder von Wartensee, 1786 *	183
Hotham	7s, 8 lines	Martin Madan, 1776 *	150
Howard	C. M.	Mrs. Cuthbert *	41
Hummel	C. M.	Charles Zeuner ("American Harp"), 1832	239
Hursley	L. M.	From Francis Joseph Haydn. Arr., William Henry Monk, 1861.	7
ILLINOIS	L. M.	Jonathan Spilman *	126
Inverness	S. M.	Lowell Mason, 1835	122
(Iowa)	S. M.	(See "Kentucky.")	172
Irish	C. M.	Isaac Smith, cir. 1760 *	197
Italy	6s & 4s	Felice Giardini, 1760	30
(Ives)	7s, 8 lines	(See "Beulah.")	255
JORDAN	C. M., 8 lines	William Billings, 1781. Arr., S. P. W. *	258
(Judgment)	L. M.	(See "Monmouth.")	254
KENTUCKY	S. M.	Aaron Chapin "Methodist Harmonist," N. Y., 1822.)	172
LABAN	S. M.	Lowell Mason, 1830	18
Land of Rest	C. M.	William B. Bradbury, 1863	260
Lanesboro'	C. M.	English melody	23
Leighton	S. M.	Henry W. Greatorex (Root and Sweetser's Coll.), 1849	186
Lenox	H. M.	J. Edson, 1782.	108
Lisbon	S. M.	Daniel Read, 1785.	10
Lischer	H. M.	German Volkslied. Arr., Lowell Mason, 1841	16
Loudon, New	C. M.	Scotch Psalter, Edinburgh, 1615 *	241
Louvan	L. M.	Virgil Corydon Taylor ("Taylor's Sacred Minstrel"), 1847	95
Loving-Kindness	L. M.	Western melody	147
Luther	S. M.	Thomas Hastings, 1835	208
Luton	L. M.	Aaron Williams' Coll., 1760	25
MADISON	8s, 8 lines	Sylvanus B. Pond, 1841	159
Maitland	C. M.	—— Allen. Western melody	155
Mannheim	8s & 7s	From Ludwig van Beethoven, 1770-1827 *	48
Manoah	C. M.	Giacomo Rossini, 1792-1868. Adapted	113
Marlow	C. M.	English melody. Arr., Lowell Mason, 1832	12
Marriott	6s & 4s	Joseph Barnby, 1867	62
Martyn	7s, 8 lines	S. B. Marsh, 1836. ("Musical Miscellany.")	106
(Martyrdom)	C. M.	(See "Avon.")	252
Martyrs	C. M.	Scotch melody, 1611 *	237
Mear	C. M.	Welsh Air. Aaron Williams' Coll., cir. 1760	22
Medfield	C. M.	William Mather, 1790	64, 153
Melody	C. M.	Aaron Chapin, ("N. Y. Selection of Sacred Music," 1823.)	211
Mendebras	7s & 6s, 8 lines	German Volkslied. Ad. by Lowell Mason ("Modern Psalmist"), 1839	15
Mendon	L. M.	German. Arr. by Lowell Mason ("Sacred Harmony"), 1832	26
Meribah	C. P. M.	Lowell Mason, 1839	118
Messiah	7s, 8 lines	Adapted by George Kingsley, 1838	84
Messiah	C. M.	Geo. Frederick Händel, 1741. Ad. from "The Messiah."	139
(Micah)	C. M.	(See "Bemerton.")	52, 205
Migdol	L. M.	Lowell Mason, 1840	156
Missionary Chant	L. M.	Charles Zeuner, 1832	223
Missionary Hymn	7s & 6s, 8 lines	Lowell Mason, 1824	225
Monmouth	L. M.	"Esist gewisslich." Joseph Klug's Gesangbuch, 1535 *	254
Monson	C. M.	Samuel R. Brown. Arr., Thomas Hastings, 1836	143
Moravian	C. M., 8 lines	German melody ("N. Y. Choralist," 1871.) *	128
Morning Star	7s, 8 lines	Lowell Mason, 1830	220
Mount Auburn	C. M.	George Kingsley, 1838	243
Mount Calvary	7s, 6 lines	Johann Rosenmüller, 1655. Adapted	107
Mozart	7s.	J. C. Wolfgang A. Mozart, 1756-91. Adapted	73
NAOMI	C. M.	Lowell Mason, 1836	188
(Nayland)	C. M.	(See "Stephens.")	154
Nearer Home	6s	John M. Evans, 1860	267
Nettleton	8s & 7s, 6 or 8 l.	Asahel Nettleton, 1825 *	132
Newcourt	L. P. M.	Hugh Bond, 1790. Altered	37
New Haven	6s & 4s	Thomas Hastings, 1833	56

NAME.	METRE.	AUTHOR OR SOURCE.	PAGE.
Nicaea	11, 12, 12, 10	John B. Dykes, 1861	5
Normanton	C. M.	"Christus der ist mein Leben." *Melchior Vulpius*, 1609. Har., Ludwig Erk, 1863	191
Nuremberg	7s, 6 lines	"Liebster Jesu wur sind hier." *Johann Rudolf Ahle*, 1664. Altered *	234
OAKSVILLE	C. M.	*Charles Zeuner*, 1839	53
Old Hundredth	L. M.	*Guillaume Franc*, 1543. (Marot and Beza's Psalter), *	31
Oliphant	8s, 7s, & 4	*Lowell Mason*, 1832*	170
Olivet	6s & 4s.	*Lowell Mason*, 1831 *	184
Olmutz	S. M.	Eighth Gregorian Tone. Ad., *Lowell Mason*, 1832	60
Olney	S. M.	*Lowell Mason*, 1830	180
Orland	L. M.	*William Arnold*, 1768–1832 *	206
Ortonville	C. M.	*Thomas Hastings*, 1837	93
Osgood	8s, 7s, & 4	Arr. from *Peter Ritter*, 1790 *	253
Otto	8s & 7s, 8 lines	*Henry K. Oliver*, 1840 *	249
PARADISE	7s & 6s, 8 lines	*Frederick A Weber* *	262
Park Street	L. M.	*Frederick M. A Venua*, cir. 1810	86
Peterboro'	C. M.	*Ralph Harrison*, 1786 *	8
(Phuvah)	C. M.	(See "Normanton.")	191
Pilesgrove	L. M.	*Nahum Mitchell*, 1812 *	201
Pleyel	7s	*Ignace Pleyel*, 1757–1831	61
Portugal	L. M.	*Thomas Thorley*, 17—	14, 232
Portuguese Hymn	11s	*John Reading*, 1760	182
QUITO	L. M.	*William Horsley*, 1774–1858 *	152
RAPTURE	C. P. M.	*Edward Harwood*, 1707–1787 *	36
Rathbun	8s & 7s	*Ithamar Conkey*, 1851	133
Rest	L. M.	*William h. Bradbury*, 1844	245
Rest for the weary	8s & 7s, with Chor.	*J. W. Dadmun*. "Revival Melodies," 1860	268
Retreat	L. M.	*Thomas Hastings*, 1822	193
Rthue	H. M.	*Thomas Hastings*, 1836 *	221
Rhine, New	C. M.	German melody *	259
Rochester	C. M.	*Aaron Williams'* Coll., cir. 1760 *	163
Rockbridge	L. M.	*Aaron Chapin*. "Methodist Harmonist," N. Y., 1822 *	68
Rockingham	L. M.	*Lowell Mason*, 1830	105
Rock of Ages	7s, 6 lines	*Thomas Hastings*, 1830	131
Rolland	L. M.	*William B. Bradbury*, 1844	137
Rosefield	7s, 4 or 6 lines	*Cæsar Malan*, 1830	89
Rothwell	L. M.	*William Tansur*, cir. 1743	50
Russia	8s & 7s, 8 lines	*Dimitri S. Bortnansky*, 1751–1825. Ad. by *Lowell Mason*	74
SABBATH	7s, 6 or 8 lines	*Lowell Mason*, 1834	11
St. Ann's	C. M.	*William Croft*, 1712	13
St. George	C. M.	"Lobt Gott, ihr Christen." *Nicolaus Hermann*, 1544. Altered *	199
St. John's	C. M.	English melody. *Aaron Williams'* Coll., cir. 1760 *	44
St. Martin's	C. M.	*William Tansur*, 1735 *	87
St. Thomas	C. M.	*William Tansur*, 1708	46, 214
Saul	L. M., 6 lines	*George Frederick Handel*, 1740. Ad. from "Saul."	246
Scotland	12s	*John Clarke (Whitfield)*, cir. 1800	109
Seasons	L. M.	*Ignace Pleyel*, 1757–1831 *	173
Seymour	7s	From *Carl Maria von Weber*, 1825 *	171
Shining Shore	8s & 7s, Tro., 8 l.	*George F. Root*, 1859	266
Shirland	S. M.	*Samuel Stanley*, 1800 *	200
Shoel	L. M.	*Thomas Shoel*, 1810 *	178
Sicily	8s, 7s, & 4	"O Sanctissima." Sicilian melody *	17
Silver Street	S. M.	*Isaac Smith*, 1770	19
Solitude	7s	*L. T. Downes* (Greatorex Coll., 1851)	167
Spanish Hymn	7s, 6 or 8 lines	Spanish melody *	166
State Street	S. M.	*Jonathan C. Woodman*, 1844	229
Stephens	C. M.	*William Jones*, obit, 1799. ("Psalmo Doxologia," 1822.)	154
Stillingfleet	S. M.	Swiss Collection	151
Stirling	L. M.	*Ralph Harrison*, 1786	27
Stonefield	L. M.	*Samuel Stanley*, 1810	32, 66
Stow	H. M.	English melody. Ad., *Lowell Mason*, 1832	85
Sunderland	C. M.	*E. M. Whitaker*, 1872 *	176
Supplication	L. M.	From *W. A. Mozart*, 1756–1791 *	111
Surrey	L. M.	— *Costello*, cir. 1810 *	222
Swanwick	C. M.	*J. Lucas*, 17—	140
Sweet Hour	L. M., 8 lines	*William B. Bradbury*, 1861	164

ALPHABETICAL INDEX OF TUNES.

NAME.	METRE.	AUTHOR OR SOURCE.	PAGE.
Tamworth	8s, 7s, & 4	Scotch melody. Ad. by *Charles Lockhart*, 1790	227
Tappan	C. M.	*George Kingsley*, 1838	256
Telemann	7s	*Charles Zeuner*. 1832	49
Thatcher	S. M.	*George Frederick Handel.* Adapted from "Sosarme," 1732...63.	161
Tucodora	7s	*George Frederick Handel* (from "Theodora,"), 1749	149
(Toplady)	7s, 6 lines	(See "Rock of Ages.")	131
Tranquillity	L. M.	—— *Marson*. English melody	261
Truro	L. M.	*Charles Burney*, cir. 1760 ("*Lock.*" Coll.)	51
Uxbridge	L. M.	*Lowell Mason*, 1830	25
Valentia	C. M.	*Maximilian Eberwein*, 1775–1831. Arr. *George Kingsley*, 1853.	127
Varina	C. M., 8 lines	*Christian Heinrich Rink*, 1770–1846. Arr., *George F. Root*, 1849.	237
(Vesper Hymn)	8s & 7s, 8 lines	(See "Russia.")	74
(Visitation)	8s, 7s, & 4	(See "Belmont.")	96
Waud	L. M.	Scotch melody. Arr., *Lowell Mason*, 1830	194
Ware	C. M.	*George Kingsley*, 1838	215
(Wareham)	L. M.	(See "All Saints.")	250
Warsaw	H. M.	*Thomas Clark*, 1804	72
Warwick	C. M.	*Samuel Stanley*, cir. 1810	92
Watchman	S. M.	*James Leach*, 1789	228
Webb	7s & 6s, 8 lines	*George James Webb* (from the "Odeon "), 1837	202
Wells	L. M.	German: before 1740. *Aaron Williams'* Coll., cir. 1760	244
Welti	L. M.	*Cæsar Malan*, 1830	33
Wilmot	8s & 7s	*Carl Maria von Weber*, 1786–1826. Adapted	54
Windham	L. M.	*Daniel Read*, 1785	136
Windsor	C. M.	*George Kirby.* (*Este's* Psalter, 1592.)	114
Woodland	C. M.	*Nathaniel D. Gould*, 1832	101
Woodstock	C. M.	*Deodatus Dutton, Jr.*, 1829	212
Woodworth	L. M.	*William B. Bradbury*, 1849	125
Yarmouth	7s & 6s, 8 lines	*Lowell Mason*, 1835	224
Yoakley	L. M.	*William Yoakley*	110
York	C. M.	Scotch Psalter, Edinburgh, 1615	144
Zephyr	L. M.	*William B. Bradbury*, 1844	103
Zerah	C. M.	*Lowell Mason*, 1837	219
Zion	8s, 7s, & 4	*Thomas Hastings*, 1830	97

METRICAL INDEX OF TUNES.

COMMON METRE.

IAMBIC 8, 6 8, 6.

	Page.		Page.		Page.		Page.
Abridge	236	Bemerton	52, 205	Christmas	71, 158	Evan	69
Antioch	70	Bethlehem	129	Clarendon	45	(Florence)	127
Arcadia	100	(Bradford)	139	Colchester	21, 209	(Fountain)	81
Arlington	112	Brattle Street, 8 lines	189	Conway	91	(French)	39, 177
Armenia	76	(Bray)	190	Coronation	90	Geer	142
Auburn	230	Broomsgrove	226	Coventry	80	Geneva	43
Avon	252	Brown	175	Cowper	81	Glasgow	99
Azmon	42	Byefield	174	Dedham	59	Heath	162
Balerma	58	Cambridge	40, 98	(Denfield)	42	Heber	77
Bangor	242	(Chelmsford)	211	Devizes	65	Henry	38
Barby	190	Chester	141	Downs	192	Howard	41
		Chesterfield	138	Dundee	39, 177	Hummel	239
		Chimes	213	(Dundee)	114	Irish	197
		China	251	(Elim)	142	Jordan, 8 lines	258

METRICAL INDEX OF TUNES.

	Page.
Land of Rest	260
Lanesboro'	23
London, New	241
Maitland	155
Manoah	113
Marlow	12
(Martyrdom)	252
Martyrs	237
Mear	22
Medfield	64, 153
Melody	211
Messiah	139
(Micah)	52, 205
Monson	143
Moravian, 8 lines	128
Mount Auburn	243
Naomi	2, 188
(Nayland)	154
Normanton	191
Oaksville	53
Ortouville	93
Peterboro'	8
(Pluvah)	191
Rhine, New	259
Rochester	163
Saint Ann's	13
Saint George	199
Saint John's	44
Saint Martin's	87
Stephens	154
Sunderland	176
Swanwick	140
Tappan	256
Valentia	127
Varina, 8 lines	257
Warwick	92
Windsor	114
Woodland	101
Woodstock	212
York	144
Zerah	219

LONG METRE.

IAMBIC, 8, 8, 8, 8.

	Page.
Alfreton	231
All Saints	250
Angels	34
Anvern	207
Appleton	195
Arnheim	76
Bera	104
Blendon	146
Brewer	238
Captivity	216
Duke Street	6
Ellenthorpe	67
Eman	124
Evening Hymn	165
Federal Street	57
(Forest)	68
Germany	179
Gratitude	157
Hamburg	83, 196
Hebron	135, 210
Hursley	7
Illinois	126
(Judgment)	254
Louvan	95

	Page.
Loving-Kindness	147
Luton	35
Mendon	26
Migdol	156
Missionary Chant	223
Monmouth	254
Old Hundredth	31
Orland	206
Park Street	86
Pilesgrove	201
Portugal	14, 232
Quito	152
Rest	245
Retreat	193
Rockbridge	68
Rockingham	105
Rolland	137
Rothwell	50
Saul, 6 lines	246
Seasons	173
Shoel	178
Stirling	27
Stonefield	32, 66
Supplication	111
Surrey	222
Sweet Hour, 8 lines	164
Tranquillity	261
Truro	51
Uxbridge	25
Ward	194
Ware	215
(Wareham)	250
Wells	244
Welton	33
Windham	136
Woodworth	212
Yoakley	110
Zephyr	103

SHORT METRE.

IAMBIC, 6, 6, 8, 6.

	Page.
Bonar, 8 lines	247
Boylston	82, 217
Braden	148
Dennis	160, 187
Detroit	134
Dover	94
Dunbar	265
Golden Hill	102
Inverness	122
(Iowa)	172
Kentucky	172
Laban	18
Leighton	186
Lisbon	10
Luther	208
Olmutz	60
Olney	180
Saint Thomas	46, 214
Shirland	200
Silver Street	19
State Street	229
Stillingfleet	151
Thatcher	63, 161
Watchman	228

LONG PARTICULAR METRE.

IAMBIC, 8, 8, 8; 8, 8, 8.

	Page.
Newcourt	37

COMMON PARTICULAR METRE.

IAMBIC, 8, 8, 6; 8, 8, 6.

	Page.
Ariel	145
Ganges	119
Meribah	118
Rapture	36

SHORT PARTICULAR METRE.

IAMBIC, 6, 6, 8; 6, 6, 8.

	Page.
Dalston	24

HALLELUJAH METRE.

IAMBIC, 6, 6, 6, 6, 8, 8.

	Page.
Bethesda	130
Darwell	88
Haddam	29
Harwich	47
Lenox	108
Lischer	16
Rhine	221
Stow	85
Warsaw	72

SIXES.

IAMBIC, 6, 6, 6, 6.

	Page.
Agatha, 8 lines	185
Nearer Home	267

SIXES AND FOURS.

IAMBIC, 6, 6, 4, 6, 6, 6, 4.

	Page.
America	235
Italy	30
Marriott	62
New Haven	56
Olivet	184

IAMBIC, 6, 4, 6, 4, 6, 6, 4.

	Page.
Bethany	169

6, 4, 6, 4, 6, 6, 6, 4.

	Page.
Hope	123

SEVENS.

TROCHAIC, 7, 7, 7, 7.

	Page.
Aletta, 4 or 6 lines	117
Benevento, 8 lines	240

	Page.
Beulah 8 lines	255
Eltham, 8 lines	204
Gethsemane, 6 lines	79
Halle	28
Hendon	20
Holley	9, 213
Hollingside, 8 lines	116
Horton	183
Hotham, 8 lines	150
(Ives) 8 lines	255
Martyn, 8 lines	106
Messiah, 8 lines	139
Morning Star, 8 lines	220
Mt. Calvary, 6 lines	107
Mozart	73
Nuremberg, 6 lines	234
Pleyel	61
Rock of Ages, 6 lines	131
Rosefield, 4 or 6 lines	89
Sabbath, 6 or 8 lines	11
Seymour	171
Solitude	167
Spanish Hymn, 6 or 8 lines	166
Telemann	49
Theodora	149
(Toplady) 6 lines	131

SEVENS AND SIXES.

IAMBIC, 7, 6, 7, 6, 7, 6, 7, 6.

	Page.
Christine	264
Ewing	263
(Goodwin)	202
Mendebras	15
Missionary Hymn	225
Paradise	262
Webb	201
Yarmouth	224

7, 6, 7, 6, 7, 7, 7, 6.

TROCHAIC AND IAMBIC.

	Page.
Amsterdam	168

EIGHTS.

8, 8, 8, 8, 8, 8, 8, 8.

ANAPESTIC.

	Page.
Madison	159

EIGHTS AND SEVENS.

8, 7, 8, 7. TROCHAIC.

	Page.
Austria, 6 or 8 lines	203
Autumn, 8 lines	121
Bartimeus, 4 or 6 lines	120
Bavaria, 4, 6 or 8 lines	78

EIGHTS AND SEVENS.

	Page.
Even me, 8 lines, (See 8, 7, 8, 7, 6, 7)	115

METRICAL INDEX OF TUNES. 283

Page.		Page.		Page.		Page.
Harwell, 6 or 8 lines, (See 8, 7, 8, 7, 7, 7).	55	**EIGHTS, SEVENS AND FOUR.**		8, 7, 8, 7, 6, 7.		11, 12, 12, 10.
Mannheim	48			Even me (See 8s & 7s) 115		Nicaea 5
Nettleton, 6 or 8 lines	132	8, 7, 8, 7, 4, 7. Trochaic.		8, 7, 8, 7, 7, 7.		**TWELVES.**
Otto, 8 lines	249					
Rathbun	133	Belmont	96	Harwell (See 8s & 7s) .. 55		12, 12, 12, 12. Anapestic.
Rest for the Weary...	268	Greenville 181,	218			Scotland 109
Russia, 8 lines	74	Oliphant............	170	**ELEVENS.**		
Shining Shore, 8 lines	266	Osgood	253			
		Sicily...............	17	11, 11, 11, 11. Anapestic.		12, 11, 12, 11.
(Vesper Hymn) 8 lines	74	Tamworth...........	227	Frederick............ 248		
Wilmot	54	(Visitation)..........	96	Portuguese Hymn ... 182		Frederick (See 11s)... 248
		Zion	97			

INDEX OF AUTHORS OF HYMNS.

Adams, Mrs. Sarah Flower (1805—1849), 472.
Addison, Joseph (1672—1719), 82, 110, 710.
Alexander, Mrs. Cecil Frances (1858), 377
Alexander, Rev. James W., D.D. (1804—1859), 384.
Allen, G—— N. (1849), 434.
Allen, Rev. James (1734—1804), 150, 334.
Allen, Rev. Jonathan (1801), 260.
Ambrose (340—397), 65, 258.
Auber, Harriet (1773—1862), 16, 21, 239, 570.

Baker, Rev. & Sir Henry Williams, Bart. (1821—), 524, 642, 750.
Bakewell, Rev. John (1721—1819), 148, 213.
Barbauld, Mrs. Anna Lætitia (1743—1825), 604, 645, 656, 690.
Barlow, Joel (1755—1812), 668.
Bathurst, Rev. William Hiley (1796—), 27, 158, 615, 627.
Beddome, Rev. Benjamin (1717—1795), 153, 171, 182, 354, 372, 531, 544, 577, 593, 602, 626, 653.
Beman, Rev. Nathan S. S., D.D. (1786—1871), 339, 713.
Bennett, Henry (1851), 745.
Bernard de Clairvaux (1091—1153), 383, 387.
Bernard de Morlaix (ab. 1150), 739—742.
Berridge, Rev. John (1716—1793), 665.
Bethune, Rev. George W., D.D. (1805—1862), 611, 695.
Bickersteth, Rev. Edward Henry (1825—), 75.
Blacklock, Rev. Thomas, D.D. (1721—1791), 81.
Boden, Rev. James (1757—1841), 149, 304.
Bonar, Rev. Horatius, D.D. (1808—), 69, 198, 518, 640, 694.
Bonar, Mrs. Horatius (1853), 342.
Borthwick, Jane (1854), 517, 743.
Bowring, Sir John, LL.D. (1792—1872), 208, 369, 617.
Brady, Rev. Nicholas, D.D. (1659—1726), See Tate.
Bridges, Matthew (1852), 261.
Brown, Mrs. Phœbe H. (1783—1861), 9, 609.

Brown, William (1822), 19.
Browne, Rev. Simon (1680—1732), 23.
Bruce, Michael (1746—1767), 693, 706.
Bryant, William Cullen (1794—), 654.
Burder, Rev. George (1752—1832), 118, 597.
Burdsall, Richard (1806), 305.
Burnham, Rev. Richard (1749—1810), 316.
Burns, Rev. James Drummond (1823—1864), 14, 326.
Burton, John (1803—), 621.
Byrom, John (1691—1763), 453.

Cary, Phœbe (1825—1871), 749.
Carlyle, Rev. Joseph Dacre (1759—1804), 54.
Caswall, Rev. Edward (1814—), 225, 385—387.
Cawood, Rev. John (1775—1852), 202.
Cennick, Rev. John (1717—1755), 25, 349, 401, 467, 712.
Chandler, Rev. John (1837), 219, 220, 258, 603.
Cleveland, Benjamin (1790), 459.
Codner, Elizabeth (1860), 321.
Coffin, Prof. Charles (1676—1749), 667.
Collyer, Rev. William Bengo, D.D. (1782—1854), 295, 624, 681, 701.
Conder, Josiah (1789—1855), 327, 364.
Cooper, J—— (1810), (?) 67.
Cotterell, Rev. Thomas (1779—1823), 157, 159, 637.
Cowper, William (1731—1800), 174, 221, 417, 446, 458, 485, 492, 526, 555, 534, 613.
Coxe, Rev. Arthur Cleveland, D.D., (1818—), 558.
Crosby, Fanny (1849), 460.
Cummins, James J. (—1867), 475.

Dana, Mrs. Mary S. B. (Palmer) (1841), 744.
Davies, Rev. Samuel (1724—1761), 588.
Davis, Rev. Thomas (1864), 738.
Deck, James George (1837), 520.
DeFleury, Maria (1806), 447.
Denny, Sir Edward, Bart. (1796—), 368, 374.
Dickson, Rev. David (1583—1663), 729.

INDEX OF AUTHORS OF HYMNS.

DOANE, REV. GEORGE W., D.D. (1799—1859), 11, 212.
DOBELL, JOHN (1757—1840), 283.
DODDRIDGE, REV. PHILIP, D.D. (1702—1751), 8, 28, 55, 90, 132, 152, 191, 192, 233, 273, 276, 373, 376, 397, 409, 443, 445, 449, 452, 501, 565, 573, 576, 589, 584, 587, 608, 620, 622, 646, 669—671, 674, 682, 736.
DRAPER, B—— H. (1816), 628.
DUFFIELD, REV. GEORGE, D.D. (1818—), 365, 629.
DWIGHT, REV. JOHN S. (1844), 661.
DWIGHT, REV. TIMOTHY, D.D. (1752—1817), 33, 285, 292, 560, 703.

EASTBURN, JAMES WALLIS (1798—1819), 66.
EDMESTON, JAMES (1791—1867), 476, 632.
ELLIOTT, CHARLOTTE (—1871), 346, 461, 500, 540.
ELLIOTT, MRS. JULIA ANNE (—1841), 18.
ELVEN, REV. CORNELIUS (1797—), 310.
ENFIELD, REV. WILLIAM, D.D. (1741—1797), 210.
EVANS, REV. JONATHAN (1749—1809), 34, 215.

FABER, REV. FREDERICK WILLIAM (1815—1863), 97, 352, 734.
FAWCETT, REV. JOHN, D.D. (1730—1817), 138, 172, 275, 491, 509, 600.
FORTUNATUS, VENANTIUS H. C. (530—609), 219.

GERHARDT, REV. PAUL (1606—1676), 523.
GIBBONS, REV. THOMAS, D.D. (1720—1785), 634, 650, 735.
GOODE, REV. WILLIAM (1762—1816), 147.
GRANT, SIR ROBERT (1785—1838), 323.
GRIGG, REV. JOSEPH (—1768), 289, 408.
GURNEY, REV. ARCHER THOMPSON (1820—), 203.
GURNEY, JOHN HAMPDEN (1802—1862), 490.

HAMMOND, REV. WILLIAM (—1783), 44, 259.
HARBAUGH, REV. HENRY (1818—1867), 416.
HART, REV. JOSEPH (1712—1768), 43, 64, 161, 214, 265, 266, 309.
HASTINGS, THOMAS, D.M. (1784—1872), 13, 204, 469, 507, 567.
HATFIELD, REV. EDWIN F., D.D. (1807—), 22, 65, 73, 664.
HAWEIS, REV. THOMAS, M.D. (1732—1820), 301, 530.
HAYWARD, —— (1806), 31.
HEATH, GEORGE (1806), 504.
HEBER, RT. REV. REGINALD, D.D. (1783—1826), 1, 205, 631, 698, 715.
HEGINBOTHAM, REV. OTTIWELL (1744—1768), 105, 117, 178, 498.
HERVEY, REV. JAMES (1714—1758), 533.
HILL, REV. ROWLAND (1744—1833), 302, 512, 704.
HOPE, HENRY (1852), 341.
HOW, REV. WILLIAM WALSHAM (1823—), 618, 643.
HUNTER, REV. WILLIAM (1857), 751.
HYDE, MRS. ANN BEADLY (—1872), 291.

JERVIS, REV. THOMAS (1795), 40.
JOHNSON, MRS. CATHERINE H. (1866), 652.
JONES, REV. EDMUND (1722—1765), 381.

KEDLE, REV. JOHN (1792—1866), 5.
KELLY, REV. THOMAS (1769—1855), 24, 35, 135, 145, 146, 244—246, 350, 569, 571, 590, 623, 638.
KEMPTHORNE, REV. JOHN (1810), 125.
KEN, RT. REV. THOMAS (1637—1711), 2, 3.
KETHE, REV. WILLIAM (1561), 77.
KEY, FRANCIS SCOTT (1779—1843), 126.
KRUGER, JOHN (1649), 300.

LAURENTI, LAURENTIUS (1660—1722), 743.
LLOYD, WILLIAM FREEMAN (1791—1853), 514.

LYTE, REV. HENRY FRANCIS (1793—1847), 109, 129, 336, 423, 454, 465, 508, 511, 630.

MACKAY, MRS. MARGARET (1832), 689.
MADAN, REV. MARTIN (1726—1790), 297.
MAITLAND, FANNY F. (1827), 513.
MANT, RT. REV. RICHARD (1776—1848), 164.
MARRIOTT, REV. JOHN (1780—1825), 167.
MASON, REV. JOHN (—1694), 10.
MASSIE, RICHARD (1859), 370.
MEDLEY, REV. SAMUEL (1738—1799), 193, 282, 406, 411.
MERCER, REV. WILLIAM (1864), 667.
MERRICK, REV. JAMES (1720—1769), 468, 691.
MIDLANE, ALBERT (1825—), 610.
MITCHELL, REV. WILLIAM (1831), 396.
MONSELL, REV. JOHN S. B., LL.D. (1811—), 87, 230.
MONTGOMERY, JAMES (1771—1854), 12, 45, 119, 130, 162, 160, 200, 216, 267, 479, 482, 486, 566, 572, 599, 579, 581, 586, 662, 651, 657, 696, 718.
MOORE, REV. HENRY (1732—1802), 92.
MOORE, THOMAS (1780—1852), 535.
MORELL, PROF. THOMAS (1781—1840), 635.
MORRISON, REV. JOHN, D.D. (1749—1798), 195.
MUHLENBERG, REV. WILLIAM A., D.D. (1826), 697.

NEALE, REV. JOHN MASON (1818—1866), 717, 739—742.
NEEDHAM, REV. JOHN (ab. 1768), 83, 357, 435.
NELSON, REV. DAVID, M.D. (1793—1844), 722, 747.
NEWTON, REV. JOHN (1725—1807), 17, 46, 315, 329, 333, 353, 398, 419, 477, 478, 481, 484, 493, 522, 508, 612, 673, 711, 675, 728.
NOEL, HON. AND REV. GERARD THOMAS (1782—1851), 393.

OCKUM, REV. SAMSON (1723—1792), 332.
OGILVIE, REV. JOHN, D.D. (1733—1814), 91.
ONDERDONK, RT. REV. HENRY U. (1789—1858), 127, 285.

PALMER, REV. RAY, D.D. (1808—), 30, 218, 280, 322, 383, 400, 413, 442, 515, 676.
PARK, REV. ROSWELL, D.D. (1807—), 367.
PEACOCK, JOHN (1776), 585.
PEABODY, REV. WILLIAM B. O., D.D. (1799—1847), 683.
PERRONET, REV. EDWARD (—1792), 247.

RAFFLES, REV. THOMAS, D.D. (1788—1863), 324, 719.
REED, REV. ANDREW, D.D. (1787—1862), 156, 165, 196, 243, 270, 410.
ROBINSON, REV. CHARLES S., D.D. (1862), 473.
ROBINSON, REV. ROBERT (1735—1790), 143, 144, 366.
RYLAND, REV. JOHN, D.D. (1753—1825), 70, 421, 432, 592.

SANTOLIUS VICTORINUS (1630—1697), 603.
SCHMOLKE, REV. BENJAMIN (1672—1737), 517.
SCOTT, ELIZABETH (ab. 1764), 619, 644.
SCOTT, SIR WALTER (1771—1832), 716.
SEAGRAVE, REV. ROBERT (1693—?), 470.
SEARS, REV. EDMUND H. (1810—), 194.
SEYMOUR, AARON CROSSLEY HOBART (1780—), 248.
SHIRLEY, SELINA, COUNTESS OF HUNTINGDON (1707—1791), 324.
SHIRLEY, HON. AND REV. WALTER (1725—1786), 36.
SHRUBSOLE, REV. WILLIAM (1729—1797), 625.
SIGOURNEY, MRS. LYDIA H. (1791—1865), 163.
SMITH, MRS. CAROLINE [SPRAGUE] (1856), 699.
SMITH, REV. SAMUEL FRANCIS, D.D. (1808—) 580, 600.
SMYTH, EDWARD (1774), 37.
SPITTA, REV. CARL J. P., D.D. (1801—1859), 370.
STEELE, ANNE (1716—1778), 52, 114, 140, 147, 173, 188, 257, 263, 274, 278, 288, 313, 314, 319, 345, 360, 378, 405, 425—427, 431, 463, 499, 525, 537, 548, 666, 672, 707, 727.

INDEX OF AUTHORS OF HYMNS.

STENNETT, REV. SAMUEL, D.D. (1727—1795), 39, 229, 234, 256, 318, 320, 391, 502, 726.
STERNHOLD, THOMAS (—1549), 95.
STOCKER, JOHN (1776), 166.
STOWELL, REV. HUGH (1799—1865), 163, 539.
STRONG, REV. NATHAN, D.D. (1748—1816), 658.
SWAIN, REV. JOSEPH (1761—1796), 268, 594.

TAPPAN, REV. WILLIAM BINGHAM (1794—1849), 720.
TATE, NAHUM (1652—1715), 47, 106, 108, 123, 454.
TATLOCK, ELEANOR (179s), 348.
TAYLOR, JANE (1783—1823), 361.
TERSTEEGEN, GERHARD (1697—1769), 483.
THEODORE (ab. 820), 717.
THOMAS, OF CELANO (1250), 716.
THOMPSON, REV. ALEXANDER R. (1869), 748.
TOPLADY, REV. AUGUSTUS M. (1740—1778), 217, 330, 393, 451, 524.
TURNER, REV. DANIEL (1710—1798), 429.

VOKE, MRS. (1806), 583.

WALLIN, REV. BENJAMIN (1711—1782), 251.
WARDLAW, REV. RALPH, D.D. (1779—1853), 112, 466, 639.
WATTS, REV. ISAAC, D.D. (1674—1748), 4, 6, 7, 15, 20, 26, 32, 38, 41, 48—51, 53, 56—63, 71, 72, 76, 78—80, 84—86, 88, 89, 93, 94, 96, 98—104, 107, 113, 116, 120—122, 124, 131, 133, 134, 136, 137, 139, 141, 151, 155, 169, 170, 175—177, 179—181, 183—187, 189, 190, 206, 207, 209, 211, 222, 224, 226—228, 235, 237, 238, 240, 242, 250, 252, 254, 260, 262, 264, 271, 272, 277, 287, 290, 296, 306, 307, 317, 340, 343, 347, 351, 355, 356, 358, 359, 379—382, 388, 389, 392, 394, 402, 403, 412, 414, 422, 428, 430, 433, 436—441, 444, 448, 450, 455—457, 462, 466, 488, 489, 494—497, 505, 519, 521, 527, 532, 536, 541, 542, 545—547, 549, 550—554, 557, 559, 561, 562—564, 575, 578, 582, 591, 601, 605, 606, 607, 614, 633, 649, 677—680, 684—688, 692, 702, 705, 708, 709, 714, 721, 723—725, 730, 731.
WESLEY, REV. CHARLES (1708—1788), 68, 74, 199, 201, 231, 232, 236, 241, 249, 253, 294, 298—300, 303, 308, 311, 312, 325, 331, 338, 392, 375, 390, 407, 420, 471, 480, 487, 503, 506, 574, 595, 596, 598, 641.
WESLEY, REV. JOHN (1703—1791), 344, 483, 523.
WESLEY, REV. SAMUEL (1662—1735), 223.
WHITE, HENRY KIRKE (1785—1806), 513.
WHITFIELD, REV. FREDERICK (1859), 395, 399.
WILLIAMS, HELEN MARIA (1762—1827), 529.
WILLIAMS, REV. WILLIAM (1717—1791), 476, 636.
WILLIS, NATHANIEL PARKER (1807—1867), 653.
WINGROVE, JOHN (1806), 337.
WORDSWORTH, RT. REV. CHRISTOPHER, D.D. (1807—), 29, 648, 752.
WRANGHAM, WILLIAM (1829), 128.
WREFORD, REV. JOHN REYNELL, D.D. (1837), 669.
AUTHORSHIP UNCERTAIN:
42, 111, 115, 154, 197, 255, 279, 284, 293, 371, 404, 415, 418, 424, 516, 538, 543, 556, 616, 733, 746.

INDEX OF AUTHORS OF TUNES.

	PAGE
AHLE, JOHANN RUDOLF (1625—1673)	234
ALLEN, ——	155
AMERICAN MELODY	119
ANON	22, 96, 151
ARNOLD, WILLIAM, Eng. (1768—1832)	206
BARNBY, JOSEPH, Organist, Lond	62
BARTNIANSKY, DIMITRI S., Russia (1751—1825)	74
BEASTALL, WILLIAM, Eng.	231
BEETHOVEN, LUDWIG VON (1770—1827)	48, 179
BILLINGS, WILLIAM, Boston (1746—1800)	258
BOND, HUGH (Lay Vicar Choral, Exeter Cathedral, 1762—1792)	37
BOST, AMI (Switzerland, Contemporary)	157
BOYCE, WILLIAM, Mus. Doc (1710—1779)	195
BRADBURY, WILLIAM B. (1816—1868), 103, 115, 117, 137, 148, 164, 175, 216, 245, 260.	
BROWN, REV. SAMUEL R., P.D., Am. Miss. to Japan	143
BURNEY, CHARLES, Mus. Doc. (1726—1814)	51
CAREY, HENRY (—1743)	235
CELTIC MELODY	69
CHAPIN, AARON, cir., 1820	68, 102, 172, 211
CLARKE, JOHN (WHITFIELD), Mus. Doc. (1770—)	109
CLARK, THOMAS, 1804	72
COLE, JOHN, Eng. (1775—), Baltimore, 1800	43
CONKEY, ITHAMAR, New York, 1851	133
COSTELLO, —— (English), 1810	222
CRAMER, JOHANN BAPTISTA (1771—1858) Arr.	181
CROFT, WILLIAM, Mus. Doc. (1677—1727)	13
CRUGER, JOHANN (1598—1662), Organist, Berlin	47
CUTHBERT, Mrs.	41
DADMUN, REV. J. W.	268
DARWELL, REV. JOHN, Eng., cir., 1750	88
DOWNS, L. T., 1851	107
DUNBAR, E. W., 1858	265
DUTTON, DEODATUS, JR., 1829	212
DYKES, REV. JOHN B., Eng., 1861	5, 116
EBERWEIN MAXIMILIAN (1775—1831)	127
EDSON, J., 1782	103
ESTE'S (THOMAS) Psalter, 1592	114
EVANS, JOHN M., Phila., (1825—)	267
EWING, RT. REV. ALEXANDER, D.D., D.C.L., Bishop of Argyll and the Isles, 1861	263
FRANC, GUILLAUME, 1543	31

INDEX OF AUTHORS OF TUNES.

	PAGE
GARDINER, WILLIAM, 1830	59
GIARDINI, FELICE, Milan (1716—1796)	30, 146
GIBBONS, ORLANDO, Mus. Doc. (1583—1625)	34
GLASER, CARL GOTTHELF (1784—1829)	42
GOULD, JOHN E. (Phila.), (1822—)	104
GOULD, NATHANIEL D. (Boston), (1781—1864)	101
GREATOREX, HENRY W	52, 142, 186, 205
GREENE, MAURICE. Mus Doc. (1695—1755)	130
GREGORIAN	60, 83, 196
HANDEL, GEORGE FREDERICK (1685—1759), 63, 70, 71, 139, 158, 161, 246.	
HARRISON, RALPH (REV.), Manchester (1748—1810)	8, 27
HART, ANDRE, Pr., Edinburgh, 1615 (Scotch Psalter)	144, 237, 177, 241
HARWOOD, EDWARD, Liverpool (1707—1787)	36
HASTINGS, EUROTAS P., 1846	134
HASTINGS, THOMAS, Conn. (1784—1872), 55, 93, 97, 100, 131, 141, 143, 157, 174, 193, 208, 221.	
HATTON, J. (See REEVE)	6
HAVERGAL, REV. WM. HENRY, Eng. (1793—1870)	69
HAWES, THOMAS (REV.), M.D., Eng. (1733—1820)	138
HAYDN, FRANCIS JOSEPH (1732—1809)	7, 28, 203
HERMANN, NICOLAUS (—1561)	199
HEROLD, L. J. F. (1791—1833)	84
HEWS, GEORGE, Boston, (1806—)	9, 213
HOLDEN, OLIVER, Mass. (—1831)	90
HOLYOKE, SAMUEL, Massachusetts (1771—1816)	76
HORSLEY, WILLIAM (1774—1858)	152
IVES, ELAM, JR., Conn. (1802—1864)	255
IVISON, H.	230
JONES, REV. WILLIAM, England (1726—1799)	154
KINGSLEY, GEORGE, Northampton, Mass., 77, 84, 127, 215, 243, 248, 256.	
KIRBY, GEORGE, Organist to Queen Elizabeth (Este's Psalter, 1597)	114
KLUG, JOSEPH, "Gesangbuch," 1535	251
KNAPP, WILLIAM, Eng. (1698—1768)	250
LEACH, JAMES, England (1762—1798)	228
LINLEY, FRANCIS, Org., Eng. (1771—1800)	67
LOCKHART, CHARLES, Org., Lond., 1790	227
LUCAS, J. (17—)	140
MADAN, REV. MARTIN, Eng. (1726—1790)	150
MADAN, DR. SPENSER (Bishop), (—1813)	129
MALAN, REV. CÆSAR, Geneva (1787—1857)	20, 33, 89
MARSH, S. B., 1836	106
MARSON, —	261
MASON, LOWELL, Mus. Doc. (1792—1872), 11, 12, 15, 16, 18, 25, 26, 29, 42, 47, 55, 60, 81, 82, 83, 85, 105, 122, 124, 135, 145, 156, 162, 169, 170, 180, 184, 187, 188, 192, 194, 196, 204, 207, 210, 217, 219, 220, 224, 225, 233, 247.	
MATHER, WILLIAM, Organist, Sheffield (1756—1808)	64, 158
MITCHELL, NAHUM, Mass., 1812	201

	PAGE
MOZART, J. C. WOLFGANG AMADEUS (1756—1791)	73, 111
NAGELI, HANS GEORGE, Switz. (1773—1836.)	160, 187
NARES, JAMES, Mus. Doc., York, Eng. (1715—1783)	168
NETTLETON, REV. ASAHEL (1783—1844)	132
OLIVER, HENRY K. (1800—)	57, 249
PERKINS, THEODORE E., New York	123
PLEYEL, IGNAZ, Austria (1757—1831)	61, 173, 189
POND, SYLVANUS B., N. Y. (1792—1871)	112, 159
RANDALL, JOHN, Mus. Doc. (1715—1799)	40, 98
READ, DANIEL, New Haven, Conn., 1785	10, 120, 136
READING, JOHN, Org., Lond. (1690—1766)	182
REDHEAD, RICHARD, Org., Lond., "Church Hymn Tunes," 1853	79
REEVE, WILLIAM, Org., Lond. (1757—)	6
RINK, JOHANN CHRISTIAN HEINRICH (1770—1846)	257
RITTER, PETER (cir. 1760—)	253
ROOT, GEORGE FREDERICK, 1820—	99, 266
ROSENMULLER, JOHANN, Saxony (cir. 1615—1686)	107
ROSSINI, GIACOMO (1792—1868)	113
ROUSSEAU, JEAN JACQUES, Swiss (1712—1778)	181, 218
SHOEL, THOMAS, Eng. (1750—1823)	178
SIMPSON, R., Scotch	58
SMITH, ISAAC ("Psalm Tunes," Lond., 1770), 19, 197, 236.	
SPILMAN, REV. JONATHAN (1835)	126
STANLEY, SAMUEL, Birmingham (1767—1822), 32, 92, 200.	
SWAN, TIMOTHY, Mass. (1760—1842)	261
TALLIS, THOMAS, Lond. (—1585)	10, 155, Arr. 165
TANSUR, WILLIAM, Eng. (1699—cir. 1774), 46, 50, 87, 190, 214, 242.	
TAYLOR, VIRGIL CORYDON (1817—)	95
THORLEY, THOMAS, 17—	14, 232
TUCKER, ISAAC, Eng. (1761—1825)	45, 65
VENUA, FREDERICK M. A., Paris (1788—)	86
VULPIUS, MELCHIOR, Ger. (cir. 1560—)	191
WARREN, SAMUEL P.	75, 264
WARTENSEE, XAVIER SCHNYDER VON (1786—)	183
WEBB, GEORGE JAMES (1803—), New York	202
WEBBE, SAMUEL, SEN., Lond. (1740—1824)	240
WEBER, CARL MARIA, VON (1786—1826)	54, 171, 135
WEBER, FREDERICK A., Eng.	262
WHITAKER, E. M., Washington, D. C.	176
WILLIAMS, AARON, Lond. (1731—1776), Coll. cir., 1760; 21, 22, 24, 35, 44, 163, 209, 244.	
WILLIAMS, THOMAS, Lond., cir., 1768	226
WILSON, HUGH, Eng., 17—	252
WOODMAN, JONATHAN C.	229
YOAKLEY, REV. WILLIAM, Eng.	110
ZEUNER, CHARLES, Boston (—1857)	49, 53, 223, 239

INDEX TO HYMNS.

		HYMN.
A broken heart, my God, my King	*I. Watts.*	307
A charge to keep I have	*C. Wesley.*	480
A few more years shall roll	*H. Bonar.*	694
Ah! wretched, vile, ungrateful	*Miss A. Steele.*	499
Alas! and did my Saviour bleed	*I. Watts.*	222
All hail, incarnate God!	*Miss E. Scott.*	619
All hail the power of Jesus' name	*E. Perronet.*	247
All people that on earth do dwell	*W. Kethe.*	77
Almighty Maker, God!	*I. Watts.*	120
Amazing grace—how sweet the sound	*J. Newton.*	353
Amazing sight! the Saviour stands	*Vill. Hymns.*	279
Am I a soldier of the cross	*I. Watts.*	536
Amid the splendors of thy state	*Rippon's Coll.*	115
An earthly temple here we	*Mrs. C. H. Johnson.*	652
And can I yet delay	*C. Wesley.*	338
And dost thou say,—"Ask what	*J. Newton.*	484
And must I part with all I have	*B. Beddome.*	354
And now another week begins	*T. Kelly.*	24
And will the Lord thus condescend	*Miss A. Steele.*	319
And will th' offended God again	*S. Stennett.*	502
Angels! lament, behold your	*Tr., J. Chandler.*	220
Approach, my soul! the mercy-seat	*J. Newton.*	315
Arise, arise! with joy survey	*T. Kelly.*	623
Arise, my soul! arise	*C. Wesley.*	362
Arise, my soul! my joyful powers	*I. Watts.*	359
Arise, O King of grace! arise	*I. Watts.*	50
Arise, ye people! and adore	*Miss H. Auber.*	239
Arm of the Lord! awake, awake	*W. Shrubsole.*	625
Around the Saviour's lofty throne	*T. Kelly.*	135
As Jesus died and rose again	*M. Bruce.*	706
As pants the hart for cooling str'ms	*H. F. Lyte.*	434
Ascend thy throne, almighty King!	*B. Beddome.*	626
Asleep in Jesus!—blessed sl'p	*Mrs. M. Mackay.*	689
Assemble! at thy great command	*W. B. Collyer.*	624
At thy command, our dearest Lord!	*I. Watts.*	381
Awake, and sing the song	*W. Hammond.*	259
Awake, my heart! arise, my tongue!	*I. Watts.*	358
Awake, my soul! and with the sun	*T. Ken.*	2
Awake, my soul! in joyful lays	*S. Medley.*	411
Awake, my soul! stretch every	*P. Doddridge.*	443
Awake, my tongue! thy tribute	*J. Needham.*	83
Awake, our souls! away, our fears!	*I. Watts.*	438
Awake, ye saints! and raise your.	*P. Doddridge.*	674
Awake, ye saints! to praise your King.	*I. Watts.*	107
Awaked by Sinai's awful sound	*S. Ockum.*	332
Away from earth my spirit turns	*R. Palmer.*	442
Away from every mortal care	*I. Watts.*	62
Away, my unbelieving fear	*C. Wesley.*	503
Before Jehovah's awful throne	*I. Watts.*	76
Begin, my soul! th' exalted lay	*J. Ogilvie.*	91
Begin, my tongue! some he'v'nly theme	*I. Watts.*	175
Behold! a stranger 's at the door	*J. Grigg.*	289
Behold! the blind their sight receive	*I. Watts.*	207
Behold the glories of the Lamb	*I. Watts.*	137
Behold! the lofty sky	*I. Watts.*	169
Behold! the morning sun	*I. Watts.*	170
Behold the Saviour of mankind	*S. Wesley.*	223
Behold the sure foundation stone	*I. Watts.*	559
Behold the throne of grace	*J. Newton.*	481
Behold the western evening	*W. B. O. Peabody.*	683
Behold! what condescending love	*J. Peacock.*	585
Behold! what wondrous grace	*I. Watts.*	448
Behold where, in the Friend of man	*W. Enfield.*	210
Bless, O my soul! the living God	*I. Watts.*	85
Blest are the sons of peace	*I. Watts.*	601
Blest are the souls that hear and know	*I. Watts.*	177
Blest be the dear uniting love	*C. Wesley.*	596
Blest be the tie that binds	*J. Fawcett.*	600
Blest be thou, the God of	*H. U. Onderdonk.*	127
Blessed Saviour! thee I love	*G. Duffield.*	365
Blest Comforter divine	*Mrs. L. H. Sigourney.*	163
Blest is the man, whose heart doth move	*I. Watts.*	649
Blest is the man whose	*Mrs. A. L. Barbauld.*	645
Blest Jesus! come thou gently down	*Luth. Coll.*	616
Blow ye the trumpet, blow	*C. Wesley.*	303
Bread of heaven! on thee I feed	*J. Conder.*	364
Brief life is here our portion	*Tr. J. M. Neale.*	739
Bright and joyful is the morn	*J. Montgomery.*	200
Bright King of glory, dreadful God!	*I. Watts.*	131
Brightest and best of the sons of the	*R. Heber.*	205
Brightness of the Father's glory	*R. Robinson.*	144
Broad is the road that leads to death	*Watts.*	550
Calm on the listening ear of night	*E. H. Sears.*	194
Cast thy burden on the Lord	*R. Hill.*	512
Children of the heavenly King	*J. Cennick.*	467
Christ and his cross is all our theme	*I. Watts.*	575
Christ, of all my hopes the ground,	*R. Wardlaw.*	466
Christ, the Lord, is risen to-day	*C. Wesley.*	232
Come, all ye saints of God	*J. Boden.*	149
Come, bless Jehovah's name	*E. F. Hatfield.*	73
Come, blessed Spirit, Source of,	*B. Beddome.*	153
Come, dearest Lord! descend and dwell	*I. Watts.*	60
Come, every pious heart!	*S. Stennett.*	234
Come, happy souls! approach your God	*I. Watts.*	272
Come, heavenly love! inspire my	*Miss A. Steele.*	257
Come hither, all ye weary souls	*I. Watts.*	287
Come, Holy Ghost! my soul inspire	*Vill. Hymns.*	556
Come, Holy Spirit! calm	*H. F. Burder's Coll.*	154
Come, Holy Spirit! come	*J. Hart.*	161
Come Holy Spirit, heavenly Dove!	*I. Watts.*	155
Come, humble sinner! in whose breast	*E. Jones.*	281
Come in, thou blessed of the Lord!	*T. Kelly.*	590
Come, let our voices join to raise	*I. Watts.*	290
Come, let us join in songs of	*Campbell's Coll.*	253
Come, let us join our cheerful songs	*I. Watts.*	141
Come, let us join our friends above	*C. Wesley.*	595
Come, let us lift our joyful eyes	*I. Watts.*	250
Come, let us lift our voices high	*I. Watts.*	394

INDEX TO HYMNS.

	HYMN.
Come, Lord! and tarry not - - - - *H. Bonar.*	640
Come, Lord! and warm each - - *Miss A. Steele.*	52
Come, my fond fluttering heart - *Miss J. Taylor.*	361
Come, my soul! thy suit prepare - - *J. Newton.*	477
Come, O my soul! in sacred lays - *T. Blacklock.*	81
Come, sacred Spirit! from above - *P. Doddridge.*	152
Come, Saviour, Jesus! from above *Tr., J. Wesley.*	344
Come, shout aloud the Father's *O. Heginbotham.*	117
Come, sound his praise abroad - - - *I. Watts.*	41
Come, thou almighty King! - - - *C. Wesley.*	74
Come, thou Fount of every - - *R. Robinson.*	366
Come, thou soul-transforming Spirit! *J. Evans.*	34
Come to Calvary's holy mountain *J. Montgomery.*	267
Come, we that love the Lord! - - - *I. Watts.*	38
Come, weary souls, with sin - - *Miss A. Steele.*	288
Come, ye lofty! come, ye lowly! *A. T. Gurney.*	209
Come, ye sinners, poor and wretched - *J. Hart.*	265
Come, ye souls! by sin afflicted - *J. Swain.*	268
Come, ye that know and fear the - - *G. Burder.*	118
Come, ye that love the Saviour's *Miss A. Steele.*	140
Come, ye weary, heavy-laden - - - *J. Hart.*	266
Come, ye weary sinners! come - - *C. Wesley.*	299
Commit thou all thy griefs - - *Tr., J. Wesley.*	523
Crown him with many crowns - - *M. Bridges.*	261
Crown his head with endless blessing *W. Goode.*	147
Crowns of glory, ever bright - - - *T. Kelly.*	245
Day of judgment, day of wonders! - *J. Newton.*	711
Dearest of all the names above - - - *I. Watts.*	254
Death cannot make our souls afraid - *I. Watts.*	684
Deep in the dust before thy throne - *J. Watts.*	185
Depth of mercy!—can there be - - *C. Wesley.*	325
Descend from heaven, immortal Dove! *I. Watts.*	264
Did Christ o'er sinners weep - - *B. Beddome.*	372
Dismiss us with thy blessing, Lord! - *J. Hart.*	64
Early, my God! without delay - - - *I. Watts.*	53
Eternal source of every good! - - *B. Beddome.*	654
Eternal source of every joy! - - *P. Doddridge.*	609
Eternal Spirit, God of truth! - - *T. Cotterill.*	157
Eternal Spirit! we confess - - - *I. Watts.*	151
Eternal wisdom! thee we praise - - *I. Watts.*	100
Faith adds new charms to earthly - *D. Turner.*	429
Far as thy name is known - - - *I. Watts.*	561
Far from my thoughts, vain world! - *I. Watts.*	61
Far from the world, O Lord! I flee - *W. Cowper.*	458
Far from thy fold, O God! my - *Miss E. Tutlock.*	348
Father! how wide thy glory shines - - *I. Watts.*	113
Father! I long, I faint to see - - - *I. Watts.*	730
Father of eternal grace - - - *J. Montgomery.*	479
Father of heaven above! - - *E. H. Bickersteth.*	75
Father of heaven! whose love - - *J. Cooper (?).*	67
Father of mercies! bow thine ear - *B. Beddome.*	577
Father of mercies! in thy house, *P. Doddridge.*	576
Father of mercies! in thy word - *Miss A. Steele.*	173
Father of mercies! send thy - - *P. Doddridge.*	647
Father! whate'er of earthly bliss, *Miss A. Steele.*	525
For ever here my rest shall be - - *C. Wesley.*	390
For ever with the Lord! - - - *J. Montgomery.*	696
For thee, O dear, dear country *Tr., J. M. Neale.*	741
Frequent the day of God returns - *S. Browne.*	23
From all that dwell below the skies - *I. Watts.*	63
From every stormy wind that blows *H. Stowell.*	539
From Greenland's icy mountains - - *R. Heber.*	631
From the cross uplifted high - - *T. Haweis.*	301
From the table now retiring - - *Exeter Coll.*	371
From thee, my God! my joys shall rise, *I. Watts.*	456
Gently, Lord! Oh! gently lead us - *T. Hastings.*	507
Gird on thy conquering sword - *P. Doddridge.*	620

	HYMN.
Give me the wings of faith to rise - - *I. Watts.*	444
Give thanks to God most high - - - *I. Watts.*	124
Glorious things of thee are spoken - *J. Newton.*	568
Glory be to God on high - - - - *C. Wesley.*	68
Glory, glory to our King - - - - *T. Kelly.*	244
Glory to God on high, - - - - - *J. Allen.*	150
Glory to thee, my God! this night - - *T. Ken.*	3
Go, and the Saviour's grace proclaim, *T. Morrell.*	635
"Go preach my gospel," saith the - - *I. Watts.*	578
Go to dark Gethsemane - - - *J. Montgomery.*	216
Go, worship at Immanuel's feet - - - *I. Watts.*	136
God bless our native land - - - *J. S. Dwight.*	661
God, in the gospel of his Son - - *B. Beddome.*	182
God is a spirit just and wise - - - *I. Watts.*	553
God is the Refuge of his saints - - - *I. Watts.*	542
God moves in a mysterious way - *W. Cowper.*	534
God, my Supporter and my Hope - - *I. Watts.*	457
God of my life! through all my - *P. Doddridge.*	90
God of our salvation! hear us - - *T. Kelly.*	35
God of the universe! to thee *Miss Mary C——.*	656
Grace, like an uncorrupted seed - - *I. Watts.*	654
Grace! 'tis a charming sound - *P. Doddridge.*	373
Gracious Spirit, Dove divine! - - *J. Stocker.*	166
Great Creator! who this day *Mrs. J. A. Elliott.*	18
Great Father of each perfect - - *P. Doddridge.*	55
Great God! attend while Zion sings - *I. Watts.*	59
Great God! how infinite art thou - - *I. Watts.*	98
Great God! the nations of the earth - *T. Gibbons.*	634
Great God! we sing thy mighty - *P. Doddridge.*	670
Great God! whose universal sway - - *I. Watts.*	663
Great High Priest! we view thee - - *J. Hart.*	214
Great Prophet of our God! - - - *I. Watts.*	242
Great Shepherd of thine Israel - - - *I. Watts.*	607
Guide me, O thou great Jehovah! *W. Williams.*	474
Hail! great Creator, wise and *Gent's Magazine.*	111
Hail! mighty Jesus! how divine - *B. Wallin.*	251
Hail! my ever blessed Jesus! - - *J. Wingrove.*	537
Hail the day that sees him rise! - - *C. Wesley.*	231
Hail! thou once despised Jesus! - *J. Bakewell.*	213
Hail to the brightness of Zion's - *T. Hastings.*	204
Hail to the Lord's Anointed! - *J. Montgomery.*	566
Hail to the Prince of life and - - *P. Doddridge.*	132
Happy soul! thy days are ended - *C. Wesley.*	700
Happy the man whose cautious feet - *I. Watts.*	545
Hark! from the tombs a doleful sound - *I. Watts.*	680
Hark! hark! the notes of joy - - - *A. Reed.*	196
Hark, hark! the voice of praise - *Lyra Cœlestis.*	746
Hark! how the choral song of - *R. S. M——.*	737
Hark! my soul! it is the Lord - - *W. Cowper.*	417
Hark! ten thousand harps and voices *T. Kelly.*	146
Hark the glad sound! the - - - *P. Doddridge.*	191
Hark! the herald angels sing - - - *C. Wesley.*	109
Hark! the judgment trumpet *N. S. S. Beman.*	713
Hark the notes of angels singing - - *T. Kelly.*	145
Hark! the song of jubilee - - *J. Montgomery.*	572
Hark the sound of holy voices - *C. Wordsworth.*	752
Hark! the voice of love and mercy - *J. Evans.*	215
Hark! what celestial notes - - *Salisbury Coll.*	197
Hark! what mean those holy voices *J. Cawood.*	202
Hast thou within a care so deep *Ryle's S. Songs.*	543
Hasten, Lord! the glorious time, *Miss H. Auber.*	570
He lives—the great Redeemer - *Miss A. Steele.*	263
Hear what God, the Lord, hath - *W. Cowper.*	613
Hear what the voice from heaven - - *I. Watts.*	721
Hearts of stone! relent, relent - - *C. Wesley.*	300
Here at thy table Lord! we meet - *N. Stennett.*	291
Here in thy name, eternal God! *J. Montgomery.*	651
High in yonder realms of light - - *T. Raffles.*	719
High let us swell our tuneful - - *P. Doddridge.*	192
Ho! every one that thirsts! draw - *C. Wesley.*	294

INDEX TO HYMNS. 289

Hymn	Author	No.
Holy Father! hear my cry	H. Bonar.	69
Holy Ghost! my soul inspire	R. Mant.	164
Holy Ghost! with light divine	A. Reed.	165
Holy, holy, holy! Lord God Almighty!	R. Heber.	1
Holy, holy, holy Lord! Self-existent	J. Ryland.	70
Hosanna to the Prince of light	I. Watts.	240
How beauteous are their feet	I. Watts.	582
How blest the righteous	Mrs. A. L. Barbauld.	600
How blest the sacred tie	Mrs. A. L. Barbauld.	601
How can I sink with such a prop	I. Watts.	433
How charming is the place	S. Stennett.	39
How condescending and how kind	I. Watts.	392
How did my heart rejoice to hear	I. Watts.	48
How far beyond our mortal sight	Miss A. Steele.	727
How firm a foundation, ye saints of the	K——.	510
How gentle God's commands	P. Doddridge.	521
How heavy is the night	I. Watts.	260
How helpless guilty nature lies	Miss A. Steele.	188
How oft, alas! this wretched	Miss A. Steele.	313
How oft have sin and Satan strove	I. Watts.	441
How pleasant, how divinely fair	I. Watts.	58
How pleased and blessed was I	I. Watts.	56
How precious is the book divine	J. Fawcett.	172
How sad our state by nature is!	I. Watts.	187
How shall the young secure their	I. Watts.	176
How short and hasty is our life	I. Watts.	679
How sweet and awful is the place	I. Watts.	388
How sweet, how heavenly is the sight	J. Swain.	591
How sweet the name of Jesus sounds	J. Newton.	398
How sweet to bless the Lord	Urwick's Coll.	42
How sweetly breaks the Sabbath	E. P. Hatfield.	22
How sweetly flowed the gospel's	J. Bowring.	208
How vain are all things here below	I. Watts.	497
I have a home above	H. Bennett.	745
I hear a voice that comes from far	T. Kelly.	350
I'll praise my Maker with my breath	I. Watts.	94
I love thy kingdom, Lord!	T. Dwight.	560
I love to steal awhile away	Mrs. P. H. Brown.	9
I'm not ashamed to own my Lord	I. Watts.	355
I send the joys of earth away	I. Watts.	343
I would not live alway; I ask	W. A. Muhlenberg.	697
If Christ is mine, then all is mine	B. Beddome.	531
If human kindness meets return	G. T. Noel.	393
In all my Lord's appointed ways	J. Ryland.	592
In all my vast concerns with thee	I. Watts.	531
In robes of judgment, lo! he comes	I. Watts.	714
In the Christian's home in glory	W. Hunter.	751
In the cross of Christ I glory	J. Bowring.	369
In the morning hear my voice	J. Montgomery.	12
In vain my fancy strives to paint	J. Newton.	728
Indulgent Sovereign of the skies!	P. Doddridge.	622
Infinite excellence is thine	J. Fawcett.	133
Inquire, ye pilgrims! for the	P. Doddridge.	276
It is not death to die	G. W. Bethune.	695
It is thy hand, my God!	J. G. Deck.	520
Jehovah reigns, his throne is high	I. Watts.	84
Jerusalem, my happy	Williams & Boden's Coll.	733
Jerusalem, the glorious	Tr., J. M. Neale.	742
Jerusalem, the golden	Tr., J. M. Neale.	740
Jesus! and shall it ever be	J. Grigg.	408
Jesus! hail! enthroned in glory	J. Bakewell.	148
Jesus! how sweet thy memory	J. W. Alexander.	384
Jesus! I come to thee	N. S. S. Beman.	339
Jesus! I live to thee	H. Harbaugh.	416
Jesus! I love thy charming name	P. Doddridge.	397
Jesus! I my cross have taken	H. F. Lyte.	336
Jesus, immortal King! arise	A. C. H. Seymour.	248
Jesus! Lord of life and glory!	J. J. Cummins.	475
Jesus, Lord! we look to thee	C. Wesley.	508
Jesus, Lover of my soul!	C. Wesley.	426
Jesus! merciful and mild	T. Hastings.	469
Jesus, my All, to heaven is gone	J. Cennick.	349
Jesus! my heart within me burns	R. Palmer.	413
Jesus, my Lord! how rich thy	P. Doddridge.	646
Jesus shall reign where'er the sun	I. Watts.	564
Jesus spreads his banner o'er us	R. Park.	367
Jesus, the name high over all	C. Wesley.	249
Jesus, the name I love so well	F. Whitfield.	395
Jesus! the very thought of	Tr., E. Caswall.	385
Jesus! the word of mercy give	C. Wesley.	574
Jesus! these eyes have never seen	R. Palmer.	400
Jesus! thou art the sinner's	R. Burnham.	316
Jesus, thou everlasting King!	I. Watts.	382
Jesus, thou Joy of loving hearts!	R. Palmer.	383
Jesus! thy church, with longing	W. H. Bathurst.	627
Jesus! thy love shall we forget	W. Mitchell.	396
Jesus! thy name I love	Ryle's S. Songs.	516
Jesus! who knows full well	J. Newton.	522
Joy to the world, the Lord is come	I. Watts.	190
Judge me, O Lord! and prove	I. Watts.	546
Just as I am, without one plea	Miss C. Elliott.	346
Lead us, heavenly Father! lead us	J. Edmeston.	476
Let every mortal ear attend	I. Watts.	277
Let every tongue thy goodness speak	I. Watts.	102
Let everlasting glories crown	I. Watts.	181
Let others best how strong they be	I. Watts.	678
Let party names no more	B. Beddome.	602
Let sinners take their course	I. Watts.	423
Let songs of praises fill the sky	T. Cotterill.	159
Let Zion and her sons rejoice	I. Watts.	614
Let Zion's watchmen all awake	P. Doddridge.	573
Life is a span, a fleeting hour	Miss A. Steele.	707
Life is the time to serve the Lord	I. Watts.	686
Lift up to God the voice of praise	R. Wardlaw.	112
Like sheep we went astray	I. Watts.	226
Listen, sinner! mercy hails you	A. Reed.	270
Lo! he cometh, countless	J. Cennick.	712
Lo! God, our God, has come	H. Bonar.	198
Lo! on a narrow neck of land	C. Wesley.	331
Lo! what a glorious sight appears	I. Watts.	557
Long as I live, I'll bless thy name	I. Watts.	104
Look down, O Lord! with	P. Doddridge.	609
Look up, my soul! with cheerful	Miss A. Steele.	426
Lord! as to thy dear cross we	J. H. Gurney.	400
Lord! dismiss us with thy blessing	E. Smyth.	37
Lord! dismiss us with thy blessing	W. Shirley.	36
Lord God, the Holy Ghost	J. Montgomery.	162
Lord! I am thine, entirely thine	S. Davies.	588
Lord! I cannot let thee go	J. Newton.	478
Lord! I hear of showers of	Miss E. Codner.	321
Lord! in the morning thou shalt hear	I. Watts.	49
Lord of all power and might	H. Stowell.	168
Lord of the Sabbath! hear our	P. Doddridge.	28
Lord of the worlds above!	I. Watts.	32
Lord! thou hast called thy grace to	I. Watts.	606
Lord! thou hast scourged our guilty	J. Burlow.	668
Lord! thou hast searched and seen me	I. Watts.	547
Lord! thou hast won at length	J. Newton.	329
Lord! 't is an infinite delight	I. Watts.	731
Lord! we adore thy vast designs	I. Watts.	541
Lord! we come before thee now	W. Hammond.	44
Lord! what a heaven of saving grace	I. Watts.	412
Lord! when thou didst ascend on high	I. Watts.	237
Lord! when we bend before thy	J. D. Carlyle.	54
Lord! where shall guilty souls retire	I. Watts.	552
Lord! while for all mankind we	A. R. Wreford.	603
Lord! with glowing heart I'll praise	S. F. Key.	126
Loud hallelujahs to the Lord	I. Watts.	78

INDEX TO HYMNS.

	HYMN.
Majestic sweetness sits enthroned - *S. Stennett.*	256
Mercy, O thou Son of David! - - *J. Newton.*	333
Mighty God! while angels bless - *R. Robinson.*	143
Mine eyes and my desire - - - - *I. Watts.*	505
Mortals, awake! with angels join - *S. Medley.*	194
Much in sorrow, oft in woe - - *H. K. White.*	513
Must Jesus bear the cross alone - *G. N. Allen.*	434
My country! 't is of thee - - - *S. F. Smith.*	660
My days are gliding swiftly by - *D. Nelson.*	747
My dear Redeemer and my Lord? - *I. Watts.*	209
My faith looks up to thee - - - *R. Palmer.*	515
My God! accept my early vows - *I. Watts.*	6
My God and Father! while I - *Miss C. Elliott.*	540
My God! how endless is thy love - *I. Watts.*	4
My God! how wonderful thou art - *F. W. Faber.*	97
My God! is any hour so sweet - *Miss C. Elliott.*	461
My God! my King! thy various praise *I. Watts.*	80
My God, my Life, my Love! - - *I. Watts.*	414
My God, my Portion, and my Love! - *I. Watts.*	402
My God! permit me not to be - - *I. Watts.*	462
My God! the Spring of all my joys - *I. Watts.*	403
My God! thy boundless love I praise *H. More.*	92
My God! 't is to thy mercy-seat - *Miss A. Steele.*	537
My gracious Lord! I own thy - *P. Doddridge.*	376
My Helper, God! I bless his - - *P. Doddridge.*	671
My Jesus! as thou wilt - - - *Tr., J. Borthwick.*	517
My Lord, my God, my Love! - - *Lyra Catholica.*	415
My rest is in heaven, my rest is not *H. F. Lyte.*	511
My Saviour! I am thine - - - - *P. Doddridge.*	449
My Shepherd will supply my need - *I. Watts.*	428
My soul I be on thy guard - - - *G. Heath.*	504
My soul I repeat his praise - - - *I. Watts.*	519
My soul triumphant in the Lord *P. Doddridge.*	445
My spirit longs for thee - - - - *J. Byrom.*	453
My spirit on thy care - - - - *H. F. Lyte.*	423
My thoughts surmount these lower - *I. Watts.*	455
Naked as from the earth we came - - *I. Watts.*	527
Nature with open volume stands - - *I. Watts.*	228
Nearer, my God! to thee - - *Mrs. S. F. Adams.*	472
No more, my God! I boast no more - *I. Watts.*	347
Nor eye has seen, nor ear has heard - *I. Watts.*	725
Not all the blood of beasts - - - - *I. Watts.*	224
Not all the outward forms on earth - *I. Watts.*	180
Not to condemn the sons of men - - *I. Watts.*	296
Not with our mortal eyes - - - - *I. Watts.*	450
Now begin the heavenly theme - *M. Madan (?).*	297
Now be my heart inspired to sing - - *I. Watts.*	206
Now be the gospel banner - - - *T. Hastings.*	567
Now, by the love of Christ, my God - *I. Watts.*	605
Now for a tune of lofty praise - - - *I. Watts.*	235
Now, from labor and from care - - *T. Hastings.*	13
Now, from the altar of our hearts - *J. Mason.*	10
Now, gracious Lord! thine arm - - *J. Newton.*	673
Now, I have found a Friend - - - - *H. Hope.*	341
Now I resolve with all my heart, *Miss A. Steele.*	345
Now is th' accepted time - - - - *J. Dobell.*	283
Now let my soul, eternal King! *O. Heginbotham.*	178
Now let our souls, on wings sublime, *T. Gibbons.*	735
Now let our voices join - - - - *P. Doddridge.*	453
Now may He, who from the dead - *J. Newton.*	46
Now to the Lord a noble song - - *I. Watts.*	134
Now to the Lord, that makes us know - *I. Watts.*	252
Now to thy sacred house - - - *T. Dwight.*	33
O Christ, our Hope, our hearts, *Tr., J. Chandler.*	258
O day of rest and gladness! - - *C. Wordsworth.*	20
O God of mercy! hear my call - - *I. Watts.*	317
O God! we praise thee, and - *Tate and Brady.*	106
O holy, holy, holy Lord! - - *J. W. Eastburn.*	66

	HYMN.
O Jesus, bruised, and - - *Mrs. C. F. Alexander.*	377
O Jesus, full of grace! - - - - *C. Wesley.*	506
O Jesus, King most wonderful! *Tr., E. Caswall.*	386
O Jesus! sweet the tears I shed - *R. Palmer.*	218
O Jesus! thou the beauty art - *Tr., E. Caswall.*	387
O Lord! how joyful 't is to see, *Tr., J. Chandler.*	603
O Lord! I would delight in thee - *J. Ryland.*	432
O Lord! my best desire fulfill - *W. Cowper.*	526
O Lord of heaven and earth and *C. Wordsworth.*	648
O Lord, our God! arise - - - - *R. Wardlaw.*	639
O Lord, our heavenly King! - - - *I. Watts.*	121
O Lord! thy perfect word - - - *B. Beddome.*	171
O Lord! thy work revive - *Mrs. P. H. Brown.*	609
O Love divine! how sweet thou art, *C. Wesley.*	407
O mother, dear, Jerusalem! - - *D. Dickson.*	729
O my soul! what means this sadness, *J. Fawcett.*	509
O paradise eternal! - - - - - - *T. Davis.*	738
O paradise! O paradise! - - - *F. W. Faber.*	734
O Saviour, who didst come - *Songs for the Sanc.*	424
O Thou, from whom all goodness - *T. Haweis.*	530
O thou God, who hear'st prayer! - *J. Conder.*	327
O Thou, that hear st prayer! - - *J. Burton.*	621
O Thou, that hear'st the prayer *A. M. Toplady.*	330
O Thou, that hear'st when sinners - *I. Watts.*	306
O Thou, the contrite sinner's - *Miss C. Elliott.*	500
O Thou, to whose all-searching *Tr., J. Wesley.*	483
O Thou, who driest the mourner's tear! *T. Moore.*	535
O Thou, whose own vast temple *W. C. Bryant.*	655
O Thou, whose tender mercy - *Miss A. Steele.*	314
O'er the gloomy hills of darkness *W. Williams.*	636
O'er the realms of pagan darkness - *T. Cotterill.*	637
Overwhelmed in depths of woe, *Tr., E. Caswall.*	225
Oh! blessed souls are they - - - *I. Watts.*	340
Oh! could I find from day to day, *B. Cleveland.*	459
Oh! could I speak the matchless - *S. Medley.*	406
Oh! could our thoughts and - *Miss A. Steele.*	431
Oh! for a closer walk with God - *W. Cowper.*	492
Oh! for a glance of heavenly day - *J. Hart.*	309
Oh! for a heart to praise my God - *C. Wesley.*	467
Oh! for a shout of sacred joy - - *I. Watts.*	238
Oh! for a sweet inspiring ray - *Miss A. Steele.*	463
Oh! for a thousand tongues to sing - *C. Wesley.*	253
Oh! for an overcoming faith - - - *I. Watts.*	685
Oh! for the happy hour - - - *G. W. Bethune.*	611
Oh! gift of gifts! Oh! grace of - *F. W. Faber.*	362
Oh! happy day, that fixed my - *P. Doddridge.*	589
Oh! how divine how sweet the joy *J. Needham.*	357
Oh! if my soul were formed for woe, *I. Watts.*	496
Oh! let me, heavenly Lord! extend *J. Merrick.*	691
Oh! may my heart, by grace - - *J. Fawcett.*	491
Oh! might I once mount up and see *I. Watts.*	464
Oh! praise our God to-day - - *W. H. Bathurst.*	642
Oh! sing to me of heaven, *Mrs. M. S. B. Dana.*	744
Oh! that I could for ever dwell - - *A. Reed.*	410
Oh! that my load of sin were gone - *C. Wesley.*	308
Oh! that the Lord's salvation - *H. F. Lyte.*	630
Oh! that thou wouldst, the heavens *C. Wesley.*	312
Oh! that thy statutes every hour - - *I. Watts.*	488
Oh! the delights, the heavenly joys - *I. Watts.*	139
Oh! 't was a joyful sound to hear - *N. Tate.*	47
Oh! what amazing words of grace - *S. Medley.*	282
Oh! what, if we are Christ's - - *H. W. Baker.*	524
Oh! where are kings and empires - *A. C. Coxe.*	558
On Jordan's stormy banks I stand - *S. Stennett.*	726
Once more, before we part - - - *J. Hart.*	43
Once more, my soul! the rising day - *I. Watts.*	8
Once more the solemn season *Tr., W. Mercer.*	667
One sweetly solemn thought - *Miss P. Cary.*	749
Our heavenly Father! hear - *J. Montgomery.*	482
Our Lord is risen from the dead - *C. Wesley.*	236

INDEX TO HYMNS. 291

Hymn	Author	No.
Pass away, earthly joy!	Mrs. H. Bonar.	342
Peace! 't is the Lord Jehovah's	P. Doddridge.	682
People of the living God	J. Montgomery.	599
Pleasant are thy courts above	H. F. Lyte.	465
Plunged in a gulf of dark despair	I. Watts.	252
Pour out thy Spirit from on	J. Montgomery.	581
Praise, everlasting praise, be paid	I. Watts.	86
Praise the Lord, his glories show	H. F. Lyte.	129
Praise the Lord, his power	W. Wrangham.	128
Praise the Lord, ye heavens!	John Kempthorne.	125
Praise to God, immortal	Mrs. A. L. Barbauld.	657
Prayer is the soul's sincere	J. Montgomery.	486
Prostrate, dear Jesus! at thy feet	S. Stennett.	318
Rejoice, all ye believers!	Tr., Miss J. Borthwick.	743
Rejoice, the Lord is King	C. Wesley.	241
Return, my roving heart! return	P. Doddridge.	501
Return, O God of love! return	I. Watts.	494
Return, O wanderer! return	W. B. Collyer.	295
Revive thy work, O Lord!	A. Midlane.	610
Rise, my soul! and stretch thy	R. Seagrave.	470
Rise, O my soul! pursue the path,	J. Needham.	435
Rock of ages, cleft for me!	A. M. Toplady.	363
Safely through another week	J. Newton.	17
Salvation! Oh! the joyful sound	I. Watts.	271
Saviour! I follow on	C. S. Robinson.	473
Saviour! teach me, day	M. E. S. S. Hy. Book.	418
Saviour! visit thy plantation	J. Newton.	612
Saviour! when, in dust to thee	R. Grant.	323
Say, sinner! hath a voice	Mrs. A. B. Hyde.	291
See, gracious God! before thy	Miss A. Steele.	666
See Israel's gentle Shepherd	P. Doddridge.	587
See, Oh! see what love the	Tr., R. Massie.	370
Shall man, O God of life and light!	T. Dwight.	703
Shine, mighty God! on Zion shine	I. Watts.	633
Show pity, Lord! O Lord! forgive	I. Watts.	184
Since all the varying scenes of time,	J. Hervey.	533
Since Jesus freely did appear	J. Berridge.	665
Sing, O heavens! O earth!	J. S. B. Monsell.	230
Sing to the Lord a joyful song,	J. S. B. Monsell.	87
Sing to the Lord Jehovah's name	I. Watts.	101
Sing to the Lord, ye heavenly hosts!	I. Watts.	99
Sinners! the voice of God regard	J. Fawcett.	275
Sinners! turn, why will ye die?	C. Wesley.	298
Sinners! will you scorn the message,	J. Allen.	269
So let our lips and lives express	I. Watts.	439
Softly now the light of day	G. W. Doane.	11
Soldiers of Christ! arise	C. Wesley.	641
Soldiers of the cross! arise	W. H. Howe.	618
Songs of immortal praise belong	I. Watts.	103
Songs of praise the angels sang,	J. Montgomery.	130
Sons of men! behold from far	C. Wesley.	201
Sons of Zion! raise your songs	T. Kelly.	246
Soon as I heard my Father say	I. Watts.	532
Sovereign of worlds! display thy,	B. H. Draper.	628
Sovereign Ruler, Lord of all!	T. Raffles.	324
Sovereign Ruler of the skies!	J. Ryland.	421
Spirit Divine! attend our prayers	A. Reed.	156
Spirit of holiness! look down,	W. H. Bathurst.	158
Spirit of peace and holiness	S. F. Smith.	580
Spirit of power and might!	J. Montgomery.	160
Stand up, and bless the Lord	J. Montgomery.	119
Stand up, my soul! shake off thy fears,	I. Watts.	437
Stand up, stand up for Jesus	G. Duffield.	629
Stay, thou insulted Spirit! stay	C. Wesley.	311
Still, still with thee, my God!	J. D. Burns.	14
Sun of my soul, thou Saviour dear!	J. Keble.	5
Sure, the blest Comforter is nigh,	Miss A. Steele.	548
Surely, Christ thy griefs hath	A. M. Toplady.	217
Sweet feast of love divine	E. Dendy.	374

Hymn	Author	No.
Sweet hour of prayer! sweet	Miss F. Crosby.	460
Sweet is the memory of thy grace	I. Watts.	116
Sweet is the work, my God, my King!	I. Watts.	26
Sweet is the work, O Lord!	Miss H. Auber.	16
Sweet land of rest! for thee I sigh	G. M——.	732
Sweet peace of conscience!	O. Heginbotham.	498
Sweet the moments, rich in blessing	J. Allen.	334
Sweet the time, exceeding sweet	G. Burder.	597
Sweet was the time, when first I felt,	J. Newton.	493
Sweeter sounds than music knows	J. Newton.	419
Swell the anthem, raise the song	N. Strong.	659
Take me, O my Father! take me	R. Palmer.	322
Take, my soul! thy full salvation	H. F. Lyte.	508
Tarry with me, O my Saviour!	Mrs. C. L. Smith.	699
Thank and praise Jehovah's	J. Montgomery.	658
That awful day will surely come	I. Watts.	708
That day of wrath, that dreadful day,	W. Scott.	716
That fearful day, that day of	Tr., J. M. Neale.	717
The God of harvest praise	J. Montgomery.	662
The heavens declare thy glory, Lord!	I. Watts.	179
The hour of my departure 's come	M. Bruce.	693
The law commands and makes us know,	I. Watts.	180
The Lord descended from above	T. Sternhold.	95
The Lord! how fearful is his name!	I. Watts.	96
The Lord! how wondrous are his ways,	I. Watts.	89
The Lord Jehovah reigns, And	I. Watts.	57
The Lord of glory is my light	I. Watts.	515
The Lord, the Judge, before his throne,	I. Watts.	709
The Lord will come, the earth shall	R. Heber.	715
The Lord will happiness divine	W. Cowper.	555
The mercies of my God and King	H. F. Lyte.	109
The perfect world by Adam trod	N. P. Willis.	653
The promise of my father's love	I. Watts.	389
The royal banner is unfurled	Tr., J. Chandler.	219
The Saviour calls, let every ear	Miss A. Steele.	278
The spacious firmament on high	J. Addison.	82
The Spirit breathes upon the word,	W. Cowper.	174
The Spirit, in our hearts	H. U. Onderdonk.	286
The voice of free grace cries	R. Burdsall.	305
Thee, King of saints! we praise	C. Wesley.	375
Thee, thee we praise, O God! and,	E. F. Hatfield.	65
Thee we adore, eternal Name!	I. Watts.	677
There is a blessed home	H. W. Baker.	750
There is a fountain filled with blood,	W. Cowper.	221
There is a land of pure delight	I. Watts.	723
There is a name I love to hear	F. Whitfield.	399
There is an hour of peaceful rest,	W. B. Tappan.	720
These glorious minds, how bright they,	I. Watts.	724
Think, O ye who foully languish,	W. B. Collyer.	701
This day the Lord hath called	W. H. Bathurst.	27
This is the day the Lord hath made	I. Watts.	20
This is the word of truth and love	I. Watts.	183
This world is poor from shore to shore,	D. Nelson.	722
Thou art gone to the grave, but we will,	R. Heber.	608
Thou art my Portion, O my God!	I. Watts.	489
Thou art the Way, to thee alone	G. W. Doane.	212
Thou dear Redeemer, dying Lamb!	J. Cennick.	401
Thou lovely Source of true delight,	Miss A. Steele.	405
Thou only Sovereign of my heart!	Miss A. Steele.	425
Thou, who did'st on Calvary bleed!	J. D. Burns.	326
Thou, who roll'st the year around	R. Palmer.	676
Thou, whom my soul admires above	I. Watts.	380
Thou, whose almighty word	J. Marriott.	167
Through all the changing scenes of life,	N. Tate.	108
Through every age, eternal God!	I. Watts.	688
Thus far the Lord has led me on	I. Watts.	7
Thy bounties, gracious Lord!	Miss E. Scott.	644
Thy holy day's returning	R. Palmer.	30
Thy name, almighty Lord!	I. Watts.	562
Thy way, not mine, O Lord!	H. Bonar.	518

INDEX TO HYMNS.

Hymn	HYMN
"'T is finished!" so the Saviour cried, *S. Stennett.*	229
'T is thine alone, almighty Name! *E. F. Hatfield.*	664
To-day, if you will hear his voice - *Kent's Coll.*	293
To-day, the Saviour calls - - - *Spir. Songs.*	284
To him that chose us first - - - - *I. Watts.*	72
To Jesus, our exalted Lord - - *Miss A. Steele.*	378
To Jesus, the Crown of my hope - *W. Cowper.*	446
To our Redeemer's glorious name, *Miss A. Steele.*	142
To thy pastures fair and large - - *J. Merrick.*	468
To thy temple I repair - - - *J. Montgomery.*	45
To us a Child of hope is born - - - *M. Bruce.*	195
To whom, my Saviour! shall I go, *Vill. Hymns.*	404
Triumphant Zion! lift thy head, *P. Doddridge.*	565
'T was on that dark, that doleful night, *I. Watts.*	379
Unshaken as the sacred hill - - - - *I. Watts.*	430
Unveil thy bosom, faithful tomb! - - *I. Watts.*	692
Vain, delusive world! adieu! - - - *C. Wesley.*	471
Wait, my soul! upon the Lord - *W. F. Lloyd.*	514
Wait, O my soul! thy Maker's will, *B. Beddome.*	544
Watchman! tell us of the night! - *J. Bowring.*	617
Wayfarers in the wilderness - *A. R. Thompson.*	748
We bid thee welcome in the - - *J. Montgomery.*	538
We bless thee for thy peace - *Songs of the Chh.*	538
We give immortal praise - - - - *I. Watts.*	71
We give thee but thine own - - *W. W. How.*	643
We sing his love who once was slain - *R. Hill.*	704
Welcome, delightful morn - - - *Hayward.*	31
Welcome, sacred day of rest - - - *W. Brown.*	19
Welcome, sweet day of rest! - - - *I. Watts.*	15
Welcome, welcome, dear Redeemer! *W, M——.*	335
What are these in bright array - *J. Montgomery.*	718
What equal honors shall we bring - - *I. Watts.*	133
What shall I render to my God - - *I. Watts.*	591
What shall the dying sinner do - - *I. Watts.*	186
What sinners value I resign - - - *I. Watts.*	702
What various hindrances we meet - *W. Cowper.*	485
When all thy mercies, O my God! - *J. Addison.*	110
When at this distance, Lord! we, *P. Doddridge.*	409
When bending o'er the brink of life, *W.B.Collyer.*	681
When God revealed his gracious name, *I. Watts.*	356
When I can read my title clear - - *I. Watts.*	436
When I survey the wondrous cross - *I. Watts.*	227
When Jesus dwelt in mortal clay - *T. Gibbons.*	650
When Jesus left his Father's - *J. Montgomery.*	586
When languor and disease invade, *A.M.Toplady.*	528

Hymn	HYMN
When, O dear Jesus! when shall I - *J. Cennick.*	25
When, rising from the bed of death, *J. Addison.*	710
When shall the voice of singing - *J. Edmeston.*	632
When sins and fears prevailing - *Miss A. Steele.*	427
When thou, my righteous Judge! *Mrs. S. Shirley.*	328
While beauty clothes the fertile, *Miss A. Steele.*	672
While in sweet communion feeding - *E. Denny.*	368
While life prolongs its precious light, *T. Dwight.*	292
While on the verge of life I stand, *P. Doddridge.*	736
While, with ceaseless course, the sun, *J.Newton.*	675
Whilst thee I seek - - - *Miss H. M. Williams.*	529
Who are these that come from far? *T. Kelly (?).*	571
Who can describe the joys that rise - *I. Watts.*	351
Who shall ascend thy heavenly place, *I. Watts.*	549
Who shall the Lord's elect condemn? *I. Watts.*	440
Why do we mourn departing friends - *I. Watts.*	705
Why should the children of a King - *I. Watts.*	495
Why should we start and fear to die - *I. Watts.*	687
With all my powers of heart and - - *I. Watts.*	88
With broken heart and contrite sigh - *C. Elvin.*	310
With joy we hail the sacred day, *Miss H. Auber.*	21
With joy we lift our eyes - - - - *T. Jervis.*	40
With joy we meditate the grace - - *I. Watts.*	211
With tears of anguish I lament - - *S. Stennett.*	320
Witness, ye men and angels! now, *B. Beddome.*	593
Wouldst thou eternal life obtain - *R. Palmer.*	280
Ye angels who stand round, *Miss M. De Fleury.*	447
Ye boundless realms of joy! - - - *N. Tate.*	123
Ye dying sons of men! - - - - *J. Boden.*	304
Ye glittering toys of earth! adieu! *Miss A. Steele.*	300
Ye hearts, with youthful vigor - *P. Doddridge.*	273
Ye holy souls! in God rejoice - - - *I. Watts.*	93
Ye humble souls! approach your, *Miss A. Steele.*	114
Ye messengers of Christ - - - *Mrs. Voke.*	583
Ye nations round the earth! rejoice - *I. Watts.*	79
Ye saints! your music bring - - - *A. Reed.*	243
Ye servants of the living God! *W. H. Bathurst.*	615
Ye servants of the Lord! - - - *P. Doddridge.*	584
Ye sinners! fear the Lord - - - *T. Dwight.*	285
Ye that in his courts are found! - - *R. Hill.*	302
Ye tribes of Adam! join - - - - *I. Watts.*	122
Ye wretched, hungry, starving - *Miss A. Steele.*	274
Yes, I will bless thee, O my God! *O. Heginbotham.*	105
Yes, the Redeemer rose - - - *P. Doddridge.*	233
Yes, we trust, the day is breaking - *T. Kelly.*	638
Your harps, ye trembling saints! *A. M. Toplady.*	451
Zion is Jehovah's dwelling - - - - *T. Kelly.*	569

THE CHURCH HYMN BOOK,

Contains 1464 Hymns, 30 selections for chanting, and 439 metrical tunes, besides chants. Price at Retail—Hymns and Tunes $2.00, without tunes $1.50.

TESTIMONIALS.

By far the best collection of hymns in existence. (Rev. Herrick Johnson, D.D., Phila., Pa.)

Dr. Herrick Johnson is justified in his verdict that it is the best Hymn book in the world. (Rev. James S. Kemper, Dayton, O.)

The hymns and the tunes, both in themselves and in their mutual adaptation, are admirable. Attracted by the signal excellence of the book, we have adopted it for use in our church. (Rev. Henry Martyn Scudder, D.D., Brooklyn, N. Y.)

I am delighted with its appearance and arrangements. (Rev. Samuel J. Nicolls, D.D., St. Louis, Mo.)

The best selection in existence. A selection unrivaled on earth. (Rev. Joel Jewell, Sylvania, Pa.)

I heartily wish our Assembly would adopt it. (Rev. Edward P. Humphrey, D.D., LL.D., Louisville, Ky.)

I am prepared to assign the work the first place, and call it the latest and the best for congregational use. (Rev. Epher Whitaker, Southhold, L. I.

It surpasses any and every other work of the kind ever issued from the press. (Mr. E. M. Whitaker, Washington, D. C.)

It bears evidence throughout of unusual study and care. (Rev. Frederick M. Bird, Spotswood, N. J.)

It will be highly appreciated by hymnologists. (Rev. Zachary Eddy, D.D., Chelsea, Mass.)

Altogether, the completest book of hymns that has ever been issued; a monument of great labor, sound judgment and true lyrical taste. Then, the skill and judgment that have been used in the musical arrangement, with such admirable taste, contribute to make the book about as near perfection as we can expect to come. (Rev. J. M. Bachelder, Albia, Iowa.)

Dr. Hatfield's work seems past criticism. I feel satisfied that the Church Hymn and Tune Book is THE book. (Rev. J. Augustine Hood, Marva, Ill.)

It meets my full and cordial approbation. Its peculiarities are its excellencies. (Rev. Wm. Patton, D. D., New Haven, Ct.)

I am deeply impressed with its extraordinary excellence. (Rev. Aaron Rittenhouse (M. Ep.), Hestinville, W. Phila., Pa.)

It approves itself to us by its careful and copious selection of valued hymns, and by its rescue and preservation of the good old tunes. The body, as well as the soul of the book, is so attractive that it does its part in giving tone and character to our chapel singing. (Chancellor Howard Crosby, D.D., LL.D., New York.)

I can hardly overstate the satisfaction which a thorough examination of the book has given me. I do not hesitate to pronounce it, in my judgment, by far the best Hymn and Tune Book in existence. (Rev. Wm. L. Gaylord, Meriden, Ct.)

One of the latest and richest of the hymn books—rich both in its dainty paper and type, and in its collection of hymnologic wealth. An admirable hymn book. (Rev. Theodore L. Cuyler, D.D., Brooklyn, N. Y.)

All that can be desired, and I hope and believe it will become the standard collection of the Presbyterian and Congregational churches. (Mr. J. M. Tibbits, Windham, Ct.)

A valuable contribution to the hymnology of our country. Equal, if not superior, to any other hymn and tune book we have seen. (Rev. Robert W. Patterson, D.D., Chicago, Ill.)

It fills my ideal of what such a book should be better than anything I have seen. The selection of hymns is admirable. (Rev. Joseph T. Smith, D.D., Baltimore, Md.)

Having examined carefully both the hymns and the music of this collection, I do not hesitate to pronounce it, in both these respects, one of the very best extant. The collection of hymns is very large, yet there is not one of them that has not a fair claim to the place it occupies. The information given, in respect to the authorship and dates of hymns and tunes, is more extensive and satisfactory than is elsewhere to be found in any single volume that has come under my observation. In short, the book is unsurpassed. (Rev. Raymond H. Seeley, D.D., Haverhill, Mass.)

The Church Hymn Book is an uncompromising *Congregational Singing Book*. Every tune has apparently been selected for that purpose and no other. There is not a musical composition in the entire book which will not in time become available for Congregational use. Great care has been bestowed upon the harmony and phrasing of the tunes to impart to each, as far as possible, that sonority and choiral quality in its rendering analogous to the orotund voice in Oratory. This merit was noticed by the writer in playing through the music of the book in score, and the impression has been verified by the singing of the congregation. The effect of the music cannot fail to be the education of any congregation who may employ it, in the execution and appreciation of true Choral Psalmody. The best of congregational singing books, and one that will discourage any further attempts at such compilations. (Rev. Charles W. Wood, Silver Creek, N. Y.)

I have carefully compared it with Hymn Books in common use, and have no hesitancy in pronouncing it the best Hymn Book I have ever examined, and in a ministry of almost thirty years, I have seen and used a large variety. As a Tune Book, for so large a collection, it is superior to any other book of which I have any knowledge. It would be a marvelous step in advance, if this book could be introduced into all our churches. (Rev. Silas S. Hyde, Hicksville, Ohio.)

The tunes impress me as being of a very lofty order, well adapted to the sentiment of the hymns; and the hymns embracing such a wide selection, on such a variety of subjects, seem eminently fitted to express the feelings of devotion and thankfulness of the Christian heart, both in the public services of the sanctuary and in the home circle. I do not see how our General Assembly can do better than to adopt it as our Church Hymn Book. (Rev. Wm. S. Knight, Augusta, Ill.

The Church Hymn Book deserves a place in every Christian Congregation in the land. I am greatly rejoiced that so perfect a Hymn and Tune Book should be issued, and regard it as the *ne plus ultra*. (Rev. James A. Little, Hokendaugua, Pa.)

I want to tell you how much we like your Hymn Book, of which we have 400 copies in use. Every one speaks so highly of the entire work, that I have no hesitation, in behalf of our whole people, to express to you our hearty thanks for this great and good work that you have done, and for the lasting service you have rendered to the church. (Rev. B. Sunderland, D.D., Washington, D. C.)

The adaptation of hymns to tunes is in most excellent taste, and the hymns themselves are admirably selected. In fact the whole book is first class in every respect, and surpasses, in many respects...... two of the very best works of this class hitherto published. (Charles P. Turner, M. D., Phila., Pa.)

It is without qualification the best book of the sort I ever saw. (Rev. John S. Hays, Louisville, Ky.

Dr. Hatfield, the compiler of this new Hymn book, has some unusual qualifications for the work. He has long been known as one of our best and most accurate hymnologists. He has had access to all the chief works, older and recent; and has the requisite skill and judgment to avail himself of all these, selecting the best and rejecting what is insignificant. The result is the production of a work which has already taken its place in the front rank with the best among its competitors. It cannot fail to have a cordial reception, and to be widely used. (The Presbyterian Quarterly and Princeton Review, New York.)

It has most thoroughly satisfied us in its hymns, its tunes, and its arrangement, while in its typographical appearance it is superior to any similar book yet published. We are ready to give it our unqualified commendation, as, in all respects, the best book of the kind we have ever seen. A collection that is remarkable for its richness, fullness, and adaptation for every reasonable want. The editor, publishers and the public, are to be congratulated, and we have no hesitation in recommending the Church Hymn Book most cordially and unreservedly. (The Congregational Quarterly, Boston, Mass.)

This new collection, the result of many years' careful study and preparation by one of the most learned and experienced hymnologists in our country, Rev. Edwin F. Hatfield, D D., might almost be termed a Hymnological Encyclopædia, so extensive is the selection from all sources, and at the same time so judiciously made. The book is creditable to the publishers as well as to the compiler. (New York Observer.)

Those who are aware of the scrupulous accuracy and patient investigation of the Stated Clerk of our General Assembly, will naturally regard with confidence the result of his studies, and many of them are aware of the great attention which for many years he has paid to the past as well as to the present hymnology of the church. The result is a book which contains the selectest gems of our Christian lyric literature, while it is claimed by the author that no similar compilation can compare with this in the "number, variety, availability and general excellence of its tunes." (New York Evangelist.)

A collection which, in some important particulars, has no rival. It includes a larger number of hymns than is found in any similar compilation; and yet, by careful economy of space, this volume scarcely exceeds the proportions of others. We give the book great credit for its selection of tunes. The Church Hymn Book is beautifully printed. We wish it large success, for it is designed to promote singing by the whole congregation, and it is admirably adapted to its end. (The Christian Intelligencer, New York.)

The examination of a new hymn book, of any degree of merit, is always a pleasant task to us, and it is doubly so when all parts of the work have been so carefully and well executed as in the volume before us, of which Dr. Hatfield is the editor. The number of hymns is large, but we have noticed nothing that seemed to us unworthy of its place. Evidently, a taste at once devout, refined and catholic, has guided the selection. It seems to us an unusually valuable addition to the works of its class. (The Christian Union, H. W. Beecher, Ed., New York.)

In several respects it is superior to any similar publication with which we are familiar. It is a most rich and varied compilation, containing, in all its departments, an abundance of poetical and singable hymns. We know of no hymn and tune book which, in its musical arrangement, is superior to this one. It is issued in a style which gives great credit to its publishers. The typography is splendid. We do not hesitate to commend it to the churches, believing that it is destined to secure extensive use, as it is an attractive book, and every way worthy of patronage. (The Independent, New York.)

It is well calculated to supply the want which has been so long and so deeply felt. It has certainly reached a much higher point of excellence than any that have gone before it; so high that, with our present state of hymnology, it would be difficult to exceed it. It will bear the closest scrutiny, and if it has faults it is not easy to find them. The whole work shows immense research, careful discrimination, sound judgment and refined taste. This volume is a gem of poetry and music. (The Eclectic Magazine, New York.)

The Church Hymn Book is a splendid production. It must have cost many years of loving and assiduous labor, and, taken as a whole, we deem it superior to any other hymn book we are acquainted with. (The Union Advocate, New York.)

The writer has used this book for the last few Sabbaths, and with a growing feeling that as a manual of Praise it is not surpassed by anything hitherto brought under his notice. (The Illustrated Christian weekly of the American Tract Society, New York.)

We can, without hesitation, pronounce the book before us to be *one of the very best* of the hymn and tune books thus far produced. The adaptation of the tunes to the hymns is in the main exceedingly happy and judicious. The mechanical execution deserves all praise. (The Christian World, New York.)

For half his life, Dr. Hatfield has been an enthusiastic student of psalmody, and we are ready to believe at the outset that the book he has now produced must be one of the best of its kind. He has culled from a wider field than most compilers, and with good taste. Dr. Hatfield has given the churches a standard hymn and tune book. (The Congregationalist, Boston, Mass.)

We regard it as one of the best published. It is much to be preferred to anything published by our Board of Publication, and anything that will be likely to come from the best committee that can be appointed. Dr. Hatfield's book would be used in many churches if its merits were known. (The Herald and Presbyter, Cincinnati, Ohio.)

Dr. Hatfield is unusually well qualified for such a work as this, by his natural taste, his musical acquirements, his long pastoral experience, and his possession of the largest collection of hymn books in this country. To the preparation of this book he has devoted much labor and care during many years. This admirable book of Praise is one of very great merit, and will be highly prized by all the lovers of sacred music. The compiler and publisher deserve the gratitude of all the friends of sacred music and of congregational singing, for the manner in which they have discharged their respective duties. (The Presbyterian Banner, Pittsburg, Pa.)

Dr. Hatfield's new and beautiful Hymn Book, with Tunes, is winning golden opinions from the best quarters, and is, in the view of many, to become speedily THE Hymn Book of the Presbyterian Church. (The Interior, Chicago, Ill.)

IVISON, BLAKEMAN, TAYLOR, & Co., Publishers,

138 & 140 Grand Street, New York; 133 & 135 State St., Chicago.

www.ingramcontent.com/pod-product-compliance
Lightning Source LLC
Chambersburg PA
CBHW032056220426
43664CB00008B/1020